Prophecy

Prophecy

Essays presented to Georg Fohrer
on his sixty-fifth birthday
6 September 1980

Edited by

J. A. Emerton

Walter de Gruyter · Berlin · New York
1980

Beiheft zur Zeitschrift für die alttestamentliche Wissenschaft

Herausgegeben von Georg Fohrer

150

CIP-Kurztitelaufnahme der Deutschen Bibliothek

Prophecy : essays presented to Georg Fohrer on his 65th birthday
6. September 1980 / ed. by J. A. Emerton. — Berlin, New York : de
Gruyter, 1980.
   (Zeitschrift für die alttestamentliche Wissenschaft : Beih. ; 150)
   ISBN 3-11-007761-2
NE: Emerton, John A. [Hrsg.]; Fohrer, Georg: Festschrift

1980

by Walter de Gruyter & Co., vormals G. J. Göschen'sche Verlagshandlung — J. Guttentag,
Verlagsbuchhandlung — Georg Reimer — Karl J. Trübner — Veit & Comp., Berlin 30
Alle Rechte des Nachdrucks, der photomechanischen Wiedergabe,
der Übersetzung, der Herstellung von Mikrofilmen und Photokopien,
auch auszugsweise, vorbehalten.
Printed in Germany
Satz und Druck: Arthur Collignon GmbH, Berlin 30
Bindearbeiten: Lüderitz & Bauer, Berlin 61

Preface

The present volume is a tribute to Professor Georg Fohrer on the occasion of his sixty-fifth birthday, 6 September 1980. All who were associated with the Zeitschrift für die alttestamentliche Wissenschaft, whether as members of the editorial board or as those who have helped by writing for the Zeitschriftenschau or Bücherschau or in other ways, were invited to contribute essays, but some had regretfully to decline because of infirmity or pressure of other duties. I am indebted to Herr Claus Petersen for his help in editing the volume.

Professor Fohrer has edited ZAW since 1960, originally in association with Professors O. Eissfeldt and J. Hempel, and after 1966 on his own. His achievements as editor are well known: the standard of the articles has been maintained at a high level; the international character of the journal has been strongly emphasized; the Zeitschriftenschau and Bücherschau have been further developed and are a valued tool of Old Testament scholars. The number of works included in the Beihefte has grown considerably, and they include some that are of great importance for biblical studies.

Despite the time and energy that the editorship of ZAW has demanded, Professor Fohrer has made other substantial contributions to Old Testament scholarship. Many pupils have studied at his feet, and many dissertations have been prepared under his supervision. He has also managed to write numerous books and articles, and the list of publications later in this volume is one that might have seemed scarcely possible even for a scholar without his editorial duties. They include standard works on different aspects of the books of the Old Testament, and on the religion and history of Israel, and some of his writings have helped to change the direction of Old Testament studies in recent years. While his publications cover most aspects of the Old Testament, it is perhaps to the study of the prophets that he has made his most substantial contribution. It has, therefore, been thought appropriate that this volume in his honour should be concerned with Old Testament prophecy.

The contributors to this book, together with his other colleagues and friends, express their thanks to him for his many and varied contributions to the study of the Old Testament. They wish him a long and happy retirement.

J. A. Emerton

Contents

Preface	V
M. J. Buss: The social psychology of prophecy	1
J. A. Emerton: Notes on two verses in Isaiah (26 16 and 66 17)	12
E. Jacob: La dimension du prophétisme d'après Martin Buber et Abraham J. Heschel	26
W. McKane: משא in Jeremiah 23 33–40	35
J. Maier: Die Hofanlagen im Tempel-Entwurf des Ezechiel im Licht der »Tempelrolle« von Qumran	55
A. Malamat: A Mari prophecy and Nathan's dynastic Oracle	68
R. Martin-Achard: Esaïe 47 et la tradition prophétique sur Babylone	83
A. Marx: A propos des doublets du livre de Jérémie. Réflexions sur la formation d'un livre prophétique	106
S. Segert: Syntax and style in the Book of Jonah: six simple approaches to their analysis	121
J. A. Soggin: Hosea und die Außenpolitik Israels	131
J. J. Stamm: Der Name des Propheten Amos und sein sprachlicher Hintergrund	137
J. V. M. Sturdy: The authorship of the »prose sermons« of Jeremiah	143
G. Wanke: Jeremias Besuch beim Töpfer. Eine motivkritische Untersuchung zu Jer 18	151
A. S. van der Woude: Seid nicht wie eure Väter! Bemerkungen zu Sacharja 1 5 und seinem Kontext	163
W. Zimmerli: Das Phänomen der »Fortschreibung« im Buche Echeziel	174
List of Professor Georg Fohrer's publications	192

The Social Psychology of Prophecy

By Martin J. Buss

(Emory University, Atlanta, Georgia)

The appropriate use of science in theology — including biblical study — is one the crucial issues of the present day. By the end of the nineteenth century, historical criticism had provided a new view of biblical literature which will probably remain an integral part of biblical scholarship. Nevertheless, that procedure was one-sided, so that many attempts have been made to transcend the limitations — especially the particularism — of historical criticism. In most disciplines, newer movements turned toward science[1]. A weakness of twentieth-century theology lies in its lack of adequate participation in this turn.

Although it is not altogether easy to define the term »science«, or the somewhat broader German term »Wissenschaft«, two characteristics of what is designated are especially important: attention to data (a feature shared with historical study), and a concern with generality (not just the particular for its own sake). Scientific and historical concerns do not exclude each other in a given discipline. On the contrary, physics, geology, and biology include a very strong historical dimension. The same holds true for the social sciences, when adequately pursued. Similarly, the humanities need to take account of general considerations. In all realms, specific features can be examined in the light of processes shared with other phenomena.

Skepticism toward the use of science in theology appears to be based in large part on a belief that the scientific approach undermines faith, just as historical criticism has been thought to do. According to some theorists the truth of biblical faith is supported by its peculiarity i.e., by its not being subject to general categories[2]. Indeed, if biblical events or beliefs can

---

[1] E.g., ca. 1885, interest within the study of music moved from music history to »Musikwissenschaft«, with attention to ethnology, psychology, physiology, and acoustics (T. Georgiades, RGG, IV 1963³, 1224f.). M. Buss, Understanding Communication, in: M. Buss, ed., Encounter with the Text, 1979, e.g., 3. 32, points out that the over-all shift is connected with concerns for general social welfare.

[2] E.g., O. Procksch, Theologie des Alten Testaments, 1950, 16; T. Vriezen, Outline of Old Testament Theology, 1958, 12 (Dutch original, 1949); G. E. Wright, The Old Testament Against its Environment, 1950, 15, in part following W. Eichrodt, JBL 65 (1946), 211–213, and holding that »the Israelite mutation, which made the particular and peculiar evolution of Biblical faith a possibility« represents »a radical revolution, as

be shown to be more unique than other phenomena, then their contravening of normal processes may furnish a proof for divine action or revelation. Yet it is unlikely that such a special uniqueness can be shown, nor is there any reason to believe that divine activity occurs only, or even especially, in the unnatural.

A different criticism of scientific — such as psychological or sociological — examinations of biblical literature which can be made is that they succeed in dealing with only limited aspects of the literature and do not enter deeply into its structure. This criticism is partially valid and reflects the fact that all intellectual endeavors (except theology?) deal with only certain aspects of existence. In part for the sake of convenience, the study of human life has become specialized; psychology focuses primarily on the individual, and sociology primarily on group processes. Human existence, however, is always at once individual and social, so that it can be treated adequately only in a perspective which combines both of these sides — in other words, by social psychology. Similarly, it is now clear that many nonhuman phenomena need to be apprehended through approaches, such as biochemistry, that draw together disciplines which had become separated.

Social psychology, as a science, has been practiced continuously since the turn of the century. An early pioneer was G. Simmel, a colleague of H. Gunkel in Berlin and one of the founders of modern sociology. His »formal sociology« described »forms of sociation«, i.e., processes of interaction — such as exchange, conflict domination, and sociability[3]. One can apply its framework by conceiving, for example, the life-situation of a genre as lying in a process (such as conflict and its resolution) rather than in an externally described organization (such as the meeting of elders at a city gate). Theoretical explorations of social psychology were furnished especially by the philosopher G. H. Mead. A considerable amount of conceptual and empirical work has been carried out in this area in the present century, although often with a primarily psychological or sociological orientation[4]. It is of course not possible to discuss within a short compass

---

    opposed to evolution, which is not entirely explainable by the empirical data«. Continuity is accepted by H. Huffmon in: Magnalia Dei, 1976, 183.

[3] Über sociale Differenzierung: Sociologische und psychologische Untersuchungen, 1890; Die Religion (Die Gesellschaft: Sammlung sozialpsychologischer Monographien, ed. M. Buber, 2), 1906; Soziologie: Untersuchungen über die Formen der Vergesellschaftung, 1908.

[4] Major contributors to social psychology include: S. Freud, A. Adler, H. S. Sullivan, G. Allport, B. F. Skinner, A. Maslow, in psychology; K. Lewin, W. I. Thomas, G. C. Homans, A. Schutz, L. Festinger, and E. Goffman, in sociology. Cf. also I. King, The Development of Religion: A Study in Anthropology and Social Psychology, 1910, and W. C. Graham and H. G. May, Culture and Conscience, 1936, 140 (treating of the Bible).

the many issues raised in this general field so far as they are relevant to prophecy. Nevertheless, some concerns can be examined.

Role

One of the topics frequently discussed in social psychology is that of *role*. This topic deals with the activity of individual persons as expected by, and carried out in, a group. It is natural in describing roles to highlight a positive or harmonious relation between individuality and the social order. Yet some balance is required. Neither a view setting individuals and society in continuous opposition to each other nor one which assumes an almost complete harmony is correct. In fact, according to some theorists (such as G. Simmel) a considerable amount of conflict is constitutive of the social order. Thus the reality of conflicting roles and even roles embodying conflict (as in games or law) must be considered within social relations. Indeed, one of the advantages of the concept of »role« is that it allows considerable flexibility in describing a wide variety of relations.

The actual (or »enacted«[5]) role played by a human being emerges from an interplay between role expectations present in a community and the history and inclination of the actor. General observations and experimental studies show that cultural expectations and given situational factors have great power[6]; yet individual dispositions and abilities also affect social behavior[7]. In fact, role expectations may grant considerable latitude in regard to the details of a prescribed activity. The playing of a role, then, is not only one of »role-taking« but also one of »role-making«[8]. Furthermore, social prescriptions appear to be in general no more rigid and precise in smaller societies than in larger ones[9], so that it would be erroneous to picture »primitive« life as highly inflexible.

---

[5] M. Deutsch and R. Krauss, Theories in Social Psychology, 1965, 175.

[6] C. Haney, W. Banks, and P. Zimbarno, Interpersonal Dynamics in a Simulated Prison, International Journal of Criminology and Penology 1 (1973), 69—97, describe a striking experiment in which participants quickly adopt the roles of prisoners and guards (although one must recognize that events in real life may be somewhat different).

[7] E.g., J. Yinger, Toward a Field Theory of Behavior, 1965, 111; D. Cartwright and A. Zander, Group Dynamics, 1968³, 523.

[8] R. Turner, Role-Taking: Process Versus Conformity, in: A. M. Rose, ed., Human Behavior and Social Processes, 1962, 22. Similarly, for role flexibility, T. Parsons, The Social System, 1951, 39. 234f.; T. Sarbin and V. Allen, Role Theory, in: G. Lindzey and E. Aronson, eds., Handbook of Social Psychology, I 1968², 499.503.

[9] Not only is there no evidence that existence in small groups is relatively more rigid than in larger ones, but there is some contrary evidence; see, e.g., L. Greenbaum, Possession Trance in Sub-Saharan Africa: A Descriptive Analysis of Fourteen Societies, in: E. Bourguignon, ed., Religion, Altered States of Consciousness, and Social Change,

As communities grow in size, an increasing specialization can be observed. In a very small group, all adult members — perhaps under the leadership of one person, such as the head of the household or a chieftain — may exercise the various operations required or thought useful for a group's existence: religious, judicial, economic, recreational, etc.; indeed, these operations are not sharply delineated from each other[10]. As a group increases in size, at first a single part-time or full-time religious specialist emerges (often called a »shaman«[11]), then religious duties are divided between priests and diviners, and finally several classes of priests and diviners or prophets are formed. This pattern of development also appears in Israelite society. Although early Israel existed within the orbit of elaborately organized states, its constituent groups were small enough so that there was little occasion for assigning priestly, prophetic, and judicial functions to different persons. Thus early figures — including the patriarchs, Moses, and Samuel — are appropriately pictured as executing a variety of tasks[12].

It is, in fact, likely that early Israelite seers or prophets stood in close connection with cultic processes as well as with wisdom[13]. Such

---

1973, 80—84. Of course, the total number of options is greater in a more complex society.

[10] E. Gerstenberger, Wesen und Herkunft des »apodiktischen Rechts«, 1965, 95—99, comes close to this by locating the source of so-called apodictic law in clan ethos; such a background in a compact group — not necessarily a clan organization — holds for virtually all facets of Israelite literature. B. Malinowski wrote: »The fundamental institutions of human culture have changed not by way of sensational transformations but rather through increasing differentiation of form in accordance with increasingly different functions« (Culture, Encyclopaedia of the Social Sciences, IV 1931, 624). Weak in the area of sociology, H. Gunkel assumed an early division of functions, so that he had to account for the overlapping of spheres, such as in prophecy, as a secondary phenomenon.

[11] A. Schutz and T. Luckmann, The Structures of the Life-World, 1973, 325; R. Jones, Limbu Spirit Possession and Shamanism, in: J. Hitchcock and R. Jones, Spirit Possession in the Nepal Himalayas, 1976, 29. Thus K. Goldammer, Elemente des Schamanismus im Alten Testament, in: Ex orbe religionem: Studia Geo Widengren, II 1972, 266—285, can find shamanistic elements in traditions concerning Moses, patriarchs, judges, and prophets.

[12] On the roles of Moses, cf. J. Lindblom, Die Vorstellung vom Sprechen Jahwes zu den Menschen im Alten Testament, ZAW 75 (1963), 266f. It is true, descriptions of the early figures owe a number of details to an imagination based on later practices, but this recognition should not lead one to deny those persons a richness of functions. M. Noth, Amt und Berufung im Alten Testament, 1958, 25, moved in the right direction when he regarded kingship and prophecy as reflecting different sides of an earlier office (even though his description of that office was hardly accurate).

[13] S. Mowinckel, Psalmenstudien III: Die Kultpropheten und prophetische Psalmen, 1923, 9—11, held that the ancient Israelite seers were at the same time priests even though

association reflects a social condition in which major concerns are not sharply separated from each other. For instance, in such a condition ritual action occurs on many types of occasions throughout life[14]. In Israel, cultic specialization increased sharply with Josiah's reform, when the sacrificing of animals was limited to the Jerusalem temple and made the preserve of priests. But since cult consists of more than sacrifice — e.g., prayer — a prophet could take part in cultic activity even after that event. Similarly, the involvement of prophecy with wisdom never ceased, although it took on new forms. Indeed, if institutions are understood as aspects of culture, not as exclusive domains or as highly professionalized operations, they can be seen as interacting with each other in Israel as well as elsewhere[15]. The prophetic role should therefore be described in terms of a certain kind of activity, not in terms of a full-time or exclusive profession[16]. For in its basic features that activity precedes its professionalization, and it is never rigidly marked off from other spheres of life.

---

by then a distinction between these two classes was emerging; without adequate reason, however, he regarded the ecstatic prophet as different from the seer-priest in origin, 16. A similar position is developed by H. M. Orlinsky, Essays in Biblical Culture and Bible Translation, 1974, 39—65 (and in earlier versions of that essay); with S. Mowinckel, he also rightly draws scribal activity and thus »wisdom« into the orbit of the seer-priest.

[14] E.g., G. Widengren, Religionsphänomenologie, 1969, 209—257. S. Mowinckel failed to carry through adequately in his analysis of cult; although defining cult as the visible, ordered aspect (not a distinct realm) of religion (Religion und Kultus, 1953, 13; RGG IV 1963³, 120f.), he proceeds to describe it as a specialized activity, executed above all on regular occasions by official representatives. According to the broad definition, virtually all prophecy has a cultic aspect; but according to the narrower description, few prophets would be cultic. G. Fohrer, Der heilige Weg, Inaugural-Dissertation Bonn, 1939, discussed cultic or holy »paths« as an expression of religion.

[15] The word »institution« can be used both narrowly for a rigid, professionalized organization and more broadly for a system of social relations; e.g., M. Olson, The Process of Social Organization, 1968, 79, favors the narrower definition over the broader one, which he recognizes as widely current. Thus when G. Fohrer, Einleitung in das Alte Testament, 1965, 27, argues that a Sitz im Leben is not necessarily connected with an institution or an office, his point is not very different from the one made by M. Buss, The Prophetic Word of Hosea, 1969, 1, which relates life-situations only to institutions in a broad sense. In anthropology, a well-known set of analyses by E. E. Evans-Pritchard examined the major institutions (economics, politics, kinship, and religion) of the Nuer, treating each of these as aspects of a social order. That such domains interact even in a modern society can be seen, for instance, in many a wedding ceremony — although specific focal organizations (institutions in a narrow sense, e.g., banks and churches) have been developed for them.

[16] For instance, »prophetic« words were given both by specialized persons and by others at Mari (as emphasized by E. Noort, Untersuchungen zum Gottesbescheid in Mari, 1977, 51.73) and in early Christianity (J. Panagopoulos, Prophetic Vocation in the New Testament and Today, 1977, 8).

The role of a prophet or seer can be characterized as the receiving and transmitting of communications not available to ordinary conscious sensitivity, which are held to come from a source (the divine) or through a form of perception transcending normal spatiotemporal limitations (e.g., I Sam 9 20 10 2–6). Subjectively, such communications occur in many forms, including visions, the hearing of voices, and a (less easily described) sense of insight into reality. The precise nature of these experiences is a fascinating topic which cannot be explored here in detail. Recently, however, considerable attention has been paid to altered states of awareness, including various forms of ecstasy, so that much has been learned about their physiological and social aspects[17]. To a greater or lesser extent, all human beings share in such states. Yet some persons develop a predilection toward special experiences and thus naturally enter a role in which these are prized. Furthermore, some one who has accepted such a role may well actively seek — and perhaps simulate — an appropriate state.

One can ask for what purpose such communications are valued. The answer is that, for the most part, they serve the making of decisions and the handling of problems[18]. This is the human situation to which they primarily belong. Individuals and groups are constantly faced with more or less important choices and more or less serious crises. They do not have immediate knowledge, however, of all the relevant considerations that would enable them to make a wise decision or to take effective action. Indeed, »practical reasoning« involves an holistic grasp of the state of reality as it impinges on the present moment; one can call such an apprehension an »intuition«[19]. Individuals can receive such insight personally, for instance in a dream (as in Gen 31 3.11), or they may accept it from some one else, who may be a professional in giving guidance.

---

[17] See, e.g., J. White, ed., The Highest State of Consciousness, 1972; C. Tart, ed., Altered States of Consciousness, 1969; E. Bourguignon op. cit.; S. Walker, Ceremonial Spirit Possession in Africa and Afro-America, 1972, 147; and n. 30 below.

[18] E.g., I Sam 23 1–13 I Reg 22 5–28. G. Park, Divination and its Social Context, The Journal of the Royal Anthropological Institute 93 (1963), 208, calls divination (broadly conceived) »the midwife of decision«. R. Lannoy, The Speaking Tree, 1971, 199, and J. Hayes, An Introduction to Old Testament Study, 1979, 383, relate prophetic and similar activity to »crises«; of course, some of the problems dealt with are quite minor. G. Fohrer (Studien zur alttestamentlichen Prophetie, 1967, 30f. etc.) is notable for stressing the relation of prophecy to the decisions of recipients in their present.

[19] On the holistic nature of practical reasoning, see M. Buss, Understanding Communication, 27. There is some reason to believe that holistic or intuitive perception is carried out especially in the right hemisphere of the human brain; see, e.g., R. Ornstein, The Psychology of Consciousness, 1972, 50–72, and still somewhat more speculatively, D. Loye, The Knowable Future: A Psychology of Forecasting and Prophecy, 1978, 51–65, pointing to the use of perception for decisions.

In content, prophetic messages — like more mechanical divinations — deal especially with the assessment of the actual, which contains elements of particularity and of the new[20]. A general insight — also a concern of revelation — does not need to be rediscovered constantly; once gained (e.g., through a figure such as Moses), it can become a part of the cultural heritage of a group and may be guarded by priests who are not themselves viewed as revelatory persons. Laws, for instance, are general in principle and have become highly changeable only in modern times, because of rapid technological developments. Confrontation with actual conditions, however, has always been subject to considerable uncertainty, so that continuing light is valued for dealing with them. It can be noted that the words of a prophet or seer are inherently new and unpredictable, for no revelation would otherwise be required. Thus we have here an interesting paradox, namely that the role-expectation for prophecy is the presentation of a word that cannot be specifically anticipated.

Prophetic words serve both individual and social needs. Most of the individual and many of the social concerns are naturally brought to a prophet, seer, or diviner as an inquiry. A society, however, can also benefit from the unasked giving of advice and judgment. That may or may not take place during ritual occasions. In any case, it is not true that cultic processes deal only with general and repeatable matters. Thus, for instance, in a Voodoo ceremony, the gods, through a possessed person, »threaten sinners, and gladly give advice«[21]. An important use of oracles lies in the detection of sources of evil, so that remedial steps can be taken. In what may be called the judicial realm, that includes the identification of evil-doers and determinations of guilt[22].

In Israel, as is well known, a significant aspect of prophetic activity consisted in the evaluation of kings and of the nation as a whole. Such a role is unusual in the degree to which it was carried out and, indeed,

---

[20] »Divination« (in a broad sense, including prophecy) has been described by J. P. Vernant, Paroles et signes muets, in: J. P. Vernant, et al, Divination et rationalité, 1974, 17, as being concerned with the »knowledge of singular events«; D. Napier, Prophet, Prophetism, The Interpreter's Dictionary of the Bible, III, 1962, 905, characterized prophecy as »address to history«. See, further, M. Buss, Hosea, 116–118; in part, J. Muilenburg, The »Office« of the Prophet in Ancient Israel, in: J. P. Hyatt, ed., The Bible in Modern Scholarship, 1965, 97; and R. E. Clements, Prophecy and Tradition, 1975, 25.

[21] A. Métraux, Voodoo in Haiti, 1959, 125 (cf. 129–131). Similarly, for a hill tribe in South India, D. Mandelbaum, Social Trends and Personal Pressures, in: Language, Culture, and Personality: Essays in Honor of Edward Sapir, 1941, 221; for the Near East, cf. e.g., ANET, 26. Such dealing with specific problems in a ritual context must be distinguished from general, repeatable oracles found in some biblical psalms. (It is unlikely that a recitation of the latter was called »prophesying«, except so far as inspired singing as such was designated by that term, as in Ex 15 20 I Chr 25 1–3.)

[22] E.g., A. Retel-Laurentin, Oracles et ordalies chez les Nzakara, 1969, 34.

expected there; but it stands in continuity with the tasks of seers and diviners in general, as well as with provisions made in different societies for the criticism of authorities[23]. Israelite prophets not only engaged in advice and denunciation, but, according to biblical narratives, were instrumental in the founding[24] and ending[25] of dynasties. With the passing of kingship, the functions relating to royalty became irrelevant, of course. That does not mean, however, that prophecy itself ceased. On the contrary, it remained for the rest of the biblical period, although dealing with somewhat different problems and participating in new forms of organization of life and expression.

The prophetic role persists to the present day, although its operation has been transformed and to some extent its functions have been dispersed. For in all probability holistic perception and guidance for decision are inescapable ingredients of human existence. The words of the biblical prophets also continue to be relevant because they dealt with life at such a fundamental level that their assessments transcend some of the more incidental differences between events.

---

[23] Jesters attached to many African kings expressed jokes, praise, and criticism (M. Gluckman, Politics, Law and Ritual in Tribal Society, 1965, 103). Aztec and Ashanti kings could be deposed; see, P. Radin and P. Akoi in: Sacral Kingship, 1959, 89. 146). In China criticism of kings occurred formally and informally, deposing or killing a king was legitimated, and a dynasty could be held to lose its heavenly mandate (e.g., M. Weber, Gesammelte Aufsätze zur Religionssoziologie, I 1920, 303. 312; and H. H. Rowley, Prophecy and Religion in Ancient China and Israel, 1956, 57–73). These examples are by no means exhaustive.

[24] I Sam 10 1.21 (Saul) 16 13 (David) I Reg 11 31 (Jeroboam) II Reg 9 6 (Jehu). On the dynastic character of kingship, cf. now T. Ishida, The Royal Dynasties of Ancient Israel, 1977.

[25] The rejection of a king did not imply his being deposed, but the end of the dynasty. I Sam 13 14 15 26, rejecting Saul, who remains king; I Reg 14 7–14, announcing the end of the »house of Jeroboam«; I Reg 16 2–4, against «Baasha and his house« (16 2 may imply an unrecorded prophetic designation of Baasha as king); I Reg 21 21.29, ending the »house« of Ahab, but granting it an extension of one generation because of Ahab's repentance. The sons of Saul, Jeroboam, and Baasha were killed in revolts (the latter two within two years), perhaps in part as a result of the reported prophetic rejections, insofar as these are historical. Similarly, the »house« of Jeroboam II, against which God will rise with the sword according to Amos 7 9, ceased with a revolt six months after that king's death. The fact that this prophetic role pattern is only partially recorded in the books of Samuel and Kings indicates that it represents the view of one or more sources used by those books rather than specifically a conception of the final editors. (For discussions of some of these traditions, see W. Dietrich, Prophetie und Geschichte, 1972, 10. 26. 51; and S. J. De Vries, Prophet Against Prophet, 1978, 58. 85. 127.)

Selfhood and Other Concepts

Almost as prominent in social psychology as the notion of role is the concept of the *self*. One might imagine that this is a strictly psychological, not a sociological, topic. Yet a central thesis for investigators of this phenomenon is that selfhood arises only in a social context[26]. Selfhood involves reflexivity, i. e., self-reference, which requires an imaginative standing outside of oneself. Such a stand is aided by awareness that one becomes an object to another. Not a purely self-centered individual, then, but rather one that is »decentered«[27], truly has a self. In other words, self-transcendence is an integral part of selfhood.

This conception is of major importance for an understanding of religion, especially if religion is defined in terms of beliefs and practices relating directly to an over-all view of existence. In referring to a reality (or to a group of realities) which is ultimate, one finds a center of orientation outside of oneself — unless, of course, one identifies oneself with the ultimate, a position which for social and reflective reasons is normally considered pathological. From the perspective of such an ultimate reference point the actions of an individual or group can be evaluated so that a framework is given for self-evaluation, including self-criticism. Clearly, biblical references to deity and the fact that Israelites allowed themselves to be judged by high standards for existence are made possible by this sociopsychological process. Quite generally in human life, a fairly conscious adoption of social values, often in connection with religious belief[28], takes the place of inherited instincts serving the welfare of a species.

Prophecy exhibits self-transcendence both in the form of its experience and in its content. The prophet may experience a form of possession, in which another power is believed to take over one's consciousness[29]. Thus the prophetic word arrives, at least in part, through a receptive attitude to the divine. In content, the great Israelite prophets stress the

---

[26] Crucial theoretical contributions include those of C. Cooley, Human Nature and the Social Order, 1902, 152; G. H. Mead, Mind, Self and Society, 1937; S. Duval and R. Wicklund, A Theory of Objective Self-Awareness, 1972.

[27] J. Piaget and B. Inhelder, The Psychology of the Child, 1969, 94f.

[28] Religion tends to have two poles; on the one hand, an orientation toward the comprehensive and ethical (with belief in a high god or fundamental spiritual reality), and on the other hand — shading over into what is often called magic — an involvement in limited, even competitive, concerns (with beliefs in multiple spirits and highly concrete cults). See, e.g., A. Lang, Magic and Religion, 1901, 51; P. Radin, Primitive Religion, 1937, 258; E. Evans-Pritchard, Nuer Religion, 1956. The former pole is emphasized in biblical prophecy.

[29] For data and views, cf. S. Parker, Possession Trance and Prophecy in Pre-exilic Israel, VT 28 (1978), 271–285.

concern of human beings for one another in such a way that social oppression is criticized. In this emphasis they do not stand alone. For ecstatic — and similarly mystical — religion frequently stands in opposition to stratification in society[30]. It can be noted, of course, that through presumed contact with the divine the prophet or ecstatic person gains, rather than loses, power and authority and is thus able to present a challenge or promise for a transformation of life.

The ultimate reference point of prophecy emerges in the concept of an »end«. Insofar as a prophetic word confronts existence on a fundamental level — as happened in Israel[31] — it raises the question of a solution as such. The acuteness of this issue rises both with the degree of self-reflection and with the seriousness of tensions present in a society at a given time. Both of these elements appear to have been fairly high in the sphere of the Bible — the former aided by an increasingly widespread use of writing, the latter by the development of aristocratic organization and empire building. It is then understandable that a divine victory over evil, establishing a truly good state, is announced in biblical prophecy. Such an end embodies self-transcendence and, at the same time, fulfilment[32].

It has often been observed that many of the words of Israelite prophets considerably exceed in profundity those of most shamans and diviners. Such a comparison needs to be set into the context of two considerations, which are related to each other: the relative complexity of societies in which they operate and the fact that biblical words represent not simply views of momentary situations, but analyses of human life which were preserved in writing because of their potential for a continuing significance. In societies comparable to Israel in terms of technological and cultural development, critical reflections concerning the self and society, together with a groping toward a better reality, became quite important. Most of the major religious traditions that arose under those conditions indeed were skeptical of mechanical divination[33].

---

[30] I. Lewis, Ecstatic Religion, 1971, argues that ecstacy provides a vehicle for protest. Bhakti (ecstatic devotion), Tantra, and many other forms of mysticism in India as well as elsewhere have sought to transcend class distinctions (see, e.g., T. Hopkins and E. Dimock in: M. Singer, ed., Krishna, 1966, 14—22. 53).

[31] H. Saggs, The Encounter with the Divine in Mesopotamia and Israel, 1977, 151, finds this the most peculiar feature of biblical prophecy within the context of the Near East, in that it prescribes behavior for »mankind«.

[32] The transcendence of boundaries and of self in the victory of life was noted by G. Simmel, Lebensanschauung, 1918, 1—27. Theology needs a view of eschatology which is theoretical and practical at once; cf. G. Fohrer, Studien, 293f.; M. Buss, Hosea, 129—140; and, for the terminology, G. Wanke, »Eschatologie«, KuD 16 (1970), 300—312.

[33] E.g., T. Fahd, La divination arabe, 1966, 64; L. Epstein, Causation in Tibetan Religion, Diss. Washington, 1977, 227. Neither the Bible nor Eastern religion, however, entirely eschewed mechanical oracles.

Besides ideas of role and selfhood, there are other topics of social psychology which can be explored fruitfully in relation to biblical study[34]. One of these is that of communication; the use of writing, a special subtopic already touched upon, involves not only specific questions regarding the transmission of prophetic words but also the nature of human life within societies employing this medium. Another is that of a group's or person's cognitive structure, including some issues (such as responses to dissonance) which are currently quite controversial. Finally, one can point to attempts to determine the origin and dynamics of a sense of justice, whose relevance to biblical study is yet unclear. Because of the importance of these questions to theology, one may hope that they will receive careful attention with the aid of appropriate data.

---

[34] Useful surveys of the field can be found in W. Sahakian, Systematic Social Psychology, 1974, and K. Shaver, Principles of Social Psychology, 1977.

Notes on two verses in Isaiah (26 16 and 66 17)

By J. A. Emerton

(St John's College, Cambridge, CB2 1TP, England)

Among the parts of the Old Testament to whose understanding Professor Georg Fohrer has made a valuable contribution is the book of Isaiah, on which he has published a commentary in three volumes. The requirements of the series, Zürcher Bibelkommentare, make it primarily an exegetical work, rather than a textual and philological one, although it is, of course, based on a careful and well-informed study of the Hebrew text. The following notes discuss the text of two difficult verses in Isaiah and the principal solutions that have been suggested to their problems, and also make new attempts to overcome the difficulties.

(1) Isaiah 26 16

יהוה בַּצַּר פְּקָדוּךָ

צָקוּן לַחַשׁ מוּסָרְךָ לָמוֹ

This difficult verse speaks of *ṣăr* and of God's *mûsar*, and thus appears to belong in sense with verses 17–18, which describe the people's distress. Unlike them, however, it has verbs in the third person plural, not the first person plural, although there is a variant reading *pᵉqădnûka*. Some manuscripts of the LXX have the first person plural reading ἐμνή-σθημέν σου instead of the singular reading ἐμνήσθην σου (see Ziegler), but it is doubtful how much weight should be attached to the Greek evidence. The question of the person of the verb has been much discussed, and I have nothing new to add to the discussion, and so I shall not go into the problem or the related question whether *lamô* should be emended to *lanû* on the basis of the LXX's ἡμῖν or whether M. Dahood, Biblica 47 (1966), 409f., is right in thinking that *lmw* can be understood as a preposition with a first person plural suffix. To read the first person plural in verse 16 as in verses 17–18 makes the text run more smoothly, but it is by no means certain that the abrupt transition from third to first person is not original.

The problems of the first part of the verse are less difficult than those of the second. It is questionable whether the divine name at the beginning of the verse should be regarded as secondary on metrical grounds (so Duhm and Cheyne), for the metre of this part of the chapter does not appear to be regular. In any case, the deletion depends, in part at least, on emendation of the second part of the verse, and we shall see below that the change proposed there is doubtful.

The main difficulty of the first part of the verse is to explain the meaning of the verb *pqd*[1], which appears to be used in a unique way. It denotes an action of people directed towards God, and a meaning like »entreat« or »seek« would fit the context, but the verb does not have such a meaning elsewhere in the Hebrew Bible. It has been thought by some (e.g. Delitzsch, Gesenius—Buhl, and Zorell) to have a meaning comparable to »miss« in I Sam 20 6 25 15 Isa 34 16 Jer 3 16 — »*desiderat rem absentem*« (Zorell) — but the supposed semantic development is far from certain. Not to find something is not so easily to be identified with desiring or seeking God. Another suggestion is that the verb here means »aufsuchen, besuchen«, and Drechsler compares Judg 15 1 and I Sam 17 18. Once again, however, the contexts are so different that the suggestion is scarcely convincing. It may be better to postulate a meaning akin to »care for, pay attention to«, which is perhaps found in I Kings 9 34 Zech 10 3 11 16 Ps 8 5. Perhaps the people »pay attention to« God, almost »turn to« God. In any case, it may be noted that the Syriac cognate not only means »to visit«, etc., but has acquired the meaning »to entreat« (Payne Smith), whatever the precise semantic development may have been. While it would be rash to suggest that the Hebrew verb must have followed the same semantic development as its Syriac cognate, such a development cannot be excluded as impossible, and it fits the needs of Isa 26 16. Therefore, although the verse is unique in that God is the object of the verb, it is probably better to retain the text than to emend it. If, however, the text is corrupt, the solution to the problem that keeps closest to the Massoretic Text, and therefore the best solution, is to follow Hylmö and read $b^e\check{s}ar\ p\mathring{a}qd^eka$. It is also possible to read $b^e\check{s}ar\ p^equddat^eka$ with Kaiser or $\check{s}ar\ p^equddat^eka$ with Leibmann, but both suggestions are farther from the M.T., and the latter is less close than the former. The phrase »in the distress of thy visiting, or punishing«, that is, the distress caused by God's punishment, must be construed with the later part of the verse, whether it be a verbal or a nominal clause. That makes good sense, and it is difficult to see why Wildberger objects to Kaiser's emendation on

---

[1] Talmon 125 thinks that 1QIs^a read the word as a noun *pqdyk*, and that it was taken with *ṣqwn*, which was understood to be a contraction of *ṣ^eqwn*: »Lord, in distress they call out your precepts«. Even if he is right in his reading of 1QIs^a's text, in holding that *ṣqwn* is likely to have been regarded as a contraction, and in supposing that *pqdyk* would have been thought to be a suitable object of the verb *ṣ^eq*, such a way of understanding this part of the verse can scarcely have been original — and Talmon does not claim that it was, but speaks only of the meaning intended in 1QIs^a.

the ground that »ein Verb ist unentbehrlich«. Rudolph's emendation *buṣṣār* (or *quṣṣār*) *bipᵉquddatᵉka* also involves the second part of the verse, where he changes *ṣaqûn* to *qaṣenû*: »abgeschnitten (vermindert Ps 76, 13) wurde durch deine Heimsuchung unser Ende (unsere Grenze, unser Gebiet, vgl קצוי 15)« (p. 20). Ehrlich's reading *bǎṣṣarā nôdækka . . . lanû* goes farther from the M.T. The change of *pᵉqadûka* to *puqqᵉdû* in the first edition (1941) of Kissane's commentary is less drastic: »with trouble were they visited«. The second edition (1960) was published posthumously, and Isa 26 16 is one of the places where the textual notes have not been revised in keeping with the writer's most recent judgement about the text (cp. p. vii), but the translation he gives seems to presuppose a return to the traditional text: »in distress they appealed to thee«. It may be suspected that the Good News Bible accepts Kissane's emendation of 1941 for its translation »You punished your people, LORD«; the passive construction in Hebrew may have been replaced by an active construction in English. If, however, *pᵉqadûka* or *pᵉqădnûka* is defensible, there is no need to make any change to the first part of the verse, unless there is anything in the second part to make it necessary.

The second part of the verse is more difficult. It is best to start with the traditional rendering, which is based on Jewish exegesis as it is represented by Rashi, Ibn Ezra, and Qimḥi. It is well illustrated by the Revised Version: »they poured out a prayer [mg. Heb. whisper] *when thy chastening was upon them*«. The last two words in the Hebrew are treated as a circumstantial clause. The first word, *ṣaqûn*, is regarded as the third person plural of the perfect of the verb *ṣûq*, a by-form of *yaṣăq*, and *lăḥăš* is thought to mean »whisper« and to be used in the sense of »whispered prayer«. There are several difficulties in such a way of understanding this part of the verse.

Two difficulties are raised by *ṣaqûn*. First, the use of paragogic *nun* with the perfect is anomalous (G. K. § 44 l). The only two other examples are in Dtn 8 3. 16, where we find *yᵉdaʿûn* – and the presence of *yodh* at the beginning of the root may have suggested an external resemblance to the imperfect. Second, the figurative use of this by-form of *yaṣăq* to mean »to pour out (prayer)« is strange, notwithstanding the analogous employment of *špk* in Ps 102 1, where we find *yišpok śiḥô*. Moreover, none of the ancient versions understands the word as a verb. The LXX (ἐν θλίψει), Vulgate (*in tribulatione*), Peshitta (*wᵉbaḥᵉbušyaʾ*), and Targum (*bᵉʿaqaʾ*) all translate it as a noun meaning »distress« with a preposition meaning »in«. It is doubtful whether they all used a Hebrew text with *b* at the beginning of the word, for they may have supplied it from the preposition in *bǎṣṣār* earlier in the verse. It is clear, however, that the word was thought to be a noun, and it has been compared with such nouns as *śaśôn*, *zadôn*, and *laṣôn*, which are derived from hollow roots. The Hebrew verb *ṣûq* is used in the hi. to mean »to constrain, bring into straits, press upon«, and there are cognate nouns ṣûqâ, mûṣaq, maṣôq, and mᵉṣûqâ, denoting »distress« or the like.

The understanding of lăḥăš as a »whisper« goes back a long way. The Vulgate translates this part of the verse *in tribulatione murmuris doctrina tua eis*, and a similar understanding underlies the Targum's »in their troubles they used secretly [*buḥšay*] to teach the instruction of thy law« (Stenning). The Peshitta's rendering »and in straitness they whispered thy chastisement« has a verb *lḥšw* corresponding to the M.T.'s noun, and it may have been based on a variant Hebrew reading *lḥšw*, which is found in 1QIs$^{a\,2}$. The hitp. of the verb is used of whispering in the Hebrew Bible, and the pi. appears in the more specialized sense of trying to charm a snake. The noun *lăḥăš* is also used of snake-charming in Jer 8 17 and Koh 10 11, and either in that sense or in the more general sense of incantation in Isa 3 3; and in Isa 3 20 the plural apparently denotes »amulets« or »lucky charms«. The noun does not appear to denote any other kind of whispering in the Hebrew Bible, but that may be a matter or chance. It is possible that a noun meaning »whisper« came to mean »prayer«, and von Soden records for the Gt of the Accadian verb *laḥāšu* the rendering »flüsternd beten«, but there is no evidence for a comparable semantic development in Hebrew. It would, moreover, be strange if a noun normally meaning »a charm« or the like were employed without further explanation or definition as a word denoting a prayer to God. The LXX, the only major version that has not been considered so far in the discussion of *lăḥăš*, raises a further problem when it renders the first two words of the second part of the verse by ἐν θλίψει μικρᾷ. It is unlikely that the underlying Hebrew text had a word as different from *lăḥăš* as *qaṭôn*. Conceivably, *qṭwn lḥš* was read in place of *ṣqwn lḥš* (cp. Gray), but the suggested Hebrew is not very close to that of the received text. Nor does the Greek adjective seem a likely rendering of *kăḥăš*, which is one of Ottley's two suggestions. His other suggestion, *ḥăllăš*, is better, but it is still doubtful whether it would have been rendered »little«. Driver (1958) has suggested — not very convincingly — that the translator understood *lăḥăš* »as a figure of speech for a very small amount (cp. Fr. *soupçon*)«. Oort, however, put forward the view that μικρᾷ is an inner-Greek corruption of πικρᾷ, »bitter«, and he has been followed by Cheyne and Fischer[3]. Unfortunately, the suggestion involves the further hypothesis that *lāḥaṣ* was read in place of *lăḥăš*; and it is hazardous to base an emendation of the Greek on an imagined different reading of the Hebrew, particularly if the emended Greek text

---

[2] Talmon 125 thinks that the scribe of 1QIs^a understood this part of the verse to mean »they whisper your commandments unto themselves«.

[3] Ziegler appears to think that the suggestion originated with Fischer (p. 20), but it was made by Oort long before.

is regarded as evidence for an emendation of the Hebrew. The LXX appears to offer us no help in our attempts to solve the problem of the word *lăḥăš*.

The first type of solution of the problem of the second part of the verse is to emend *ṣaqûn* to a form of the verb *ṣaʿaq*, »to cry out«. Houbigant suggested in the eighteenth century that we should read *ṣaʿaqû bᵉlăḥăš*, which he translated *clamant in angustia*. Since *lăḥăš* does not mean *angustia*, J. D. Michaelis (Vorzügliche Varianten 67) suggested that Houbigant really intended *lăḥăṣ*, and that noun has been read by some later commentators. Cheyne suggested two centuries after Houbigant that we should emend the text to *ṣaʿăqnû millăḥăṣ kî mûsarᵉka lanû*, »we cried out in distress when Thy discipline came on us«; and he made a questionable appeal to the LXX in partial support of *millăḥăṣ*. Cheyne has been followed by such scholars as Marti, Condamin, and Wildberger, and probably by Fohrer, whose translation of an emended text is »haben wir . . . vor Bedrängnis geschrien, da deine Züchtigung über uns kam«. Variant forms of the theory are favoured by Kaiser, who reads *ṣaʿăqnû bᵉlăḥăṣ . . . lak*, and by Hylmö, who reads *zaʿăqnû* and takes it with the first part of the verse, and then reads *millăḥăṣ mûsarᵉka ḥălnû*. As we have seen, the textual notes on this verse in the second edition of Kissane's commentary have not been revised, but a change of *ṣaqûn* is presupposed by his translation »They cried out and Thy chastisement upon them was withdrawn«; presumably, *lăḥăš* is emended to a verb meaning »was withdrawn«. The emendation is improbable, because its reference to deliverance comes too soon. The other forms of the theory make good sense and are attractive, but they involve several changes to the consonantal text, and we must hesitate to accept any of them until we have investigated other possibilities.

The second type of theory follows the ancient versions in seeing in *ṣqwn* a noun from the root *ṣwq* which, as we have seen, means »to constrain, bring into straits, press upon« in the hi. of the verb and appears in nouns with a related meaning. An early form of the theory, however, which was advanced by J. H. Michaelis (and accepted by J. D. Michaelis) derived the noun from a root *ṣqn*, which is found in Ethiopic with the meaning *munivit, circumsepsit*, and suggested that it referred to a defence against sorcery; but it would be better to postulate a noun from a root that is well-attested in Hebrew, if possible, rather than to make use of a root that is otherwise known only in Ethiopic. Whether the noun is derived from *ṣwq* or *ṣqn*, and whether it is thought to be in the absolute or the construct state, several translations have been suggested, such as »und deine Züchtigungen sind eine Bewahrung vor dem Übel« (J. D. Michaelis), »Zauberzwang war deine Züchtigung für uns« (Koppe), »*Drangsal* [war der] *Bann Deiner Zucht für sie*, d.h. die Noth gab ihnen Augen, die Drangsal Ohren für Dich, die Noth machte sie aufmerksam, die Drangsal gehorsam gegen Dich« (Böttcher), »ein Drangsal von der Kraft eines Zauberspruchs ist uns deine Züchtigung« (Ehrlich, who reads either ṣᵉqôn lăḥăš or ṣaqôn loḥeš). A variant form of the theory is Ewald's reading ṣaqôn luḥăš, »ein zauberschuzring wurde deine züchtigung ihnen«. Koppe's theory was accepted by, among others, Dillmann and Duhm. Against such theories it may be argued that God's punishment of his people is unlikely to have been compared to magic, which was detested by the prophets. Procksch avoids the difficulty by changing lăḥăš to millăḥăš, as in the theory of Cheyne, but the need thus to make two further changes to the consonantal text is regrettable. Some forms of this type of theory retain lăḥăš unchanged but give it a meaning other than »sorcery«. The American Jewish translation The Prophets (1978) returns to the old view that lăḥăš denotes a prayer (»Your chastisement reduced them // To anguished whispered prayer«), but the difficulty in understanding the noun thus remains. Driver has advanced two different explanations. He suggested in 1937 that lăḥăš is related to the Accadian verb laḥāšu, »to be bowed down«, and offered the rendering »thy chastisement (has been) a humiliating constraint unto us«. By 1958, however, he had abandoned his own suggestion, perhaps because the existence of the relevant meaning for the Accadian verb is questionable (it is not listed by von Soden). Instead, he favoured the view, which was mentioned above as his explanation of the LXX, that it means »whisper« and is used »as a figure of speech for a very small amount«. The clause means, in his opinion, »(for) the least (whisper of a) rebuke from Thee (was) distress(ful) to them«, and his interpretation has been accepted in the New English Bible, which says that »we« were »chastened by the mere whisper of thy rebuke«. Driver's explanation is questionable for two reasons. First, the figurative sense he gives to »whisper« (a meaning which, in any case, the noun has nowhere else in the Hebrew Bible) is an unproven guess. Secondly, it is not clear why God's rebuke should be thought to be »a very small amount«. While a small rebuke might well have distressed the Jews, the context suggests that his judgement had, in fact, been much more severe.

Thirdly, the other suggestions do not belong to either of the two groups considered above. Hitzig abandoned the traditional understanding of lăḥăš, but sought to retain the M.T.: he thought it said that the people »Ergossen sich in Gebet, das deine Züchtigung beschwöre«. In addition to giving a dubious meaning to ṣaqûn, his rendering is improbable in a description of the effect of God's punishment of his people. Several scholars have emended ṣaqûn to a form of the noun ṣûqâ, lăḥăš to lăḥăṣ, and lamô to lanû. Thus, Oort suggests bᵉṣûqâ lăḥăṣ (»in de benauwdheid was de verdrukking ons eene bestraffing van u«), Liebmann ṣûqăt lăḥăṣ (1905, p. 168; cp. 1904, pp. 77—80), and Fischer bᵉṣûqăt lăḥăṣ. The first edition of Kissane's commentary reads maṣôq wᵉlăḥăṣ but does not change *lamô* (»Distress and oppression were Thy chastisement to them«). Rudolph goes farther: in addition to emending *ṣaqûn* to *qaṣenû* and taking it with the first part of the verse (see above), he reads *ḥalăšnû mûsarᵉka lanû*, »wir wurden geschwächt, da deine Züchtigung uns traf«. It is not clear what has been done with the Hebrew text by those responsible for the Good News Bible, where this part of the verse is translated »and in anguish they prayed to you«. It may be that they adopted an emendation similar to that of Kaiser (see above), but read the third person plural in place of the first (*ṣaᶜaqû bᵉlăḥăṣ . . . lak*). There is, however, no obvious rendering of *mûsarᵉka*; perhaps they thought that, since they had referred to punishment in their rendering of the first part of the verse, there was no need to mention it again, despite the fact that there is a word for it in the Hebrew. Against all such emendations, it may be argued that they depart from the traditional text more than could be wished.

It thus seems that none of the attempts to obtain a satisfactory meaning from the M.T. is convincing, and that the emendations that have been proposed either are insufficient to yield good sense or depart too far from the traditional consonantal text. There is thus room for a new suggestion. Perhaps those scholars who follow the ancient versions in understanding *ṣqwn* to be a noun from the root *ṣwq* are right. It may also be suggested that *lăḥăš* has arisen by an accidental metathesis, and that the text should be emended to *ḥăllaš*. It was only after the emendation had occurred to me that I learned that Ottley had suggested that the LXX was based on a text with *ḥăllaš* and that Rudolph had postulated a reading *ḥalăšnû*, but the former scholar did not appear to think that the reading was original (and his theory that the LXX presupposes it is questionable), and the latter's emendation is not identical with the one I have proposed or as close to the M.T. If the reading *ṣᵉqôn ḥăllaš* is accepted, the second clause of Isa 26 16 means »thy chastening is to them affliction (brought on) a weak man«. God's punishment is likened to suffering brought on a man who is feeble and unable to bear what is imposed on him. Indeed, the weakness may be part of the punishment. The idea of the weakness of the sinner who is punished by God is found in the Psalter (especially Ps 6, 38, and 88) and in Job (e.g. 6, 13, 14).

The emendation proposed above has the advantage of keeping closer to the M.T. than is usual with emendations of the verse, for it involves only the inversion of two consonants. If *ṣᵉqôn ḥăllaš* is read in Isa 26 16, the verse may be translated:

O LORD, they entreated thee in distress;
thy chastening was to them like the affliction of a weak man.

Postscript

The above discussion of Isa 26 16 had been completed and submitted for publication when W. H. Irwin's article, Syntax and style in Isaiah 26, CBQ 41 (1979), 240—61, reached me. He considers Isa 26 16 on pp. 250—252 and, after emending the vocalization of one word, translates the verse as follows:

Yahweh, in Confinement may they be placed by you,
Be restrained by the press of your correction on them.

Several comments may be made on the translation and Irwin's justification of it.

First, $p^eqadûka$ is emended to $puqqadûka$ and understood to be a third person plural perfect pu. with a second masculine singular suffix, and the suffix is thought to be a »dative suffix expressing agency«. There is no need to discuss here the disputed question whether a precative perfect existed in Hebrew, and it would be possible to modify the translation so that the verb was understood to describe a state of affairs rather than to express a wish. Irwin's understanding of the suffix as an expression of agency may, however, be contested. He appeals to M. Bogaert, Les suffixes verbaux non accusatifs dans le sémitique nord-occidental et particulièrement en hébreu, Biblica 45 (1964), 220—247, where the question is discussed on pp. 240f. Bogaert mentions only four examples of the use of a suffix to express the agent of a passive verb: Ps 63 11 91 15 119 14 (Ps 50 15 is not, as Irwin supposes, cited as an instance) Job 31 18. We need not linger over Ps 119 14, which Bogaert himself regards as »moins sûr«. The text of the opening words of Ps 63 11 has long been suspect: $yăggîruhû\ ʿăl-y^edê-ḥaræb$. Bogaert wishes to read the verb as a passive, presumably in the third person masculine plural, and thinks that the third person masculine singular suffix refers to Sheol as the agent: the evildoers will be delivered by Sheol into the power of the sword. Against Bogaert's theory, it may be maintained that Sheol has not been mentioned (unless $l^ešôʾâ$ in v. 10 is emended) except in the form $b^etăḥtiyyôt\ hāʾaræṣ$, which is unlikely to have been represented by a masculine suffix. Moreover, Sheol is the place to which the evildoers will go, rather than the agent that delivers them into the power of the sword. In Ps 91 15 Bogaert wishes to emend $wăʾăkăbb^edehû$ to $wăʾăkubb^edehû$, »et je serai glorifié par lui«. The change is unnecessary, however, for the pi. of kbd can be used with God as the subject and man as the object (I Sam 2 30), as Bogaert concedes, and there is no need for Ps 91 15 to have the same meaning as the corresponding part of Ps 50 15. In Job 31 18 Bogaert changes $g^edălănî$ to $gudd^elănî$ and translates the first part of the verse: »Car depuis *son* jeune âge, il (l'orphelin) a été élevé par moi comme un père«. Yet the difficulty of the verse, for which several solutions have been proposed (see, for example, Fohrer's commentary), is such that it cannot serve as evidence for the hypothesis that a pronominal suffix could represent the agent of a passive verb — and Bogaert's suggestion is not helped by his questionable view that the first person singular suffix of *minnᵉʿûrāy* is to be given a third person masculine singular meaning. A theory about the existence of a Hebrew idiom must be based on unambiguous evidence if it is to be convincing, and Irwin's treatment of *pᵉqadûka* in Isa 26 16 must be rejected because it thus lacks a firm foundation.

Secondly, *ṣaqûn* is also understood to be a precative perfect: »[may they] Be restrained«; and Irwin wishes to keep the verb unchanged. He admits that the paragogic *nun*, is suspicious, but he does not attempt to justify it.

Thirdly, *lăḥăš* is understood to be a by-form of *lăḥăṣ*, as was suggested by M. Dahood in Orientalia NS 45 (1976), 343. Dahood believes that a comparison of I Kings 22 27 with Isa 30 20 »reveals that« *lăḥăṣ* and *ṣăr* »are a fixed pair«, and that, since Isa 26 16 contains *ṣăr*, we should understand *lăḥăš* to be equivalent to *lăḥăṣ*. He adduces as evidence for the interchange of *ṣ* and *š* Ugaritic *mḫṣ* and *mḫš*, and Hebrew »*ḥrṣ* and *ḥrš*, both signifying ›to cut, engrave‹«. The equation of *lăḥăš* with *lăḥăṣ* is not quite as simple as he appears to suppose. Two references are insufficient to prove that *lăḥăṣ* and *ṣăr* are a fixed pair and, even if they were, it would not necessarily follow that *lăḥăš* is to be identified with *lăḥăṣ* in Isa 26 16 simply because the other half of the verse contains *ṣăr*. Indeed, if *lăḥăṣ* and *ṣăr* were a fixed pair, we might ask why the verse has *lăḥăš* instead of *lăḥăṣ*, which is, ex hypothesi, the fixed partner of *ṣăr*. As far as Ugaritic *mḫṣ* and *mḫš* are concerned, Irwin himself draws attention to M. Held's article, *mḫṣ/*mḫš* in Ugaritic and other Semitic languages (a study in comparative lexicography), JAOS 79 (1959), 169—176. Held points out on p. 173 that *mḫš* is found only in the form *mḫšt*, and he suggests that »in this sequence the emphatic *ṣ* became *š* through partial assimilation to the following *-t*«, and he draws attention to Accadian analogies. »In other words,« he says, »this would not be a question of a regular change of *ṣ* to *š*, but rather one of strictly positional variation«. No influence likely to have changed *ṣ* to *š* has been pointed out in Isa 26 16. Dahood's other example is even less satisfactory. Hebrew *ḥaraš*, »to engrave«, is normally, and doubtless rightly, thought to be related to Arabic *ḥaraṯa*, Aramaic *ḥᵉrăṯ*, and Ugaritic *ḥrṯ*, »to plough«, etc., and so it appears that the third radical was not originally a sibilant at all. It is thus far from certain that the root *ḥrṣ* is a by-form.

Fourthly, Irwin suggests that the preposition in *băṣṣăr* »extends its force to« *lăḥăš*. If so, the preposition is used in two different senses, for it is thought by Irwin in the first part of the verse to mean »in«, but in the second to mean »by«.

Irwin's translation of Isa 26 16 thus involves several dubious, or even unlikely, hypotheses, and it must be rejected as improbable.

(2) Isaiah 66 17

This verse speaks of people who engage in pagan religious practices. The present note is not concerned with all the problems of the verse, but only with three difficult words, and the last part of the verse will be ignored:

המתקדשים והמטהרים אל־הגנות אַחַר אַחַת (אחד כתיב) בַּתָּוֶךְ אכלי בשר החזיר וגו׳

This part of the verse is translated as follows in the Revised Version (I ignore the marginal variants):

> They sanctify themselves and purify themselves *to go* unto the gardens, behind one in the midst, eating swine's flesh . . .

It is unnecessary for the present purpose to discuss whether the R.V. is correct in understanding the preposition in the phrase 'æl-hăggănnôt in a pregnant sense, for the words with which this note is concerned are 'ăḥăr 'ăḥăt băttawæk. The *kethibh* of the second word is the masculine 'ḥd, and the *qere* is the feminine 'ăḥăt, which is the reading of 1QIs[a] and many Hebrew manuscripts, and has the support of the Vulgate's rendering *post unam intrinsecus*. The variant reading *ianuam* is probably an inner-Latin corruption of *unam*, notwithstanding the fact that it recalls the LXX, which will be discussed below. In contrast, the Peshitta appears to support the masculine 'ḥd, for it has ḥăd bătăr ḥăd bᵉmeṣʿtaʾ. The first ḥăd may be the result of free translation, but it is also possible that the Syriac presupposes a Hebrew text with 'ḥd 'ḥr 'ḥd btwk. Similarly, according to Jerome's commentary on Isaiah, Theodotion and Symmachus had *alter post alterum* (of which only the words ὀπίσω ἀλλήλων have been preserved in Greek), but they translate *btwk* as if it were in the construct state before the words that follow. The Targum has as its counterpart to the M.T.'s 'ḥr 'ḥd (or 'ḥt) btwk the words sîʾaʾ bătăr sîʾaʾ, »one company after another«, and it is not clear on what Hebrew reading it is based. The LXX's καὶ ἐν τοῖς προθύροις, »and in the porches«, is obscure. Oort has suggested that the underlying Hebrew had 'ăḥăr without 'ḥd or 'ḥt, and that instead of btwk it read pᵉtaḥîm or pætăḥ (Klostermann bᵉpætăḥ; Cheyne băppætăḥ). Ottley's suggestion is that the LXX's *Vorlage* either read 'ăḥăr pætăḥ or »omitted the two difficult words« 'ḥr 'ḥd and read bitrăʿ (Dan 2 49) in place of btwk — and Fischer also favours the latter theory. Gesenius offers two suggestions. The first is that the translator ignored 'ḥr 'ḥd and gave twk the meaning »court«, which, in Gesenius's opinion, is found in II Sam 4 6 (baʾû ʿād tôk hăb-bāyit). The second is that btwk was ignored and ʾḥr ʾḥd translated, and that ʾḥd was associated by the translator with Syriac ʾeḥadaʾ, »Thür« (cp. Isa 57 8). It may be added that the Syriac word can mean »bolt«, and Jewish Aramaic ʿᵃḥadaʾ has the same meaning, and that »behind bolts in the midst« might conceivably have been paraphrased »in the porches«[4]. None of the suggested explanations of the LXX, however, is completely convincing, and it is unwise to make use of the version when trying to make sense of this verse.

It is not easy to find a satisfactory explanation of the phrase ʾăḥăr ʾăḥăt (or ʾæḥad) băttawæk. The rabbinical idea that ʾăḥăt or ʾæḥad here denotes an Ashera or a tree is unlikely (why should not the fact have been stated plainly in the text?), and the view that the word was the name of a deity has long been shown by commentators to be without a reliable foundation. The most plausible explanation of the M.T. is that the whole phrase means »after one in the midst«, that ʾăḥăr is not used in a local but a temporal sense, and that it refers to pagan worshippers copying the action of a priest or priestess standing in their midst as they sanctify and purify themselves. Such an interpretation cannot be described as impossible, and there may be a reference to a cultic practice that was familiar in ancient Palestine, although it is obscure to us. Fohrer's translation »hinter einem in der Mitte« understands the expression thus, but he adds a question mark, and his comment expresses doubt about the text. Similarly, while the American Jewish translation The Prophets (1978) has »imitating one in the center«, it adds a note »Meaning of Heb uncertain«. Such renderings are certainly preferable to that of the Good News Bible, which has »those who purify themselves for pagan worship, who go in procession to sacred gardens«; if the »one« is in the midst of the worshippers, it is hard to see how they can be following him, or her, in a procession. Yet even the better translations, such as that of Fohrer, make us wonder why the leader of the cult is referred to simply as »one«, and the text looks suspicious.

It is not surprising that attempts have been made to solve the problem by emendation. The reading ʾæḥad ʾăḥăr ʾæḥad, which was suggested by Schelling, has been accepted by some, including the translators responsible for the New English Bible, and it is possible to appeal for support to the Peshitta and Targum, as well as to Theodotion and Symmachus, unless they are merely translating freely. The loss of ʾḥd before ʾḥr could easily be explained on the ground of the words' similarity in appearance. J. D. Michaelis's suggestion is slightly different: ʾæḥad ʾăḥăr ʾăḥăt, understood in an obscene sense. Luzzatto, however, does not add a word, but postulates the confusion of daleth with resh and reads ʾæḥad ʾæḥad. He

---

[4] Cp. G. R. Driver in Vetus Testamentum 1 (1951), 244.

presumably understands the participle *hammitqaddᵉšîm* in a reciprocal sense: they sanctify one another. While the hitp. can have such a reciprocal sense (G. K. § 54f), it does not, however, have it elsewhere with the verb *qdš*. Fischer and Kissane also read *'æḥad 'æḥad*, but they go farther from the M.T. and change *băttawæk* into a verb: *batarû*, »einer nach dem andern zerschneidet (sein Opfer)« (Fischer), or *yikkarᵉtû*, »one by one [shall be cut off]« (Kissane). Other emendations are less plausible. Klostermann offers the ingenious emendation *'ăḥăd 'ăḥăd băttᵉnuk,* »Einen den anderen am Ohrzipfel«, in which he has been followed by Cheyne: *'ăḥăd 'æḥad* [cp. Isa 27 12] *băttᵉnuk,* »the one consecrating the other on the tip of his ear« (cp. Ex 29 20 Lev 8 23 14 14), but the guess is more bold than convincing. Houbigant emends the verse too drastically: . . . *'æl-'ăgganôt 'ăḥăr hăddᵉlatôt, & qui purgant se super pollubra post ostia*. There is even less to be said for Oort's view that *pætăḥ* means »woman« here and in Isa 3 17, and that 66 17 originally read *'ăḥăr pᵉtaḥîm* or *pætăḥ,* »de vrouwen achterna«. Nor is it possible to take seriously the theory of Doederlein, which was advanced about a century earlier, that *'ḥr* should be pointed as the first person singular imperfect of the pi. (contracted from *'ᵃ'ăḥer*), that *'ḥd* should be regarded as the equivalent of *yăḥdaw*, and that *băttawæk* should be changed to the construct state and read with what follows: *Qui initiari et lustrari semet patiuntur ad sacra in lucis, eos tollam: inter eos qui porcinis et muribus vescuntur . . .* Quite apart from other objections to the theory, the verb *'ḥr* has the required meaning nowhere else. After considering such attempts to solve the problem of Isa 66 17 one is tempted to conclude with Ehrlich that the words *'ḥr 'ḥd btwk* »sind heillos verderbt«.

Although it is not certain that the M.T. is impossible, its reading is suspect, and we have seen that a variety of suggestions have been made. A possible solution to the problem was once suggested to me orally by the late Professor D. Winton Thomas. He did not record the suggestion in his edition of Isaiah in BHS, and it may have occurred to him later. As far as I am aware, it has never been published, but it is possible that he came across it in his wide reading of literature concerned with the text of the Hebrew Bible. It seems to me that it deserves to be put before Old Testament scholars.

Thomas suggested that the words *'ḥr 'ḥd btwk* originated by vertical dittography from some words of similar appearance in the preceding verse, Isa 66 16, which is translated as follows in the Revised Version (the relevant Hebrew words have been added in brackets):

For by fire will the LORD plead, and by his sword, with all flesh (*ûbᵉḥărbô 'æt-kâl-baśar*), and the slain of the LORD shall be many.

If we suppose that *'ḥd* in verse 17 has arisen by dittography from *'ḥr* (and that the reading *'ḥt* is secondary), then we are left with the words 'ḥr btwk, which have much in common with wb]ḥrbw 't k[l bśr. Thomas spoke of vertical dittography, but it is possible to present his theory in a slightly different form. Verse 16 has the words 't kl bśr (»all flesh«), and verse 17 'kly bśr (»eating the flesh of«). Perhaps a scribe copying verse 17 got as far as 'l hgnwt and should have written 'kly bśr next. It is possible that he was interrupted for a moment, and that, when he returned to what he was copying, his eye fell on the superficially similar phrase 't kl bśr in the previous verse, which he had copied shortly before, and he started to write the phrase again, together with wbḥrbw, which immediately precedes it. He saw his mistake as soon as he had got as far as wbḥrbw 't k, and he put a mark on the scroll to indicate that the erroneous words should be deleted. A later scribe failed to understand what had happened, and he reproduced as best he could what he was able to read of the text before him. Either he or a later scribe was responsible for adding 'ḥd.

If Thomas's suggestion is correct, then the obscure words 'ḥr 'ḥd (or 'ḥt) btwk are not an original part of the text, but have entered the verse as the result of scribal error. The strength of the case is the resemblance between the phrase and what follows it in verse 17 to words in verse 16. Whether or not Thomas's theory wins wide acceptance, it deserves to be made known.

List of works cited

This list excludes some well-known works such as lexicons.

F. Böttcher and F. Mühlau, Neue exegetisch-kritische Aehrenlese zum Alten Testamente 2, 1864, 132–133.
T. K. Cheyne, The Book of the Prophet Isaiah. A New English Translation, 1898.
—, The Book of the Prophet Isaiah. Critical Edition of the Hebrew Text, 1899.
A. Condamin, Le livre d'Isaïe, 1905.
F. Delitzsch, Commentar über das Buch Jesaia, ⁴1889.
A. Dillmann, Der Prophet Jesaja, 1890.
J. C. Doederlein, Esaias, ³1789.
M. Drechsler, Der Prophet Jesaja II.1, 1891.
G. R. Driver, Linguistic and textual problems: Isaiah i–xxxix, JTS 38 (1937), 36–50.
—, Notes on Isaiah, in: Von Ugarit nach Qumran, BZAW 77, 1958, 42–48.
B. Duhm, Das Buch Jesaia, 1892.
A. B. Ehrlich, Randglossen zur hebräischen Bibel, IV 1912.
H. Ewald, Die Propheten des Alten Bundes, III ²1868.
J. Fischer, In welcher Schrift lag das Buch Isaias den LXX vor?, BZAW 56, 1930.
G. Fohrer, Das Buch Jesaja, 1960–64.
W. Gesenius, Der Prophet Jesaia, 1820–21.
G. B. Gray, A Critical and Exegetical Commentary on the Book of Isaiah, I–XXVII, 1912.
F. Hitzig, Der Prophet Jesaja, 1833.
C. F. Houbigant, Notae criticae in universos Veteris Testamenti libros, 1777.

G. Hylmö, De S. K. Profetiska Liturgiernas Rytm, Stil och Komposition, 1929.
Jerome's commentary on Isaiah, Corpus Christianorum. Series Latina LXXIII and LXXIII A, 1963.
O. Kaiser, Der Prophet Jesaja. Kapitel 13–29, 1973.
E. J. Kissane, The Book of Isaiah I, ¹1941, ²1960, II, 1943.
A. Klostermann, Deuterojesaia hebräisch und deutsch mit Anmerkungen, 1893.
J. B. Koppe, D. Robert Lowth's . . . Jesaias . . . mit Zusätzen und Anmerkungen 3, 1780.
E. Liebmann, Der Text zu Jesaia 24–27, ZAW 22 (1902), 1–56; 23 (1903), 209–86; 24 (1904), 51–104; 25 (1905), 145–71.
S. D. Luzzatto, Il Profeta Isaia, 1867.
K. Marti, Das Buch Jesaja, 1900.
J. D. Michaelis, Deutsche Uebersetzung des Alten Testaments 8, 1779.
–, Vorzügliche Varianten im Propheten Jesaia, in: Orientalische und Exegetische Bibliothek 14 (1779), Anhang, 3–223.
–, Supplementa ad lexica hebraica, 1792.
J. H. Michaelis, Biblia Hebraica, 1720.
H. Oort, Jezaja 24–27, Theologische Tijdschrift 20 (1886), 166–194.
–, Jezaja 3:16–4:4, TT 20 (1886), 561–568.
R. R. Ottley, The Book of Isaiah according to the Septuagint (Codex Alexandrinus) I and II, 1904 and 1906.
Peshitta: I have used the Urmia edition of 1852 with G. Diettrich, Ein apparatus criticus zur Pešitto zum Propheten Jesaia, BZAW 8, 1905.
O. Procksch, Jesaja I, 1930.
W. Rudolph, Jesaja 24–27, 1933.
J. F. Schelling, Animadversiones philologico-criticae in loca difficiliora Iesaiae, 1797.
J. Payne Smith, A Compendious Syriac Dictionary, 1903.
J. Stenning, The Targum of Isaiah, 1949.
S. Talmon, DSIa as a witness to ancient exegesis of the book of Isaiah, Annual of the Swedish Theological Institute 1 (1962), 62–72; reprinted in: F. M. Cross and S. Talmon (ed.), Qumran and the History of the Biblical Text, 1975, 116–126. I have cited the article according to the page numbers of the reprint.
H. Wildberger, Jesaja 13–27, 1978.
J. Ziegler, Isaias, Septuaginta. Vetus Testamentum Graecum auctoritate Societatis Litterarum Gottingensis editum 14, 1939.

La dimension du prophétisme d'après Martin Buber et Abraham J. Heschel

Par E. Jacob

(2 Avenue du Général de Gaulle, Strasbourg, France)

Martin Buber et Abraham Heschel seront sans doute retenus par la postérité comme les plus grands penseurs juifs du 20ème siècle. La forte personnalité de l'un et de l'autre ne permet pas de les confondre, mais dans leurs différences ils sont très proches. Ils sont contemporains, bien que la carrière de Heschel ait été beaucoup moins longue que celle de son aîné (1907—1972). L'un et l'autre ont eu des liens avec l'Europe orientale et ont été marqués par le hassidisme; Heschel était, dit-on, apparenté par son père au Rabbi Dov Ber de Meseritz, dit le Grand Maggid, et par sa mère au fameux Rabbi Levi Issac de Berditshev. Heschel a succédé à Buber à la tête du Jüdisches Lehrhaus de Francfort en 1937 pour une période très courte interrompue par la guerre, qui le mena aux Etats-Unis, alors que Buber se fixa à Jérusalem; mais le sionisme de Heschel ne le cède en rien à celui de Buber et s'est exprimé en des accents particulièrement lyriques dans un de ses derniers écrits »Israël, un écho de l'éternité« (1969). Au point de vue philosophique ils peuvent être qualifiés l'un et l'autre d'existentialistes croyants, Buber étant dans une assez large mesure influencé par Kierkegaard, tandis que l'existentialisme de Heschel a des accents tantôt platoniciens tantôt spinozistes. Profondément juifs l'un et l'autre, ils ne se situent ni dans la ligne dogmatique, ni dans la ligne halachique; l'essentiel pour eux n'est pas l'observation de la torah, mais la vie avec Dieu dont les prophètes constituent le meilleur exemple, encore qu'ils n'aient jamais ni l'un ni l'autre considéré qu'il y avait opposition entre loi et prophètes. »Partager la foi d'un prophète«, écrit Heschel, »signifie davantage que percevoir ce que le sens commun ne parvint pas à percevoir, cela signifie être ce que l'homme ordinaire ne parvint pas à être: un miroir où se réfléchit Dieu. Partager la foi d'un prophète, c'est s'élever au niveau de son existence« (Dieu en quête de l'homme, trad. franç. 264). Cette foi est consignée dans la Bible. Buber et Heschel se situent dans la Bible envisagée comme un tout. La Bible est la semence, Dieu est le soleil et l'homme est le sol; cette image de Heschel pourrait également convenir à Buber qui soulignerait davantage ce troisième aspect, mais pour l'un et l'autre il ne saurait y avoir une théologie qui ne déboucherait pas sur une éthique. L'un et l'autre sont éloignés du littéralisme; la Bible est moins un livre qu'une voix: »Pensons-nous au livre? Nous pensons à la Voix. Il importe moins d'apprendre à lire qu'à écouter«[1] et Buber en a fait l'application magistrale dans sa traduction de la Bible, et lui faisant écho, Heschel a pu écrire: »La présence de Dieu dans la Bible est plus décisive que l'origine de la Bible en Dieu« (Dieu en quête . . . 265). Mais la voix passe par les mots et l'un et l'autre ont été sinon des exégètes, du moins des lecteurs attentifs des textes bibliques. Heschel a conquis son grade de docteur par une dissertation présentée à la Faculté de philosophie de Berlin en 1935 consacrée à la conscience prophétique et publiée l'année suivante sous le titre ›Die Prophetie‹. Il prenait place dans le débat suscité en particulier par le livre de Hoelscher de 1914 et qui mettait au centre des études sur les prophètes leur caractère extatique, que Heschel propose de remplacer par l'expérience du *pathos* et de la sympathie. Dans son ouvrage sur les prophètes, paru en anglais en 1962, Heschel reste fidèle aux positions défendues dans son premier ouvrage, en tenant compte de tout ce que les recherches récentes avaient apporté pour l'intelligence du phénomène prophétique. Buber s'est occupé des prophètes à plus d'une reprise, mais c'est dans son livre intitulé »La Foi des prophètes« (Der Glaube der Propheten) qu'il a donné une vue d'ensemble qui est pour lui l'occasion, à partir des prophètes, de tracer les grandes structures de la foi d'Israël. La première édition de ce remarquable livre a paru en néerlandais en 1940, suivie en 1942 d'une traduction en hébreu, en 1949 en anglais et en 1950 en allemand. Les ouvrages de Heschel et de Buber sur les prophètes peuvent être considérés comme des classiques tant à cause de la personnalité de leurs auteurs que par le souci de dégager les questions essentielles qui, malgré les tendances nouvelles, ne cesseront de se poser à tous ceux qui s'attachent à l'interprétation des prophètes. Nous n'avons voulu parler que d'auteurs disparus, mais nous ne pouvons passer sous silence les travaux consacrés aux prophètes par notre collègue A. Neher, en particulier ses monographies sur Amos et Jérémie et sa synthèse sur l'Essence du prophétisme, que l'histoire placera un jour à côté de ceux de Buber et de Heschel.

Le prophétisme dans l'histoire d'Israël

Pour Buber le prophétisme est vraiment le centre de l'histoire d'Israël. Ses débuts coïncident avec les débuts d'Israël, et tout au long de l'histoire le prophète est celui qui incarne la vocation d'Israël et qui est chargé de la rappeler lorsqu'elle est oubliée. Il y a deux modes de la révélation de Dieu: il se manifeste dans l'histoire comme celui qui marche avec son peuple sur un chemin dont le but est le royaume de Dieu. La grande thèse bubérienne sur la royauté de Dieu (Königtum Gottes) est fondée

---

[1] Der Mensch von heute und die jüdische Bibel, Werke II: Schriften zur Bibel, 1964, 869.

sur l'étude des livres des Juges et de Samuël et sur les données de l'histoire des religions, mais on peut dire que Buber en a trouvé les racines profondes dans son contact avec les prophètes. Dieu se manifeste ensuite en s'adressant à des individus particuliers qui doivent se faire auprès du peuple les interprètes de cette parole. Cette double expérience, collective et individuelle, apparait aux origines mêmes de l'histoire dans la figure d'Abraham, car si l'on fait la synthèse des différentes traditions à son sujet, on constate qu'elles mettent en relation avec lui a) l'origine du peuple, b) le lien de l'histoire d'Israël avec l'histoire de l'humanité, c) l'origine de la prophétie. Le titre de *nabî* donné à Abraham en Gen 20 7 n'est pas la projection dans le passé d'une tendance unificatrice, mais correspond au sens profond de l'histoire d'Abraham qui est d'être un médiateur. Cet intermédiaire est aussi un visionnaire; la vie d'Abraham (cf. Abraham der Seher, in: Werke II: Schriften zur Bibel, 1964, 871 ff.) est rythmée par sept visions qui sont les sept étapes de la révélation qui le conduit vers l'achèvement parfait de la relation entre l'homme et Dieu. On pourrait penser que Buber introduit ici des considérations philosophiques étrangères au texte, mais il appuie sa démonstration sur la fréquence du verbe *ra'ā* qui est le mot-clé (Leitwort) du récit et cela mérite que l'exégète y prête attention. Le prophète est donc d'abord un voyant et les termes de *ro'æ* et de *ḥozæ* n'ont jamais été entièrement oblitérés par celui de *nabî* qui reste susceptible d'explications diverses qui ne se laissent pas ramener uniquement à celle par la parole. Les visionnaires constituent une chaîne continue d'Abraham à Samuel, ligne de laquelle émerge la figure de Moïse. Le »Moïse« de Buber est un des ouvrages les plus suggestifs de ceux qui dans le dernier demi-siècle aient été consacrés à Moïse[2]. L'expérience de Moïse est celle des prophètes à son degré maximum. Moïse voit Dieu dans les phénomènes de la nature aussi bien que dans ceux de l'histoire, et Dieu lui communique sa parole avec une telle intensité et une telle précision que ce prophète devient la bouche même de Dieu et se trouve revêtu de son esprit et devient capable de réaliser l'œuvre de Dieu. A l'encontre de ceux qui parlaient d'une coloration prophétique tardive des récits sur Moïse, il pense que la vision de Dieu et le don de l'esprit appartiennent aux plus anciennes traditions sur Moïse, en qui se conjuguent le rôle des extatiques saisis par l'Esprit et celui des voyants qui voient les choses cachées à l'œil ordinaire. On peut estimer que Buber fait la part trop grande aux récits concernant Moïse, homme de l'Esprit dans le livre des Nombres, mais on ne saurait mécon-

---

[2] L'originalité du livre de Buber est bien caractérisée par R. Smend, Das Mosebild von Heinrich Ewald bis Martin Noth, 1959, 66: »Das eindrucksvollste Mosebuch verdanken wir Martin Buber . . . Sein ›Mose‹ ist schwer auf eine Formel zu bringen. Er ist eine reiche Gestalt, reich nicht in seiner Individualität, wie der Mose der Romane, sondern reich in der Beziehung zu seinem Gott und in seinem Werk an Israel.«

naître, pour la reconstruction de l'histoire de Moïse, ce qu'il y a sans doute de vrai dans la puissance de l'esprit qui était telle qu'il suffisait d'une petite partie de cet esprit pour faire prophétiser les soixante-dix anciens et pour déborder largement le cadre institutionnel: le souhait que tout le peuple devienne un peuple de prophètes sur qui repose l'esprit est le meilleur commentaire de l'expression de ›peuple saint‹ (cf. Nb 11 29). Il n'est pas évident que les oracles de Balaam aient pour principale intention de montrer par contraste que Moïse est un voyant supérieur à ceux des autres peuples, mais là encore l'intuition de Buber rejoint l'histoire dans ses profondeurs cachées. Ce qui est certain, semble-t-il, c'est que l'esprit a continué à agir non dans l'institution représentée par Josué (cf. Nb 11 28), mais dans les Juges qui maintiennent Israël dans sa vocation spécifique de peuple à part; le šopeṭ est proche du nabî' et la frontière entre les deux fonctions est plutôt floue, comme chez Déborah et Gédéon. Le prophète Osée dans un texte qu'il n'y a pas lieu de suspecter de correction théologique, appelle Moïse un prophète (12 14) et Amos, sans nommer Moïse, dit la même chose en parlant des n^{e}bî'îm et des nazirîm comme des artisans et garants de l'élection d'Israël (2 11). Mais c'est surtout dans la figure de Samuel que se concrétise l'œuvre mosaïque. La tradition qui s'est formée autour de lui est la preuve qu'il a joué un rôle historique considérable. Il est, selon Buber, d'abord prophète, il se situe dans la ligne des Juges et autres inspirés, mais il a vécu à une période de transition. Les n^{e}bî'îm s'étaient réfugiés dans les manifestations extatiques et n'étaient plus capables de produire des chefs sachant galvaniser les énergies du peuple pour résister au danger philistin. Le sacerdoce qui avait réussi à maintenir un pouvoir central autour du sanctuaire de l'arche manquait d'envergure; le régime royal apparaît pour beaucoup comme la solution souhaitable. Conscient que la parole de Dieu était rare et les visions peu fréquentes (I Sam 3 1), Samuel accepta à son corps défendant le passage du prophétisme charismatique à une forme de pouvoir plus institutionalisée. L'onction de Saül est une onction prophétique; ce n'est que lorsqu'il fut entré en contact avec les n^{e}bî'îm que l'onction par l'esprit devint véritable et que Saül fut changé en un autre homme. L'avènement de la royauté ne signifie pas la disparition du prophétisme. A Jérusalem les prophètes ont leur place à la cour royale et ils lui apportent une franche collaboration, mais ils s'opposent au roi lorsque celui-ci oublie qu'il n'est que le détenteur de la royauté de Dieu. Les récits sur Samuel et Saül montrent bien en quoi il y a eu entre les deux collaboration et conflit; sous le règne de David Nathan est prophète de cour et fait en quelque sorte partie du gouvernement, mais lorsque le droit du roi prend le pas sur le droit de Dieu, il passe à l'opposition. Dans le royaume du Nord le prophétisme s'est plus difficilement intégré au régime royal. Une royauté qui prenait modèle sur ce qui se passait dans les pays voisins, qui favorisait les cultes étrangers ou du moins la baalisation du yahvisme, suscita l'opposition farouche des prophètes. Elie autour de qui devait se constituer un groupe de *nebî'îm* fidèles à l'esprit mosaïque[3], et un Michée ben Yimla condamnent les rois et une royauté qui au lieu d'être le ciment du peuple l'avait réduit au rang de moutons qui n'ont point de berger I Rois 22 17). Dans le royaume de Juda le prophétisme connut une résurgence de son indépendance au moment du danger de la puissance assyrienne. Aucun prophète de cette époque ne rejette la royauté comme illégitime, tout en faisant preuve à son égard d'une totale indépendance. Esaïe est en tous points fidèle à la promesse faite à David concernant l'éternité de sa dynastie, mais en face d'un roi qui refuse de faire la politique conforme à cette promesse, il est amené à prendre le contrepied du roi et à se faire le défenseur de l'idéal ›théopolitique‹ qui veut que le peuple soit soumis à la souveraineté de Dieu pour qu'il soit les prémices du royaume de Dieu. Désormais il n'appartient plus au roi, mais au prophète de dire qui fera partie de ce peuple de Dieu, et c'est la thèse du reste qui aura, selon les circonstances, une connotation soit plus religieuse soit plus nationale. C'est en somme le retour à la dynamique prophétique du temps des Juges, car si Esaïe refuse la guerre sainte en tant qu'institution, il en conserve toutes les virtualités spirituelles. L'eschatologie, contenue en germe dans la révélation de Dieu à Moïse, donne alors au prophétisme une nouvelle dimension, mais elle est plus existentielle que temporelle, et le Messie n'est pas d'abord le roi idéal de l'avenir plus ou moins mythique, mais celui qui répond à l'exigence actuelle de la souveraineté de Dieu et dont le prophète est le prototype. Cette nouvelle dynamique du prophétisme ne pouvait manquer de rejaillir sur les institutions. Le trône de David ne connut pas que des Achaz, mais des rois selon le cœur de Dieu tels que Ezéchias et Josias qui firent un instant refleurir l'esprit mosaïque. Mais en même temps surgit de nouveau le risque pour le prophétisme de chercher sa réalisation dans l'institution. Le prophétisme est un mouvement qu'il est difficile de suivre et que dans un désir de sécurisation on est toujours à nouveau tenté d'arrêter; c'est ce qui explique l'apparition et le grand succès des faux prophètes. Ceux-ci se cramponnent aux institutions garanties par Dieu, le Temple et la permanence de la promesse davidique, mais ils ne voient plus les signes des temps ni le moment existentiel de l'histoire qui veut qu'à temps nouveaux il y ait des exigences nouvelles. Cette division à l'intérieur du prophétisme, qui fut tragique, posera le problème de la place de l'échec et de la souffrance dans la réalisation du plan de Dieu. Jérémie, Job et le Second Esaïe font, chacun à sa manière, la preuve que la souffrance donne un sens nouveau à l'existence et que la souffrance permet à Israël de réaliser sa

---

[3] Buber pense que les cercles prophétiques autour d'Elisée ont eu un rôle important dans la fixation des traditions sur Moïse considéré comme le prototype de leur propre maître (Schriften zur Bibel 75).

vocation d'instrument de salut pour les nations. Aussi Buber consacre-t-il de fort belles pages au serviteur souffrant, figure à la fois individuelle et collective, en qui se concentrent et s'incarnent et la destinée d'Israël et la vocation des prophètes.

Heschel a aussi mis en lumière cette permanence du prophétisme dans l'histoire: »La prophétie en Israël n'était pas un épisode dans la vie d'un individu mais une illumination dans l'histoire du peuple. Une chaîne d'expériences liant ensemble des événements s'étendant sur des siècles est un fait sans parallèle dans l'histoire de l'humanité« (The Prophets II 252). Dans sa théologie du *pathos* il met en évidence l'importance de la souffrance de Dieu, mais il a moins insisté que Buber sur le prophétisme comme étant la clé révélatrice de cette histoire spécifique, et il n'a pas inséré des témoins comme Abraham ou Job dans la tradition prophétique. Un point commun aux deux auteurs c'est qu'ils arrêtent l'exposé de l'histoire du prophétisme avec le Second Esaïe, ce qui peut paraître étonnant chez des penseurs juifs. Ils n'accordent qu'une place très mince à Ezéchiel, en qui Buber voit le père de l'apocalyptique qui par son déterminisme aliénant la liberté de l'homme se situe à l'opposé du prophétisme où l'appel à la conversion et à la liberté de cette conversion tient une place primordiale[4]. Heschel ne parle pas des apocalypses, parce qu'il ne voit pas ce qu'une nouvelle ›révélation‹ pourrait ajouter de plus à celle qui est parfaite chez les prophètes.

L'expérience prophétique

Sur ce point Heschel est bien plus explicite que Buber qui dans son souci de réalisme théopolitique n'est guère sensible à l'aspect psychologique des prophètes. Dans sa thèse de 1935 Heschel prend position dans le débat sur la conscience prophétique. Contre G. Hoelscher, H. Gunkel, B. Duhm, W. Jacobi et bien d'autres qui cherchent l'originalité du prophétisme dans l'extase, étudiée avec les ressources de la magie et de la psychanalyse, il situe l'explication du prophétisme non pas dans l'extase, mais dans la théophanie (cf. Die Prophetie 29). Il est assez remarquable de constater que ce dernier thème a reçu ces dernières années, indépendamment de Heschel, une attention plus grande dans les études vétérotestamentaires[5]. La théophanie se situe tout à l'opposé de l'extase; l'ex-

---

[4] Buber s'est exprimé dans un texte de 1954 sur la différence entre Prophétie et Apocalyptique (Schriften zur Bibel 927–942). En plus du caractère déterministe, il insiste sur le fait que l'apocalyptique est purement livresque et il l'oppose à la voix vivante de Dieu à travers une personne.

[5] Les textes les plus importants sont groupés dans l'ouvrage de J. Jeremias, Theophanie, 1965, qui s'en tient à la structure littéraire des récits théophaniques. L'intérêt renouvelé

périence première du prophète c'est ce qu'il voit, et il cherche ensuite à connaître et à comprendre ce qu'il voit; la vision n'est pas le résultat d'une marche ascendante, mais elle est une réalité qui descend et qui s'impose. Et c'est bien cela qui est le chemin de Dieu vers l'homme, mais dans et derrière la vision se manifeste le *pathos* de Dieu qui est l'attention que Dieu accorde au monde, attention qui n'est pas un sentiment seulement, mais un acte, un mouvement en Dieu, déterminé non par l'arbitraire ou la colère, mais par l'attitude que l'homme prend hic et nunc à l'égard de cette sympathie de Dieu. Les prophètes sont ceux qui répondent pleinement au *pathos* de Dieu et en sont par leurs paroles et leurs actes la vivante démonstration. Il est normal que le psychisme du prophète se ressente de cette force qui tombe sur lui, mais il en est avant tout saisi et émerveillé. Le premier stade de la philosophie et de la théologie est selon Heschel l'émerveillement. On peut comparer ce que Heschel dit du *pathos* à l'action de l'esprit. Le terme de *rûaḥ* est absent de l'étude de 1936; dans celui de 1962 l'esprit est identifié au *pathos*; ainsi il peut écrire: »Les actions de Dieu sont faites par ceux qui sont remplis de la *ruach*, du pathos« (II 38). »Le *ish haruach* de Os 9 7 est l'homme rempli du pathos de Dieu« (ib. 97), mais, curieusement, dans les quelques pages succinctes consacrées à l'esprit (ib. 96s.) il parle de la *rûaḥ* de l'homme au sens psychologique de sentiment ou d'émotion. En revanche le silence de Buber sur le pathos semble attester qu'il ne donnait pas une grande portée à la thèse centrale de Heschel. Il parle une seule fois de ›l'intense pathos prophétique‹ (Schriften zur Bibel 398), mais il l'entend dans le sens courant d'exagération de sentiments et du langage et non dans le sens heschélien.

Le *pathos* au sens où l'entend Heschel, est certainement apte à rendre ce qui qualifie le prophète comme homme de Dieu. Mais était-il nécessaire de recourir à ce terme grec, et au surplus plein d'ambiguïté, pour rendre une réalité hébraïque? Il y a, nous semble-t-il, deux termes hébreux qui recouvriraient assez exactement tout ce que Heschel met dans le *pathos*: le premier est celui de connaissance qui, lorsqu'il a Dieu pour sujet, exprime une relation intime d'où ne sont exclues ni l'affection ni la sympathie; le second est la jalousie, la *qin'ā*, qui n'est pas restreinte au domaine de l'amour conjugal, mais qui englobe, selon B. Renaud dans son excellente monographie sur le sujet[6], les réalités de l'alliance, de l'amour, de la sainteté et de la violence. Connaissance et jalousie sont sans doute des termes plus adéqats pour définir la religion biblique qui est fondée sur l'alliance et non sur la parenté entre Dieu et les hommes,

---

pour le sujet va de pair avec la redécouverte de l'importance du langage mythique et rejoint la définition bubérienne du mythe comme un récit issu de l'impression profonde produite par un événement réel, ce qui était précisément le cas au Sinaï.

[6] Je suis un Dieu jaloux. Etude d'un thème biblique, 1963.

car même le langage anthropomorphique ou anthropotropique, qui est employé tout au long de la Bible, veut mettre l'accent sur l'alliance, non sur la parenté. Buber avec son insistance sur le dialogue et sur la distinction entre le Je et le Tu comme principes de pensée et de vie est plus proche de la dialectique biblique. Il y a une notion voisine de la sympathie et du pathos, sur laquelle nos deux auteurs ont eu l'occasion de s'exprimer, c'est celle de l'imitation de Dieu[7]. Ce thème dont Buber a dit qu'il était un paradoxe dans le judaïsme est assez proche du thème central de Heschel; pourtant la sympathie et l'imitation ne sauraient être réduites l'une à l'autre: l'imitation est une attitude pratique, tandis que la sympathie est une attitude spirituelle; l'imitation suppose un modèle fixe, le *pathos* est changeant et conditionné par chaque nouvelle situation particulière; dans le *pathos* il y a expérience, dans l'imitation il y a transmission d'un modèle. Buber met l'imitation en relation avec le thème de l'image de Dieu et les conséquences éthiques qu'en ont tirées les rabbins; par ailleurs, la seule imitation est celle de la marche avec Dieu qui ne peut être qu'une obéissance sur le chemin de Dieu, mais jamais Buber n'y voit une attitude type du prophète, alors que Heschel par sa note plus mystique qu'éthique serait disposé à faire une plus large place à la »Nachahmung« qu'à la »Nachfolge«.

Conclusion

Buber et Heschel situent le prophétisme au centre de la religion; c'est à dire qu'ils n'en font pas un phénomène à part, sporadique ou marginal, mais qu'ils voient dans le prophétisme la vraie relation entre Dieu et l'homme. Pour l'un et l'autre, la religion ne se définit pas par les termes de transcendant et d'immanent, d'objet et de sujet, de saint et de pécheur, mais par ceux de rencontre et de sympathie. Le prophète est celui qui rappelle que cette rencontre est non seulement possible, mais qu'elle est antérieure à toute explication rationnelle. Dans l'état actuel des recherches sur le prophétisme les travaux de Buber et de Heschel n'ont rien perdu de leur actualité. Tout d'abord l'exégète n'écoute jamais sans profit l'avis du philosophe et du poète, qui voient les choses avec plus de recul et chez qui l'érudition est moins importante que la pénétration en profondeur et qui prennent quelque distance par rapport aux modes et aux écoles. La théologie de la parole qui a remplacé la théologie de l'expérience a certes contribué à une meilleure intelligence des prophètes, et

---

[7] M. Buber, Nachahmung Gottes, 1926, in: ders., Schriften zur Bibel, 1053—1065. L'étude la plus complète sur le sujet avec de multiples références de la littérature postbiblique est celle de H. Kosmala, Nachfolge und Nachahmung Gottes, a) im griechischen Denken, ASTI 2, 38—85, b) im jüdischen Denken, ASTI 3, 65—110.

a provoqué des études fort précieuses sur l'expression, la structure et la transmission de cette parole. Mais l'accent mis unilatéralement sur la parole n'a-t-il pas rétréci quelque peu la dimension prophétique en faisant du prophète avant tout le messager? Sans doute a-t-on souligné que la parole est toujours action et mis en lumière l'importance des actions symboliques. Sans vouloir retomber dans une théologie de l'expérience, ne faut-il pas dire que le prophète est plus qu'un homme qui parle, qu'il participe à ce *pathos* de Dieu qui est une intervention de Dieu dans le monde, une révélation qui rend l'homme capable de recevoir une révélation et de prendre conscience qu'il est, lui, une expérience de Dieu. Si le prophète est la manifestation la plus probante du »Dieu en quête de l'homme« (Heschel), on prend aussi mieux conscience de la dimension humaine des prophètes. L'engagement du prophète dans la vie sociale et politique fait partie intégrante du message du prophète. La politique des prophètes fait aujourd'hui de nouveau l'objet d'études[8], et on prend de plus en plus conscience que politique et foi ne s'opposent pas, mais se conditionnent réciproquement, et que l'eschatologie, si elle est partiellement une utopie, entend donner à cette utopie une expression concrète dans les réalités terrestres. On voit combien la lecture de nos deux auteurs, et de Buber en particulier, s'avère actuelle.

Il faut ajouter que Buber et Heschel ont été préoccupés par le fait chrétien; ils ont senti et fait sentir qu'entre le Dieu de la sympathie et du dialogue et le Dieu de l'Evangile, qui est pleinement à la quête de l'homme, il ne pouvait y avoir d'antinomie[9]. Ils ont été l'un et l'autre fortement engagés dans un dialogue sincère et constructif avec le christianisme. Aussi lire les prophètes sous leur direction prend-il la signification d'un pélerinage aux sources.

---

[8] C'est principalement Esaïe qui a été étudié sous l'angle de la politique. Parmi la littérature la plus récente signalons deux ouvrages: W. Dietrich, Jesaja und die Politik, 1976 et G. Brunet, Essai sur l'Isaïe de l'histoire, 1975. Les deux insistent sur le réalisme de la politique du prophète, et le second va même jusqu'à écrire qu'Esaïe était moins un personnage religieux qui a joué un rôle politique qu'un homme politique dont le rôle fut pour une bonne part religieux (243)! On peut dire qu'aujourd'hui deux tendances se fassent jour: les uns dans la ligne de H. Winckler insistent sur le réalisme concret de la prédication politique des prophètes, les autres parlent de son caractère utopique en opposant politique et utopie. Le terme de ›théopolitique‹ forgé par Buber permet de concilier les deux points de vue: ainsi selon lui l'exhortation d'Esaïe à Achaz de se tenir tranquille est une exigence religieuse, mais au moment précis de l'histoire où elle se situe, elle était aussi le meilleur programme politique possible et efficace.

[9] On a fait à Heschel la critique que sa théologie du pathos était plus chrétienne que juive, mais il l'a trouvée chez les prophètes et même dans des textes midrashiques et hassidiques, et il peut à bon droit affirmer qu'elle fait partie intégrante de l'héritage israélite, même si elle n'y est pas devenue normative. Cf. E. Berkovits, A. J. Heschel's Theology of pathos, Tradition 6, 1964, 67–104, et la réponse de S. Tanenzapf, Abraham Heschel and his critics, Judaism 23, 1974, 276–286.

משׂא in Jeremiah 23 33—40

By W. McKane

(51 Irvine Crescent, St. Andrews)

Jerome[1] refers to Aq ἄρμα which he elucidates as *onus* (Vulg), *pondus*. He supposes that משׂא at the beginning of a prophetic oracle is a technical term for a prophecy of doom: hence it is »heavy«, »burdensome«, and other words are used (*visio* = חזון and דבר יהוה) where prosperity is predicted or better times following disaster are foreseen. Hence it was clear from the title of a prophecy what kind of prediction would follow. Jerome explains v. 33 as a play on משׂא, so that when Jeremiah is asked מה משׂא יהוה, the intention is to poke fun at his unfulfilled prophecies of doom. Jerome has a second way of explaining משׂא which is founded on the assumption that LXX λῆμμα means *donum* »gift« or *munus* »provision«, »favour«. משׂא then becomes the prosperity for which the questioners are looking and it is this expectation which Jeremiah dashes with his reply: »He tells them that they are no longer to utter משׂא, for they are unworthy of God's gifts and kindnesses; much rather should they be cast out and cut off from God's help.«[2] Jeremiah is asked for a שׁלום prophecy, but playing on the ambivalence of משׂא (LXX λῆμμα), favour/burden, he makes a doom-laden prediction.

The first of Jerome's opinions has been influential and requires close scrutiny. He has built a case on the foundation of Vulg *onus* and Aq ἄρμα, but it is doubtful whether the versions lend support to the view that an ambivalent or homonymic משׂא is being exploited in the question מה משׂא יהוה. Thus *onus* (Vulg) is the normal rendering of משׂא, where משׂא refers to a prophetic utterance, and the same state of affairs is indicated by Pesh (*ptgm'*) and Targ (נבואה). Moreover, it is doubtful whether Aq ἄρμα, derived from αἴρω »take up«, »lift up«, means »burden«. On this J. D. Michaelis[3] remarks: ἄρμα perquam etymologicus reddere Aquila solebat, ab αἴρω *tollo*, incertum, utrum hic de *onere*, an de *prolato sermone*, *elata voce*, cogitans, ut in ejusmodi etymologicis interpretibus incerta multa et obscura. Sed de *onere* accepit Hieronymus. According to J. D. Michaelis there are the two possibilities of »lifting up a burden« or »lifting up the voice«, but he is disposed to avoid etymological speculations.

---

[1] S. Reiter (ed.), Sancti Eusebii Hieronymi in Hieremiam Prophetam, CSEL 59, 1913, 290f.
[2] Op. cit. 293.
[3] T. C. Tychsen (ed.), Supplementa ad Lexica Hebraica, 1792, 1685.

It is likely that Aq's intention was to be as faithful as possible to the literal sense of משא; in that case it should not be supposed that ἄρμα indicates a meaning significantly different from λῆμμα which is the usual rendering of Symm and Theod in prophetic contexts (also in v. 33, *assumtio*, according to Jerome) and which is the rendering of LXX in v. 33. J. D. Michaelis[4] urges that λῆμμα means *vaticinium*, but that it may be taken to indicate a particular elucidation of משא, namely, that which the prophet appropriates from God: LXX, Symmachus, Theodotion, λῆμμα vertere solent, i. e., *vaticinium*, sed ab accipiendo, quod ipsum נשא significare potest, dictum, *acceptum a deo*.

An examination of LXX renderings of all the occurrences of משא in contexts of prophetic utterance yields the following results:

(a) in five passages (Isa 14 28 15 1 17 1 22 1 23 1) משא is translated by ῥῆμα; in 22 1 and 23 1 J. Ziegler[5] prefers ὅραμα to ῥῆμα.

(b) ὅρασις is the translation of משא in three passages (Isa 13 1 19 1 30 6) and ὅραμα in two passages (Isa 21 1.11).

(c) There is a division of attestation as between ῥῆμα and ὅραμα in Isa 15 1 21 1.11 22 1 and 23 1[6].

(d) There is a group of passages where משא is rendered by λῆμμα (Jer 23 33.34.36.38 Nah 1 1 Hab 1 1 Zech 9 1 12 1 Mal 1 1). If the occurrences in Jer 23 are set aside for the present, it will be seen that there are special features in the remaining passages which account for the rendering λῆμμα. It is a literal, non-committal rendering of משא which has not been adopted in LXX except in those passages where further definitions make its sense transparent. Thus in Nah 1 1 משא נינוה (λῆμμα Νινευή) is supplemented by ספר חזון נחום האלקשי (Βίβλιον ὁράσεως Ναοὺμ τοῦ Ἐλκεσαίου). In Hab 1 1 המשא is elucidated by אשר חזה חבקוק הנביא (ὃ εἶδεν Ἀμβακουμ ὁ προφήτης). In the remaining passages (Zech 9 1 12 1 Mal 1 1) the phrase משא דבר יהוה (λῆμμα λόγου Κυρίου) elucidates משא as דבר יהוה. Part of H. S. Gehman's[7] argument that משא means »burden« is that otherwise משא דבר יהוה is a tautology, but this is not a point which should be pressed. משא דבר יהוה could be explained as »announcement of the word of Yahweh«, but the function of the fuller phrase is, probably, to define more explicitly the term משא. Another LXX passage, outside the prophetic literature, where the rendering of משא by λῆμμα may be accounted for by the circumstance that the sense of משא is given by the context, is II Kings 9 25: ויהוה נשא עליו את המשא הזה leads on to the utterance in v. 26 and so משא is elucidated as »announcement« or »sentence« (NEB).

---

[4] Op. cit. 1686.

[5] J. Ziegler, Isaias, Septuaginta Vetus Testamentum Graecum Auctoritate Societatis Litterarum Gottingensis editum 14, 1939, in loc.

[6] See J. Ziegler, op. cit. in loc.

[7] H. S. Gehman, The »Burden« of the Prophets, JQR NS 31 (1940–41), 118.

From this review it may be concluded that LXX was concerned not to under-translate משׂא; that it consequently opted for renderings which were transparent and gave a clear indication of sense (ῥῆμα, ὅρασις, ὅραμα), and that it used the more literal and less luminous λῆμμα only where there were contextual helps which fixed the sense of משׂא. The translations ὅρασις and ὅραμα, in all probability, owe something to the firm indication of Nah 1 1 and Hab 1 1 that a משׂא is a vision. These passages function like a glossary and it is unlikely that the renderings ὅρασις and ὅραμα are uninfluenced by them. On the other hand, such a particular relation between ῥῆμα and דבר יהוה משׂא (Zech 9 1 12 1 Mal 1 1) need not be postulated, because ῥῆμα is not a rendering which calls for a special explanation in the way that ὅρασις or ὅραμα does. It is obvious from the contexts where ῥῆμα is used that משׂא is connected with prophetic utterance, and this is a sufficient explanation of the rendering of משׂא as ῥῆμα. There are, however, no indications in the passages where ὅρασις and ὅραμα are used that משׂא is related to visionary experience and the question why such a translation was selected is an entirely proper one. How did the translators reach the conclusion that משׂא was a vision? It is in order to answer this question that the clues offered by Nah 1 1 and Hab 1 1 have to be taken into account.

If this reasoning were accepted, it would follow that in those passages (Isa 15 1 21 1.11 22 1 23 1) where LXX manuscripts are divided between ῥῆμα and ὅραμα, the latter represents a correction of ῥῆμα influenced by Nah 1 1 and Hab 1 1, reflecting the conviction that ὅραμα is a more precise rendering of משׂא than ῥῆμα[8].

The above discussion has shown that apart from Vulg, which invariably renders משׂא as *onus*, the versions, particularly the Greek versions, do not support Jerome's view that the nuance of »burden« attaches to משׂא in prophetic contexts and that משׂא consequently denotes a heavy and menacing prophetic prediction. The opinion that משׂא means hard prophecies is found in S. Muenster[9] and J. Buxtorf[10] whose entry runs, *prophetia, propriè, onerosa, calamitatum ac poenarum onus de-*

---

[8] Cf. P. A. H. de Boer, An Inquiry into the Meaning of the Term משׂא, OTS 5 (1948), 203. P. A. H. de Boer supposes that J. Ziegler (op.cit. 96), in the final paragraph, is making statements about the relations between λῆμμα, ῥῆμα and ὅραμα in the 11 Isa occurrences which are listed on the same page. But J. Ziegler is referring only to משׂא in Isa 21 13 which, as he remarks, is missing from the »old Septuagint texts«. Hence the line of development which J. Ziegler postulates (λῆμμα − ῥῆμα − ὅραμα) applies only to 21 13 and its point of departure is Symm and Theod. J. Ziegler is not arguing that λῆμμα is the original rendering of משׂא in LXX and that it has been replaced by ῥῆμα and ὅραμα.

[9] S. Muenster, Dictionarium Hebraicum, 1539, s. v. נשׂא.

[10] J. Buxtorf, Lexicon Hebraicum et Chaldaicum, 1631[4], 488.

nuncians. It is firmly set aside by J. D. Michaelis[11] who observes: Jam dudum monuit Coccejus, non esse vertendum, *onus*, quem significatum vocabulo per lusum et jocum dederant Judaei, Jerem. xxiii 30–40, sed *prolatio*, i. e., *effatum* Jehovae, *oraculum*, a נשא *proferre, eloqui*. The most decisive argument against the contention that משא means oracle of doom is the circumstance that it is used to designate prophetic utterances which are not oracles of doom: maxime cum מַשָּׂא etiam ponatur, ubi nihil molesti aut adversi portenditur, ut Proverb xxxi 1. ubi de doctrina ponitur, quam filius a matre accepit benevolentissimam, Thren ii 14. ubi blanda et fallacia pseudoprophetarum vaticinia sunt, משאות שוא, Zachar. xii 1. ubi laeta portenduntur[12]. J. D. Michaelis also postulates a semantic connection which separates משא from »burden« and associates it with raising the voice or producing an utterance.

An understanding of משא disengaged from the sense »burden« is found in Ibn Janah, and a semantic connection between משא and the raising of the voice is reported by Kimchi[12a] to have been the opinion of his father. Ibn Janah[13] glosses משא with *khiṭāb* »speech« and *kalām* »utterance«. Kimchi, explaining his father's position, says, »Prophecy is called משא, because it is lifted up in the mouth of the prophet«. Ibn Janah has the same understanding of the functioning of משא in Jer 23 33 as Rashi and Kimchi. He remarks that those who said מה משא יהוה pretended that they were enquiring concerning God's revealed word, but that they were insinuating another meaning, that of burden, and were making fun of the prophet. Neither Ibn Janah nor Rashi nor Kimchi supposes that this word-play rests on the circumstance that משא »utterance« has the nuance »burden«. It rests on nothing more than the existence of a homonym, namely, משא »burden«.

This is also the lexicography of W. Gesenius[14] who, like J. D. Michaelis, notes that the connection of משא with oracles of doom was made by Jerome and who adds Luther and Hengstenberg to the list of culprits. He explains משא »utterance« in terms of the lifting up of the voice; he gives the sense as *effatum divinum, vaticinium,* and, following Michaelis, he considers that the use of משא in connection with prophetic utterances which are not threatening tells decisively against the view that משא is a term for oracles of doom. On the Jeremiah passage he remarks: Ceterum in utroque, *vaticinii* et *oneris*, significatu luditur apud Jer. xxiii, 33 sqq. quo loco vetantur Israëlitae uti hac voce, qua ut ambigua

---

[11] Op. cit. 1685.
[12] Op. cit. 1685.
[12a] Rashi and Kimchi are cited from מקראות גדולות.
[13] A. Neubauer (ed.), Abu'L Walîd Marwān ibn Janāh, The Book of Hebrew Roots, 1875, 456 ff.
[14] W. Gesenius, Thesaurus philologicus criticus linguae hebraeae et chaldaeae, II 1840, 918.

profani homines abuti soleant, ut prophetis irrideant. This is how the matter stands in BDB[15] and KB[16]. The way in which the entries are made establishes that these lexicons regard משא »utterance« and משא »burden« as homonyms, even although both are derived from נשא: in BDB II משא »burden« is differentiated from III משא »utterance« and I משא »burden« is similarly distinguished from II משא »utterance« in KB. In both משא »utterance« is elucidated in terms of נשא קול or the like. Whether or not this is a correct semantic explanation of משא »utterance« is not the main consideration, although it has been generally followed by commentators on Jer 23 33–40 and has been associated by B. Duhm[17] and P. Volz with the impressive tones in which a prophetic oracle was declaimed. Thus B. Duhm: »Die Gottheit schweigt gewöhnlich, bisweilen aber erhebt sie ihre Stimme; wenn das geschieht, so ist das ein Ereignis und alle Welt ist neugierig.« And P. Volz: »Der Ausdruck stammt wohl vom Orakelwesen, wo das gefragte Numen bzw. der Priester aus der Verborgenheit und Schweigsamkeit heraus die Stimme erhob.« The main position to be established is that משא »utterance« does not have the nuance »burden« and that משא »utterance« and משא »burden« are homonyms. Many scholars have subscribed to this view (Rashi, Kimchi, C. F. Houbigant, H. Venema, B. Blayney, E. Henderson, K. H. Graf, F. Hitzig, C. W. E. Naegelsbach, E. H. Plumptre, C. von Orelli, F. Giesebrecht, B. Duhm, A. S. Peake, P. Volz, W. Rudolph, A. Weiser, J. Bright, A. van Selms, N. C. Habel)[18].

The opinion that משא »utterance« has the nuance »burden«, and that it denotes menacing oracles which are heavy with doom, has, nevertheless, not been eclipsed. It is asserted by J. Calvin (Onus autem significat prophetiam, quae terret Dei contemptores, dum illis vindictam minatur) and it is found in W. Lowth: »The Word *Massa* or *Burden*, signifies a burdensome prophecy, big with Ruin and Destruction.« L. Elliott Binns posits a semantic connection between burden and oracle and maintains that the latter sense is derived from the former: the oracle is a burden because the prophet takes up or appropriates the word of God which is revealed to him. This conforms with part of J. Calvin's interpretation which is adopted lock, stock and barrel by H. S. Gehman. J. Calvin incorporates the sense »raising up a word« into his »burden« interpretation and connects אשר אנכי נשא עליכם קינה (Am 5 1) with the assumption of a burden by the prophet and the laying of it on the people as a

---

[15] F. Brown, S. R. Driver, C. A. Briggs, Hebrew and English Lexicon of the Old Testament, 1907, 672.
[16] L. Koehler and W. Baumgartner, Hebräisches und Aramäisches Lexikon zum Alten Testament II, 1974³, 604.
[17] Full bibliographical information on commentaries is given at the end of the article.
[18] The order accords with the date of publication of the commentaries.

prophecy of doom. H. S. Gehman remarks: »The reformer has a correct insight into the passage; the ominous warning received by the prophet is raised and laid upon the nation.«[19] H. S. Gehman cites J. Calvin on Mal 1 1 with approval: »For prophecy is not everywhere called a burden; and whenever this word is expressed, there is ever to be understood some judgement of God.«[20]

P. A. H. de Boer[21] has argued against the two entries in the lexicons for משׂא »burden« and משׂא »oracle« and, in particular, against the explanation of משׂא »oracle« in terms of נשׂא קול. He explains II Kings 9 25 as »The Lord laid this burden on him«, and urges that משׂא in prophetic contexts often suggests the idea of judgement and catastrophe: »This ominous sense, however, although suited to the purpose, and a comprehensible evolution of the original sense, is not inherent in the term itself, but will be linked up with the catastrophic feature of so many prophecies.«[22] If then משׂא »burden«, in prophetic contexts, does not necessarily denote doom prophecies, what is its »original sense« in these contexts? It is not clear what answer P. A. H. de Boer is giving to this question. He has said of λῆμμα that it means the commission received by a prophet and so the »burden« assumed by him[23]. This is part of J. Calvin's account of the matter and agrees with L. Elliott Binns. But P. A. H. de Boer also says: »In the headings of prophetic oracles משׂא means »burden imposed on . . .«. These headings show us that the term had acquired a technical sense. This technical sense as »argument, thesis, title« of the passage following preserves the original sense of the term, indicating the character of the prophecy, and must be understood as λῆμμα in Greek.«[24] The sense »imposing a burden on« does not fit the prophecies which are not burdensome and the argument of J. D. Michaelis and W. Gesenius prevails. The sense »argument«, »thesis«, »title« has not been established by Hebrew lexicography but by registering the various senses of λῆμμα which are found in H. G. Liddell and R. Scott[25].

The conclusion to be drawn is that משׂא »burden« and משׂא »utterance« are homonyms, that no nuance of »burden« attaches to משׂא »utterance and that the interpretation of Jer 23 33–40 should proceed on this foundation.

---

[19] Op. cit. 113 f.
[20] Op. cit. 120.
[21] Op. cit. 209 ff.
[22] Op. cit. 214.
[23] Op. cit. 203.
[24] Op. cit. 214.
[25] Op. cit. 203 n. 7.

II

That the word-play in the question מה משא יהוה (v. 33) rests on nothing more than the existence of a homonym is the view of Ibn Janah, Rashi, Kimchi, J. D. Michaelis and W. Gesenius, but among the scholars listed above there are some (C. F. Houbigant, B. Duhm, A. S. Peake, P. Volz, W. Rudolph, A. Weiser, N. C. Habel) who do not suppose that there is any word-play in מה משא יהוה. If there is a play on the homonymic משא, Jeremiah's questioners are enquiring in a derisory way what new burdens he proposes to heap on them by means of his utterances in the name of Yahweh. He is being chaffed as one who sees disaster round every corner and who confuses his own jaundiced condition with Yahweh's word. C. W. E. Naegelsbach, who supposes that the question is full of scorn, nevertheless, introduces the thought that this was a stock question to address to a prophet and that it was a way of asking whether there was any news on the prophetic front — whether there had been any new disclosure from Yahweh. This idea, invested with greater seriousness and urgency, is read into the question by those who suppose that it was genuine and that it was an honest request for guidance from Yahweh.

A second opinion, therefore, is that the question has no aspect of taunt or derision and that there is no play on the homonym משא »burden«. The question is a bona fide request for the word of Yahweh. addressed to a prophet whose stock had risen because his earlier predictions had been fulfilled or partly fulfilled. V. 33 is then located in the reign of Zedekiah (cf. 21 1–10) when Jerusalem was under siege and the prophet's help was sought. He is solicited out of a sense of fear and helplessness and there is no satirical intention. This comes in only with the brusque and harsh nature of Jeremiah's reply: it is he who imports sarcasm into the context by playing on the homonymic משא and introducing the nuance »burden«. So C. F. Houbigant: Ludit Jeremias in vocabulo משא, quod significat et *vaticinationem*, et *onus* propriè dictum, quod onus Dominus à se projecturus est. The presence of this »bitter irony« (W. Rudolph) in the answer is taken as evidence that v. 33 is a genuine saying of Jeremiah. The hardness of the answer is explained by the circumstances in which it was uttered: Yahweh's patience is at an end; he has »carried« his people long enough and now he is about to unburden himself of them (A. Weiser).

According to H. Torczyner[26] and H. M. Weil[27] משא (MT משׂא) should be read as מַשָּׁא »loan« or »pledge« (Neh 5 7.10 10 32; cf. משאה, Dtn 24 10 and Prov 22 26; also משׁה Dtn 15 2). H. M. Weil's argument is

---

[26] משא יהוה, MGWJ 76 (1932), 273–284.
[27] Exégèse de Jérémie 23 33–40 et de Job 34 28–33 (Jérémie 44 9), RHR 118 (1938), 201–208.

that משׂא (v. 33) means »pledge« and that נשׂא אתכם (הנני ונשׁיתי אתכם) (v. 39) can be related to the usages of משׂא in vv. 33.34.36 and 38 only on this assumption. נטשׁ (vv. 33.39) is used with משׂא in Neh 10 32 with the sense of forgoing a pledge and it is this usage which obtains in Jer 23 33.39. The reason why Jeremiah replies so sharply is that the question מה משׂא יהוה is insulting and contains the inuendo that he is Yahweh's »pawn« (How is Yahweh's pledge?). The reply אתם המשׂא ונטשׁתי אתכם (emending MT, see below), »You are the pledge and I shall forgo you« (that is, leave you unredeemed) is picked up in v. 39: הנני ונשׁיתי אתכם נשׂא ונטשׁתי אעכם, »I shall lend you out and not redeem you« (this goes back to Hitzig who interpreted v. 39 as »I shall lend you out and not temporarily«). The present form of MT, according to H. M. Weil, is the result of dogmatic alterations: the representation that Yahweh was a lender was felt to be objectionable, but the »lending« reference was allowed to stand in v. 39 because there was no mention of Yahweh.

H. Torczyner's account, although it has a similar lexicographical foundation, proceeds differently, but H. Torczyner also urges that נטשׁ in vv. 33 and 39 is a synonym of עזב and cannot denote the casting down of a burden. עזב and נטשׁ are synonyms in Neh 5 10 and 10 32 and, in association with משׂא, they refer to the renouncing of a claim. Vv. 33—40 represent the popular view that Israel is Yahweh's possession or property. He may temporarily allow her to fall into alien hands (»lend her out«) but she will always be redeemed. The people are being lulled into a false sense of security by the שׁלום prophets and it is this which makes Jeremiah angry. Hence his retort that Israel will be given as a pledge and will be abandoned: the loan will not be temporary and there will be no redemption.

But is the representation that Israel is loaned out by Yahweh (even if the loan is only temporary) an appropriate or even a credible symbol for a sense of security or an unshakable expectation of שׁלום? It is rather a symbol which makes Israel into a chattel at Yahweh's disposal and which builds into the relation between Yahweh and Israel a measure of recurring insecurity. H. Torczyner knows that vv. 35—37 presuppose the sense »oracle« for משׂא and do not fit into his pattern of interpretation for vv. 33—34.38—39: מה ענה יהוה and מה דבר יהוה, as substitutions for משׂא in vv. 35 and 37 respectively, presuppose משׂא »oracle«. Hence H. Torczyner assumes that the original sense of the passage has been deflected by an editorial superimposition or by a commentary which misses the point. It is striking that H. Torczyner does not indicate how מה משׂא יהוה (v. 33) can be accommodated to his interpretation. If משׂא means »loan« or »pledge«, what is intended by the question which is addressed to the prophet? Weil can make an effort at answering this, because he assumes that משׂא is being applied in a derisory way to Jeremiah. Even so, »How is Yahweh's pledge?« is an improbable sense for מה משׂא יהוה. H. Torczyner is in greater difficulty, because if משא is being used as a symbol of שלום prophecy to which the questioners are attached, what can they possibly mean by asking Jeremiah מה משא יהוה? A great deal has to be read into the question in order to make it sensible. We have to suppose that they were asking Jeremiah why he constantly failed to take account of the ultimate security of Judah as a משא יהוה. This stretches credibility beyond tolerable limits (cf. W. Rudolph), but if it is allowed, the point of Jeremiah's answer is that his consistent note of doom is justified, because Yahweh is about to loan his people out or deposit them as a pledge and leave them permanently in pawn.

An important element in the argument of H. Torczyner and H. M. Weil, in respect of vv. 33 and 39 is that נטש is a synonym of עזב and cannot denote the throwing down of a burden (also van Selms, »opgeven«, »geen aandacht meer geven«). נטש and עזב are synonyms in Neh 5 10 and 10 32, where, in association with משא, they refer to the renouncing of a claim. But the sense »casting out« or »casting down« is indicated for נטש in v. 33 by LXX (καὶ ῥάξω ὑμᾶς), Vulg (*proiiciam quippe vos*) and, probably, Targ (וארטוש יתכון). Even if Targ means »And I will abandon you«, the figure of laying down a burden is not precluded. This is clear from the exegesis of Rashi and Kimchi who gloss ונטשתי (v. 33) with ועזבתי and yet suppose that Jeremiah's reply indicates that Yahweh will unburden himself of his people. The argument that »forsake« or »abandon« cannot be stretched to include the laying down of a burden was not accepted by them. In addition, Kimchi suggests that נטש may be regarded as a variant of נתש; this has apparently been assumed by the Syriac translator (*d°'qwrkwn* »uproot«, »demolish«) and is found in S. Muenster and W. Lowth: »The Hebrew reads thus, ›And I will cast you‹ . . . for the verb נטש writ with a ט is equivalent with the verb נתש, with a ת.«

Ibn Janaḥ[28] represents the sense »cast out« (*'iṭrāḥ*) for נטש, but he does not discuss any passage in which נטש has this sense. Contrasting with this is the detailed treatment of the matter in W. Gesenius who adumbrates a theory of biliteral roots by urging that ט and שׁ are the fundamental constituents of the root. He cites Arabic *waṭasa* »crush«, »smash«, *laṭasa* »knock«, *raṭasa* »slap« and Hebrew רטש »dash in pieces«, »cast away«. The semantic development is from »shatter«, »cast out«, to »abandon« and he illustrates this with special reference to רטש: hebr. et chald. diffregit, quod apud Chaldaeos eodem modo ad abiiciendi et derelinquendi potestatem transfertur, atque hebr. נטש[29]. He is aware that the occurrences to which he has assigned the sense »cast off« are usually explained as »abandoned«, but he argues that the association of נטש and

---

[28] Op. cit. 433.
[29] Op. cit. 879.

הִשְׁלִיךְ in Jer 7 29 indicates the sense »cast off« and that this was how נטשׁ was understood, for the most part, by the ancient versions: Sed fortiorem *abiiciendi reiiciendique* potestatem non solum suadet et primaria verbi potestas et veterum interpretum auctoritas, qui plerisque locis hanc vim exprimunt . . . sed adeo flagitant loci Jer. vii, 29, ubi נטשׁ respondet verbo הִשְׁלִיךְ, et xxiii 39, ubi coniunguntur verba נטשׁ מֵעַל פְּנֵי et relinquendi potestatem non admittunt[30].

Even if this account of the semantic development of נטשׁ were rejected and »forsake«, »abandon« were taken to be the central sense of נטשׁ (J. Buxtorf[31], BDB[32], KB[33]), this would not rule out the possibility that there is a reference to unburdening in Jer 23 33. 39. To lay down a burden is to abandon it and the sense »cast out«, »throw down« can be derived from »abandon (to exile)«. That נטשׁ means »throw down«, »cast off« in Jer 23 33. 39 is indicated by the versions and is maintained by J. Calvin, B. Blayney, K. H. Graf, C. F. Keil, E. H. Plumptre, C. von Orelli, F. Giesebrecht, B. Duhm, A. S. Peake, L. Elliott Binns, P. Volz, W. Rudolph, A. Weiser, J. Bright, N. C. Habel, S. B. Freehof, NEB.

The argument so far has been that משׂא »burden« and משׂא »utterance« are homonyms and that their homonymic character is exploited both in the question מה משׂא יהוה and in the rejoinder to it. The question means »What is Yahweh's utterance?«, or »What disclosure do you have from Yahweh?«, but through a play on the sense »burden« there is an overtone of scorn and derision: »What is your latest gloomy prognostication?« The answer appears in MT as ואמרת אליהם את מה משׂא, but את מה משׂא has been read by LXX (ὑμεῖς ἐστε τὸ λῆμμα) and Vulg (*vos estis onus*)[33a] as אתם המשׂא. P. Wernberg-Møller[34] urges that the text should be read as אתמה משׂא, אתמה being a form of the pronoun attested by IQ[Is.a]. He then supposes that in addition to the play on משׂא there is a deliberate echoing of the interrogative מה of מה משׂא יהוה in אתמה משׂא. Targ. has fudged the difficulty of את מה משׂא by paraphrasing it as ותימר להון כדין נבואתא. Pesh (*'nt hnw ptgmh dmry'*) has read את as אַתְּ, »You are the very word of Yahweh« (the sense is obscure). Kimchi supposes that את מה משׂא refers back to מה משׂא יהוה, and so he comments on ואמרת אליהם את מה משׂא, »You will answer the question which they

---

[30] Op. cit. 880.
[31] Op. cit.
[32] Op. cit. 643 f.
[33] Op. cit., 1958², 613 f.
[33a] Cf. Liber Hieremiae et Lamentationes, Biblia Sacra 14, 1972, 144: *ut quid vobis onus* is preferred to *vos estis onus*; *ut quid vobis onus* is apparently an attempt to render MT את מה משׂא (anti. secundum hebr. non habent »vos estis onus« sed »ut quid vobis onus«).
[34] The Pronoun אתמה and Jeremiah's Pun, VT 6 (1956), 315 f.

have asked«. The answer then follows, ונטשתי אתכם נאם יהוה. The sense of יהיה... ואמרת, according to Kimchi, is: »You will answer the question which they have asked (מה משא יהוה) as follows, ›I shall unburden myself of you‹. This is Yahweh's word.« Ewald's explanation, which K. H. Graf notes, follows Kimchi: את מה משא is elucidated as *Was betrifft diese Frage was* משא *sei*. K. H. Graf's comment that this justification of MT does not supply a proper connection for ונטשתי אתכם is to the point (Dabei fehlt aber für ונטשתי die rechte Verbindung und Beziehung). An unconvincing modern attempt to justify MT urges that את is used emphatically before a nominative in את מה משא: »What, do you suppose (את), is a burden (to me)«[35]. C. F. Houbigant adopts אתם המשא (*onus ipsi vos*) and comments: Nec aliter legendum; nam את מה interrogationem habet, ubi opus est responsione.

The weakness of the view that there is no nuance of taunt or derision in the question מה משא יהוה is that it does not account adequately for the sharpness of Jeremiah's (Yahweh's) reply. If the prophet had been approached with a genuine request for a »word of God«, he would not have been required to round on his interlocutors as he does in the latter part of v. 33 (reading, אתם המשא ונטשתי אתכם). So far as H. Torczyner is making the point that there is an incongruence between the assumption of an honest approach to the prophet and the rough nature of the answer which it gets, his contribution has value, but his contention that משא »loan« or »pledge« is to be read in vv. 33.34.38.39 should be rejected. To the extent that he is urging that vv. 33—40 revolve around a conflict between doom and שלום prophecy, he is in accord with the interpretation of v. 33 which I have adopted. This is found in Lowth (»The false prophets . . . derided the true ones whose predictions were full of threatenings, as if God's messages were a burden they were weary of hearing, and made a jest of these words.«) and in P. A. H. de Boer (»It is the prophet who scoffs at the people because of the שלום prophets«).

»What is your latest burdensome word from Yahweh?« is the intention of the question in v. 33, to which Jeremiah gives Yahweh's answer, »You are the burden and I am about to unburden myself of you«. This implies dissent from an account of the relation between vv. 33 and 34 which rests on the assumption that there is no satirical nuance in מה משא יהוה (B. Duhm, P. Volz, W. Rudolph, A. Weiser). According to this view v. 34 has misunderstood the point of v. 33 by supposing that it hinged on the impropriety of the term משא, and so has introduced a foreign terminological fussiness or hair-splitting pedantry concerning the right word to use in describing a communication received by a prophet from Yahweh. Rather, v. 34 is an interdict arising out of the satirical exploitation of the

---

[35] N. Walker, The Masoretic Pointing of Jeremiah's Pun, VT 7 (1957), 413.

homonymic character of מִשָּׁא in the question מַה מַשָּׁא יהוה, and is connected with a substantial theological issue: the conflict between doom and שָׁלוֹם prophecy. Those who deride a prophet of doom by asking tongue in cheek מַה מַשָּׁא יהוה will suffer for it. The versions, which do not detect any play on מַשָּׁא in v. 33, similarly give no indication of it in v. 34, since LXX λῆμμα, Vulg *onus* (the normal rendering of מַשָּׁא in prophetic contexts), Pesh *ptgm'* and Targ נבואתא are innocent of any ambivalence. If there is a lack of coherence between vv. 33 and 34, it does not consist in the circumstance that an interdict on the use of מַשָּׁא has no foundation in v. 33, but rather on the change from a national context to one restricted to individuals and their families (עַל הָאִישׁ הַהוּא וְעַל בֵּיתוֹ). If v. 33 reflects a polemical situation obtaining between doom and שָׁלוֹם prophecies, the outcome should be described as a judgement which will fall on the nation – dispersion and exile – and not as a judgement which will fall on an individual and his household.

Vv. 35–37 can be considered together conveniently: v. 36 presents considerable difficulties, whereas vv. 35 and 37, which have much in common, and the first part of v. 36, reiterate the proscription on the use of מַשָּׁא. לֹא תִזְכְּרוּ (MT לֹא תִזָּכְרוּ) should be read as לֹא תַזְכִּרוּ (LXX μὴ ὀνομάζετε). The sense of not mentioning or using the term מַשָּׁא any more has been secured by the use of the passive in Vulg (*non memorabitur*) and Pesh (*l' ttdkrwn*). Vv. 35 and 37 furnish unambiguous ways of referring to a prophetic oracle (v. 35) or of asking a word of God from a prophet (v. 37). מַשָּׁא, because of its satirical associations and debunking intent, is to be avoided. In conversation one should say
and in addressing a prophet, מַה עָנָךְ יהוה וּמַה דִּבֶּר יהוה.

J. G. Janzen[36] is right to conclude that in jumping from לְאִישׁ דְּבָרוֹ (v. 36) to וּמַה דְּבַר יהוה (v. 37) LXX has left the latter »high and dry«, and that it has the appearance of a torso rather than an »original« shorter text to which additions have been made in MT. Whether LXX was the result of »the accidental loss of a line in the Hebrew text which was translated«, that is, a defective Hebrew *Vorlage*, as J. G. Janzen supposes, or the carelessness of the Greek translator, may be left open. The difficult part of v. 36 consists of כִּי הַמַּשָּׂא יִהְיֶה לְאִישׁ דְּבָרוֹ. Both LXX (ὅτι τὸ λῆμμα ἔσται τῷ ἀνθρώπῳ ὁ λόγος) and Vulg (*Quia onus erit unicuique sermo suus*) suppose that דְּבָרוֹ is subject and the sense of Vulg is certainly »For his own word will be הַמַּשָּׂא to each man«. The sense of LXX, which renders דְּבָרוֹ as ὁ λόγος, is obscure, but it is clear that Pesh (*mtl dptgm' nhw' lgbr' nbywth'*) has understood דְּבָרוֹ differently from Vulg: »Because his prophecy (i.e., the word which he receives from Yahweh) will be הַמַּשָּׂא to a man«. This is not altogether transparent, but perhaps מַשָּׁא is

---

[36] J. G. Janzen, Studies in the Text of Jeremiah, 1973, 99 f. 223 n. 35.

being defined as a term which should be reserved for »word of God« (*nbywth'*) and not used satirically. The Hebrew grammar presupposed by Targ is different, since לאיש דברו is taken as a construct relationship (»to the man of his word«), and the suffix then refers to Yahweh: »And you will take no further account of prophecy (נבואה) in the name of the Lord, because prophecy (נבואתא) will be the possession of the man who fulfils the words which he (= the Lord) has willed.« »The man who fulfils the words which the Lord has willed« is a paraphrase of איש דברו.

Rashi, who has the same grammar as Targ, comments that the meaning of משא is נבואה (= Targ) which God speaks to איש דברו and divulges to איש עצתו. Kimchi explains כי המשא יהיה לאיש דברו as לכל איש מהם יהיה המשא דברו and adds, »As if to say, by his (i.e., Yahweh's) word alone he (the prophet) speaks a משא«. This is close to Pesh and has the same grammar: משא is defined as Yahweh's word which is then equated with prophecy (נבואה). The twisting of God's word is, according to Targ, a nullifying of his words, and, according to Kimchi, a reference to the mocking of prophecies of doom by importing the nuance of »heaviness« and attributing them to the constitutional gloominess of the prophet Jeremiah: »In your minds you twist them from prophecy to heaviness.« Two interpretations of כי המשא יהיה לאיש דברו have so far been encountered and the first has two variants:

1. (a) A משא is a word of God revealed only to true prophets who are bearers of his word (Targ, Rashi). Hence Rashi supposes that vv. 33—40 are an elaboration of the accusation that false prophets steal oracles from true prophets which he finds in v. 30. This exegesis of v. 36 is founded on the grammar »man of his word«.

(b) This is founded on a different grammar — דברו is subject. משא means נבואה »prophecy« and this comes to expression in Yahweh's word (Pesh?, Kimchi).

2. משא (Yahweh's word) is being confused with the private opinions of individual men which they give out as if they were word of God (Vulg).

When the history of interpretation is studied, it becomes evident that, for the most part, דברו has been taken as »his own word« rather than »Yahweh's word« and that it has been regarded as subject rather than as an element of a construct relationship (איש דברו). The interpretation of Vulg, namely, that human opinions are being confounded with the word of God, is present in A. S. Peake (»The oracle he utters has no source higher than himself«). Comparable with this is B. Duhm's supposition that כי המשא יהיה לאיש דברו is a philological gloss, the intention of which is to establish that there is no longer any occasion for using the term משא, since only human opinions are being expressed for which דבר will serve perfectly well.

If יהיה is translated as a future and משא as »burden« (»For every man's own word shall be his burden«, so L. Elliott Binns), a note of threat is introduced, and this is an interpretation which has commanded widespread support. Those who have made משא a vehicle of their satire will indeed experience God's word as a »burden« when the judgements which it predicts fall on them. This is found in J. Calvin (Nam alioqui unicuique vestrum onus erit sermo suus), H. Venema (Quod ipse sarcastice de verbo Dei protulit, acsi esset onus grave et molestum, *illud vere* fit experturus), W. Lowth (»You shall be severely accountable for your loose and profane Speeches, wherewith you deride and pervert the Words and Messages of God himself«), and B. Blayney (»That is, every man shall have most reason to regard his own word as hurtful and prejudicial to him«). It is followed by a large number of later scholars (e. g., E. Henderson, K. H. Graf, F. Hitzig, C. W. E. Naegelsbach, C. F. Keil, C. von Orelli, F. Giesebrecht).

Another view, which is represented by W. Rudolph and J. Bright, derives from a proposal of A. B. Ehrlich that המשא should be read as הַמַּשָּׂא. The other part of A. B. Ehrlich's[37] proposal that דברי should be emended to דברי is not taken up, because it is assumed (so W. Rudolph) that Jeremiah and not Yahweh is the speaker in vv. 35–40. If כי המשא יהיה לאיש דברו is translated as »For is his word (or »my word«, if A. B. Ehrlich is followed) a burden to anyone?«, the supposition is that there is a reference to the exploitation of the homonyms משא »utterance« and משא »burden«, and that it is the nuance of »burden« attached to God's word which is indicated by the reference to the twisting of the words of the living God. But is this a probable interpretation of והפכתם את דברי אלהים חיים? Does not this refer to a tampering with or distortion of the content of God's word rather than simply a satirical use of the term משא, whereby doom oracles are written off as heavy tidings deriving from Jeremiah's melancholy rather than from God?

The grammar of v. 36 which best supports this line of thought is found in Targ and Rashi and has reappeared in NEB: »You shall never again mention ›the burden of the Lord‹; that is reserved for the man to whom he entrusts his message.« Those addressed are »false prophets« who have not been commissioned by Yahweh and who have no prophetic authority. They have no right to preface their utterances with the term משא (»oracle«, »word of God«), for the claim which this embodies is reserved for those to whom God reveals his word (לאיש דברו). Hence their claim is false and the שלום prophecies which they utter are a perversion of the words of the living God. It is those who change doom to שלום and who claim Yahweh's authority for what they say that are guilty of twisting Yahweh's words. A different exegetical use of this grammar is S. D. Luzzato's assumption that there is a nuance of »heavi-

---

[37] A. B. Ehrlich, Randglossen zur Hebräischen Bibel, IV 1912, 304 f.

ness« in משא and so an allusion to the heavy burden of the prophetic vocation.

It is a delicate task mediating between these differing interpretations of כי המשא יהיה לאיש דברו. The grammar and the associated interpretation of Targ, Rashi and NEB are attractive, but they introduce new ideas to v. 36 which are a departure from the controversy in vv. 33—35 and which are not continued in vv. 37—40. The evidence elsewhere in the passage suggests that it is the satirical use of משא and the attaching of the nuance »burden«, as a device for lampooning prophecies of doom, which constitutes the subject matter of vv. 33—40, and it is the exegesis represented by A. B. Ehrlich and W. Rudolph which best achieves this end in v. 36. The question »Is his word a burden to any man?« can be related to it and the difficulty of reconciling with it »For you have twisted the words of the living God« is not insuperable. The insinuation, involved in the play on the homonym, that prophecies of doom disclose more of the constitutional gloom of those who utter them than they do of Yahweh's word is the device by which the words of the living God are twisted. The »man of his word« type of exegesis, on the other hand, introduces into v. 36 a kind of opposition between authentic prophets, who are bearers of Yahweh's דבר, and false prophets which is foreign to the remainder of the passage. It presents a different antithesis in respect of משא, namely, that משא, prefacing an utterance, is a claim which true prophets may make but from which false prophets must refrain.

J. G. Janzen[38] holds that ואם משא יהוה תאמרו is superfluous in v. 38 and that the shorter LXX text, which does not represent these words, is superior. This deserves serious consideration, but there is not much at stake exegetically: ואם משא יהוה תאמרו does not entirely cohere with יען אמרכם. Vv. 38—40 deliver a threat in view of a refusal to abstain from a use of משא which amounts to a satire on prophets of doom, and the main problems are in v. 39. The opinion that נטש cannot refer to the casting down of a burden has already been discussed[39], but it is introduced by J. G. Janzen[40] in connection with v. 39 and is the foundation of his argument that מעל פני (not represented by LXX) is not original. He contends that if ונטשתי אתכם means »And I shall abandon you«, it is not appropriately associated with מעל פני: ונטשתי . . . מעל פני would have to be translated »And I shall cast you out from my presence«, but נטש does not have this sense.

It has been noted that נטש is understood as »cast out« or »cast down« by LXX and Vulg in v. 33 and as »uproot« by Pesh. In v. 39 LXX uses the same word to render ונטשתי (καὶ ῥάσσω); Pesh, with

---

[38] Op. cit. 223 n. 35.
[39] Above, 43 f.
[40] Op. cit. 44. 206 n. 22.

another word, indicates »cast out« (*w'šdykwn*), whereas Vulg indicates »desert« (*derelinquam*) as opposed to »cast out« (*proiiciam*) in v. 33. Targ's וארחיק for ונטשתי (v. 39) points to »removal (into exile)«. Hence the versions, except Vulg, represent »casting out« or »casting down« for נטש rather than simply »desertion«, but Vulg, which renders ונטשתי as »desert«, does not discern any incompatibility in the combination of this with מעל פני (*a facie mea*). Why has Vulg varied its translation of נטש as between v. 33 and v. 39? The change may be connected with the reference to Jerusalem in v. 39 and the associated thought that Yahweh will desert Jerusalem. This would be in accord with the reference in Ezekiel to the departure of the »Glory« of Yahweh from Jerusalem (11 22f.) and with Kimchi's exegesis of 39, »I shall forsake you and the city from which I shall remove my שכינה«. According to Kimchi, however, נטש refers both to Yahweh's forsaking of Jerusalem and to Israel's exile away from Jerusalem (cf. Jerome, non solum autem vos, sed et urbem vestram, quam dedi patribus vestris — et dabo, inquit, in opprobrium et ignominiam sempiternam, quae numquam oblivione delebitur[41]).

What has emerged is that the problem is bigger than מעל פני: one sense of נטש, »cast out« or »cast down« suits ונטשתי אתכם (= v. 33) and another, »desert« suits ולאבותיכם . . . ואת העיר אשר נתתי. The supposition that there is a deliberate ambivalence of נטש to accommodate this should not be seriously entertained. Even if it is urged that the sense »cast out« or the like is a development from »desert«[42], two different senses of »desert« or »abandon« are involved. The first is either »abandoning (a burden)« or »abandoning (to exile)« and this (ונטשתי אתכם) has been reinforced by מעל פני. The second sense of »abandon« involves not the removal of Israel but Yahweh's desertion of Jerusalem (ונטשתי את העיר). J. G. Janzen's contention that מעל פני does not combine credibly with the sense »desert« is correct, because if נטש means »desert« ונטשתי אתכם is complete and מעל פני adds nothing to it — it is redundant or incongruous. Since LXX does not represent מעל פני, the conclusion should be drawn that this was the final addition made to v. 39 in the process of forming the extant Hebrew text (MT). It is appropriate in relation to ונטשתי אתכם and inappropriate in relation to ונטשתי את העיר which requires the sense »desert«. But the latter is a further disturbing factor in the verse and should be regarded as a secondary elaboration, introducing the new idea that Yahweh would »desert« Jerusalem. The original sense of v. 39 was the same as that of v. 33 and the verse terminated like v. 33 with ונטשתי אתכם. Hence J. G. Janzen's view that מעל פני will not combine with the sense »desert« should be accepted, but his

---

[41] Op. cit. 293.
[42] Above, 44.

opinion that נטש cannot have the sense »cast out« or »throw down« should be rejected.

אתכם נשא is not indicated by LXX and J. G. Janzen[43] supposes that it is a corruption of what was originally »a marginal variant to ונשיתי«. Over against MT נשיתי and נשא there is support from Hebrew manuscripts for נשיתי and נשא. Kimchi derives ונשיתי and נשא from נטש »forget«, in which case there is a substitution of א for ה in נשא. Kimchi comments: »Just as you are forgetful of my words and signs which I perform by the hand of my prophets — and now you are rejecting my prophetic witness and despising it — so I will forget you, although I purchased you and made a covenant with you, for you have made my covenant of no effect from the beginning.« This is in general accord with Targ which, however, paraphrases ונשיתי אתכם נשא as וארטוש יתכון מרטש, »And I will utterly abandon you« (using the verb which translated נטש in v. 33). This is an interpretation which is in KJV and NEB (footnote), which is noted by J. Bright and has been revived by A. van Selms.

LXX (Aq, Symm) read ונשיתי as ונשיתי=ונשאתי; Vulg (*Propterea ecce ego tollam vos portans*) and Pesh (*mṭl hnʾ ʾškwlkwn mšql*) have similarly understood ונשיתי אתכם נשא. This assumes a further play on משא and is an explanation of v. 39 which has been widely followed (Jerome, J. Calvin, H. Venema, W. Lowth, B. Blayney, E. Henderson, C. von Orelli, K. H. Graf, F. Giesebrecht, B. Duhm, A. S. Peake, L. Elliott Binns, P. Volz, W. Rudolph, A. Weiser, J. Bright, NEB, N. C. Habel). It is on this assumption that v. 39 is interpreted by Jerome: »Since you say what I forbid and do not say what I commanded by many prophets whom I sent, I shall fulfil for you your own word (משא = *onus, pondus*). I shall take you (LXX λαμβάνω) and lift you and carry you and cast you down; I shall make you tumble from the heights to the ground.« Those who use משא satirically, as an indication of their refusal to take prophecies of doom seriously, will themselves be carried off into exile. Blayney remarks: »It is obvious that according to the Hebrew idiom נשיתי and נשא ... are the same verb repeated with an allusion to the ›burden‹ before spoken of in ver. 33 ... נשיתי is put for נשאתי according to the form of the verbs quiescent in ה which is often assumed by those quiescent in א.« E. Henderson, adopting the readings נשיתי and נשא, remarks: »The former ... is found in two of de Rossi's MSS and has been in four more originally and has the suffrages of LXX, Syr. and Vulg.; and, the latter in seven of de Rossi's MSS, originally in eight more.«

The view that v. 33 is a kernel attributable to Jeremiah which has been elaborately expanded and that vv. 34—40 is one of the latest passages in the Hebrew bible is found in B. Duhm and is further represented by

---

[43] Op. cit. 99 f.

P. Volz, W. Rudolph, A. Weiser, J. Bright, J. P. Hyatt and W. Thiel[44]. According to B. Duhm, v. 36b (כי המשׂא יהיה ... אלהינו) is a gloss and v. 37 a doublet of v. 35; vv. 34–36a have more credibility than vv. 38–40, because the author of the former addressed himself to the circumstances of his own times, whereas the latter contains the absurd proposition that the downfall of Judah was the consequence of the misuse of משׂא. According to P. Volz, vv. 34–40 may not be attributed to Jeremiah since he did not share the view that judgement overtook Judah because משׂא rather than דבר was used to designate »word of God«. Since משׂא was still an acceptable term for »word of God« in the period when the book of Malachi was written (1 1), vv. 34–40 must be very late, and the passage betrays Talmudic niceties: it illumines the piety of certain circles in the time of Jesus.

B. Duhm and P. Volz reconcile this interpretation of משׂא in vv. 34–40 with the occurrences of משׂא in prophetic contexts in the Hebrew bible in different ways. There is a problem here for both of them, because if those responsible for vv. 34–40 were so pedantic and so fussy about terminological niceties as is claimed, it is strange that they did not feel uncomfortable about the firmly established position of משׂא »word of God« in the prophetic literature. Would they, being the kind of scholars they are alleged to have been, have proscribed the use of a word which had »canonical« authority? The answers given by B. Duhm and P. Volz are different in character. B. Duhm appears to say that they were unaware of these usages of משׂא in the Hebrew bible, but it is odd that scholars who, on his hypothesis, were so precise and excessively scrupulous displayed such ignorance. P. Volz, on the other hand, builds his argument for the lateness of vv. 34–40 on the presence of משׂא in these other prophetic contexts, and the implication is that a sufficient time must have elapsed after the latest of these occurrences to permit the development whereby משׂא became a suspect word. Neither of these arguments is satisfactory; it will be recalled that all those mentioned above who separate v. 33 from vv. 34–40 do so on the assumption that there is no satirical intent in the question מה משׂא יהוה and that the point of v. 33 is taken wrongly in v. 34. I have dissented from these reasons for disengaging v. 34 from v. 33, but there are two other considerations which make it probable that the separation of v. 33 from the remainder of the passage is a correct move:

(a) The suggestion that או הנביא או כהן has been imported into v. 33 from v. 34 (W. Rudolph, A. Weiser) should be supplemented by the observation that the word order of these three terms (כהן; נביא; עם) differs in the two verses: in v. 33 it is עם, נביא and כהן; in v. 34 נביא, כהן and עם. It is not merely that או הנביא או כהן has been tagged on to העם הזה in v. 33. A more significant factor is that העם הזה (v. 33) has a different sense

---

[44] W. Thiel, Die deuteronomistische Redaktion von Jeremia 1–25, 1973, 253.

from העם (v. 34): העם הזה means the Judaean community in an all-inclusive sense, and so או הנביא או כהן is an unconvincing and superfluous supplementation, whereas העם means the »laymen« in the community — those who are neither prophets nor priests.

(b) ופקדתי על האיש ההוא ועל ביתו (v. 34) does not cohere with v. 33, if, as I have argued, that verse reflects a conflict of doom and שלום prophecy, for in that case the matter at stake is not the fate of individuals or households, but the fate of the nation. Hence it is likely that from v. 34 on we have to reckon with attempts of later generations, living in historical circumstances greatly different from those of the late pre-exilic period, to elucidate the conflict between Jeremiah and the prophets, in the course of which they seek to identify themselves with the pre-exilic prophet of doom. Thus the נביא who appears in association with הכהן in v. 34 is a שלום or establishment prophet and may be identified with the prophets who opposed Jeremiah and commanded popular support. V. 34 and what follows is a way of asserting that Jeremiah was right and the שלום prophets were wrong, and of acknowledging that his words have been vindicated by events, that later generations must absorb them and order their lives in the light of them. על האיש ההוא ועל ביתו reveals a situation where individuals and households are seen as severally and separately determining their own destinies by whether or not they accept the witness of a pre-exilic prophet of doom. This is not a decision on which the fate of the nation hangs, but rather a type of decision made by individuals which creates distinctions within the community and divides it into different categories, into those who decide for Yahweh and those who expose themselves to judgement by deciding against him. The exile is viewed (v. 40; cf. 20 11) as inflicting a humiliation on God's people which will never be effaced; it is a chapter of shame which will always testify against them.

Nevertheless, the development of v. 33 in vv. 34–40 possesses a substantial cohesiveness, because it is explicable as a drawing-out of the satirical use of משא which represented the pre-exilic doom prophet, Jeremiah, as a pathological pessimist whose utterances reflected his own fits of depression and were not »word of God«. Hence the supposition that there is nothing in vv. 34–40 but terminological fussiness or tedious word-chopping or incredible representation is mistaken. There is an attempt to recapture the significance of the conflict between doom and שלום prophecy in the time of Jeremiah, and so the contention (W. Rudolph, A. Weiser, W. Thiel[45]) that vv. 33–40 do not cohere well with a section (v. 9–32) which deals with true and false prophecy is not altogether correct. What is intended by vv. 33–40 is an acknowledgement that Jeremiah was vindicated by events: the post-exilic (?) Jewish community must

---

[45] Op. cit. 253.

confess that this prophet of doom spoke the word of God and identify themselves with him over against the prophets whose assurances of שלום were proved false by destruction, defeat and exile. But this is now a matter of individual responsibility and is a decision which presses on individuals and families. Those who do not affirm his witness and take their stand with him are ripe for judgement before God.

Commentaries cited

Blayney, B., Jeremiah and Lamentations: A New Translation with Notes critical, philological and explanatory, 1784.
Bright, J., Jeremiah: Introduction, Translation and Notes, AB 21, 1965.
Calvin, J., Praelectiones in Librum Jeremia et Lamentationes, 1589³.
Duhm, B., Das Buch Jeremia, KHCAT 9, 1901.
Elliott Binns, L., The Book of the Prophet Jeremiah, Westminster Commentaries, 1919.
Freehof, S. B., Book of Jeremiah, 1977.
Giesebrecht, F., Das Buch Jeremia, HKAT III 2:1, 1894.
Graf, K. H., Der Prophet Jeremia, 1862.
Habel, N. C., Jeremiah, Lamentations, Concordia Commentary, 1968.
Henderson, E., The Book of the Prophet Jeremiah and that of the Lamentations, 1851.
Hitzig, F., Der Prophet Jeremia, KEHAT 3, 1866².
Houbigant, C. F., Biblia Hebraica cum notis criticis, IV: Prophetae Posteriores, 1753.
Hyatt, J. P., The Book of Jeremiah, IB 5, 1956.
Keil, C. F., The Prophecies of Jeremiah, I, 1873.
Lowth, W., A Commentary upon The Prophecy and Lamentations of Jeremiah, 1718.
Luzzato, S. D., Commentary on Jeremiah, 1870.
Naegelsbach, C. W. E., The Book of the Prophet Jeremiah, 1871.
von Orelli, C., Der Prophet Jeremia, KK A 4:2, 1905³.
Peake, A. S., Jeremiah and Lamentations I, The Century Bible, 1910.
Plumptre, E. H., Jeremiah-Malachi, 1884.
Rudolph, W., Jeremia, HAT I 12, 1968³.
van Selms, A., Jeremia I, Die Prediking van het Oude Testament, 1972.
Venema, H., Commentarius ad Librum Prophetiarum Jeremiae, 1765.
Volz, P., Der Prophet Jeremia, KAT 10, 1928².
Weiser, A., Das Buch Jeremia, ATD 20/21, 1969⁶.

Die Hofanlagen im Tempel-Entwurf des Ezechiel im Licht der »Tempelrolle« von Qumran

Von Johann Maier

(Chlodwigstr. 2, Brühl)

Die von Y. Yadin edierte »Tempelrolle«[1] (im folgenden: TR) enthält in den Kolumnen 3—48 Vorschriften und Angaben über den Tempel und den Tempelkult, und zwar als Offenbarung Gottes am Sinai. Es handelt sich also nicht um den Entwurf eines endzeitlichen Tempels, sondern um einen als Gotteswort deklarierten Entwurf für den Tempel, der nach der Landnahme gebaut werden sollte, um eine kritische Alternative zum realen 1. und 2. Tempel, engstens verbunden mit ganz bestimmten Kulttraditionen, die zur Zeit der Abfassung bereits länger kontrovers gewesen sein dürften. Für das Folgende sind nur jene Kolumnen von Interesse, in denen die Tempelanlage selbst entworfen wird, das sind außer Kol. 3—13 (für das Tempelhaus und den Brandopferaltar) insbesondere Kol. 30—46 für die Tempelhöfe.

Die Tempelanlage der TR besteht aus 3 architektonisch jeweils als quadratische Quadriportikus-Komplexe gestalteten Hofumfassungen: 1. Innerer Hof, der Funktion nach Priesterhof (wie bei Ez).

2. Ein Mittlerer Hof, der Funktion nach Männerhof, möglicherweise auch der äußere Hof Ezechiels (jedenfalls im Verständnis Späterer), zumal das Ausmaß 500×500 beiden gemeinsam ist.

3. Der Äußere Hof, der Funktion nach Israelitenhof (für kultfähige Männer und Frauen), im 2. Tempel der Bereich hinter der Abgrenzung mit den Warntafeln für Fremde (für Ez vgl. 44 6—9).

Im Groben haben der Ez-Entwurf und die TR folgende Anliegen und architektonische Grundvorstellungen gemeinsam:

a) Die Neigung zu quadratischen Hofflächen mit Umfassungsbauten.
b) Die Fläche von 500×500 Ellen für den Äußeren Hof bei Ez bzw. den Mittleren Hof der TR.
c) Die Abtrennung des allein für Priester zugänglichen Bereiches als eigenen architektonischen Innenhof-Komplex.

---

[1] Y. Yadin, M^{e}gillat ham-miqdaš. The Temple Scroll (Hebrew Edition), I: Introduction, II: Text and Commentary, III: Plates and Text, IIIA: Supplementary Plates, 1977. Deutsche Übersetzung der TR: Johann Maier, Die Tempelrolle vom Toten Meer, 1978.

Während die Art und Weise der architektonischen Realisierung der Abgrenzung der Heiligkeitsbereiche in der TR klar ersichtlich ist, bleiben bei Ez manche Angaben über die Hof-Verbauung undeutlich bzw. unvollständig. Da jedoch das Grundanliegen, die eindeutige Abgrenzung der Heiligskeitsbereiche, beiden Entwürfen gemein ist, ist zu fragen, wieweit auch für die architektonischen Vorstellungen ähnliche Züge angenommen werden können. Da beide Entwürfe als Korrektur der realen historischen Tempelanlage verfaßt worden sind, darf man davon ausgehen, daß auch die jeweils ideale Lösung en detail anzunehmen ist. Darum ist es äußerst unwahrscheinlich, daß z.B. im Blick auf die »großen Tempelsakristeien« Ez 42 1ff. die von K. Galling[2] wie von K. Elliger[3] u. a. angenommenen »Geländeschwierigkeiten« mit »Felsvorsprüngen« (s. unten) wirklich in Betracht kommen. Dergleichen paßt nicht zu einem Ideal-Entwurf, wie ja auch in bezug auf die Arealeinfassung von 500 × 500 Ellen (bei Ez 42 15 45 2) keine solchen Schwierigkeiten auftauchen —, obschon sie von den topographischen Gegebenheiten her hier eher zu erwarten wären als bei den »Sakristeien«, wo zudem die erheblichen Niveauunterschiede — 3 Terrassen bzw. 3 Stockwerke! — ja die natürlichen weit übersteigen würden, es sei denn, man identifiziert mit K. Galling[4] Stockwerke und Terrassen nicht.

Als Mittel der Abgrenzung der Heiligkeitsbereiche bzw. Höfe kennt die Tempelrolle Einfassungsmauer und Umfassungsbauten, letztere ringsum der Einfassungsmauer entlang, nur durch die Torbauten unterbrochen. Niveauunterschiede, wie sie bei Ez durch die Angabe der Stufenzahl der zu den Torbauten hinaufführenden Treppen vorausgesetzt sind, werden in der TR innerhalb des Areals nicht erkennbar. Bautechnisch bedeutet dies für den Ez-Entwurf immerhin, daß die nach dem Zentrum der Heiligkeit zu jeweils höher werdenden Areale durch eine Einfassungsmauer oder eine Böschung umgeben sein müssen, wobei das erstere wahrscheinlicher ist, denn für die äußere Einfassung ist offensichtlich eine Mauer und nicht eine Böschung vorgesehen (Ez 40 5), wobei sich das seltsame Ausmaß (6 Ellen hoch und 6 Ellen stark) durch die Doppelfunktion als Einfassung des erhöhten Hofareals und als Teil-Fundament für die Umfassungsbauten des Hofkomplexes erklärt. Eine durch die Torbauten unterbrochene Einfassung durch Böschungen, auf denen dann erst die »Hallen« des Innenhofbereiches ständen, ist für Ez kaum wahrscheinlich, obwohl dies oft an-

---

[2] K. Galling in: G. Fohrer, Ezechiel (HAT I/13), 1955, 235ff. (mit Skizze am Ende des Bandes).
[3] K. Elliger, Die großen Tempelsakristeien im Verfassungsentwurf des Ezechiel (Ez 42 1ff.), in: Geschichte und Altes Testament, 1953 (= Festschrift A. Alt), 79–103. Ihm folgte im wesentlichen H. Gese, Der Verfassungsentwurf des Ezechiel (Kap. 40–48), 1957, 26ff.
[4] A.a.O. (Anm. 2).

genommen wird. Es ist auch hier mit einer Einfassungsmauer zu rechnen, deren Minimalhöhe das Innenhofniveau erreicht. Dies bedeutet zugleich, daß der Innenhof bei Ezechiel nur durch die 3 Torbauten betreten werden konnte — im Grunde logisch, denn diese dienen ja gerade der Kontrolle und Regulierung des Verkehrs zwischen den Heiligkeitsbereichen. Dies wieder ist für die Frage von Belang, wie sich der Verfasser den Zugang zu den »Hallen« vorgestellt hat (s. unten).

Hofanlagen als architektonische Abgrenzung von Heiligkeitsbereichen sind in der Umwelt Israels nicht unbekannt gewesen, wenngleich erst verhältnismäßig spät so konsequent angelegt worden, wie es der Ezechiel-Entwurf oder die TR fordert. Im Städtebau sind vom 6. Jh. v. Chr. an Einfassungen von Hofplätzen mit Säulenhallen eine ständig zunehmende Erscheinung gewesen. Das Verhältnis zur TR in der Sache und im Blick auf die Chronologie bedarf noch genauerer Untersuchungen, doch scheinen sowohl Ez-Entwurf wie TR architekturgeschichtlich beachtliche Beiträge darzustellen. Nun ist freilich die erhebliche Differenz zwischen Idealentwürfen und den durch die topographischen und kostenmäßigen Bedingungen bestimmten Realisierungen immer mitzubedenken. Schon ein oberflächlicher Blick auf die herodianische Tempelanlage zeigt, daß sie der Tendenz nach durchaus vergleichbare Ziele verfolgte, diese aber trotz riesigen bautechnischen Aufwands nur begrenzt erreichen konnte. Man darf ferner annehmen, daß die recht komplizierte und wenig durchsichtige Baugeschichte des 1. und 2. Tempels auch durch Überlegungen und Bedürfnisse mitbestimmt war, wie sie in den Idealentwürfen Ezechiels und der TR — wenn auch mit Unterschieden — systematisiert wurden, bei Ezechiel in einer weniger geschlossenen Weise, weil nur die besonderen Anliegen und umstrittenen Daten genauer behandelt bzw. erwähnt werden, in der TR in einem viel weitergehendem Maß, so daß die architektonische Gesamtanlage zumindest grundrißmäßig mit ziemlicher Sicherheit festzustellen ist. Angesichts der nicht zahlreichen Möglichkeiten, die Abgrenzung der Heiligkeitsbereiche architektonisch durchzuführen, und anhand der archäologisch belegbaren Beispiele für die Gestaltung von Hofanlagen dürfte es erlaubt sein, von der TR her einige Rückschlüsse auf den Ezechiel-Entwurf zu ziehen.

Auf eine vergleichende archäologische Studie muß in diesem Rahmen verzichtet werden, doch einige Hinweise seien erwähnt. Abgesehen von ägyptischen Hofanlagen sind schon früh kleinasiatische, syrische und phönikische Anlagen belegt (z. B. in Sendschirli und Byblos). Von Interesse sind dann auch das Iseum von Savaria, der Astarte-Tempel von Umm el-ʿAmed, der von Stoen umgebene Tempelhof von Larissa aus dem 6. Jh., wobei zu vermerken ist, daß 2-geschossige Anlagen zu der Zeit immer häufiger auftauchen, z. B. auch in Amrit. Es sind architektonische Muster, die dann im späthellenistischen und römischen Städtebau große Bedeutung erlangen (Gestaltung des Forums, Paläste und Villen, Thermen). Quadratische Flächen erreichen besonders in der Achaemenidenzeit besondere Bedeutung, haben aber eine weitere Verbreitung und auch ältere Tradition, teils im Städtebau und Festungsbau (auch Militärlager), teils in der Sakralarchitektur. Für die TR wäre abgesehen von der herodianischen Gesamtanlage in Jerusalem vor allem ein Vergleich mit den Anlagen von Baalbek und Palmyra, aber auch von Hatra wichtig.

Der Komplex des »Äußeren Hofes«

1. In der Tempelrolle

Die Außenhofanlage der TR besteht aus einem geschlossen umbauten Hofquadrat. Auf jeder Quadratseite befinden sich 3 Torbauten von 50 × 50 Ellen im Grundriß, die den Gesamt-Hofflügel in 4 Teile zu je 360 Ellen Länge unterteilen. Diese Teile bilden mit den Torbauten zusammen also einen architektonischen Komplex, insgesamt stellt sich die Hofanlage als Quadriportikus mit je 3 Eingängen auf jeder Seite (also mit 12 Toren nach den 12 Stämmen Israels) dar. Der Tiefe nach besteht dieser Umfassungsbau abgesehen von den Torbauten aus folgenden Elementen: Außenmauer (7 Ellen stark, 49 Ellen hoch), 10 Ellen Hinterraum (ḥdr), 20 Ellen Vorderraum (nškh) und 10 Ellen Galerie (prwr), und zwar in 3 Stockwerken, die an den Torbauten durch (im Grundriß quadratische) Stiegenaufgänge im Bereich der Säulengänge verbunden sind.

Die Hoffläche erscheint also durch 3-stöckige Galerien umgeben, unterbrochen durch die Torbauten. Die Galerie-Teile enthalten pro Stockwerk jeweils 18 Raumeinheiten (mit je 1 Hinter- und Vorderraum), deren Türen auf die Galerien münden, also 54 pro Teilstück, ausgenommen auf der Nord- und Südseite an den Ecken, wo jeweils 2 Raumeinheiten wegfallen, weil sie offenbar mit den Küchenanlagen in den Eckbauten zusammenhängen, so daß mit 12 Teilkomplexen zu 54 und 4 Teilkomplexen zu 52 Raumeinheiten (insgesamt 856 Raumeinheiten) in den Einfassungsbauten des Äußeren Hofes zu rechnen ist, je 216 an der Ost- und Westseite, je 208 an der Nord- und Südseite. Damit ist ein zugleich optimaler Abgrenzungs- wie Raumnutzungseffekt gewährleistet. Man wird davon ausgehen dürfen, daß die Einrichtung von solchen Zellenbauten (lškwt/nškwt) bereits in der Königszeit mit der Tendenz auf dieses Ziel hin einsetzte, wenngleich architektonisch offenbar erst Herodes mit seiner Heidenhofumbauung die völlige Einfassung nicht nur mit Mauern sondern auch mit nutzbaren Bauten, in diesem Fall mit hellenistischen Säulenhallen, erreichte.

2. Bei Ezechiel

Von der Gesamtaußenlänge des Äußeren Hofes von 500 Ellen (Ez 42 15 45 2)[5] verbleiben nach Abzug der (lichten!) Torbauweite von 25 Ellen 475, wovon noch auf beiden Ecken das Ausmaß der Kücheneckbauten abzuziehen ist, das Ez 46 21 ff. mit 30 × 40 Ellen (Innenmaß) angegeben ist, wobei man bei diesem Eckbau, der ja als unbedacht und damit als unverstrebt (als eine Art Turmbau) vorzustellen ist, mit erheblichen Mauerstärken rechnen muß. Dabei ist vorauszusetzen, daß die eigentliche Küchenfläche 30 × 30 Ellen beträgt und die 10 überschießenden Ellen auf einer Seite die übliche ezechiel'sche Zugangbreite bedeuten. Der Zutritt würde aus der Galerie erfolgen. Bei differierenden Mauerstärken wäre also ein Gesamtflächenmaß von 40 × 40 Ellen denkbar, die Symmetrie gewahrt. Somit blieben 395 Ellen, geteilt in 2 Komplexe zu beiden Seiten des Torbaues, also à 187.5. Die 7.5 Ellen könnten die Mauerstärke des Torbaues sein, der damit ohne Vorhalle ein Außenmaß von 40 × 40 hätte — wie die Torbauten des Priesterhofs in der TR (Kol. 36). So blieben 180 Ellen pro *lškh*-Komplex, eventuell noch verkürzt um den Raum des Stiegenaufgangs (10 Ellen breit?), den man wohl wie in der TR seitlich an den Torbauten lokalisieren darf. Die Zahlenangabe von Ez 40 17, die 30 *lškwt* auf der *rṣph* nennt, bezieht sich schwerlich auf die Gesamtzahl im Hofbereich, denn dies ergäbe gewaltige Hallen, architektonisch unwahrscheinlich. Wahrscheinlicher zählt jeder Einzelkomplex 30 *lškwt* insgesamt, also 10 pro Stockwerk, so daß im Erdgeschoß ringsum insgesamt 6 × 10 und 2 × 5 (diese im Westen), also 70, anzusetzen sind, insgesamt bei 2 Geschossen 140, bei 3 Geschossen 210. Die Zahl 30 allein auf die Erdgeschoßzellen eines Teilkomplexes zu beziehen, ergäbe zu schmale Einheiten. Somit ergibt sich für die Einzel-*lškh* eine Länge von 18 oder 17 Ellen inkl. Trennwandstärke, nicht viel weniger als in der TR (20 Ellen). Die Tiefe des Umfassungsbaues ist teils durch die Kücheneckbauten und teils durch die Achsenlänge der Torbauten (50 Ellen) angegeben. Da die Maßangaben für die Bauten im Westen des Tempelhauses eindeutig voraussetzen, daß die 6 Ellen starke Einfassungsmauer von Ez 40 5 zugleich Fundamentmauer für die Außenwand der Umfassungsbauten ist, muß dies auch für die übrigen Seiten gelten. Offen ist die Stärke dieser Außenwand, sie betrug wohl mindestens 6 Ellen, in den Kücheneckbauten, wie schon bemerkt, gewiß mehr. In der TR ist die Außenmauer 7 Ellen stark (Kol. 40 9). Daß die *lškwt*-Komplexe mit der inneren Torbautenfront auf einer Fluchtlinie

---

[5] Das Ausmaß von 500 × 500 Ellen für das Hofareal (Ez 42 15 45 2), in der TR Kol. 38 auf den Mittleren Hof bezogen, begegnet auch in Angaben über den 2. Tempel, und zwar für den Fremden nicht mehr zugänglichen Teil (vgl. mMiddot II,1). Aber auch die Terrasse des Zeustempels von Palmyra weist in etwa diese Fläche auf. Es dürfte sich um eine sakralarchitektonische Konvention handeln.

lagen, wird Ez 40 18 nahegelegt, obschon die Möglichkeit besteht, daß nur die Torbautiefe selbst (40 Ellen) und nicht auch die Vorhalle gemeint ist. Aber die planerische Gestaltung der Hoffläche spricht dagegen, bildet die Fläche des Äußeren Hofes doch höchstwahrscheinlich 10 Quadrate zu je 100 × 100 Ellen. Bei einer Außenwand von nur 6 Ellen Stärke und einer Tiefe der Säulengalerie von 10 Ellen (stereotype Zugangsbreite) blieben 34 Ellen *lškh*-Tiefe, das Doppelte der oben erhobenen Länge, im Innenmaß wohl 15 × 30 (2 Ellen Trennwand, 4 Ellen Hofseitenwand), ein stattlicher Raum, sofern nicht noch an eine Unterteilung gedacht war, etwa wie in der TR in Vorder- und Hinterraum. Sollte die Galerie auf der *rṣph* aber zurückgesetzt sein, würde sich die Tiefe der *lškwt* eben verringern, die Vorhalle der Torbauten aber um die Torbauecken herum erstrecken. Jedenfalls weisen die archäologischen Beispiele von Hofumfassungsbauwerken ebenso wie die TR darauf hin, daß es sich um eine geschlossene Umbauung handelt, nicht um für sich stehende Gebäude für je 1 *lškh*, im ganzen 30, wie gelegentlich angenommen wurde. Die LXX haben insofern richtig interpretiert[6], mögen sie dabei auch bereits eine hellenistische Ausführung im Sinn gehabt haben.

In diesem Zusammenhang ist auch von Bedeutung, wie das hebräische *rṣph* in Ez 40 17f. und 42 3 aufgefaßt wird, das man meist als »Pflaster(ung)« übersetzt, jedoch schon in der LXX mit *peristylon* und *stoai* wiedergegeben wurde. Die syr. Version hat, wie H. Gese[7] auch bereits vermerkt, dabei auch einen Stockwerkaufbau im Sinn, und auch Salomo b. Isaak (»Raschi«) erläutert in diesem Sinn: Galerie und Obergeschoß. Möglicherweise ist *rṣph* bei Ezechiel tatsächlich ein architektonischer terminus technicus, der später so nicht mehr verwendet wurde. Y. Yadin meinte zuletzt[8], er sei durch *prbr/prwr* ersetzt worden, da in der TR für den Galerievorbau – wie überhaupt für Säulenvorbauten – *prwr* verwendet wird, wozu der Sprachgebrauch in II Reg 23 11 paßt (wo die LXX aber nur transkribieren). Möglicherweise ist Ezechiels term. techn. mesopotamischer Herkunft, denn im Akkadischen bedeutet *raṣāpu* »aufschichten, (Bauten) aufführen«[9], *riṣpu* »Bau« und *riṣiptu* »Errichtung«[10], und vielleicht ist eine ähnliche Bedeutung auch vereinzelt im nordwestsemitischen Bereich belegt[11]. Von einer Grundbedeutung »aneinanderfügen« her ist die Anwendung sowohl auf horizontale Vorgänge (Pflasterung) wie auf Aufbauten einleuchtend, dabei muß nicht speziell an eine Säulenfront gedacht sein, wie Y. Yadin a.a.O. annimmt, sondern an Gebäude mit größeren

---

[6] Vgl. dazu auch Y. Yadin a.a.O. (Anm. 1) I 204f.
[7] A.a.O. (Anm. 3) 151f.
[8] A.a.O. (Anm. 1) I 204f.
[9] W. v. Soden, Akkadisches Handwörterbuch, 1959ff., II, 959f.
[10] Ebd. 989.
[11] J. Hoftijzer, Dictionnaire des inscriptions sémitiques de l'ouest, 1965, 282.

Fluchten überhaupt. Unbedingt notwendig ist diese Deutung aber nicht, sofern der Umstand zu erklären ist, warum dem Seher eine *rṣph* ins Auge fällt, denn eine Pflasterung hat es sicher auch im Inneren Hof gegeben. Möglicherweise ist an ein augenfällig erhöhtes »Pflaster« gedacht und dafür spricht das Verhältnis zwischen der Treppenstufenzahl des Torbauaufgangs außen — 7 Stufen — und der Höhe der Einfassungsmauer, 6 Ellen. 7 Stufen können diesen Niveauunterschied nicht überwinden, das Torbauniveau — 6 Ellen über dem Außenniveau — muß aber wohl das Niveau der Äußeren Hoffläche sein, so daß bis zur Höhe der Einfassungsmauer noch etwas mehr als 1 m fehlt, der vielleicht an die Einfassungsmauer anschließend als Fundament für die *lškh*-Komplexe bis vor an die Hoffront der Torbauten als *rṣph* aufgemauert werden soll. In diesem Fall wären die *rṣph*-Komplexe im Erdgeschoß von den Vorhallen der Torbauten aus über eine Treppe von etwa 4 Stufen zu erreichen, während im rechten Winkel dazu, an den Torbauflanken, jeweils die Stiegen in die oberen Galerien zu denken wären. In diesem Fall könnte die Vorhalle in ihrer Länge eigentlich über die Torbaubreite (inkl. Mauerstärke) hinausgehen, also noch auf jeder Seite die Breite der Stiegenaufgänge verdecken, die vielleicht ebenfalls je 10 Ellen Breite haben, so daß, wie noch bemerkt werden soll, die 60 Ellen Frontbreite des Portikus in Ez 40 14 nicht absurd erscheinen.

Lage und Funktion der Torbau-Vorhallen

In der TR wird für die Torbauten im Unterschied zu Ez 40 keine Vorhalle erwähnt. Da sich in dem Punkt der ezechiel'sche Torbau auch von den bekannten Stadttorbauten unterscheidet, muß diesem Gebäudeteil eine wichtige Funktion zukommen. Dabei fällt vor allem auf, daß die Vorhallen der Außenhof-Torbauten innen liegen, also aus dem Tordurchgang auf die Fläche des Äußeren Hofes führen, während die Vorhallen der Innenhof-Torbauten außen liegen, ebenfalls an der Fläche des Äußeren Hofs. Diese Anordnung vis-à-vis muß einen plausiblen Grund haben — und dieser kann eigentlich nur darin bestehen, daß die Vorhallen eine konkrete Funktion in der Regelung und Kontrolle des Verkehrs zwischen bestimmten Bereichen erfüllen[12]. Nichts rechtfertigt die vorherrschende Meinung, daß die Vorhalle seitlich geschlossen sein soll, also nur den Tordurchgang hat. Bei den Außenhoftorbauten ist zunächst an die Galerien zu denken, die der jeweiligen *lškwt*-Flucht auf der *rṣph* entlangführen, aber auch zum Stiegenaufgang zu den oberen Galerien, wie ja auch in der TR (Kol. 42 6ff.) die Stiegenaufgänge an die Torbauten angeschlossen sind,

---

[12] Die bei G. Fohrer – K. Galling a.a.O. (Anm. 2) 226 gebotene theologische Deutung (Übergangsraum zwischen Heiligkeitsbereichen) trifft zwar das Grundanliegen, erklärt aber nicht die konkrete architektonische Funktion.

nur daß, wie erwähnt, hier keine Vorhalle angesetzt wird. Meint Ez 40 also, daß man von den Vorhallen der Torbauten des Äußeren Hofes aus zu den Galerien gelangt? Wenn ja, wäre unter Umständen die Vorhalle sogar breiter zu denken als die Innenweite des Torbaues von 25 Ellen mit den beiden Torbaumauerstärken ausmacht, nämlich noch die Breite der Stiegenaufgänge dazu. So ergäbe sich folgendes Bild: Der eigentliche Torbau ohne Vorhalle bildet ein Quadrat von 40 × 40 Ellen Außenmaß, wie auch die Torbauten des Innenhofes in der TR (Kol. 36), die Vorhallenfront insgesamt mißt 60 Ellen: 40 Ellen vor dem eigentlichen Torbau und darüber hinaus auf jeder Seite die stereotype Gangbreite von 10 Ellen für den Raum, von dem aus man Galerie bzw. Stiegenaufgänge erreicht. Nun bietet der Text von Ez 40 14 (vgl. v. 30) in der Tat eine Angabe, die allgemein als Produkt einer Textverderbnis betrachtet wird[13], jedoch dazu passen könnte: »Und er machte (maß?) die Vorhalle 60 Ellen ...«, wobei die LXX-Hauptüberlieferung mit *kai to aithrion tou ailam tēs pylēs hexekonta pēcheis* noch deutlicher wird. Hier heißt es dann ferner: »zwanzig Nischen des Torbaues ringsum«, so daß man zur Schlußfolgerung kommt, im Vorhallenbereich und an den Vorderen Seitenwänden der Torbauten außen wären insgesamt 20 Abteilungen (Nischen) vorgesehen. Das Targum deutete die 60 Ellen auf die Höhe der Pfeiler, ebenso Raschi z. St., doch dürfte dies nicht zutreffen: v. 14 gibt das innere Front-Breitenmaß und v. 15 das Achsen-Längsmaß des Gesamttorbaukomplexes an, und dafür bieten die LXX den vernünftigsten Text, wie auch in v. 16, wo angegeben wird, daß der Torbau innen wie die Vorhalle voller blinder Fensternischen war — zur Ablage von Gegenständen. Daß $hallonôt$ $^{a}tumôt$[14] nicht wirkliche Fenster sein können, ergibt sich schon daraus, daß sie auch an den Pfeilern vorgesehen sind, und die TR gibt über diesen terminus technicus endgültig Aufschluß[15].

Verblüffend ist nun, daß die Innenhoftore ihre Vorhallen auf der Außenhofseite haben, ein Umstand, der kaum beachtet wurde, aber einen praktischen Grund haben muß. Da man die Toreingänge über 8 Stufen (Ez 40 37) erreicht, liegt das Niveau des Innenhofes mehr als mannshoch über dem des Außenhofes. Es ist ferner naheliegend, daß auch beim Innenhofkomplex die äußere Einfassung mit der Torbautenfront auf einer Fluchtlinie liegen, also ein Rechteck von 200 Ellen Breite im Osten und

---

[13] Zur textkritischen Diskussion s. H. Gese a.a.O. (Anm. 3) 145 ff.; G. Fohrer – K. Galling a.a.O. (Anm. 2) z. St.; W. Zimmerli, Ezechiel (BK XIII), II 1969, 985. 1003; L. Vincent, Jerusalem, II–III 1956, 672. Die Ausklammerung von v. 14 zieht notwendigerweise jene von v. 30 nach sich.

[14] Zu diesem terminus technicus s. zuletzt G. Molin, Ḥalonoth 'aṭumoth bei Ezechiel, BZ NF 15 (1971), 250–253; J. Ouelette, 'Aṭumim in 1 Kings 6 4, Bulletin of the Institute of Jewish Studies 2 (1974), 99–102.

[15] Y. Yadin a.a.O. (Anm. 1) I 174 f.

Westen und von 350 Ellen Länge im Norden und Süden bilden soll, im Westen mit der Gesamtumfassung abschließend. Im Ostteil innerhalb der Einfassungsbauten wäre, falls diese wie die Torbauten mit 50 Ellen Tiefe anzusetzen sind, nur mehr die 100 × 100 Ellen große Innenhoffläche frei, im Grunde der Kultdienstbereich, den man nur zu den vorgeschriebenen Verrichtungen und in Dienstkleidung betritt. Von wo aus sollen aber die Räume der Einfassungsbauten betreten werden? Die Antwort ist möglicherweise: Durch die Vorhallen der Torbauten. In ihnen wird kontrolliert, wer den heiligen Innenhofkomplex betritt, z. B. um zu den »Sakristeien« (Ez 42 1ff.) zu gehen und sich für den Priesterdienst umzukleiden, dann in die Vorhalle des Torbaues zurückzukehren und von dort – nach Kontrolle – durch den Torbau die Innenhoffläche zu betreten.

Einen eindeutigen Hinweis darauf, daß man von der Vorhalle aus in einen Umfassungskomplex gelangt, gibt Ez 40 38: Auf einer Seite des Torbaues gibt es einen Zugang zu einer $lškh$, wo man die Opferstücke zubereitet. Denkbar ist ein Streifen, ein Gang, der oben auf der Einfassungsmauer des Innenhofkomplexes und an den Umfassungsbauten selbst außen entlang führt – wie es in Ez 42 1ff. im Zusammenhang mit den »Sakristeien« geschildert wird. Da der Seher nur erwähnt, was ihm nötig erscheint, um bestimmte Anliegen durchzusetzen, also keine komplette Baubeschreibung bietet, ist die Ergänzung im Anschluß an Ez 42 9 in dem Sinn berechtigt: Man gelangt zu den »Sakristeien« im Westen, indem man aus der Vorhalle des Torbaues den Gang Richtung Westen geht, der dann innerhalb des Sakristeigebäudekomplexes an den Erdgeschoßzellen entlang führt. Der eigentliche Innenhofbereich bleibt damit von all dem Kommen und Treiben der nicht Diensthabenden unberührt, ein bemerkenswertes Anliegen, das auch in der TR zum Ausdruck kommen dürfte, wenn auch die Beschreibung des Inneren Hofes Kol. 36–38 stark fragmentarisch ist. Kol. 37 8ff. grenzt nämlich offenbar ebenfalls die priesterlichen Küchen- und Eßeinrichtungen vom Kultdienstbereich ab, wenn auch nicht so strikt wie Ez, nicht an der Außenseite lokalisierend, sondern innen durch eine Mauer abschirmend. Was die übrigen Teile des Umfassungsbaues bei Ez betrifft, so erwähnt nur mehr 40 44ff. die nach Altardienst und Hekaldienst getrennten Diensträume der Priester am Süd- und Nordtor ohne nähere Bauangaben, und Ez 40 38 erwähnt ebenfalls eine besondere $lškh$, die dann wohl auf der anderen (östlichen?) Torbauseite liegen müßte.

Offen bleibt die Gestaltung der Ostseite. Auffällig ist auch, daß der Seher die »großen Tempelsakristeien« vom Äußeren Hof aus beschreibt, diese Priesterdienst-$lškwt$ aber offenbar vom Innenhof aus (LXX expressis verbis), dessen Hofplatzfläche ja v. 47 gemessen wird und von wo aus es v. 48 zur Tempelvorhalle weitergeht. Das heißt aber, daß im Gegensatz zu den »Sakristeien« von Ez 42 1ff. die Eingänge zu diesen Priesterdienst-$lškwt$ an der Innenhoffläche liegen, was ja auch funktional sinnvoll ist, sind sie doch für die Diensthabenden bestimmt, die vor Dienstantritt durch die Vorhallen der Torbauten im Norden und Süden den Gang auf der Einfassungsmauer entlang nach Westen zu den Sakristeien gegangen sind und von dort in Dienstkleidung (Ez 42 14) zurück zur Vorhalle kommen, um von dieser aus durch den Torbau in den Innenhof zu treten, von dem aus sie in die erwähnten Diensträume gelangen konnten. Bei Dienstschluß nehmen sie denselben Weg, um sich vor dem Verlassen des Heiligkeitsbereiches wieder umzukleiden.

Die »großen Tempelsakristeien« Ez 42 1ff.

Für Ez 42 1ff. stehen einige neuere Rekonstruktionsversuche im Vordergrund der Diskussion, nämlich von K. Galling[16], K. Elliger[17], L. Vincent[18] und von M. Haran[19]. Vorweg ist an einige bisher erhobene, wahrscheinliche Punkte zu erinnern: Der Innere Hof liegt 8 Stufen, also übermannshoch, über dem Äußeren, ist daher nur durch die Torbauten zu erreichen. Die angegebene Gesamttiefe der Torbauten und Baukomplexe von 50 Ellen läßt es schwerlich zu, daß dieses beträchtlich erhöhte Areal wechselnd teils durch eine Einfassungsmauer, teils durch eine Böschung begrenzt wird, vielmehr ist wie beim Äußeren Hofkomplex an eine rechteckige Mauer-Einfassung zu denken, was auch der Flächeneinteilung und der Symmetrie am besten entspricht. Wahrscheinlich soll auch der gesamte Innenhof-Bereich ringsum von Einfassungs-Baukomplexen umgeben sein, jedoch von unterschiedlicher Art und Zweckbestimmung, wobei Ezechiel nur jene erwähnt, mit denen er ein besonderes Anliegen verbindet. Der Zugang zu einem Teil der Umfassungsbauten lag offenbar außen, über der Einfassungsmauer, den Umfassungsbauten entlang und nur durch die Torbau-Vorhallen erreichbar, die eben darum hier auf der Seite des Äußeren Hofes liegen. In hellenistischer Zeit hätte man auf der Einfassungsmauer ein Peristyl angelegt.

Äußerst wichtig ist die Aussage Ez 42 13-14: Die sog. »Sakristeien« liegen in dem Heiligkeitsbereich, der allein Priestern zugänglich ist, also

---

[16] K. Galling in: A. Bertholet, Hesekiel (HAT I/13), 1936. Anders 1955 a.a.O. (Anm. 2), wo weitgehend K. Elligers Ergebnisse vorausgesetzt werden.

[17] A.a.O. (Anm. 3). Auf der Skizze S. 103 ist K. Gallings Rekonstruktion mitabgebildet. Die Lage des Gebäudes mit der westlichen Schmalseite an der West-Außeneinfassung wird dem Text am ehesten gerecht, vgl. K. Galling, K. Elliger und H. Gese a.a.O.

[18] L. Vincent, Jerusalem, II—III 1956, 484ff. Er deutete die ʿattîqîm richtig als Terrassen- bzw. Galeriegänge vor den Zellenfluchten, legt den Zugang aber in der Mitte der Schmalseite an, was dem Text nicht entspricht. Alle erwähnten Autoren lassen die Priesterküchen von Ez 46 19ff. unberücksichtigt, weil dieses Stück meist als sekundär betrachtet wird. Vgl. H. Gese a.a.O. (Anm. 3) 88ff.; W. Zimmerli, a.a.O. (Anm. 12) 1180ff.

[19] M. Haran, Encyclopaedia Biblica (hebr.), V 1968, 304—360 (347f.: Skizze).

im Priesterhof-Komplex. Es versteht sich eigentlich von selbst, daß dies einen unmittelbaren Zugang vom Äußeren Hof her ausschließt, der Zu- und Abgang also durch die Torbau-Vorhalle erfolgen muß, abgesehen davon, daß der große Niveauunterschied ja Treppen erfordern würde. Rekonstruktionen, nach denen der Zugang auf Außenhofniveau liegt, sind daher schwerlich zutreffend[20]. Entsprechend der strengen Konzeption sind auch die Fluchtlinien zu beachten, durch die Torbautentiefe von 50 Ellen vorgegeben, was für den Innenhofkomplex ein Rechteck ergibt, das außen 200 × 350 Ellen ausmacht. Die umbaute Fläche beträgt, da der »Bau« im Westen 80 Ellen tief ist (41 12ff.)[21], 100 × 220 (100 Ellen vor dem Tempelhaus, 100 Ellen Tempelhaus, 20 Ellen hinter dem Tempelhaus). Der Tempelhaus- und Altardienstbereich ist somit gegenüber außen vollständig abgegrenzt – eben ein Grundanliegen, das auch in der TR zutagetritt, wenngleich dort die Westseite den übrigen Seiten gleich konzipiert ist. Ez trennt jedoch den eigentlichen Dienstbetrieb architektonisch strenger vom sonstigen priesterlichen Tun und Lassen im Priesterbereich ab und zwar mit Hilfe der Verlagerung von Eingängen an die Außenseiten der Umfassungskomplexe, die somit eigentlich nur 40 Ellen Tiefe haben – wie der Torbau ohne Vorhalle. Von diesen Voraussetzungen her ergibt sich für die sog. »großen Tempelsakristeien« von Ez 42 1ff., daß sie auf dem Innenhofniveau standen und die Breitenangabe von 50 Ellen das Gesamtmaß inklusive vorgelagertem Gang angibt, weil die Abgrenzungsmauer auf der Einfassungsmauer hier mit zum Gebäude zählt. Diese Abgrenzungsmauer sollte die Zellen mit ihren Öffnungen gegenüber dem Außenhof ausreichend abschirmen, während bei den übrigen Einfassungsbau-Komplexen nicht solche Zellenfluchten anzunehmen sind, so daß sich eine solche Mauer erübrigt und eine niedrigere Einfassung oder ein Geländer genügt. In hellenistischer Zeit hätte man hier eine Stoa eingeschaltet. Man könnte also vom Außenhof aus sehen, wie die Priester von der Torbau-Vorhalle aus auf dem über der Einfassungsmauer (Innenhofniveau) liegenden Umgang vor den Umfassungsbauten gegen Westen gehen und hinter der Mauer verschwinden, die die Zelleneingänge der »großen Sakristeien« abschirmt (wobei diese Mauer nach 50 Ellen Länge an die innerste *lškh*-Wand der Außenhof-Umbauung anschließt), bzw. den umgekehrten Weg nehmen.

Die bautechnische Hofkomplexgestaltung der TR und die Analogie zum Umfassungsbau des Äußeren Hofes in Ez 40 läßt aber auch die Anlage der Sakristeien deutlicher erscheinen, wie Y. Yadin festgestellt hat[22]:

---

[20] So K. Galling und K. Elliger sowie M. Haran a.a.O.
[21] Allerdings ist ungewiß, ob die Mauerstärke von 5 Ellen einzubeziehen ist. M. Haran rekonstruiert so (Anm. 19) und läßt daher im N und S des West-»*Binjan*« einen Gang von je 5 Ellen frei.
[22] A.a.O. (Anm. 1) I 205.

Es handelt sich um ein Gebäude mit 3 Stockwerken, Erdgeschoß, Mittelgeschoß, Obergeschoß, die aus Zellenfluchten bestehen, deren Ein- bzw. Ausgänge an der dem Äußeren Hof zugewandten Seite auf einen 10 Ellen breiten Gang führen. Über die Begrenzung dieses Ganges wird nur für das Erdgeschoß etwas ausgesagt, soweit sich dieses über die Tiefe der Außenhof-Umbauung (50 Ellen) hinaus erstreckt. Diese 3 Gänge vor den 3 Zellenflucht-Geschossen liegen jedoch nicht — wie bei den säulengetragenen Galerien des Äußeren Hofes voll übereinander, sondern terrassenförmig gestaffelt, so daß die Tiefe der Zellen des Mittelgeschosses sich um 10 und die Tiefe der Zellen des Obergeschosses sich um weitere 10 Ellen verkürzt. Das bedeutet konkret: Für das Erdgeschoß 10 Ellen Gangbreite und 40 Ellen Zellentiefe, für das Mittelgeschoß 10 Ellen Terrassengangbreite und 30 Ellen Zellentiefe, für das Obergeschoß 10 Ellen Terrassengangbreite und 20 Ellen Zellentiefe. Gegen den Inneren Hofraum zu ist dieser Bau völlig abgeschlossen, 80 Ellen lang sowieso durch den »Binjan« im Westen (41 12ff.), aber wohl auch den 20 Ellen tiefen Platz (*gzrh*)[23] hinter dem Tempelgebäude entlang, hier ist schwerlich ein Gang zwischen Sakristei und Westbau anzunehmen (Ez 42 10bff. bezieht sich auf die andere Hofseite) sondern ein geschlossener Umbauungskomplex.

Ein weiteres Detail für die Rekonstruktion der »Sakristeien« bietet Ez 46 19ff. Der Seher wird durch den Eingang an den Torbau-Seiten geführt — also doch wohl durch die Vorhalle — und dann — auf dem Torbau- bzw. Innenhofniveau (also über der Einfassungsmauer entlang) nach Westen zu den »Sakristeien« von Ez 42 1ff., diesmal aber in den von der Außenmauer abgeschirmten Gang hindurch bis an das westliche Ende zwischen Außenhof-*lškwt* und West-»*Binjan*«. Dort befinden sich die Küche und die Backstube für die Priester, wobei wieder ausdrücklich festgehalten wird, daß die Anlage ein Betreten des Außenhofes verhindert. Ausmaße werden nicht genannt, doch ist anzunehmen, daß der größte Teil der westlichen Hälfte des 100 Ellen langen »Sakristei«-Gebäudes für die Küchen- und Backstubenanlagen dient. In diesem Fall könnte von hier aus auch ein Zugang zu dem rätselhaften »*Binjan*« im Westen des Tempelhauses geplant sein, der sich sehr gut für Vorratsräume eignen würde. Für den Seher bilden diese Küchen- und Backstubenanlagen samt den heiligen Priesterzellen einen Gebäudekomplex von 100 × 50 Ellen Grundrißausmaß, wovon vom Äußeren Hof aus aber nur 50 Ellen sichtbar sind, der dreigeschossige Terrassenteil, während der Küchenteil hinter dem westlichen Außenhof-*lškwt*-Komplex (wahrscheinlich auch 3-geschossig) verschwindet. Es ist anzunehmen, daß diese Anlage für die Süd- wie für die Nordseite vorgesehen ist, wenngleich Ez 46 19ff. nur eine beschreibt.

---

[23] Zu *gzrh* s. K. Elliger a.a.O. (Anm. 3) 81ff.

Wie schon erwähnt[24], wird dieser Passus in der Regel gegenüber Ez 42 1ff. als sekundär angesehen und daher erscheinen die Küchen in den Rekonstruktionen meist nicht. Ob dieses literarkritische Urteil zutrifft oder ob M. Harans Analyse[25] eines planvollen literarischen Aufbaues von Ez 40—48 vorauszusetzen ist, bleibt in einer Hinsicht irrelevant: Für die Späteren und damit auch für die weiteren architektonischen Planspiele und Realisierungen war der Ezechieltext maßgebend, wie er jeweils vorlag. Was noch aussteht, ist eine gründliche Untersuchung des LXX-Textes im Lichte der archäologischen und architekturgeschichtlichen Daten und im Verhältnis zur TR, einschließlich einer umfassenden und detaillierten und vergleichenden Untersuchung der termini technici. Erst auf dieser Basis wäre eine sachgerechtere Beurteilung der masoretischen Textgestalt möglich.

---

[24] S. Anm. 18.
[25] M. Haran, Ezekiel's Code (Ezek. XL—XLIII) and its Relation to the Priestly School (hebr.), Tarbiz 44 (1974/75), 30—53.

A Mari Prophecy and Nathan's Dynastic Oracle

By Abraham Malamat

(1 Rashbastreet, Jerusalem, Israel)

The Mari Letters known to deal with prophecy and oracles at present number twenty-eight[1]. Of this group, one of the most interesting (the second to have been published) is of particular relevance for a comparative study with prophecy in the Bible. The document in question (A. 1121) has been published by G. Dossin only in transliteration and (French) translation[2]. Since this initial publication, various translations and treatments have appeared, mostly in the general context of Mari prophecy[3]. Amongst these is a specific study by the present author (published in Hebrew, with a brief English abstract), giving a Hebrew translation of the document, with a discussion of the text, its historical background and its implications for biblical prophecy[4].

One facet with which we have not previously dealt has curiously been unappreciated till now (except for some passing remarks): the nature of the prophecy in this document as a »dynastic oracle«, and its impact on the study of the parallel material in the Bible. It is this facet which occupies our attention here, our ultimate aim being a comparison with Nathan's oracle on the Davidic dynasty, in II Sam 7, also referred to as Yahwe's covenant with David.

As the basis of our discussion, we present a revised English translation of the Mari document, with brief annotations. This is followed

---

[1] The most recent comprehensive survey on Mari prophecy is E. Noort, Untersuchungen zum Gottesbescheid in Mari 1977; for the previous literature, see p. 5, n. 1, there; and for the list of the 28 texts, on p. 8, Fig. 1 there. For the most recently published text (A. 222, and cf. J. G. Heintz, VT 21, 1971, 529, n. 1), see now G. Dossin, RA 69 (1975), 28–30 (»Le songe d'Ayala«).

[2] In A. Lods, Une tablette inédite de Mari, intéressante pour l'histoire ancienne du prophétisme sémitique, in: Studies in Old Testament Prophecy Presented to T. H. Robinson (H. H. Rowley, ed.), 1950, 103–107.

[3] See W. von Soden, WO 1 (1947–52), 403; H. Schmöckel, ThLZ 76 (1951), 55; G. Rinaldi, Aevum 28 (1954), 1–9; J. J. Roberts, Restoration Quarterly 10 (1967), 124 f.; F. Ellermeier, Prophetie in Mari und Israel, 1968, 48–53; H. B. Huffmon, BA 31 (1968), 106f. (= BA Reader 3, 1970, 204f.); W. L. Moran, ANET³, 1969, 625. I was unable to consult J. G. Heintz's unpublished doctoral dissertation (Strasbourg 1968) on the Mari prophecies.

[4] A. Malamat, History and Prophetic Vision in a Mari Letter, Eretz-Israel 5 (1958), 67–73 (Hebrew; English Summary on pp. 86*f.).

by an English translation of a fragmentary letter (A. 2731)[5] which parallels
part of the first text. It is thus of considerable aid in restoring and
providing certain details missing there — including the salutation
mentioning Nur-Sin, Zimri-Lim's »ambassador« at Halab (Aleppo) as
sender and the king of Mari himself as recipient. For convenience, we
shall henceforth refer to these two documents as A and B, respectively.

A
(A. 1121)

(Opening broken — salutatory formula of Nur-Sin, »ambassador« of
Zimri-Lim at Halab.)

> Concerning [the delivery of] the *zukrum*,
> Abi [. . .], in the presence of Zuḫatnim,
> spoke to me, as follows: »[Deliver] the *zukrum*;
> also deliver the cattle. My lord, in the presence of [. . .]-men,
> 5 told me to deliver the *zukrum*, as follows:
> ›Never shall he break (his agreement) with me.‹
> I have brought witnesses for him.« Let my lord know this.
> Through oracles, Adad, Lord of Kallassu,
> [spoke] to me, as follows: »Am I not
> 10 [Ad]ad, Lord of Kallassu, who
> reared him (the king) between my loins and restored him to the throne
> of his father's house? After I restored him to the throne
> of his father's house, I have again given him a residence.
> Now, since I restored him to the throne of his father's house,
> 15 I will take from him an estate.
> Should he not give (the estate),
> am I not master of throne, territory and city?
> What I have given, I shall take away. If (he does) otherwise, and
> satisfies my desire, I shall give him throne upon throne,
> 20 house upon house, territory upon territory,
> city upon city.
> And I shall give him the land
> from the rising (of the sun) to its setting.«
> This is what the *āpilū*-diviners said, and in the oracles
> 25 it »stands up« constantly. Now, moreover,
> the *āpilum*-diviner of Adad, Lord of Kallassu,
> is standing guard over the tent-shrine of Alaḫtum to (be) an estate.
> Let my lord know this.

---

[5] As no transliteration has been published, we must rely on G. Dossin's French translation in: La Divination en Mésopotamie ancienne, 1966, 78 (where it is erroneously designated as A. 2925; cf. now ARM XVII/1, 29).

Previously, when I was residing in Mari,
30 every word the *āpilum*-diviner or *āpiltum*-diviner
told me, I would report back to my lord.
Now that I am living in another land,
that which I hear and which they tell me,
would I not communicate to my lord?
35 If ever anything remiss should occur,
let not my lord speak thus, as follows:
»The word which the *āpilum*-diviner has spoken to you — while over your tent-shrine
he is standing guard — why have you not
communicated to me?« Herewith I communicate (it)
40 to my lord. Let my lord know this.
Moreover, the *āpilum*-diviner of Adad, Lord of Ḥalab,
came [to Abu]ḫalum and spoke thus to him,
[as follows:] »Communicate to your lord
(broken off; speech of the god missing)

[from the rising (of the sun)] to its setting,
[it is I] who will give (it) to you.«
[This] is what Adad, Lord of Ḥalab,
told me in the presence of Abuḫalum.
50 Let my lord know this.

Annotations to Text A

ll. 1–7	Our suggested punctuation here remains conjectural, and is in part contrary to that of G. Dossin.
l. 1	CAD Z, 153, translates *zukrum* as »pasture-land (?)«. But this otherwise unknown word more probably denotes a male animal, as G. Dossin claims. It is difficult, however, to decide whether *zukrum* connotes »oxen« (as G. Dossin seems to hold), or »stud bull« or possibly »rams/he-goats«. For the word *lâtu* (in l. 4), paired with *zukrum* here, does not only designate the fem. pl. »cows« (pace G. Dossin), but also »cattle« collectively (CAD L, 218).
l. 2	Regarding Zuḫatnim, a high official at Mari during the reign of Zimri-Lim and, inter alia, emissary (»chargé de missions«) to Ḥalab, see now ARM XVI/1, 244.
l. 4	A new examination of the text of this letter (cf. J. G. Heintz, Biblica 52, 1971, 546) has led to the reading of the last preserved words in this line as $awī[le^m]^{eš}$ $ù[...$ (= ... »men«), rather than the published reading $šarr[āni^m]^{eš}ù[...$ (=»kings and ...«). »Men« may refer to the representatives of a certain city, or rather may serve as a determinative signifying tribal chieftains or the like.

l. 6 Here, Abi . . . seems to be quoting the words of his lord (the king of Mari, or the author of the letter?). It is also possible that the subject of this sentence is a god, who would never break his covenant with the ruler.

l. 8 *ina têrētim*, »through oracles«, is preferable to »through visions«, as in our earlier (Hebrew) translation. W. L. Moran translates: »at (the inspection of) omens« (by the *āpilū* mentioned below?).

l. 11 The words here refer to the king of Mari. The usual translations of *paḫalli* (lit. »my testicles«) are, euphemistically, »genoux«, »Schoss«, »thighs«, etc., which blur the realistic imagery which the speaker had in mind. The god Adad is here depicted primordially in the form of a bull. In Mesopotamian art, Adad is sometimes shown standing upon the back of a bull, or even personified as a bull.

l. 13 *ašar šubti*, lit. »dwelling-place«, here referring to the palace.

ll. 15, 27 *niḫlatum*, translated by us as »estate«, is taken by G. Dossin as a place name, an alleged town Niḫlatum near Halab. The appearance of this word in l. 27, defined by the post-determinative KI, might tend to support this assumption, though it is by no means decisive. First, the usage of KI is not restricted to toponyms, but it may be affixed to other geographical designations as well. Furthermore, in l. 15 the KI is missing, and in l. 27 it might simply be a scribal error, influenced by the place name Alaḫtum, mentioned immediately before. As a matter of fact, in the parallel letter (cf. J. G. Heintz, op. cit., ad loc.), *niḫlatum* actually occurs without the KI. Following upon a discussion with B. Landsberger, we suggested in our Hebrew article (and cf. my remark in JAOS 82, 1962, 149) that this is a West Semitic idiom for an »estate«, »hereditary property«, »patrimony« – an interpretation now widely accepted. The noun *niḫlatum* (and cf. ARM I 91: 6'; V 4:5), and the verbal form *naḫālum*, »inherit«, »apportion«, attested in several Mari documents, do not exist in standard Akkadian. But in turn these forms do have cognates in Hebrew (*nāḥªlā* and *naḥăl*), as well as in Ugaritic (*nḥl*; and see below, p. 81). They should be added to the various other West Semitic terms in Mari relating to tribal heritage (cf. BA 34, 1971, 14 ff.). The noun *naḫalu* is also found as a West Semitism in the Akkadian documents from Ugarit (cf. PRU III, 109, No. 16.251:7).

l. 17 *epi/erum*, »territory«, »land«, is not a West Semitic term, strictly speaking, as G. Dossin holds – cf. CAD E, 189b. It occurs in the documents from Alalaḫ, level VII, originating in approximately the same period and area as our letter. There,

	too, it occurs in combination with the words »house« and »city«, as in our ll. 20—21 below (cf. Wiseman, AT, Selected Vocabulary, s.v. *epirum*).
ll. 20—21	The syntactic structure X upon (*eli*) X, Y upon Y, and so forth, seems to be of West Semitic character. For similar examples in Biblical Hebrew (e.g. Jer 4 20), Phoenician (Azitawadda I, 6—8) and Aramaic (Sefire I B, 30), cf. J. C. Greenfield, JSS 11 (1966), 103 ff.
l. 23	The idiom *ṣitiša . . . erbiša*, »from the rising (of the sun) to its setting«, i.e. from east to west, is parallel to the expressions in Hebrew: *mimmôṣaʾ ûmimmāʿᵃrab* (Ps 75 7; and cf. Ps 50 1 113 3 Isa 45 6 Mal 1 11); in Phoenician: *lmmṣʾ šmš wʿd mbʾy* (Azitawadda A II, 2/3); and in Aramaic: *mn mwqʾ šmš wʿd mʿrb* (Panamu, l.13).
l. 24	The *āpilum* (fem. *āpiltum*, pl. *āpilū*), lit. »answerer« (derived from the Akkadian verb *apālum*, »to answer«), designates a divinatory prophet or some sort of cultic functionary. This sense is attested in Mari only, cf. CAD A II, 170a. For a discussion of the significance of the *āpilum*, see our remarks in VT Suppl. 15, 210 ff., and below, pp. 76—78.
l. 25	*ittanazzaz*, from *izuzzum* (W. von Soden, GAG, 154, § 107, 8b; AHw, 410), »to stand«, in the Gtn form (iterative), signifying »continuously, constantly standing«. Generally this verb has been translated here as if the *āpilū*-diviners were the antecedent of the verb, consequently the verb is emended and read as a plural, and it is assumed that the prophets continuously resided at the site of the oracle. Thus G. Dossin: »or ils [?] se tiennent continuellement dans les oracles«; W. L. Moran: »they are constantly appear(ing) at the omens«; and our own Hebrew translation, rendered into English: »they insist upon (or stand by) the vision«. W. von Soden, without emending the verb to the plural, translates: »hält er sich immer wieder bei den Orakeln auf«. However, the antecedent of *ittanazzaz* is not *āpilū*, but rather *annitam*, »this matter«. Thus H. B. Huffmon: »It continues to stand up in the extispices«, as well as our present rendering: »and in the oracles it (*annitam*) ›stands up‹ constantly«.
l. 27	The true connotation of *maškānum* as used in our letter (here and in l. 37) seems to have eluded those who have translated it according to one of its usual Akkadian meanings (»région«, »threshing-floor«, »dépôt«; cf. CAD M I, 369 ff.). It would seem, however, that it is used here in the specialized meaning of its Hebrew cognate, the biblical *miškan*, »tent-shrine«, »tabernacle«. If so, this is yet another illustration of West

Semitic influence on vocabulary and religious practice at Mari, especially in the »prophetic« letters there. It must be noted, however, that in the Bible, too, threshing-floors proper were used as cultic places; cf. II Sam 24 18ff. (David's altar at the threshing-floor of Araunah), and I Kings 22 10 (the prophets at the threshing-floor near the gate of Samaria).

ll. 27, 37/38 The idiom *maškānam . . . inaṣṣar*, »stand guard over the tent-shrine«, has its equivalent in the biblical (*šamăr*) *mišmæræt miškan*, »keeping watch over the tabernacle« (e.g. Num 1 53; and cf. II Kings 11 5). For the biblical phrase, see J. Milgrom, Studies in Levitical Terminology, I 1970, 8ff.

This new interpretation of the words *maškānum* and *niḫlatum* thus yields: ». . . the *āpilum*-diviner . . . is standing guard over the tent-shrine . . . to (be) a (sacred) estate«.

l. 37 The conjunction *ū* introduces a circumstantial clause and would yield the best sense if translated »while« (cf. A. Finet, L'accadien des lettres de Mari, 1956, 225f., § c, d). W. von Soden translates (p. 403): »Das Wort ⟨des Gottes⟩ [supplying *ša ilim*] sagte der ›Beantworter‹ dir, während er deine Tenne (?) bewacht.«

ll. 3'—4 ' The speaker, of course, is the *āpilum*-diviner of Adad.

B
(A. 2731)

»To my lord, speak: Thus Nur-Sin, your servant. Once, twice, five times have I communicated to my lord concerning the delivery of the livestock to Adad and concerning the *niḫlatum* which Adad, Lord of Kallassu, demands from you. (Several lines missing. Reverse:) ʿAm I not Adad, Lord of Ḫalab, who has raised you . . . and who made you regain the throne of your father's house? I never demand anything of you. When a wronged man or woman cries out to you, stand and let his case be judged[6]. This is what I demanded from you, and what I have communicated to you, you will do. You will heed my word and the land from the ri[sing (of the sun) to its setting] and the land of . . . [I will give you]'. This is what the *āp[ilum*-diviner of Adad, Lord of Ḫalab spoke to me.«]

Each of these documents originally contained two oracles intended for Zimri-Lim — in both texts, the first by Adad, Lord of Kallassu, and the second by Adad, Lord of Halab. Chance would have it that the two

---

[6] Based on G. Dossin's transliteration of this one sentence, in M. Anbar, UF 7 (1975), 517f., who cites as a biblical parallel Jer 22 3a. For further parallels of prophetic utterances on kingly obligations and conduct, cf. Jer 21 11–12 22 15–16.

tablets were preserved in a complementary manner, the first oracle being preserved in its entirety in the one, and the second oracle having survived in the other. The damaged state of the first seven lines in text A precludes a clear understanding of the precise matter there. In the light of text B, however, it is evident that the passage relates to the oracle following, and that the animals to be delivered were apparently intended for sacrifice[7].

The relationship between the two gods, whether they are merely two aspects of a single Adad or truly separate deities, is not clear, for we know practically nothing of the locale of Kallassu, which is generally considered to be in the vicinity of Halab, if not an actual quarter of that city, sacred or otherwise[8]. In any event, though both deities claim to have restored Zimri-Lim to his throne, there is an interesting difference between the two in the demands put to him: in both documents, the Lord of Kallassu claims a *niḫlatum*, while in B (the relevant passage in A is broken) the Lord of Halab presses for a just hearing for the downtrodden.

A brief analysis of the historical context of these texts can now add certain details which have been made known since our previous (Hebrew) treatment of the matter[9]. Adad's oracle must be interpreted against the backdrop of the evolving ambivalent political relationship between the land of Yamḫad (with Halab as its capital) and Mari, after Zimri-Lim's accession[10]. Though the general picture is obscure, we now know that Zimri-Lim — after almost two decades of exile in Yamḫad (at any rate, somewhere in Northern Syria) — succeeded in regaining the throne of Mari after forcing out Yasmaḫ-Adad, the Assyrian viceroy[11]. He was

---

[7] For the offering of sacrifice prior to the delivering of an oracle, see ARM XIII 23, 4ff. (where the diviner is designated *aplûm*, a variant of *āpilum*), and A. 455 (G. Dossin op. cit. [above, n. 5] 79f.).

[8] On Adad of Halab, see H. Klengel, JCS 19 (1965), 87ff.; and Adad of Kallassu, ibid., 89. For Zimri-Lim's devotion to Adad of Halab, see his year formula, No. 20, G. Dossin, Studia Mariana, 1950, 57; and cf. Syria 19 (1938), 115 n. 3, for an oracle obtained by one of Zimri-Lim's functionaries at Halab. See now also ARM XIV, 9, where Yaqqim-Adad, governor of Sagarātum, assures Zimri-Lim that sacrifices will be offered to Adad, Lord of Halab, in every town of his district.

The tablets recently discovered at Ebla (only 70 km south of Halab) may attest a long-standing tradition of prophecy in the Halab region, over half a millennium prior to Mari, as shown, by the words there for prophet (*nabi'ūtum*, Hebrew *nabî'*) and ecstatic (*maḫḫūm*); cf. G. Pettinato, BA 39 (1976), 49.

[9] See above, n. 4.

[10] On relations in general between Yamḫad and Mari, see H. Klengel, Geschichte Syriens im 2. Jahrtausend v.u.Z., I 1965, 102ff.; III 1970, 146ff., and cf. P. Artzi and A. Malamat, Orientalia NS 40 (1971), 86ff.

[11] For Zimri-Lim's recovery of Mari, see a very fragmentary victory stele published by G. Dossin, Syria 48 (1971), 1ff.; and cf. J. M. Sasson, RA 66 (1972), 177f. For an allusion to Yasmaḫ-Adad's flight from Mari, see ARM X, 140.

aided by Yarim-Lim, king of Yamḫad (who, at one stage or another, became his father-in-law). To this effect, we now have the final publication of a letter (A. 1153) in which Zimri-Lim quotes Yarim-Lim as having said: »Is it not I who made Zimri-Lim regain his throne, who consolidated his strength and the foundation of his throne?« (ll. 8—10). Later in the letter, Zimri-Lim addresses his »father« — that is, his suzerain, Yarim-Lim: »It is my father who made me regain my throne; it is he himself who strengthened me and fastened the foundation of my throne« (ll. 24—25)[12]. This immediately recalls the similar phrasing of Adad, Lord of Kallassu (A: 9—13) and Adad, Lord of Halab (B), surrogating for Yarim-Lim of Yamḫad, or rather, Yarim-Lim standing proxy for the deity.

Mari's inferior status vis-à-vis Yamḫad, at least at the time of these oracles, is further emphasized by the harsh tone of Adad, Lord of Kallassu, towards Zimri-Lim, threatening to depose him if he does not fulfill the deity's demand. But we can learn of the looseness of Yamḫad's superiority from the fact that, even after the five appeals to Zimri-Lim, noted in B (surely A was one of the five), the deity's ultimatum was ignored — regardless of whether these events were in the days of Yarim-Lim or under his son and successor, Hammurapi[13].

The crux of the matter lies in the nature of the object demanded by Adad, Lord of Kallassu — the *niḫlatum*. Although its precise meaning here is elusive, it may well have been some sort of estate, real or otherwise; here, coveted as it is by a deity, it would have been dedicated to sacred purposes — perhaps a temple precinct or even the sanctuary itself. This can further be inferred from A: 26—27, which states that »the *āpilum*-diviner of Adad, Lord of Kallassu, is standing guard over the tent-shrine at Alaḫtum, to (be) a *niḫlatum*«. That is, the tent-shrine was apparently an interim, anticipatory expedient to be superseded by the eventual *niḫlatum*.

Alaḫtum, site of the tent-shrine, was perhaps situated near Halab or between Halab and Yamḫad's border with the kingdom of Mari. This town appears in the Mari documents, in three published instances[13a]. In

---

[12] Cf. G. Dossin, La voix de l'opposition en Mésopotamie, 1973, 179—183; for earlier reports on this document, cf. Bull. Acad. Royale Belgique (Classe des lettres . . .) 38 (1952), 235; Proceedings, 23rd Congress of Orientalists, 1954, 121f.

[13] The death of Yarim-Lim and the accession of Hammurapi at Halab must have occurred about the middle of Zimri-Lim's reign. For the date in terms of Zimri-Lim's year formulas (i.e. his tenth year, at least), see now M. Birot, Syria 55 (1978), 342. Our texts A and B are certainly not from early in his reign, as sometimes contended, since Nur-Sin had resided at Mari for a period prior to his appointment to Halab (see A: 29—31).

[13a] It may also appear in ARM K, 9:12, spelled *A-la-i-tum*, as suggested by J. Sasson, cited by M. C. Astour, »The Rabbeans: A Tribal Society . . .«, Syro-Mesopotamian Studies 2/1 (1978), 4; Astour locates Alaḫtum on the right bank of the Euphrates, between Emar and

addition to our text A, an administrative text (ARM IX, 9) records a shipment of oil from Alaḫtum, sent to Mari by Nur-Sin, Zimri-Lim's »ambassador« to Halab — and a letter (ARM X, 176) notes Mari ladies at Alaḫtum, in the presence of several junior clerks (*ṣuḫārū*). More revealing are several unpublished texts, sent by Nur-Sin to Zimri-Lim, kindly brought to my attention by Professor G. Dossin[14]. These letters (A. 1257, A. 1496 and A. 4445) show that Alaḫtum had been ceded to Zimri-Lim by Hammurapi who, in the meantime, had succeeded Yarim-Lim to the throne of Yamḫad (about the middle of Zimri-Lim's reign). In one letter, it is reported that »Hammurapi constantly pesters me concerning the construction of the city of Alaḫtum«[15], and he entreats Zimri-Lim to provide the necessary funds as well as masons for that purpose. Can we thus presume that the oracle in A (and B) was invoked to induce Zimri-Lim to provide Adad, Lord of Kallassu, with a tangible estate at Alaḫtum, in the stead of the tent-shrine there? Or was this *niḫlatum* to be located at Kallassu, in or near Halab — or even at Mari itself? Only further evidence will tell.

Turning now to the *āpilū*-diviners — an intrinsic and specific part of the Mari milieu — in A we find them, female as well as male (A:30), as spokesmen for deities, acting also in groups (A: 24), like the groups of prophets in the Bible (cf. I Sam. 10 5 19 20 I Kings 20 35ff.). We have previously summarized our views on the *āpilum* and the implications for biblical prophecy (in a study on the »prophetic« texts in ARM XIII)[16]. Here, we may note briefly that an *āpilum*-diviner apparently received oracles while serving at a tent-shrine, within a cultic framework (A: 37—38). Therefore, in biblical terms he can be considered a »cult-prophet«. The very meaning of the Akkadian word *āpilum*, »answerer«, »respondent«, further recalls biblical terminology concerning divine revelation — i.e. the Hebrew verb ʿnh, »to respond«, frequently employed for divine responses to prophetic appeals. Significantly, this Hebrew verb

---

the Baliḫ confluence (cf. his map on p. 3). But for *a-la-i-tum* as »city resident« see now G. Dossin ARM X ad loc. and p. 253.

[14] Personal communication, dated 19. X. 1979.
[15] This passage in A. 1496, ll. 5—7, reads: *a-na ka-a-ia-an-tim Ḫa-m[u-ra-pí]/ aš-šum a-lim A-la-aḫ-tim / ba-ni-e-em ú-da-ab-ba-ba-an-ni*. Cf. also G. Dossin's report of a text concerning the transfer of Alaḫtum to Zimri-Lim, the appointment of new officials there, and the poor condition of the palace buildings there (see A. Pohl, Orientalia, N.S. 22, 1953, 108).

For the cylinder-seal of Nur-Sin, »servant of Zimri-Lim«, see W. Nagel, AfO 18 (1958), 323f.
[16] Cf. our Prophetic Revelations in New Documents from Mari and the Bible, VT Suppl. 15, 1966, esp. 210—214; and see now E. Noort op. cit. (above, n. 1) 142, index, s.v. *āpilum, āpiltum*; and also L. Ramlot, Le prophétisme, Dictionnaire de la Bible, Suppl. VIII, 1972, 884ff.

is not restricted to specifically solicited responses from the divinity, but may at times refer to revelatory messages per se.

Admittedly, the biblical text often makes no mention of any intermediary in such contexts, but the »answerer« must have been a diviner or some other mortal messenger of God. Furthermore, peculiar appellatives for cultic functionaries are noted in Mal 2 12 – ʿ*er* w*ᵉʿonǣ* »arouser and answerer« (sic). In Mic 6 5, referring to Balaam's oracles, we read – ». . . what Balak king of Moab devised and what Balaam the son of Beor *answered* him«. In this last context, the recently published wall inscriptions from Deir ʿAlla (late 8th–7th century BC) – which tell of visions of Balaam son of Beor – mention an ʿ*nyh*, »she who answers«, that is, a female diviner – in effect, an *āpiltum*[17]. The Aramaic Zakur inscription (ca. 800 BC) also employs this same root: »Baʿalshamayn answered me (*wyʿnny*) . . . through seers and through diviners« (side A, ll. 11–12)[18].

Hence, the prime function of the *āpilum/āpiltum*-diviner appears to have been to reveal unsolicited divine messages, though he or she may occasionally also have been the medium for responses to enquiries addressed to the deity (as sometimes were the biblical prophets).

Since our earlier treatments of prophecy at Mari, four additional Mari prophecy texts have become known, containing messages revealed by *āpilum/āpiltum*-diviners: A. 4260 (only through a French translation); ARM X, 9; ARM X, 53; and ARM X, 81[19]. These instances shed light on Nur-Sin's statement (our A: 29–31) that, while still resident at Mari, he had had contacts with such diviners there. A. 4260 is addressed to Zimri-Lim by an *āpilum*-diviner (of Shamash at Sippar) himself, without any lay intermediary – a unique occurrence in the Mari prophetic texts. In ARM

---

[17] Cf. the editio princeps, J. Hoftijzer and G. van der Kooij, Aramaic Texts from Deir ʿAlla, 1976, 174, I:13, translating (p. 180): »she who transmits divine messages«; and the reference there to *āpiltum*, p. 212. For such an interpretation, cf. also H. Ringgren, Balaam and the Deir ʿAlla Inscription, in: I. L. Seeligmann Anniversary Volume (in the press). The word ʿ*nyh*, however, could also mean »the poor one (fem.)«, as preferred by A. Caquot and A. Lemaire, Syria 54 (1977), 200.

The biblical Balaam seems particularly close to the *āpilum*-diviners of our two Mari texts. He and Balak repeatedly sacrificed and constantly tended the oracle (Num 23 3. 6. 14ff. 29); cf. M. Weinfeld, VT 27 (1977), 186f. In any event, Balaam should not be compared with the Mesopotamian *barû*, as has frequently been done, since the latter was expert specifically in haruspicy, but was not distinctly a prophet or seer.

[18] For the Zakur inscription in this context, cf. A. Malamat op. cit. (above, n. 16) 213, and n. 1. For the tie between Mari prophecy and that at Hamath in Zakur's time, cf. J. F. Ross, HThR 63 (1970), 1–28.

[19] For A. 4260, cf. G. Dossin op. cit. (above, n. 5) 85. For the other letters, cf. now the renderings by G. Dossin (in collaboration with A. Finet), Correspondance féminine, ARM X, 1978, a considerable improvement over the earlier readings.

X, 9, an *āpilum*-diviner comes to the palace gate to convey his message to the queen, Shibtu, for delivery to Zimri-Lim. These and other factors[20] show that the *āpilū*-diviners were in more intimate contact with the royal palace than any other type of diviner-prophet at Mari. This relationship brings the *āpilū* into closer analogy with the biblical court-prophets of the type represented by Gad and Nathan. With this, we arrive at the principal theme of our discussion, that is, the bearing of the Mari documents given above (our A and B) on similar prophetic messages in the Bible, specifically Nathan's oracle concerning the kingship.

Nathan's prophecy on the Davidic dynasty, often known as the »Davidic Covenant«, should preferably be regarded as a dynastic oracle. The text of this prophecy, in II Sam 7 1–17, is paralleled (with minor variations) in I Chr 17 1–15; its poetic counterpart appears in Ps 89, an interpretative exposition of the original[21], while Ps 132 would seem to be a poetic reflection of the same oracle. It has been the subject of a voluminous literature — especially since L. Rost's pioneer study in 1926[22]. The specific problems of textual analysis of II Sam 7 — such as the various literary strata, the Deuteronomistic redaction and the dating of the several compositional layers — are beyond our present scope, and can be consulted in the literature noted above. Suffice it here to say that the prophecy *per se* comes from the period of the United Monarchy, with a Davidic nucleus and an adaptation under Solomon.

An oft-applied comparison with extra-biblical sources perceives this literary type of prophecy as a sort of Königsnovelle on the Egyptian

---

[20] See ARM IX, 22:14, where an *āpilum* is listed as receiving a garment from the royal stores.

[21] For the assumption that all three biblical sources are different recensions of an original source, and for an attempt to reconstruct that source, see J. L. Mc-Kenzie, The Dynastic Oracle: II Sam. 7, ThSt 8 (1947), 187–218. But for the literary dependence of Ps 89 on II Sam 7, see, e.g., N. M. Sarna, in A. Altmann, ed., Studies and Texts I: Biblical and Other Studies, 1963, 29–46. A divergent view regards Ps 132 as containing the earliest conception of the »Davidic covenant«; see F. M. Cross, Canaanite Myth and Hebrew Epic, 1973, 232ff., esp. 233.

[22] L. Rost, Die Überlieferung von der Thronnachfolge Davids, 1926, 47–73 (Nathanweissagung). Of the vast literature on II Sam 7, we shall mention only some of the more recent books, which can also be consulted for the earlier literature, including articles and commentaries: R. A. Carlson, David the Chosen King, 1964, 97–128; R. E. Clements, God and Temple, 1965, 56ff.; P. J. Calderone, Dynastic Oracle and Suzerainty Treaty, 1966; N. Poulssen, König und Tempel im Glaubenszeugnis des Alten Testaments, 1967, 43–55, 118ff., 171–174; F. M. Cross op. cit. (above, n. 21) 241–265; T. Veijola, Die ewige Dynastie. David und die Entstehung seiner Dynastie nach der deuteronomistischen Darstellung, 1975, 68–79; T. N. D. Mettinger, King and Messiah, 1976, 48–63; J. Bright, Covenant and Promise, 1977, 49ff.; T. Ishida, The Royal Dynasties in Ancient Israel, 1977, 81–117; K. Ruprecht, Der Tempel von Jerusalem, 1977, 62–78. Cf. also the literature in the following notes.

pattern[23]. This has rightly been refuted, most recently by T. Ishida[24], who instead looks toward Mesopotamia, drawing on comparative material from the neo-Assyrian and neo-Babylonian royal inscriptions. He intimates even a possible early West Semitic tradition underlying Nathan's oracle[25]. In our present study, we focus upon the relevant comparative material in Mari and in the Bible, neither implying nor excluding the diverse possibilities of influence.

Nathan's oracle displays several basic elements held in common with our Mari prophecy, despite several other features distinctly contrastive. Amongst the latter, the promise of Adad, Lord of Kallassu, is conditional upon Zimri-Lim's meeting the deity's demand, whereas the solemn pledge given to David is unconditional, for even if David strays from the way of the Lord, God »will not take my steadfast love from him« (II Sam 7 15, and cf. Ps 89 33–37 [MT v. 34–38]; but see the conditional reinterpretation in Ps 132 12). In other words, the one is obligatory while the other is promissory[26]. Another fundamental contrast appears in the eventual divine rejection of David's intention to build a temple, whereas Adad was adamant in the fulfilment of his desire by Zimri-Lim (see A: 15 ff., and B).

Despite such divergences, there is much common ground, and the distinctive parallel patterns reveal a typology of dynastic oracles; the common features can be outlined under the following headings:

Motif	Adad, Lord of Kallassu (A. 1121 [A], A. 2731 [B])	Yahwe, Lord of Hosts (II Sam 7 1–17)
(a) Installation	»(I) restored him to the throne...« (A: 10–11)*	»I took you from the pasture ... that you should be prince over my people« (v. 8)
(b) Father-son imagery	»(I) reared him* between my loins ...« (A: 11)	»I will be his father and he shall be my son« (v. 14)

---

[23] See S. Herrmann's study entitled »Die Königsnovelle in Ägypten und Israel«, WZ Leipzig 3 (1953/54; Ges.-sprachwiss. Reihe, I), 51–62. Among his many adherents is, recently, M. Görg, Gott-König-Reden in Israel und Ägypten, 1975, 178–271.

[24] T. Ishida op. cit. (above, n. 22) 83 ff.; and cf., e.g., E. Kutsch, ZThK 58 (1961), 137–153, esp. 151 ff.; and more recently T. Veijola op. cit. (above, n. 22) 71 f.

[25] T. Ishida op. cit. (above, n. 22) 92.

[26] For terminology, see, e.g., M. Weinfeld, JAOS 90 (1970), 184–203; idem, IDB Suppl. Vol., 1976, 188–192 (s.v. Covenant, Davidic). M. Weinfeld employs the term »grant« for the unconditional form of the covenant with David, but »treaty« for the conditional type. And now cf. J. D. Levenson, CBQ 41 (1979), 208 f. Several scholars assume that the Davidic covenant (that is, Nathan's oracle) was originally conditional, but that it became unconditional as the result of later reinterpretation; see, e.g., M. Tsevat, HUCA 34 (1963), 71–82; and now F. M. Cross op. cit. (above, n. 21) 241 ff., and in both the relevant biblical passages. In contrast, for an original, unconditional covenantal royal ideology, see T. N. D. Mettinger op. cit. (above, 22) 276 ff.

(c)	Tent-shrine	maškānum (A: 27, 37)	'ohæl and miškan (v. 6)
(d)	Sanctuary as house or estate	niḫlatum (A: 15; B)	băyit (v. 5. 6. 13; cf. nāḫᵃlā, Ex 15 17 Ps 79 1)
(e)	House as palace/ dynasty	ašar šubti (A: 13); bitum (A: 20)	bǎyit (v. 11. 16)
(f)	Throne	kussû (A: 11f., 19)*	kisse' (v. 13. 16)
(g)	Land/ kingdom	ēpirum (A: 20); mātum (A: 22)	mămlakā (v. 12. 16)
(h)	Extent of rule	Spatial: »from the rising (of the sun) to its setting« (A: 22–23)*	Temporal: 'ăd 'ôlam, »for ever« (v. 13b. 16)

*Theme employed by Adad, Lord of Halab, in second oracle in A and B.

(a) In either case the installation of the king marked the beginning (David) or renewal (Zimri-Lim) of a dynasty.

(b) This is a conventional metaphor throughout the ancient Near East for the relationship between deities and mortal rulers, as well as between overlords and their vassals. The metaphor takes on a legal connotation, for it implies the legitimation of the ruler. This imagery appears in the Bible for the Israelite king in general, in Ps 2 7; for Solomon, in our oracle (cf. also I Chr 20 10 28 6); and for David, in Ps 89 26–27, where the motif is further developed, the king becoming the »firstborn« of God[27]. The metaphor in text A from Mari remains unique, however, and implies a much more graphic imagery (see the annotation to A: 11).

(c) If we are correct in our assumption that the maškānum in A has a specialized West Semitic connotation (see the annotation to A: 25), then it refers to the sacred abode of the deity, as does the mšknt in the earlier literary stratum at Ugarit (in the epics, such as UT 128 [CTA 15]: III: 19; 2 Aqht [CTA 17]: V: 32–33), and the tabernacle in the Bible. Such tent-shrines served primarily in semi-nomadic societies, precisely as noted in Nathan's oracle: »I have not dwelt in a house since the day I brought up the people of Israel from Egypt to this day, but I have been moving about

---

[27] See the apt remarks by G. Fohrer, Geschichte der israelitischen Religion, 1969, 138ff., justly divorcing this metaphor from the notion of divine descent or adoption, and regarding it merely as an expression of legitimation of rule. Similarly, F. C. Fensham, Near Eastern Studies in Honor of W. F. Albright (ed. H. Goedicke), 1971, 130f. For the father-son imagery, cf. also M. Weinfeld, JAOS 92 (1972), 469; idem, IDB Suppl. Vol., 190f.; and T. Ishida op. cit. (above, n. 22) 108f.

in a tent for my dwelling« (v. 6). This biblical tabernacle or the Tent of Meeting was not merely a cultic shrine, housing the Holy Ark, but served also as an oracular pavilion[28]. This is clearly attested concerning Yahwe's theophany before the Israelites and his revelation to Moses (cf. Ex 33 7—11 Num 14 10ff. 16 19ff.Dtn 31 14—15), and by the seventy elders prophesying at the Tent of Meeting (Num 11 16—17); and surely this was the case with the *āpilum* in text A as well.

(d) In both Mari and Israel, with the consolidation of the monarchy, an ideological reorientation occurred away from the erstwhile »tent« tradition towards a »house« tradition; in other words, the temporary, mobile shrine came to be replaced by a more elaborate installation, a permanent structure within an actual, sacred precinct[29]. This finds expression repeatedly in Nathan's oracle, the term *băyit* (v. 5.6.13) referring there specifically to a temple; as we have seen, the intended *niḫlatum* in Mari (text A) most probably also referred to real estate, including a structure proper. Significantly, the Bible, too, applies the cognate term *năḥᵃlā* (see annotation to A: 15, 27)[30] to Yahwe's permanent abode, as in the Song of the Sea, in Ex 15 17: ». . . on thy own mountain [*hăr năḥᵃlatkā*; that is, »the mount of thy estate«], the place, O Lord, which thou hast made for thy abode, the sanctuary . . .«. While the *năḥᵃlā* of God generally refers to the Holy Land or to His People, the Israelites, here it points to the Temple Mount in Jerusalem, just as the term is paired with the Holy Temple in Ps 79 1. Elsewhere, too, *năḥᵃlăt Yahwe* is restricted to some specific locale, as in II Sam 20 19, where it refers to the town of Abel Beth-Maacah. This meaning of *niḫlatum/năḥᵃlā* is greatly supported by the Ugaritic mythological texts, which several times designate the divine abode as a *nḥlt*. Of particular relevance to the biblical context is the reference to Baal's holy abode as *ġr nḥlty*, »the mountain of my *nḥlt*« (UT ʿnt [CTA 3] III: 27, IV: 64), while the abode of Kothar and Khasis, as well as of Mot, is denoted *ʾarṣ nḥlth*, »the land of his *nḥlt*« (UT ʿnt [CTA 3] VI: 16; 51 [CTA 4]:VIII: 13—14; 16 [CTA 5]: II: 16)[31].

---

[28] Cf. Y. Kaufmann, The Religion of Israel (transl. and abridged by M. Greenberg). 1960, 183 f.; M. Haran, Temples and Temple Service in Ancient Israel, 1978, 264 ff.; and cf. Encyclopaedia Biblica, V 1968, 542 f., s.v. *miškan* (Hebrew).

[29] For the age-old »tent« tradition as against the innovative »house« tradition in Israel, see F. M. Cross op. cit. (above, n. 21) 231 ff.; and cf. W. Brueggemann, JBL 98 (1979), 169 f.

[30] For the *năḥᵃlā* in the Bible, cf. Encyclopaedia Biblica V, 815 f., s.v. (Hebrew); and THAT II, 55 ff. For this term, its verbal form *naḥăl* and its counterparts at Mari, see A. Malamat, JAOS 82 (1962), 147—150.

[31] For the references, see C. H. Gordon, Ugaritic Textbook, 1965, 443, No. 1633. For the Ugaritic pair *qdš* — *nḥlt*, »sanctuary« — »estate, patrimony«, as well as its biblical correspondents, cf. Ras Shamra Parallels, I (ed. L. R. Fisher) 1972, 324, No. 484.

(e) The exegetes on II Sam 7 have generally noted the word play on *băyit*, referring here to both »temple« (v. 5) and »palace« (v. 11): »Would you build me a house (i.e. temple) to dwell in? . . . the Lord will make you a house (i.e. palace).« They also recognize the double meaning of *băyit* as both »palace« and »dynasty«. Such a twin usage is found also in Mari, in our text A where *bītum* denoted »palace« in standard Akkadian usage but, under West Semitic influence, came to denote »dynasty« as well, in the phrase *bīt abīšu*, »his father's house«, appearing in this sense in several Mari texts[32].

(f) The throne was obviously the symbol par excellence of regality, and thus it is emphasized in both texts, figuratively and literally. In another Mari prophecy directed at Zimri-Lim (ARM X, 10: 13–15), we read: »Kingship, sceptre and throne are sound«[33].

(g) The Bible employs here the Hebrew term *mămlakā*, »kingdom«, while the Akkadian used different terminology, expressed by *epirum*, »territory«, and *mātum*, »land« – specifically geographical terms. This difference in conceptualization is brought out even more boldly in the next point.

(h) Both the Mari oracle and Nathan's prophecy end with a climactic declaration of divine grace to be bestowed upon the king. In the Mari text, it is to manifest itself spatially, the royal domain is to be extended to the ends of the earth. This favour is distinctly imperial in design, as is the promise, several lines earlier, of palaces, territories and cities. In Nathan's oracle, however, Yahwe's pledge is decidedly in temporal terms, assuring the perpetuation of the Davidic dynasty: »your house and your kingdom shall be made sure for ever before me; your throne shall be established for ever« (v. 16; and cf. Ps 89 5, 30, 37f. [MT]).[34] This contrast is representative of the divergent Mesopotamian and biblical world-views, a broad and fascinating subject in itself.

---

[32] Cf. T. Ishida op. cit. (above, n. 22) 101; CAD B, 282ff., s.v. *bītu* 1. temple, palace; 6. royal house; CAD A/1, 73ff., s.v. *abu* A, in *bīt abi* 1. family. The latter surely also includes the sense of »dynasty«, usually denoted in Akkadian by *palû*.

[33] The reading *qa-ma-at*, »sound« (»sont solides«), has now been confirmed by Dossin, ARM X (1978), 10:15, and p. 254, superseding the previous readings, e.g., CAD K, 591b.

[34] For the theological implication of *'ăd 'ôlam*, cf. THAT II, 228ff., s.v. *'ôlam*, and the literature there. According to I. L. Seeligmann, Praqim 2 (1969–1974), 302ff. (Hebrew), the notion of the perpetuity of the Davidic dynasty in Nathan's oracle is a late, tendentious addition, making it a divine charter for the Israelite Monarchy.

Esaïe 47 et la tradition prophétique sur Babylone

Par R. Martin-Achard

(106 Route de Ferney, Genève, Suisse)

Cette page du livre d'Esaïe n'a pas donné lieu à beaucoup d'études particulières, bien que ses lecteurs aient reconnu à maintes reprises ses qualités artistiques exceptionnelles; ainsi G. Fohrer, dans son commentaire de 1964[1], estime que le prophète a composé là une oeuvre magistrale en utilisant toutes les ressources que lui offrait la poésie hébraïque[2].

Nous nous proposons de faire d'abord l'exégèse de ce chapitre et d'étudier ensuite l'histoire de la tradition prophétique sur l'ancienne cité mésopotamienne[3], en essayant de montrer le passage de la Babylone historique, celle de Nébucadnetsar et de Nabonide, à la Babylone apocalyptique, évoquée notamment dans l'Apocalypse johannique, thème qui n'a pas été jusqu'ici, à notre connaissance, l'objet d'une véritable enquête[4].

---

[1] G. Fohrer, Das Buch Jesaja III, ZBK, 1964, 104—110 (106).

[2] Selon L. Köhler, Esaïe 47 constitue un poème harmonieusement construit, il est fait de sept strophes, de six lignes chacune, et suit le rythme de la *qinah* du commencement à la fin. (Deuterojesaja [Jesaja 40—55] stilkritisch untersucht, 1923, 31—34).

[3] Le nom de Babylone/Babel se lit, d'après la concordance S. Mandelkern, 280 ×dans l'AT hébreu, dont 2 seulement dans la Thorah (Gen 10 10 11 9), et près de 240× dans les Prophètes (antérieurs: 31 ×; postérieurs: 206 ×) en relation avec les événements historiques qui ont mis en présence Jérusalem et Babylone (cf. par ex. II Rois: 31 ×, aux chapitres 20 et 24s.). Dans les Ecrits, Babel est peu mentionnée (28 ×dans l'oeuvre du Chroniqueur; 1 ×dans les Megilloth (Est 2 6) 3 × dans les Psaumes (87 et 137), et enfin dans Daniel, en écho lointain de la fin du royaume de Juda 17 × en Dan 2—5.
Ainsi c'est surtout dans la tradition prophétique que Babylone joue un rôle; son nom apparaît 9 × en Es 1—39 (Es 13 et 14, chaque fois 2 ×; Es 21: 1 ×; Es 39: 4 ×), 4 × en Es 40—55 et jamais par la suite; dans Jérémie il est fait mention de Babel 170 ×, à partir de Jer 20 et en particulier en Jer 27—29, sans oublier Jer 50 (18 ×) et 51 (34 ×); avec Ezéchiel Babylone est citée 20 ×, à partir d'Ez 17, cf. encore Mi 4 10 Zach 2 11 6 10. La plupart des textes se réfèrent aux épisodes qui ont précédé et suivi la chute de Jérusalem, ils en montrent les conséquences proches ou lointaines. Ainsi, selon le message prophétique, Babel apparaît à peu près au moment où les jours de la cité de David sont comptés; les deux villes sont curieusement liées, de telle sorte que les malheurs de l'une préparent ou annoncent le bonheur de l'autre. Babel est une d'Anti-Sion, comme l'expliquera l'apocalyptique juive et chrétienne.

[4] Les commentateurs de l'Apoc Jn se bornent en général à relever les divers traits qui caractérisent la Grande Babylone et à remarquer que nombreux sont ceux qui proviennent de l'AT. Comme le déclare G. Kuhn, les passages consacrés à Babylone (cf. surtout

Traduction[5]

v. 1 Descends, laisse-toi choir sur la poussière,
vierge, fille de Babel,
laisse-toi choir à terre, privée de trône[a],
fille des Chaldéens,
car tu n'arriveras plus à te faire appeler:
»Tendre et délicate«[b].

v. 2 Prends la meule et mouds la farine,
dénoue ton voile[c],
retrousse ta traîne, dévoile ton genou,
traverse les cours d'eau[d].

---

[a] *laisse-toi choir* plutôt qu'un simple *assieds-toi*; P. E. Bonnard propose *affale-toi* — *privée de trône* manque dans la LXX.

[b] *délicate*, habituée au bien-être, au plaisir, au luxe: Babel ne sera plus vantée pour sa culture raffinée.

[c] *voile*; P. E. Bonnard préfère parler de *tresses*.

[d] *traîne*, avec le texte massorétique, שֹׁבֶל, qui est un hapax; 1 Q Isa a שוליך *tes pans* (Es 6 1) (cf. F. Nötscher, VT 1, 1951, 300, et déjà J. T. Milik, Bibl 31, 1950, 216) — *cours d'eau*, litt. *fleuves*, qui arrosent la région babylonienne.

Apoc Jn 17s.) sont faits d'une mosaïque de textes et de notions bibliques (ThWNT, I 1933, 512–514 [513]) qui ne se réfèrent pas tous aux déclarations prophétiques sur Babylone.

[5] Commentaires et travaux consultés:
K. Marti, KHC, 1900; B. Duhm, HK, 1914³; E. König, Das Buch Jesaja, 1926; P. Volz, KAT, 1932; H. Frey, BAT, 1937; J. Fischer, HS, 1939; L. Dennefeld, SBPC, 1947; C. R. North, TBC, 1952; J. Muilenburg, IB, 1956; C. R. North, The Second Isaiah, 1964; G. Fohrer, ZBK, 1964; G. A. F. Knight, Deutero-Isaiah. A Theological Commentary, 1956; J. D. Smart, History and Theology in Second Isaiah, 1965; C. Westermann, ATD, 1966; C. Stuhlmueller, JBC, 1968; J. L. MacKenzie, AncB, 1968; P. E. Bonnard, Le Second Isaïe. Son disciple et leurs éditeurs. Isaïe 40–66, 1972; R. N. Whybray, NCeB, 1975; L. Köhler, Deuterojesaja (Jesaja 40–55) stilkritisch untersucht, 1923; G. Kuhn, Βαβυλών, ThWNT, I 1933, 512–514; G. R. Driver, JThS 36 (1935), 400s.; J. T. Milik, Bibl. 31 (1950), 216; F. Nötscher, VT 1 (1951), 300; P. A. H. de Boer, Second-Isaiah's Message, OTS 11 (1956); J. Blau, VT 7 (1957), 183s.; E. Ullendorf, JSS 7 (1962), 339–531; M. Dahood, Bibl 47 (1966), 414; D. N. Freedman, Bibl. 51 (1970), 538; H. Ringgren, בָּבֶל, ThWAT, I 1971, 503–507; Ch. Cohen, The »Widowed« City, The Gaster Festschrift JANES 5 (1973), 75–81; R. F. Melugin, The Formation of Isaiah 40–55, 1976; P. Höffken, Untersuchungen zu den Begründungselementen der Völkerorakel des Alten Testaments, Diss. Bonn 1977; J. Vermeylen, Du prophète Isaïe à l'Apocalyptique. Isaïe, I–XXXV, miroir d'un demi-millénaire d'expérience religieuse en Israël, I 1977; II 1978 (on trouvera dans l'ouvrage de J. Vermeylen une abondante bibliographie consacrée aux études sur le livre d'Esaïe).

v. 3   Que ta nudité soit dévoilée,
    qu'apparaisse aussi ton sexe^e!
    Je tirerai vengeance,
    et nul homme ne s'interposera^f.
v. 4   Notre défenseur, YHWH Sebaot est son nom,
    le Saint d'Israël^g.

v. 5   Laisse-toi choir en silence et entre dans la ténèbre,
    fille des Chaldéens,
    car tu n'arriveras plus à te faire appeler:
    »Maîtresse des royaumes«.
v. 6   Je me suis irrité contre mon peuple,
    j'ai profané mon héritage,
    je les ai livrés en ta main;
    tu n'as pas manifesté pour eux de compassion,
    sur le vieillard tu as appesanti
    ton joug lourdement.
v. 7   Tu as dit: »A jamais je serai,
    maîtresse à toujours!«^h
    Tu n'as pas pris ces choses au sérieux,
    tu n'as pas réfléchi à leur suiteⁱ.

v. 8   Mais maintenant, écoute ceci, jouisseuse,
    trônant avec assurance,
    qui dis dans ton coeur:
    »Moi et nul autre!«^j

---

[e] *sexe*, litt. *opprobre*: Babel subira le sort d'une femme indigne, exposée publiquement à la honte, comme Israël (Os 2 5.11s.), Jérusalem (Jer 13 22.26 Ez 16 37), Ninive (Nah 3 5) . . .

[f] Lire יִפְגַּע avec Sym et Vulg; le texte massorétique a אֶפְגַּע, d'où *»je ne rencontrerai pas d'homme«* (pour me faire obstacle) ou *je n'aurai pas recours à un homme* (pour me venger); on lit parfois aussi le ni. ou le hi.: l'idée générale est que YHWH se vengera sans l'aide ou la résistance de quiconque. La LXX a compris ces mots dans un sens positif et a lu אָמַר au lieu de אדם, d'où *Je ne te livrerai plus aux hommes, dit ton Rédempteur*.

[g] S'il n'est pas relié au v. précédent, comme le fait la LXX, le v. 4 paraît être une glose liturgique.

[h] Il faut déplacer l'*athnah*; 1 Q Isa a עוֹד, au lieu de עַד, que la LXX supprime. D. N. Freedman propose de lire: *Je serai à toujours et à jamais maîtresse* (Bibl 51, 1971, 538): Babel se croit capable de garder sans fin sa maîtrise sur les nations.

[i] *à leur suite*; quelques manuscrits hébreux et la Vulgate ont compris: *à ta suite*, c'est-à-dire *à ta fin*. — *réfléchis*, litt. *fais mémoire*, d'où *pris à coeur*.

[j] *jouisseuse*, voluptueuse, sybarite, mais pas encore prostituée, comme en Apoc Jn 17; F. Nötscher, VT 1 (1951), 300, suit 1 Q Isa et lit *encore* au lieu de *jouisseuse*. — *trônant avec assurance* (P. E. Bonnard) plutôt que *qui est assise tranquillement* — le yod de אפסי

> je ne resterai pas veuve,
>> et je ne connaîtrai pas la privation d'enfants!«
v. 9 Elles t'atteindront, ces deux,
>> en un instant, le même jour:
> Privation d'enfants et veuvage,
>> dans leur totalité, elles t'atteindront[k],
> malgré la multitude de tes sortilèges,
>> malgré la surabondance de tes talismans.

v. 10 Tu t'es confiée dans ta malignité,
>> tu as dit: »Nul ne me voit«.
> Ta sagesse et ta science,
>> elles t'ont circonvenue[l];
> Tu t'es dit:
>> »Moi et nul autre!«
v. 11 Sur toi surviendra un malheur,
>> tu ne sauras le conjurer;
> sur toi fondera un désastre,
>> tu ne pourras le neutraliser;
> sur toi surviendra subitement une dévastation,
>> dont tu n'as pas idée[m].

v. 12 Tiens-toi donc, avec tes talismans,
>> et avec la multitude de tes sortilèges,
> avec lesquels tu as peiné dès ta jeunesse[n];
> peut-être pourras-tu être de quelque utilité,
>> peut-être inspireras-tu quelque effroi!
v. 13 Tu es lasse de la multitude de tes conseils[o],

---

paraît être plutôt le vestige d'une ancienne déclinaison que le suffixe de la première personne du singulier – *connaîtrait*, 1 Q Isa a lu *verrai*, confusion entre ד et ר.

[k] *totalité*, d'une racine תמם, être complet, achevé; on propose parfois כתאמים, *comme une paire*, de pair, d'un verbe תאם, mettre au monde des jumeaux. La LXX a lu פתאם, *soudainement*. – *elles t'atteindront*, litt. *elles viendront sur, contre toi*, le futur avec les versions.

[l] au lieu de *malignité*, malice, 1 Q Isa a בדעתך, *dans ta science* (ד à la place de ר) – Vocaliser רֹאַנִי – *circonvenue*, trompée, égarée, séduite.

[m] *surviendra sur toi*, litt. *viendra sur, contre toi*; lire וּבָאָה – *conjurer*, d'après l'arabe, lire שַׁחְרָה, mais cf. G. R. Driver, JThS 36 (1935), 400 s. – *neutraliser*, en annuler les effets, de la racine כפר – *dont tu n'as pas idée*, litt. *que tu ne connaîtras pas*, que tu ne soupçonneras pas.

[n] 12b, qui se retrouve en 15a, et ne forme qu'un demi-stique, pourrait être dû à une erreur de copiste – *dès ta jeunesse*, depuis longtemps, depuis toujours.

[o] *tes conseils*, avec la LXX (lire עצתיך), 1 Q Isa a le singulier. On corrige parfois en יוֹעֲצַיִךְ *tes conseillers*: Babel ne manque ni de conseils, ni de conseillers, mais ils seront parfaitement inutiles!

qu'ils se présentent donc,
et qu'ils te sauvent, les diviseurs du ciel^p,
les examinateurs des étoiles,
les annonciateurs, aux nouvelles lunes,
de ce qu'il t'adviendra^q!

v. 14   Voici qu'ils seront comme de la paille,
un feu les brûlera;
ils ne pourront se sauver
du pouvoir de la flamme^r.
Ce ne sera pas de la braise pour les réchauffer^s,
ni un feu pour s'asseoir devant!

v. 15   Ainsi seront-ils pour toi ceux avec lesquels tu as peiné
dès ta jeunesse, tes trafiquants^t,
chacun errera de son côté,
aucun ne te sauvera!

L'aspect formel

Plus on examine Esaïe 47, plus se vérifie le bien-fondé de la remarque de G. Fohrer sur l'habileté avec laquelle le Second Esaïe a composé cet oracle sur Babylone; il y fait preuve d'une étonnante maîtrise artistique[6].

---

^p *diviseurs*, d'un hapax qu'on lit הָבְרֵי et qu'on rapproche de l'arabe; le verbe הבר signifierait couper, partager, compartimenter: les *diviseurs* fragmentent le ciel pour mieux en lire les signes. 1 Q Isa a חוברי de חבר lier, attacher, d'où ceux qui *lient* (par leurs enchantements). J. Blau, VT 7 (1957), 183s., à partir de l'ugaritique, comprend ceux qui s'inclinent, les *adorateurs* du ciel, qui désignerait de façon ironique les astrologues (cf. aussi E. Ullendorff, JSS 7, 1962, 339–351).

^q Lire אשר, sans le מ dû à une dittographie (cf. les versions) et le singulier יבוא comme les versions.

^r *se sauver*, litt. sauver leur vie; P. E. Bonnard: soustraire leur personne à la main de la flamme.

^s *réchauffer*, lire לְחֹם ou לְחָמָם.

^t Lire בַּאֲשֶׁר avec deux manuscrits hébreux et les versions (cf. aussi v. 12), d'où *avec lesquels* – סֹחֲרַיִךְ est mal placé, il faut le lire après לָךְ ou, comme ici, en apposition de »ceux avec lesquels« Babel a peiné depuis toujours. Ce sont soit *les trafiquants*, de סחר, voyager, trafiquer (P. E. Bonnard: ceux qui t'exploitent), soit, comme le veut G. R. Driver, JThS 36 (1935), 400 s. *ceux qui t'ensorcellent*, en s'appuyant sur d'autres langues sémitiques (akk. et arabe). Dans le premier cas, l'activité commerciale de Babel serait évoquée ici, dans le second, une fois encore, les pratiques de sorcellerie seraient associées à la cité mésopotamienne; de toutes façons ce qui a depuis toujours fait la force de Babylone vient à lui manquer au moment où elle en aurait besoin!

---

[6] Cf. note 1.

Le prophète sait utiliser à bon escient l'interpellation (ainsi les impératifs vigoureux des v. 1.2.5.8.12) et la répétition (la terminologie du v. 1 se retrouve au v. 5; l'arrogante déclaration de Babylone: »Moi et nul autre« se lit aux v. 8 et 10). Il affectionne les assonances contrastées (v. 1a: sons i et a; v. 3: sons é et a; v. 6a: sons a et i; etc.) et les allitérations (v. 3a. 6a. 10b. etc.)[7].

Le Second Esaïe emploie le rythme de la *qinah*, mais il n'en est pas l'esclave, il varie ses effets et adapte ses procédés à son propos[8]; ainsi au v. 2 il imite le bruit heurté et saccadé que fait l'esclave astreinte à moudre la farine[9]; au v. 11 il choisit avec soin les termes qui évoquent le malheur dont Babylone va être frappée et contre laquelle elle ne pourra rien, il met en évidence le fait que la cité païenne est particulièrement visée (cf. le triple »contre toi« qui retentit de façon cinglante), il observe un rythme régulier que vient rompre volontairement l'intrusion d'un mot (פתאם) à la dernière ligne; enfin la strophe s'achève par un verbe qui renvoie au substantif de la même racine (ידע) qui se lit à son début pour souligner l'ironie de la situation dans laquelle Babel est plongée: la Sage, ou qui se croyait telle, ne sait rien (du désastre qui fond sur elle), elle sera prise par surprise!

Le prophète aime également les contrastes, il dépeint la grande Dame dont la délicatesse est reconnue par tous et la voit obligée de se dépouiller de ses parures et de ses vêtements (v. 1ss.); il dit en termes variés l'orgueil de Babylone et sa chute brutale (v. 10ss.); il montre la cohorte de ceux qui l'assistent et leur inutilité, un feu est allumé non pour les réchauffer (v. 14c), mais pour les dévorer (v. 14b)! La confusion règne à Babel, et le poème s'achève par une formule coupante et sans appel: אֵין מוֹשִׁיעֵךְ.

La division d'Esaïe 47 en strophes n'offre pas de difficultés majeures, bien que les exégètes ne s'accordent pas sur certains points de détail. L. Köhler, par exemple, estime que ce chapitre est composé de cinq strophes, de sept lignes chacune (soit les v. 1–4. 5–7. 8–10a. 10b–12. 13–15), alors que G. Fohrer en compte six, formées de six lignes chacune (soit les v. 1–4. 5–7. 8–9. 10–11. 12–13. 14–15)[10]. Nous estimons aussi que ce

---

[7] Nous faisons ces remarques et les suivantes à tire d'exemples; cf. aussi les annotations stylistiques de R. Lack, La Symbolique du Livre d'Isaïe, Analecta Biblica 59, Rome (1973) 103–106.

[8] L. Köhler retrouve un rythme parfaitement régulier (3 + 2 accents) tout au long d'Es 47, mais cela l'oblige à une série de rectifications (adjonction ici, suppression là) qui semblent inutiles (cf. encore C. Westermann 151 s.).

[9] La présentation typographique du v. 2 par P. E. Bonnard met bien en évidence son caractère rythmique particulier (P. E. Bonnard 188).

[10] Dans B. Duhm 326ss. se retrouve la même répartition des versets que chez L. Köhler; C. Westermann 151ss., qui suit cet auteur, supprime cependant un stique dans la dernière strophe (v. 13a); par contre R. N. Whybray 118ss. et R. F. Melugin 135s. adoptent une

poème du Second Esaïe est fait de six strophes, mais leur longueur va en decrescendo: les deux premières (v. 1–3(4) et 5–7) ont chaque fois sept lignes, les deux suivantes (v. 8–9 et 10–11) n'en ont que six et les deux dernières (v. 12–13 et 14–15) seulement cinq[11]. Les articulations du texte sont assez aisément repérables: les strophes 2 et 5 commencent par un impératif, les strophes 3 et 6 par des formules caractéristiques comme ועתה (v. 8) et הנה (v. 14); la coupure est moins évidente entre les versets 9 et 10 qui appartiennent à des strophes qui, au coeur de l'ensemble, se renforcent l'une l'autre.

La forme, ici aussi, correspond au fond, puisque la division que nous proposons observe la progression de la pensée. Le Second Esaïe annonce à Babylone, dans le début de son oeuvre, le profond bouleversement qui va la frapper, et les versets 5–7 reprennent et développent le message des versets 1ss. En second lieu, le prophète établit la culpabilité de Babel et précise l'étendue du mal qu'elle doit connaître; les strophes 3 et 4 soulignent ainsi de manière convergente les fautes de la cité païenne et son juste châtiment. Enfin le Deutéro-Esaïe s'en prend, dans les versets 12–15, aux forces sur lesquelles Babylone compte et qui ne pourront en rien la secourir.

L'auteur

L'authenticité de cette page n'est pas contestée; son auteur est donc le Second Esaïe et sa déclaration a été écrite avant 539, car la prise de Babylone par Cyrus n'a pas correspondu aux prévisions du prophète. Loin d'être humiliée et détruite, la cité mésopotamienne a été bien traitée par le conquérant perse et il faudra attendre le règne de Xerxès, au Vème siècle, pour qu'elle connaisse un sort plus rigoureux[12].

Ce texte peut donc être daté avec quelque précision à l'inverse des autres passages prophétiques relatifs à Babylone que les exégètes situent, non sans quelque hésitation, entre les VIIIème et Vème/IVème siècles! Esaïe 47 fournit un point de repère fixe dans l'histoire de la tradition biblique sur Babel.

---

    disposition proche de celle de G. Fohrer, qui d'ailleurs écarte du poème original les versets 3a.4 sauf גאלנו, 7a. 14c.

[11] Nous considérons le v. 4 dans son contexte actuel comme une glose, bien que l'expression קדוש ישראל ne soit pas étrangère au Second Esaïe (Es 41 14. 16. 20 43 3. 14s. 45 11 etc.) (cf. aussi G. Fohrer 104; R. N. Whybray 120, etc. et à l'inverse C. Westermann 151ss.; P. E. Bonnard 188s.; ce dernier met les v. 3b–4 dans la bouche d'Israël 193)! Le v. 12b serait également un doublet du v. 15a, mais il est déjà attesté en 1 Q Isa; L. Köhler 33 le supprime, mais non G. Fohrer 105.

[12] Xerxès Ier a mis à sac Babylone entre 485 et 476 et l'ancienne capitale de Nébucadnetsar ne s'en est jamais relevée (cf. J. Vermeylen II 290).

Il faut cependant attirer l'attention sur l'originalité d'Esaïe 47 par rapport au reste du message du Second Esaïe. En premier lieu ce long poème est tout entier consacré à une puissance étrangère, cas unique dans les chapitres 40—55 d'Esaïe, ce qui l'apparente à une catégorie spéciale des déclarations des prophètes, les oracles contre les nations. Secondement le Second Esaïe utilise dans cette page un vocabulaire inédit puisqu'on a compté jusqu'à près de quarante termes qui ne se retrouvent pas ailleurs dans son oeuvre[13].

Mais ces constatations ne peuvent faire douter de l'origine de ce chapitre qui s'intègre parfaitement à l'ensemble des propos du Second Esaïe. Les contacts, au niveau du vocabulaire et des expressions, avec les oracles qui précèdent ou qui suivent, sont nets: יסף (Es 47 1. 5) se retrouve en 51 22 52 1, חשך (Es 47 5) en 42 7 49 9, יגע (Es 47 12. 15) en 40 30s. 43 22ss. 49 4, שמע (Es 47 8) en 46 3. 12 48 1. 12. 14. 16, etc. Le couple »Babel et Chaldéens« (Es 47 1) est encore attesté en Es 48 4. 20 (cf. aussi 13 19); la formule »Moi et nul autre« (Es 47 8. 10) reprend en les modifiant des expressions proches, appliquées à Yahvé (Es 45 6 46 9)[14].

Il est encore question de Babylone dans le message du Second Esaïe, en Es 43 14 48 14. 20, et indirectement en Es 44 24ss. 52 11 etc., la chute de la ville païenne étant la condition de la restauration de Jérusalem. Es 47 1ss. reprend et prolonge ce qui est annoncé en 46 1s.: à l'humiliation des divinités babyloniennes doit correspondre la déchéance de la cité de Nabonide, et Es 48 20 en tire les conséquences pour les exilés de Juda: qu'ils se hâtent de quitter Babylone avant que le jugement divin ne la frappe (cf. encore Es 52 11 Jer 51 6). Es 47 6 esquisse une interprétation théologique des événements qui ont marqué la fin de Jérusalem et d'autres déclarations du prophète (Es 42 24—43 8 43 25—44 5 54 7ss.) développeront cette théologie de l'histoire: pour le prophète de l'exil, le péché de son peuple a provoqué la colère de Yahvé qui l'a livré aux mains des Babyloniens, mais la puissance païenne sera à son tour condamnée pour avoir outrepassé ses prérogatives (cf. déjà Es 10 5ss.), tandis que Dieu prépare à Israël un nouvel avenir. Bref sans ce chapitre 47 il manquerait quelque chose au message du Second Esaïe; la disparition de Babel est la condition de la réalisation du plan de Yahvé en faveur de Jérusalem.

Le contenu

Avant d'aborder l'exégèse plus détaillée d'Esaïe 47 il s'avère nécessaire de préciser le genre littéraire utilisé ici par le prophète. On a parlé

---

[13] D'après C. R. North, The Suffering Servant in Deutero-Isaiah, 1948, 169.
[14] Cf. par ex. P. E. Bonnard 191ss. et R. F. Melugin 135ss., celui-ci souligne le rôle que joue Es 47 entre les chapitres 46 et 48.

d'un chant de triomphe (B. Duhm, K. Marti) et plus généralement d'un chant satirique (ein Spottlied: J. Begrich, J. Fischer, J. Muilenburg, G. Fohrer[15], etc.), mais si la jubilation et surtout l'ironie ne sont pas absentes de cette page, elles n'en sont sans doute pas les éléments dominants, comme l'ont fait remarquer des commentateurs récents (ainsi C. Westermann, P. Höffken, R. F. Melugin[16], etc.). Il convient de noter d'abord que le Second Esaïe, conformément à son génie poétique, sait faire appel à divers registres pour exprimer sa pensée; il ne se contente pas d'entonner à l'occasion de chute de Babel un chant funèbre qui cache mal sa satisfaction, comme le fait l'auteur d'Esaïe 14; il mêle le reproche à l'avertissement, le jugement au sarcasme, la menace à la contestation. Une analyse des formes littéraires attestées dans les diverses strophes qui forment son poème permet de mieux découvrir l'intention principale du Second Esaïe.

La première strophe (v. 1–3) s'ouvre par une interpellation qui tourne très vite à la menace, elle annonce une catastrophe qui apparaît comme une vengeance de Yahvé; la capitale babylonienne va être jugée. La strophe suivante (v. 5–7) commence comme la précédente, mais en vient rapidement à un acte d'accusation (v. 6s.) citant même, comme dans un procès, les paroles de l'adversaire (v. 7, cf. aussi plus loin v. 8. 10). Les troisième et quatrième strophes (v. 8s. et 10s.) mêlent la dénonciation des fautes de Babylone et la proclamation des sanctions prises contre elle. L'arrière-plan de cette partie décisive d'Esaïe 47 est juridique: les torts de la cité païenne sont d'abord mis en évidence (v. 8. 10), puis le verdict est prononcé (v. 9. 11). Le prophète durcit le ton, il invective la coupable, il la ridiculise (v. 11c). Dans la cinquième strophe, sa diatribe se fait caustique et méprisante, le Second Esaïe évoque la foule des devins, des magiciens, des astrologues dont Babylone aime à s'entourer et la somme avec ironie de faire appel à eux si elle veut se tirer du mauvais pas qui l'attend (v. 12 avec son double »peut-être«); enfin la dernière strophe revient sur le caractère irrémédiable de la catastrophe qui attend Babylone: tous ceux en qui elle a mis son espoir disparaissent dans les flammes (v. 14s.).

---

[15] C. R. North, 1952, 98s. parle également du ton ironique utilisé par le prophète; C. Stuhlmueller 374 souligne la virtuosité du Second Esaïe dans ce chant funèbre plein de sarcasmes qui règle le sort de Babylone; R. N. Whybray 118 insiste aussi sur le fait que l'auteur anticipe sur la disparition de la nation païenne et se moque en réalité d'elle.

[16] Pour C. Westermann 151s., Es 47 constitue un véritable oracle contre les nations (ein Völkerspruch): le Second Esaïe intervient ici comme prophète du salut et proclame un événement à venir; c'est ainsi qu'il faut interpréter ses paroles. P. Höffken 306ss. 532 met l'accent sur la menace (Drohwort) qu'il lit dans ce chapitre, le reproche (Scheltwort) et la moquerie n'en constituant que des aspects complémentaires; dernièrement R. F. Melugin, tout en soulignant le caractère ironique du poème surtout à son début et à sa fin, reconnaît qu'on y trouve aussi le style de l'oracle prophétique. On le voit, il est difficile de définir Esaïe 47 en ne recourant qu'à un seul genre littéraire.

Ce qui domine dans le poème du Second Esaïe, ce n'est ni le triomphalisme, ni la raillerie[17]. Le prophète n'est pas animé par un esprit de revanche comme Nahum qui se déchaîne contre Ninive, il ne se contente pas de régler un compte avec la ville de Nébucadnetsar; sans doute ses propos se font-ils sarcastiques à la fin de sa déclaration, mais il ne cherche pas d'abord à tourner Babylone en dérision. L'auteur d'Esaïe 47 se veut le témoin de Yahvé qui, seul, a le droit de dire son fait à la cité arrogante, il fait le procès, au nom de son Dieu, de son attitude passée et présente: menaces et jugements, dénonciations et invectives ont pour but de signifier à la grande puissance mésopotamienne qui s'enorgueillit de son pouvoir politique, économique et religieux qu'elle n'est rien devant le Dieu d'Israël. Esaïe 47 est une illustration d'un thème théologique cher au Second Esaïe: Yahvé et uniquement Yahvé conduit l'histoire, il dispose souverainement des nations et ne supporte aucun rival à des côtés. En même temps ce chapitre apparaît comme une confirmation de l'intervention du prophète qui ne cesse d'annoncer le salut à ses frères: Babylone ne sera pas un obstacle réel à leur retour en Terre Sainte.

1ère strophe (v. 1–3(4)): de la grandeur au déshonneur

Babylone est personnifiée ici sous les traits d'une jeune femme, comme d'autres villes mentionnées dans l'Ancien Testament: Sion (Es 1 8 37 22); Sidon (Es 23 12); (cf. encore l'Egypte en Jer 46 11, et les larges développements consacrés à Jérusalem en Ez 16 (et, avec Samarie, 23), etc.); sa virginité atteste son indépendance, son intégrité; aucun envahisseur ne l'a conquise à l'heure où le prophète prend la parole. Elle appartient aux Chaldéens, un peuple venu du sud qui s'est installé à Babylone vers l'an 1000 avant l'ère chrétienne, chez lequel l'étude des astres prendra un tel relief que le terme de *Chaldéens* finira par désigner une caste particulière, celle des astrologues (ainsi en Dan 2 2. 4. 10 etc.). Avant d'évoquer la puissance de Babel (v. 5. 7s.), le Second Esaïe décrit sa noblesse reconnue par tous ses sujets, son statut aristocratique, le raffinement de sa culture (v. 1c, cf. Dtn 28 54. 56). Située tout en haut de l'échelle sociale, la grande Dame du harem, comme la qualifie H. Frey, tombera au rang le plus bas[18], elle sera réduite à devenir la dernière des esclaves, dont le sort se confond presque avec celui du bétail (Ex 11 5), son travail sera dur et humiliant, puisqu'il lui faudra tourner la double meule[19], le

---

[17] Es 47 ne relève pas davantage du genre littéraire qu'affectionne pourtant le prophète, la controverse. Celle-ci cherche généralement à convaincre l'interlocuteur, à l'amener à partager le point de vue de Yahvé; ici il n'est question que d'annoncer le jugement de Babylone et de le motiver.

[18] C. Westermann 154 cite un parallèle intéressant d'Ugarit, selon lequel la divinité descend de son trône pour s'asseoir par terre.

[19] Sur la double meule, c'est-à-dire une meule faite de deux pierres, cf. K. Galling, HAT, 1937, 386s.

voile dénoué, la traîne[20] retroussée, la cuisse découverte, et sa féminité à la merci de ses maîtres (v. 2s.). Un labeur inhumain, d'incessants affronts, une situation dégradante, voilà ce que la vengeance de Yahvé réserve à la capitale de Nébucadnetsar (v. 3b), alors qu'au même moment le Second Esaïe invite Jérusalem à se relever, à secouer son joug et à revêtir des habits magnifiques (Es 52 1s.)!

2ème strophe (v. 5–7): les motifs de la chute de la maîtresse des royaumes

Le prophète continue sur le même ton et invite celle qui se fait appeler la souveraine des états[21], c'est-à-dire qui prétend étendre son hégémonie sur l'ensemble de ses voisins (v. 5), et ceci d'une façon incontestée et définitive (v. 7), à entrer dans le silence et la ténèbre[22], en clair à connaître la misère et le deuil (cf. Jer 13 18).

Le Second Esaïe justifie alors la violence de ses propos contre la ville mésopotamienne, il dit d'abord les raisons du malheur du peuple de Yahvé: les événements qui ont amené la prise de Jérusalem en 587 ne sont pas dus à la faiblesse du Dieu d'Israël, ils réalisent au contraire sa volonté (v. 5: s'irriter, profaner, livrer, 3 verbes qui ont Yahvé comme sujet), Yahvé a voulu la fin de l'état judéen, il a laissé profaner son élu[23] (cf. Es 43 28 54 7ss.).

Le prophète dénonce ensuite les crimes de Babylone qui motivent la décision du Dieu d'Israel de réduire à rien la puissance babylonienne; ils sont au nombre de trois: l'inhumanité dont Babel a fait preuve à l'heure de la victoire, comme son comportement envers les anciens en témoigne (v. 6c Thr 4 16 Dtn 28 5); l'arrogance de la cité de Nébucadnetsar qui ose s'attribuer un pouvoir qui n'appartient qu'à Yahvé en répétant ses paroles: לעולם אהיה (v. 7a) copie le אהיה אשר אהיה d'Ex 3 14; l'aveuglement et la légèreté qui la caractérisent (v. 7b). Babylone s'est montrée impitoyable envers les vaincus, ses succès l'ont égarée; elle s'est crue à jamais maîtresse de son destin; son mépris de l'homme s'est joint à son mépris de Dieu et en s'autodéifiant elle n'a pas songé que Yahvé relèverait son défi[24]!

---

[20] Sur ce mot, cf. aussi G. R. Driver, Difficult Words in the Hebrew Prophets, Studies in OT Prophecy, 1950, 58; selon P. A. H. de Boer, il s'agit de relever sa robe pour faire le travail pénible de l'esclave.
[21] K. Marti 318 traduit *la reine-mère*, cf. Es 24 2 I Rois 15 13 2 19.
[22] P. A. H. de Boer 51 estime qu'il faut comprendre que Babel sera *pétrifiée par la peur*.
[23] J. Muilenburg insiste sur le *mon* peuple, *mon* héritage utilisé ici, qui souligne le fait que Yahvé est et reste lié à Israël, bien qu'il l'ait châtié, ce que Babylone a méconnu. Sur l'irritation de Yahvé contre son peuple, cf. encore Es 54 9 57 16s. 60 10 64 4. 8 Zach 1 15 etc.
[24] La plupart des commentateurs relèvent ici et à propos des vv. 8 et 10 la démesure de Babel, son ὕβρις.

3ème strophe (v. 8–9): La démesure de Babylone et ses conséquences

Le Second Esaïe continue à interpeller la ville païenne tout en utilisant une formule (ועתה) qui introduit l'annonce de sa condamnation (v. 8a). Il rappelle que Babylone aime le plaisir et la volupté et dépeint son attitude insouciante, il cite ses propos monstrueux qui, une fois encore, témoignent de son délire, puisque, comme Dieu, elle proclame: »Moi et nul autre!« (v. 8b, cf. encore v. 10c (Soph 2 15; Es 13 14s.), qui répondent à Es 45 6 46 9)[25]. La capitale de l'empire babylonien se croit aussi à l'abri des malheurs qui ont frappé ses victimes; elle pense ignorer les effets douloureux des guerres acharnées qu'elle livre à ses ennemis et qui laissent les femmes sans mari, ni enfants (v. 8c)[26]. En réalité elle sera veuve à son tour et elle pleurera ses fils, comme aujourd'hui Jérusalem (Es 54 1–6); une catastrophe, sans doute d'ordre militaire, l'atteindra malgré toutes les forces religieuses et magiques qui travaillent pour elle, et sa fin sera aussi complète que soudaine[27] (v. 9)!

4ème strophe (v. 10–11): du danger de se croire infaillible

Le prophète continue à énumérer les erreurs de Babylone et à lui prédire les pires châtiments. Babel a cru à sa malice comme à son impunité (v. 10a); sa science et son savoir[28] lui ont tourné la tête (v. 10b), elle s'est imaginée n'avoir de compte à rendre à personne (v. 10c), aussi le malheur fondra-t-il sur elle sans qu'elle puisse parer ses coups, et avec une soudaineté[29] telle qu'elle sera prise à l'improviste (v. 11): toute la sagesse accumulée à Babylone ne lui aura même pas servi à prévoir son heure!

---

[25] Babylone n'est pas la seule puissance païenne à être victime de son désir de puissance et à sombrer dans la mégalomanie; par exemple l'Assyrie s'est enivrée de ses conquêtes (Es 10 5ss.), Tyr a cru à sa puissance économique (Ez 26 s.), le tyran d' Es 14 a voulu égaler Dieu; l'apocalyptique juive verra dans ces faits les signes avant-coureurs de l'ultime confrontation entre le Dieu de ses Pères et les forces démoniaques.

[26] Ce qu'une femme redoute le plus, être privée de son mari, qui la protège, et de ses fils, qui sont sa raison d'être. C. Cohen dans JANES 5, 1973, 75–81, a remarqué qu'il existe plusieurs sortes de veuves, le terme אלמנה désigne une femme dont le mari est mort et qui se trouve sans ressource, ni appui – une veuve-orpheline –, elle a besoin d'une protection spéciale, comme la loi assyrienne et l'AT en témoignent. La cité-veuve 7 8 s. désignerait une ville autrefois indépendante qui devient la vassale d'un autre état (cf. aussi Es 54 4 Thr 1 1).

[27] *complète,* selon le texte massorétique, *soudaine* d'après la LXX!

[28] La LXX a traduit דעת par πορνεία, la cité-prostituée se retrouve dans Apoc Jn 17 notamment.

[29] marquée par l'introduction de פתאם a la dernière ligne du v. 11 cf. p. 88.

5ème strophe (v. 12–13): *l'appel, sarcastique, aux forces spirituelles*

Le prophète développe ici un thème déjà amorcé au v. 9; il invite la cité mésopotamienne à se tourner vers les réalités religieuses qui sont à sa disposition — et précisément elle n'en manque pas! — pour essayer d'échapper au sort qui l'attend. Mais il doute fort, lui qui a fait ailleurs le procès des divinités païennes et démontré leur impuissance (Es 41 21ss. 44 6ss. etc.) et qui sait Yahvé capable de déjouer les augures et de faire divaguer les devins (Es 44 25), que magiciens, astrologues, incantateurs, prêtres et sorciers, malgré leurs calculs, leurs amulettes, leurs talismans, leurs charmes et leurs prières, puissent venir en aide à Babylone[30]. Esaïe 47 se termine justement par l'annonce de la faillite de la puissance spirituelle rassemblée dans la capitale de Nébucadnetsar[31]; toute sa piété officielle ou populaire ne lui sera d'aucun secours.

6ème strophe (v. 14–15): *le feu consumera tous les appuis de Babel*

Le poème s'achève sur la vision d'un feu qui dévore tout, d'une confusion généralisée, et d'une cité livrée sans défense à la colère de Yahvé[32]. C'en est fait de Babylone, le premier des états mésopotamiens, de Babylone si vantée pour sa culture et sa sagesse, de Babylone célèbre pour ses richesses et pour ses cultes: les officiants ont disparu dans les flammes (v. 12), les marchands se sont évanouis (v. 15), personne n'intervient pour aider la ville, qui a imposé ses lois, ses pratiques économiques et religieuses à l'ensemble de la région, à ne pas connaître à son tour la ruine et le déshonneur. »*Chacun errera de son côté, aucun ne te sauvera!*« (v. 15b)[33].

Ainsi se termine cette page du Second Esaïe qui évoque la grandeur présente de Babylone et proclame sa déchéance imminente et radicale; elle éclaire le sens des événements à venir en mettant en évidence la culpa-

---

[30] Le salut par la magie (J. Muilenburg 550) s'avérera une voie sans issue! Dès l'Antiquité Babylone s'est rendue célèbre par ses pratiques religieuses et divinatoires; on lira dans P. E. Bonnard 196 un texte révélateur sur les calculs des astrologues qui tentent de discerner l'avenir des peuples et des individus.

[31] C. Westermann 156 remarque avec raison que le fondement religieux de l'absolutisme est dénoncé ici.

[32] C. Westermann 157 souligne le sérieux de ces dernières paroles du Second Esaïe, elles rappellent les interventions des prophètes antéexiliques; l'ironie évoquée à propos des versets 12ss. ne doit pas nous masquer le caractère tragique du sort qui attend Babylone.

[33] Avec G. Fohrer il faut insister sur le caractère irrémédiable du jugement — par le feu — que Babel connaîtra; il est vraiment difficile de trouver dans ces dernières lignes du poème une note positive qui laisserait espérer à la ville de Nébucadnetsar un avenir meilleur, comme le voudrait C. Stuhlmueller 374 (cf. aussi P. E. Bonnard 197).

bilité de la cité païenne à l'égard du Dieu d'Israël; elle confirme à sa manière le plan que Yahvé a formé en faveur de Jérusalem.

* * *

L'histoire de la tradition biblique sur Jérusalem a déjà été écrite[34], celle qui concerne Babylone reste à faire, mais devant les difficultés qui se présentent pour mener à bien une telle étude, il ne peut être question ici que d'une esquisse. Ce ne sont pourtant pas les textes relatifs à la cité mésopotamienne qui manquent, ils sont plutôt nombreux et étendus — cf. notamment Esaïe 21 1–10 13 1–22 14 3–23, et la plus grande partie des chapitres 50 et 51 de Jérémie — mais ils soulèvent des problèmes délicats qui concernent aussi bien leur datation que leur composition. Les exégètes mettent souvent en question leur authenticité sans parvenir d'ailleurs à s'entendre sur leur chronologie[35] et ils soupçonnent leurs copistes de les avoir retravaillés; ce seraient donc des oracles anonymes, parfois glosés et qui n'ont été placés que tardivement dans leur contexte actuel[36].

Dans ce cas il devient périlleux de vouloir retracer de façon trop précise l'évolution de la pensée biblique au sujet de Babylone; on peut tout au plus chercher à établir quelques étapes de l'histoire qui va de la Babylone historique à la Babylone apocalyptique ou encore, de façon plus prudente, on cherchera par une enquête, même rapide, sur les passages relatifs à Babylone à relever leurs particularités.

Esaïe 21 1–10[37]

Cette page étrange du livre d'Esaïe concerne Babylone, comme le montrent le titre de l'oracle[38] et la proclamation du verset 9:

---

[34] Par exemple, par A. Causse dans deux études consacrées à Jérusalem: Le mythe de la nouvelle Jérusalem du Deutéro-Esaïe à la IIIe Sibylle, RHPhR 18 (1938), 377–414; De la Jérusalem terrestre à la Jérusalem céleste, RHPhR 27 (1947), 12–36.

[35] S. Erlandsson, The Burden of Babylon. A Study of Isaiah 13 2–14 23, CB.OT 4 (1970), 45ss., présente un tableau fort instructif sur les diverses dates proposées par les spécialistes pour une série de textes du livre d'Esaïe, celles-ci s'étendant du VIIIe (époque d'Esaïe lui-même) au IIe siècle (époque maccabéenne)!

[36] On trouvera une série d'indications sur ces oracles anonymes, leur datation, l'histoire de leur rédaction, accompagnées d'une abondante bibliographie dans J. Vermeylen, Du prophète Isaïe à l'apocalyptique. Isaïe, I–XXXV, miroir d'un demi-millénaire d'expérience religieuse en Israël, I 1977; II 1978. On complétera ces informations par l'examen de commentaires récents, comme ceux de O. Kaiser, ATD 18, 1973; P. Auvray, Isaïe 1–39, Sources Bibliques, 1972, et surtout H. Wildberger, BK X, 1978, qui se continue; on ajoutera l'étude de P. Höffken, mentionnée à la n. 5.

[37] Cf. les indications données à la note précédente.

[38] Si l'on admet l'hypothèse de E. Dhorme, reprise par P. Auvray 199 et S. Erlandsson 82, mais contestée par H. Wildberger 763, que le texte massorétique — qui n'est pas con-

»Elle est tombée, tombée, Babel,
et toutes les images de ses dieux, il les a brisées à terre.«

L'instrument de la chute de Babylone est mentionné au début de la vision, il s'agit d'Elam et du Mède (v. 2), ses anciens alliés, actuellement sans doute aux ordres de Cyrus, qui ont pour mission de prendre d'assaut, probablement de nuit[39], la capitale mésopotamienne; il est évident que c'est Yahvé[40] qui conduit les événements.

Il est probable que ce chapitre, surtout intéressant par ce qu'il révèle de l'expérience prophétique, a été composé pendant l'exil, avant l'entrée de Cyrus à Babylone par un contemporain du Second Esaïe (H. Wildberger 770—774), et non par le prophète Esaïe lui-même (S. Erlandsson 81—92) ou seulement sous Xerxès Ier (comme le suggère J. Vermeylen 326ss.)[41]. P. Auvray 202 souligne le caractère original et pittoresque de ce texte: le guetteur attend et reçoit son message, qui se concentre dans l'annonce de la fin de Babel. Il est significatif que l'expression du v. 9 (נפל) soit tirée d'une formule funéraire (cf. 11 Sam 1 18s. Jer 9 19 Am 5 2 etc.)[42]: l'oracle annonce la mort de la grande cité et de ses dieux que Yahvé brisera.

Malgré le ton mystérieux d'Esaïe 21, malgré les images extraordinaires utilisées par le prophète anonyme — le thème des douleurs de l'enfantement est familier à l'apocalyptique juive — il ne faut pas extrapoler les données de ce chapitre et le comprendre à partir de textes apocalyptiques tardifs: l'événement décrit ici a des dimensions limitées et non cosmiques, il concerne l'histoire des relations d'Israël avec ses voisins et non la fin des temps, il relève de la tradition prophétique classique[43].

Sur l'essentiel, l'auteur d'Esaïe 21 rejoint le Second Esaïe, sa théologie est fondamentalement la même, il relie comme lui la disparition de Babel à une intervention de Yahvé, qui se sert à cet effet des armées d'Elam et de Médie; par contre il ne donne pas les motifs du jugement porté contre la cité païenne, sa pensée est moins élaborée que celle de son contemporain: sa déclaration n'apporte pas d'éléments nouveaux par rapport à ceux que nous avons relevés dans Esaïe 47.

---

firmé par la LXX, ni par 1 Q Isa — »désert de la mer« doit être compris comme l'équivalent de l'expression assyrienne *mât tâmti* (terre de la mer) qui désigne les régions proches du golfe Persique.

[39] Babylone aurait été prise par surprise, la nuit, pendant un banquet; on a l'écho d'une pareille tradition dans Hérodote (1,191), la Chronique de Nabonide, et Dan 5!

[40] Yahvé se cache derrière l'expression volontairement énigmatique שֵׁבֶר.

[41] Pour plus de détails, cf. J. Vermeylen 326ss.; cet auteur pense même que l'oracle primitif aurait été tardivement relu et complété par la communauté opprimée des Juifs fidèles, opposée à leurs adversaires, juifs également; »Babylone« aurait servi à désigner alors »les mauvais Juifs«!

[42] Cf. H. Wildberger 539 et 784.

[43] Cf. dernièrement G. Fohrer 220ss. et H. Wildberger 785, et à l'inverse O. Kaiser 105.

Esaïe 13 1–22[44]

La perspective d'Esaïe 13 est différente: dans ce long poème le nom de Babel ne se rencontre que deux fois, au v. 1, dans le titre, qui pourrait être secondaire, et au v. 19 où la cité mésopotamienne est qualifiée de »parure des nations«, ce qui met en évidence la splendeur et la grandeur de la capitale de Nébucadnetsar, sa place éminente dans le concert des nations; mais le prophète ne mentionne les titres de Babylone que pour annoncer qu'elle connaîtra l'horrible sort de Sodome et Gomorrhe[45].

La date de cette page est discutée; S. Erlandsson en défend l'ésaïcité; avec la majorité des critiques H. Wildberger la situe avant 538, peut-être entre 545 et 540; pour O. Kaiser 6 comme pour J. Vermeylen 288ss., en son état actuel, Esaïe 13 est postérieur à l'exil, peut-être du Ve siècle, mais son rédacteur a pu utiliser des matériaux préexistants[46].

Ce qui frappe dès la première lecture de ce chapitre est l'ampleur de la vision: Esaïe 13 présente une perspective cosmique et pré-apocalyptique qui manque précisément à Esaïe 47, l'événement que représente la fin de Babel intéresse la terre entière et même l'univers[47]. Une grande foule est assemblée par Yahvé, des royaumes et des nations sont convoqués, des peuples viennent de l'extrémité du monde pour ravager la région babylonienne (v. 4s.); les astres ne donnent plus leur lumière, le soleil et la lune restent obscurs, l'ordre du cosmos est bouleversé à l'heure de la punition de la terre (v. 10s.). J. Vermeylen relève à juste titre l'aspect totalisant des déclarations prophétiques (cf. par exemple le v. 7 »toutes les mains«, »tous les hommes«) et l'impact universel de l'assaut final contre Babylone[48].

Un autre élément doit être relevé, qui n'apparaît pas dans l'oracle du Second Esaïe: pour l'auteur d'Esaïe 13, le sort de Babel est fixé par le Jour de Yahvé et par la guerre sainte — les deux thèmes sont unis — que le Dieu d'Israël mènera contre la cité païenne. Le début du poème évoque Yahvé consacrant ses guerriers et les mobilisant contre l'ennemi (v. 2ss.); la suite associera plus particulièrement les Mèdes incorruptibles

---

[44] Cf. n. 36, et en particulier J. Vermeylen 286–292.
[45] Cf. en particulier H. Wildberger 521s.
[46] Détails in J. Vermeylen 287ss. qui développe les arguments suivants pour une datation postexilique d' Es 13: a) ampleur de la perspective; b) inclusion des chapitres sur Babel en tête et à la fin d' Es 13–23(27); c) contacts avec Jer 50s.; d) attaches littéraires avec le livre de Joël du V/IVe siècle. G. Fohrer I 1960, 165, par contre note des liens entre Es 13 et Sophonie.
[47] G. Fohrer ibid. relève que la notion de Jour de Yahvé a été interprétée par Es 13, comme plus tard par Es 24; 34 et Joël, dans un sens eschatologique, il annonce le jugement dernier contre la puissance mondiale ennemie de Yahvé et des siens, jugement qui rend possible le salut d'Israël.
[48] J. Vermeylen 289.

et impitoyables à la destruction de Babylone (v. 17ss.), qui deviendra une région abandonnée par l'homme et livrée à des créatures étranges et malfaisantes (v. 20ss.). C'est que le Jour de Yahvé est pour ses adversaires un jour de dévastation et de terreur; les soldats seront pris de panique (v. 6ss.), le ciel et la terre eux-mêmes seront ébranlés par la colère divine (v. 13); ce sera dans les pays un sauve-qui-peut général à l'heure du massacre des nourrissons[49] et du viol des femmes (v. 14s.). La fin »de la perle des royaumes« sera vraiment atroce, et sans appel.

Ce qui domine ici et distingue ce texte d'Esaïe 47, ce sont les scènes d'horreur qui marquent la disparition de la cité mésopotamienne, la sévérité des mesures prises par le Dieu d'Israël contre celle-ci[50], bref le caractère implacable de la lutte qu'il mène contre le peuple qui s'est emparé de Sion, la cité sainte. De cette rigueur dans l'annonce du jugement et de cette ampleur de vue, certains exégètes déduisent que Babylone ne représente pas seulement la capitale du royaume de Nébucadnetsar, mais une sorte d'incarnation du mal. J. Vermeylen écrit par exemple: »Les vv. 14–22 concentrent l'attention sur la citadelle de cet empire du mal, Babylone; cette fois, l'accent est placé sur le caractère absolu de sa ruine: il n'y aura aucun survivant et la cité, dévastée de fond en comble, sera détruite pour toujours. Dans ce contexte, Babylone n'est pas la vieille ennemie dont on a souffert et dont on espère la chute comme une juste revanche, mais l'anti-Jérusalem, le centre vital d'une sorte d'anti-création.«[51] Sans aller jusque là, on doit tout de même reconnaître que la cité païenne, victorieuse jadis de Jérusalem, apparaît, à la lumière d'Esaïe 13, comme le lieu même du mal sur la terre (v. 11) et comme une figure de la puissance mauvaise avec laquelle Yahvé ne peut accepter aucun compromis[52]. Cette déclaration prophétique, qui n'est pas sans lien avec Jer 50s., marquerait ainsi une étape vers l'interprétation apocalyptique de Babylone.

Esaïe 14 3–23[53]

Le nom de Babylone n'apparaît qu'au début (v. 4) et à la fin (v. 22) de cette page, dans des passages dont l'authenticité est sérieusement mise

---

[49] Ps 137 8s.
[50] Yahvé est le sujet de toutes les actions entreprises contre Babel: il convoque ses guerriers (v. 2s.), il fait venir son Jour (v. 6.9), il punit la terre et met fin à la morgue des tyrans (v. 11s.), il suscite contre la cité mésopotamienne les Mèdes (v. 17s.).
[51] J. Vermeylen 289.
[52] W. Eichrodt, BAT, 1967, 17, attire ici l'attention sur Zach 5 11, qui ferait écho à une déclaration comme celle d' Es 13: le prophète annnonce que la Méchanceté, représentée par une femme, est déposée dans le pays de Shinear, à Babylone, comme le précisent les versions; ainsi, remarque W. Eichrodt, le nom de Babel a pris de plus en plus une signification apocalyptique.
[53] Cf. n. 36, et en particulier J. Vermeylen 292ss.

en doute par les spécialistes[54]. Le v. 4 est un titre qui dit comment il faut entendre le chant qui suit, et le v. 22, en prose, paraît une adjonction tardive due à un copiste qui se plaît à prédire l'anéantissement total de Babel (v. 22s.). Il reste un beau poème (v. 4b–20(21)) qui célèbre ironiquement, sur le mode de la *qinah*, la chute d'un tyran dont le nom demeure caché. Ce texte impressionnant, qu'il n'est pas possible d'étudier maintenant, semble utiliser des données cananéennes, il aurait été adapté par la suite à la tradition yahviste, et mis, dans son contexte actuel, en relation avec un souverain babylonien[55]; plusieurs auteurs pensent plutôt qu'il visait à l'origine quelque grand et cruel conquérant assyrien[56].

S'il est vrai que le cadre d'Esaïe 14 4b–20(21) soit postérieur au poème primitif adressé à un prince inconnu – et cela est vraisemblable – la double mention de Babylone revêt pour nous un intérêt particulier. Ces additions (v. 3–4b et 22s.), sans doute postexiliques, concerneraient alors un personnage qui ne pourrait être réellement le souverain de la métropole mésopotamienne après la conquête de Cyrus, puisqu'il a perdu son pouvoir; Babylone serait dans ce cas un chiffre et renverrait à un autre puissance[57]. Nous assisterions alors, avec cette relecture du chant satirique sur la mort de l'oppresseur, au début de la pseudonymie dont l'importance sera si évidente dans l'apocalyptique. En ce sens Esaïe 13 4bss. apporterait un élément nouveau à notre enquête en mettant en évidence le caractère symbolique que peut prendre le nom de Babel.

Appliquée dès lors à Babylone et à son roi par les gloses qui l'encadrent, l'évocation de l'entrée dans le Sheol de celui qui prétendait s'égaler au Très-Haut (v. 4bss.) confirme les vues du Second Esaïe sur le péché de la cité de Nébucadnetsar et le jugement que celui-ci lui vaut. Elle dit en d'autres termes – empruntés à la mythologie – la démesure du souverain babylonien, son orgueil dément, et le sort humiliant ou mieux abject qui l'attend: le voilà précipité à terre (v. 12), lui qui voulait hausser son trône au-dessus des étoiles de Dieu (v. 13), son cadavre est

---

[54] Cf. par exemple J. Vermeylen 294s. Celui-ci fait d'ailleurs une curieuse hypothèse à propos de cette addition qu'il attribue à un milieu piétiste en conflit avec des Juifs émancipés: Babylone désignerait ici comme dans d'autres passages tardifs l'ensemble des Juifs infidèles, persécuteurs des observateurs scrupuleux de la Loi mosaïque. Il nous semble cependant que la cité mésopotamienne doit représenter une puissance externe à Israël et non un groupe hostile au sein du judaïsme. Pour H. Wildberger 538 Babel serait l'empire perse, mais on peut objecter que dans l'ensemble les Juifs ont eu de bonnes relations avec les autorités perses. G. Fohrer, I 1960, 175, n'identifie pas cette puissance mondiale, dont un croyant d'Israël chante la déchéance.

[55] D'après G. Fohrer, I 1960, 173ss.

[56] Détails dans J. Vermeylen 292s. O. Procksch 201 par contre identifie le tyran d' Es 14 avec Nébucadnetsar et B. Duhm 117 avec Nabonide.

[57] Cf. par exemple G. Fohrer, I 1960, 175; H. Wildberger 538.

piétiné (v. 19) et il a des vers pour toute compagnie (v. 11). Que sa destinée serve de leçon[58] à toute puissance qui serait tentée de céder á la même folie, en s'imaginant imposer sa loi non seulement aux nations, mais encore au monde céleste[59]!

---

[58] H. Wildberger 561 ss. insiste sur le caractère sapiential d' Es 14 4bss.; il retrouve dans ce poème l'enseignement de la sagesse sur l' ὕβρις de l'homme qui le conduit à la catastrophe (Prov 16 18 29 23 etc.) et voit dans le personnage évoqué dans cette page — et plus tard confondu avec un souverain babylonien — une figure plus typique qu'historique.

[59] Avant de quitter le livre d'Esaïe, il faut dire un mot des chapitres 24—27 qui constituent ce qu'on appelle communément, mais peut-être à tort, l'Apocalypse d'Esaïe, et soulèvent de nombreuses difficultés. Les spécialistes sont loin de s'entendre sur l'unité et la composition d'Esaïe 24 ss., sur l'histoire de sa rédaction, sur sa datation et sa signification. On trouvera dans les récentes études de J. Vermeylen 345—381 et de H. Wildberger 885—1026 une abondante bibliographie à ce sujet. Or dans ces pages il est question à plusieurs reprises d'une ville, probablement païenne, dont le sort paraît lié au jugement du monde: ainsi la cité désolée d'Es 24 7ss. (la cité du néant, qui s'est effondrée en 24 10), la ville réduite en tas de pierres d'Es 25 2 (sur ce verset, cf. dernièrement J. A. Emerton, ZAW 89, 1977, 64—73), ou encore la ville fortifiée, mais délaissée d'Es 27 10, dont l'avenir contraste avec celui de Sion (Es 24 23 25 6ss. 27 13).

On s'interroge pour savoir de quelle cité le ou les auteur(s) de cette Apocalypse parle(nt); les hypothèses les plus variées ont été soutenues et les noms de Ninive, Carthage, Samarie, Tyr ont été prononcés en même temps que celui d'une ville de Moab, voire de Jérusalem, et naturellement, plus d'une fois, de Babylone (cf. J. Vermeylen 351; H. Wildberger 905 s.; récemment R. Hanhardt a reconnu Sion dans »die jahwefeindliche Stadt«, FS W. Zimmerli, 1977, 152—163). Certains exégètes renoncent à toute identification, ainsi O. Kaiser 143 s. et G. Fohrer, II 1962, 8, 17, car il n'est pas certain que les diverses mentions de la ville en Es 24 ss. désignent toujours la même cité; il se pourrait d'ailleurs, comme le remarque H. Wildberger 906, que celle-ci ait une signification plus exemplaire qu'historique. Néanmoins J. Vermeylen 379 estime que, dans le plus ancien noyau d'Es 24 ss. (une partie importante des chapitres 24 et 26), qui traite de la punition de la terre et de la ruine de la citadelle de l'empire païen, il est question de Babylone; ce passage pourrait se référer à la destruction de la métropole mésopotamienne par Xerxès Ier au Ve siècle. J. Vermeylen retrouve même des allusions au récit de la Tour de Babel (Gen 11 1–9) dans le chapitre 24, par exemple, l'emploi répété de נבלה au v. 7 cf. Gen 11 4, les allitérations du v. 4a! Le même auteur rapproche enfin les perspectives d'Es 24 ss. de celles d'Es 13.

On pourra conclure de ces remarques que, au cas où la ville punie par Yahvé, selon l'Apocalypse, serait Babylone, ce qui n'est pas prouvé, l'ancienne capitale de Nébucadnetsar, dans le contexte actuel, sera inclue dans le bouleversement qui frappera la terre, son sort sera lié, comme en Es 13, à un événement de portée cosmique. Cependant si le prophète, dans ce dernier texte, a insisté avant tout sur la confrontation entre Babel et les armées de Yahvé au jour aussi proche que terrible que le Dieu d'Israël a fixé, le ou les responsable(s) d'Es 24 ss. s'intéresse(nt) plutôt à la destinée du monde, au châtiment des oppresseurs et au salut des justes, comme en témoigne l'ensemble de l'Apocalypse: nous ne retrouvons pas dans ces pages les expressions les plus caractéristiques d'Es 13.

Jérémie 50 et 51[60]

Ces longs chapitres, consacrés pour la majeure partie à Babylone, posent des problèmes difficiles; leur authenticité est généralement contestée et leur date reste incertaine[61]. On admet souvent que ces pages sont contemporaines du message du Second Esaïe, elles précèdent donc la fin de l'exil, mais cela n'est pas certain, car en plus d'un endroit elles pourraient avoir été retravaillées[62].

Selon G. Fohrer, Jérémie 50 compte six déclarations sur Babel, dans lesquelles trois paroles sur Israël ont été introduites, et le chapitre se termine par une série de remarques complémentaires. Quant à Jérémie 51, il comporte une douzaine d'oracles sur la cité mésopotamienne auxquelles des annotations sur Israël et son Dieu ont été ajoutées[63]. La rédaction de ces deux ensembles s'est sans doute étendue sur une période assez longue; à des déclarations de l'époque exilique ont pu être jointes des gloses qui datent peut-être de la destruction de Babylone par Xerxès Ier, ou plus tard encore.

Trois lignes directrices se dégagent de la lecture de Jérémie 50; la première atteste la signification internationale – oecuménique serait le terme qui convient! – de Babylone; la deuxième révèle que Yahvé a déclaré la guerre sainte à l'ennemie de Jérusalem; la troisième justifie les mesures sans appel que le Dieu d'Israël prend à son égard.

Dès le début, le prophète nous avertit que le sort de Babel intéresse l'ensemble des nations (v. 2), par la suite, il évoque l'assaut général d'un groupe de peuples, קהל־גוים, contre la capitale mésopotamienne (v. 9), plus loin il rappelle le rôle que Babylone a joué, sans doute au temps de Nébucadnetsar, et qui lui vaut le titre de »marteau de toute la terre« (v. 23). Bref ces passages montrent que le bonheur ou le malheur des hommes est lié à la destinée de la métropole chaldéenne.

---

[60] Bibliographie dans les Introductions à l'Ancien Testament: E. Sellin – G. Fohrer, 1965¹⁰; O. Kaiser, 1969; H. Cazelles, II 1973²; R. Smend, 1978; les commentaires et les études de: W. Rudolph, Jeremia, HAT, 1958²; J. Vermeylen (n. 5); P. Höffken (ibid.); O. Eißfeldt, Jeremias Drohorakel gegen Ägypten und gegen Babel, FS W. Rudolph, 1961, 31–37; G. Fohrer, Vollmacht über Völker und Königreiche. Beobachtungen zu den prophetischen Fremdvölkersprüchen anhand von Jer 46–51, FS J. Ziegler, II 1972, 145–153.

[61] O. Eißfeldt (n. 60) 34s. défend l'authenticité de quelques passages; W. Rudolph (ibid.) 274ss. montre pourquoi les morceaux qui composent Jer 50s. ne peuvent être de Jérémie; cf. également O. Kaiser (ibid.) 189; R. Smend (ibid.) 164 etc.

[62] Cf. à ce propos W. Rudolph (n. 60) 274ss. et surtout G. Fohrer, FS J. Ziegler, 150ss., qui présente une étude minutieuse de l'histoire rédactionnelle de Jer 50s.

[63] Les oracles originaux concernant Babylone sont, selon G. Fohrer 105s., les passages suivants: en Jer 50, les v. 2s. 8–15. 21–24. 25–31. 31s. 35–38a; les v. 39–46 contiennent des adjonctions tardives; en Jer 51, les v. 1–4. 7–9. 11*–12a. 13–14b. 20–23. 25s. 27. 29*. 30–32. 41–43. 44–45a. 54–56. 58.

Ensuite Jérémie 50 met en évidence le fait que Yahvé mène contre Babel une lutte impitoyable. Il veut humilier et ruiner l'empire babylonien et ses dieux (v. 2s.), et dirige l'attaque de sa capitale (v. 9). Yahvé conduit ses archers au combat (v. 14); ce ne sont que bruits de guerre et fracas dans toute la région (v. 22): Babel est prise au piège (v. 2.24). Le Dieu d'Israël mobilise contre les Chaldéens des troupes qui viennent de loin pour mettre à sac Babel (v. 26). Jadis instrument de la colère divine, celle-ci est à son tour victime d'une nation »qui vient du nord« (Jer 4 6) pour la détruire (v. 4).

On remarquera l'importance significative du vocabulaire militaire dans cette page, comme en témoigne par exemple »le chant de l'épée« (v. 35ss.), — l'épée qui doit tailler dans les habitants de Babylone, dans ses devins, dans ses soldats, dans ses sages et dans ses chars ... !

Le troisième élément de ce chapitre concerne la motivation du Dieu d'Israël qui est décidé à en terminer avec la cité païenne qui a mis fin au royaume de Juda. L'heure de la vengeance a sonné: »faites-lui comme elle a fait!« (v. 4.29, cf. encore 51 6.11). A sa cruauté s'ajoute l'impudence de Babylone, son orgueil insensé: »A nous deux, impudente, ton jour est arrivé!« (v. 29ss., cf. encore 51 25ss.), Babel s'est en effet attaquée à Yahvé (v. 24), elle a osé affronter le Saint d'Israël (v. 29)[64]. Son inhumanité comme son effronterie sont une fois de plus dénoncées, ce sont elles qui causent sa perte définitive.

Nous retrouvons les mêmes données en Jérémie 51; le ton est peut-être encore plus dur, les reproches plus violents, les menaces plus vives, les expressions plus frappantes. Le chapitre s'ouvre par l'évocation de l'assaut général donné contre la ville de Nébucadnetsar: personne ne doit être épargné, Yahvé a mis l'interdit sur toute la population (v. 1ss.). C'est le temps de la vengeance (v. 6.11), celui où Babylone, qui a été jadis l'instrument du jugement des nations, doit à son tour éprouver le courroux du Dieu d'Israël: elle a servi autrefois à enivrer toute la terre (pour la châtier) (v. 7ss.), elle a été l'outil dont Yahvé s'est servi pour marteler les royaumes (v. 20ss.), maintenant vient l'heure de sa chute (v. 25s.)[65], la guerre sainte est engagée (v. 27ss.) c'est la panique dans les rangs des soldats babyloniens (v. 30ss.), déjà un chant funèbre est entonné sur la défunte Babel, sur ses villes abandonnées, sur son territoire désolé ... (v. 41ss.)! Babylone est démantelée, ses remparts abattus, ses portes incendiées (v. 58). Le chapitre 51 s'achève sur une vision de destruction et de mort d'une métropole qui fut la gloire de Nébucadnetsar!

---

[64] L'expression »le Saint d'Israël« empruntée à la tradition d'Esaïe est heureusement choisie (cf. encore 51 5).

[65] Babylone est décrite comme »la montagne cosmique« (v. 25s. 53), ce qui ne convient pas à la situation géographique de la cité, mais qui correspond à la signification mythique que celle-ci a prise pour l'auteur juif de ces passages. Le v. 53 se réfère difficilement à l'épisode de la Tour de Babel (Gen 11 1ss.), et peut-être davantage à la tradition d'Es 14.

On retrouve dans ces pages des éléments familiers à ceux qui ont lu les autres oracles sur la cité mésopotamienne; les points de contact avec Esaïe 13 sont notamment évidents[66]. Mais le ton de Jérémie 50 s. frappe par son côté vindicatif; leurs auteurs semblent se complaire dans l'évocation de la chute de la ville ennemie de Jérusalem, ils saluent l'heure de la revanche et se délectent dans la description des souffrances de Babylone en évoquant la guerre sainte et ses cruautés; on les sent exaspérés par l'oppression que la capitale chaldéenne – ou ce qu'elle représente – fait peser sur le peuple de Yahvé. Jérémie 50 s. ne se situent pas au même niveau, sur le plan théologique, qu'Esaïe 47.

* * *

Au terme de cette enquête[67] nous rappelons que nous avons relevé quelques indices de la transformation de la Babylone historique en la Babylone apocalyptique. Le rôle de l'ancienne cité de Nébucadnetsar semble s'amplifier, sa destinée passée et à venir intéresse non seulement ses voisins immédiats, mais aussi l'ensemble des nations, voire la terre entière; même l'univers paraît être partie prenante dans l'ultime conflit qui doit opposer Babylone au Dieu d'Israël; le texte d'Esaïe 13 est particulièrement éclairant sur ce point. La métropole chaldéenne tend par ailleurs à devenir une figure exemplaire, le type même de la puissance hostile à Yahvé et aux siens, la représentation du mal contre laquelle une lutte à mort doit être finalement engagée; les relectures d'Esaïe 14, et dans une certaine mesure les déclarations de Jérémie 50 s. en témoignent. Le nom de Babel sert, au terme d'une évolution qui s'esquisse avec et après l'exil, à désigner une réalité qui n'est pas simplement une cité terrestre, fût-elle la célèbre capitale de l'empire de Nébucadnetsar, mais qui peut s'incarner dans n'importe quelle forme d'absolutisme, lorsque le pouvoir se prend pour fin et s'imagine être Dieu[68]. Ce sera le cas de Rome, selon le témoignage de l'Apocalypse de Jean.

---

[66] Comme le rappelle J. Vermeylen 290 qui compare Jer 50 16 et Es 13 14 Jer 50 39 s. et Es 13 19–22 Jer 50 43 et Es 13 8 Jer 51 11. 28 et Es 13 17 Jer 51 12. 27 et Es 13 2. On admet généralement la priorité d'Es 13 sur Jer 50 s.

[67] Le nom de Babel apparaît encore en Mi 4 10, dans un passage vraisemblement exilique (cf. à ce sujet l'étude récente de B. Renaud, La formation du livre de Michée. Tradition et actualisation, 1977, 205–209).

[68] Il est intéressant de noter que les héros juifs du livre de Daniel se trouvent précisément dans l'empire babylonien, supposé être au faîte de sa gloire. Dan 4, en particulier, paraît être un écho de la tradition prophétique sur Babylone et son orgueil: Nébucadnetsar est frappé de folie pour s'être vanté d'avoir construit »Babylone la grande« (v. 25 ss.). Ici Babel et son roi sont devenus les symboles d'une puissance absolutiste, égarée par ses succès, qui doit être châtiée par le Dieu vivant. On remarquera à ce propos le peu de

Une seconde remarque s'impose: comparé aux autres passages relatifs à Babylone, Esaïe 47 se signale non seulement par la qualité de sa forme, mais aussi par la profondeur théologique de son message. Le prophète de l'exil se révèle un aussi grand penseur qu'un magistral poète, il sait dire l'essentiel à propos du sort qui attend la cité païenne, et d'une manière à la fois ferme et mesurée. Il dénonce mieux que quiconque ses crimes et dépeint avec sobriété sa fin, il vise en premier lieu à rendre à Yahvé la gloire qui lui est due, et non à se complaire de l'infortune des habitants de Babylone.

Puissent ces quelques pages rendre hommage à un spécialiste de l'Ancien Testament, le professeur Dr. Georg Fohrer, qui, par ses multiples travaux dans le domaine vétérotestamentaire, en particulier par ses recherches sur le prophétisme biblique, et également par la manière dont il dirige et anime depuis de nombreuses années la Zeitschrift für die alttestamentliche Wissenschaft, a beaucoup fait pour développer le rayonnement des sciences de l'Ancien Testament; au terme de cette étude nous lui exprimons notre reconnaissance et nos vœux les meilleurs pour les années à venir.

---

cas que les prophètes font de l'épisode de la tour de Babel (Gen 11 1ss.) pourtant significatif; ils auraient pu s'y référer pour dénoncer l'attitude constamment présomptueuse de tout ce qu'évoque le nom de Babylone. De son côté, l'apocalyptique juive, contrairement à ce qu'on pourrait attendre, utilise rarement la tradition sur la cité mésopotamienne; le texte le plus intéressant à cet égard, et constamment cité, est celui des Oracles Sibyllins (Sib 5 155ss.) qui contient une relecture d'Es 47 adaptée aux vues de l'auteur (cf. encore Apoc. Bar [syr.] 11 1ss. 67 7).

A propos des doublets du livre de Jérémie
Réflexions sur la formation d'un livre prophétique

Par Alfred Marx

(18 rue de la Paix, 67170 Brumath, France)

Le livre de Jérémie présente un certain nombre de particularités qui en font un champ d'étude particulièrement riche pour quiconque s'intéresse à la formation des livres prophétiques. Il nous est conservé dans deux versions, celle du TM et celle de la LXX qui, outre un grand nombre de variantes, diffèrent dans leur dimension et dans l'organisation des matériaux. Il contient à côté de sections poétiques d'importantes sections en prose, faites de discours et de narrations. Il donne pour certains événements une version courte et une version longue. Enfin, un certain nombre de passages — parties de verset, versets ou groupes de versets — se retrouvent ailleurs dans l'AT, ou à un autre endroit du livre.

Ce dernier point — les doublets à l'intérieur de Jérémie — n'a pas reçu beaucoup d'attention. La plupart des commentateurs se contente d'examiner le morceau dans son contexte censé primitif et, arrivé au doublet, se borne à en constater le caractère secondaire, et à renvoyer le lecteur au contexte authentique où ce texte est traité. Une telle attitude procède en définitive d'une conception de l'histoire comme une enfilade d'individus remarquables, dont il conviendra de cerner autant que possible la personnalité, et de dégager de ses scories le message authentique. Elle tend ainsi à sous-estimer la distance entre la parole prophétique, prononcée dans un contexte précis, à un moment bien défini de l'histoire, et le livre prophétique, avec tout ce que cela suppose comme choix, réorganisation, et donc partialité, en un mot comme travail rédactionnel, dont le contrôle, dans la plupart des cas, a dû échapper au prophète. Ceci reste vrai pour le livre de Jérémie, même si Jer 36 a pu longtemps donner l'illusion qu'il était possible de supprimer en partie cette distance entre le prophète et la rédaction du livre prophétique. Mais une telle attitude tend surtout à minimiser le fait que le livre fixe cette parole prophétique, lui donnant ainsi, sous cette forme, une portée qui va bien au-delà de l'horizon géographique et historique du prophète. Qu'on le veuille ou non, le livre est un précipité de la parole prophétique, dans la forme sous laquelle elle a été assimilée, adaptée, trahie peut-être, pour servir d'écriture sainte, non à un groupe restreint comme celui des disciples du prophète, mais à la société toute entière, pour qui elle devient normative, à qui elle doit permettre de vivre. C'est dire l'importance du travail de rédaction.

Or, ce qui fait l'intérêt d'une étude des doublets est qu'elle constitue l'une des voies d'approche pour cerner ce milieu des rédacteurs. La comparaison des différentes versions d'un même texte permet de juger de la fidélité de la reproduction. Surtout, la présence d'un même passage, aussi nettement délimité, en deux ou plusieurs endroits différents, constitue un excellent champ d'observation pour l'étude de ces points de suture dont H. Weippert a souligné l'importance[1]. Elle permet d'analyser les différentes techniques d'ancrage. Elle amène à s'interroger sur la nature des textes repris, les raisons de leur réutilisation, les motifs de leur insertion dans tel contexte plutôt que dans tel autre, etc. . . . Une telle étude est ainsi susceptible d'apporter un certain nombre de renseignements sur l'attitude des rédacteurs face à l'autorité de la parole prophétique, sur leur herméneutique, sur leurs préoccupations théologiques[2].

I

La présence de doublets n'est parfois qu'une conséquence de la répétition des mêmes thèmes ou de l'analogie des situations.

On retrouve ainsi en Jer 1 19 et 15 20aβ.b la même parole d'assistance divine adressée au prophète, dans le premier cas en liaison avec la mission qu'il reçoit de Yahweh, dans le second, en réponse à sa plainte[3]. En 11 20 et 20 12, dans un contexte de persécution, Jérémie exprime sa certitude d'avoir gain de cause face à ses adversaires. En 11 20, elle répond à la menace de mort proférée contre lui par les habitants d'Anathoth (11 18–19) et débouche sur une prophétie de jugement à leur encontre (v. 21–23). En 20 12, elle répond à ses adversaires qui espèrent triompher de lui (20 10b) et conduit à un appel à la louange (v. 13). Cette certitude est liée à la foi de Jérémie en la sagacité de Yahweh qui sonde les reins et les coeurs[4]. En

---

[1] Helga Weippert, Die Prosareden des Jeremiabuches, 1973, 234.

[2] Dans le cadre de cette étude, nous ne tiendrons pas compte de ceux des textes qui se présentent comme une citation d'une parole antérieure (ainsi 21 9 et 38 2, 23 5–6 et 33 14a.15aβ.b–16 27 6b et 28 14b) ou qui ne sont que la répétition d'une même formule. Il faudrait évidemment prêter une attention particulière à ces textes dans toute étude de la structure du livre de Jérémie. D'autre part, étant donné le caractère spécifique des problèmes liés à la LXX, nous nous limiterons à l'étude des doublets du TM.

[3] Sur ce texte, cf. H.-W. Jüngling, Ich mache dich zu einer ehernen Mauer. Literarkritische Überlegungen zum Verhältnis von Jer 1,18–19 zu Jer 15,20–21, Biblica 54 (1973), 1–24. En 15 20b, l'ordre des mots est différent, la formule »oracle de Yahweh« étant ici en position finale. 15 20b ajoute $l^eh\hat{o}\check{s}\hat{\imath}^{\,a}ka$. 1 18a et 15 20a ont également l'image de la muraille d'airain.

[4] Alors que 11 20a met l'accent sur le fait que Yahweh est un juste juge, $\check{s}opet\ \bar{s}\ædæq$, 20 12a insiste davantage sur l'attitude de Yahweh face au juste. Ceci a entraîné une modification des verbes.

17 10b, où Yahweh lui-même se présente comme tel (v. 10a), elle conduit à l'affirmation de la rétribution, reprise en 32 19bβ par Jérémie: parce que Yahweh connaît la voie des hommes (v. 19bα), il les rétribue selon leurs œuvres[5]. De telles séquences sont sans doute le reflet de la tradition catéchétique et liturgique d'Israël.

Les séquences suivantes, par contre, pourraient bien être des créations de Jérémie. En Jer 7 16 et 11 14 Jérémie reçoit l'ordre de ne pas intercéder pour le peuple. Dans les deux cas, cette interdiction est mise en relation avec le culte aux autres dieux, soit que la mention de ce culte vienne après cette interdiction (7 17–19), soit qu'elle la précède (11 12–13). La variante de 11 14b[6] qui se réfère à l'intercession du *peuple* vient de 11 11b, les v. 11 et 14 formant de la sorte le cadre de cette brève section. La première partie de cette interdiction d'intercéder se retrouve en 14 11b, et y est également une conséquence de l'idolâtrie (v. 10)[7]. 11 11–12 et 14 12 soulignent que ni le culte légitime, ni le culte aux autres dieux ne sauraient empêcher le châtiment. Cette séquence souligne ainsi le fait que l'idolâtrie est le crime irrémissible par excellence. La question rhétorique »ne châtierais-je pas pour ces choses ...« (5 9.29 9 8) est mise en relation avec un autre type de péché, à savoir les fautes contre le prochain (5 7b–8.26–28 9 7) qui apparaissent ainsi comme une autre raison de la catastrophe. Dans ces trois textes, cette question rhétorique finale répond à une question rhétorique initiale (5 7.22 9 6)[8].

Un inventaire de telles séquences, intentionnelles ou inconscientes, serait d'ailleurs du plus grand intérêt.

La répétition d'un même thème rend également compte du doublet suivant. 8 15 et 14 19b se réfèrent tous deux à un espoir de bonheur entretenu par les prophètes, mais qui s'avère en contradiction flagrante avec la réalité. Dans les deux passages, c'est cette idée de paix, mais surtout la métaphore de la maladie et de la guérison (8 14.17.22 14 17.19) qui ont conduit à l'utilisation de cette parole[9].

---

[5] Les deux textes diffèrent uniquement par la place de la conjonction de coordination et par l'utilisation des matres lectionis.

[6] 11 14a est un peu plus court. La comparaison entre le nombre de dieux et le nombre de villes, en 11 13a, se retrouve, de manière identique, en 2 28b. L'argumentation de 11 12 est analogue à celle de Deut 32 37–38.

[7] 14 11b, qui ne reprend pas le pronom personnel initial, ajoute *lᵉṭôbā*.

[8] Cf. W. A. Brueggemann, Jeremiah's Use of Rhetorical Questions, JBL 92 (1973), 364–366. La forme de la question est identique dans les trois textes, à ceci près que 5 29b et 9 8b ne sont pas introduits par la conjonction de coordination et que la négation y est écrite plene. 9 8a ajoute *bam* après le verbe. On retrouve la construction *hāʿal* + dém. en Am 8 8 Is 57 6 64 11. Ces questions rhétoriques ont sans doute aussi une fonction structurante (cf. aussi 50 23b = 51 41b).

[9] Les seules différences portent sur l'adjonction d'une conjonction de coordination en 14 19b et sur l'orthographe de *mărpē'*, écrit *mărpē* en 8 15 (cf. aussi le verbe en 8 11).

Il nous faut nous arrêter plus longuement au cas de Jer 6 12a. 13–14 et 8 10–12. Les deux passages offrent pour l'essentiel le même texte. Sauf pour son début, les variantes sont principalement d'ordre orthographique ou des adaptations d'expressions rares à une formulation plus courante[10]. Au ch. 6, le passage continue une annonce de jugement qui commence au v. 11b, et qui vise l'ensemble des habitants du pays. Au ch. 8, cette section est introduite par *laken*. Le v. 10 constitue ainsi le début d'une parole de jugement. Celle-ci vise ici plus précisément les sages et les scribes (v. 8–9). De là un certain nombre de modifications au v. 10: la suppression de 6 12b qui a rendu nécessaire, après *laken*, un verbe présentant Yahweh comme l'auteur du châtiment; la suppression des pronoms suffixes de 6 13a; enfin, la construction différente de 6 12a. Dans ces deux textes, c'est le mépris des instructions divines qui entraîne le châtiment (6 10 8 7b. 9b). La présence de ce doublet peut n'être que la conséquence du désir d'appliquer à un groupe spécifique ce qui vaut pour l'ensemble de la population[11], comme c'est aussi le cas pour 30 10–11 et 46 27. 28aβb, où un oracle de salut pour Israël est appliqué à ceux des juifs réfugiés en Egypte. Or, ce qui frappe dans notre doublet, c'est l'analogie thématique avec le ch. 7, et la même condamnation de l'attitude morale et de la confiance illusoire dans les institutions du culte. Notre doublet stigmatise tout particulièrement ceux qui entretiennent cette espérance illusoire, à savoir les prêtres, les prophètes, les sages et les scribes. On peut se demander si, en encadrant ainsi le ch. 7, le doublet n'a pas pour fonction de mettre en relief ce chapitre, qui constitue un résumé de la prédication de jugement de Jérémie.

Une explication de ce type pourrait peut-être également rendre compte du doublet 15 13–14 et 17 3. 4aβ. b[12].

Tous ces points devraient être repris dans le cadre d'une étude de la structure de Jer 1–25.

---

[10] Cf. l'orthographe *kullō* en 8 10a, fréquent en Jer, au lieu de *kullô*, 6 13 (et uniquement ici en Jer), et *rapā*, en 8 11a, comme au v. 15 et 6 24. Cf. aussi l'usage différent des matres lectionis. 8 12bα a *kalăm* ni. (également en 3 3 et, en relation avec *bôš*, 22 22 31 19) au lieu du hi. (uniquement en 6 15, cf. ho. en 14 3). 8 12bβ lit *pᵉquddatam*, ce qui est une harmonisation avec une expression fréquente chez Jer (10 15 46 21 50 27 51 18). Enfin, 8 11a ajoute *băt* devant *ʿămmî*, comme aux v. 19. 21. 22. 23.
[11] Cf. aussi 4 4b et 21 12b et surtout 9 14aβ. b et 23 15aβ.
[12] Sur ce texte, cf. E. Gerstenberger, Jeremiah's Complaints. Observations on Jer 15 10–21, JBL 82 (1963), 393–408; H. Reventlow, Liturgie und prophetisches Ich bei Jeremia, 1963, 212–219. Pour les problèmes textuels, cf. L. C. Allen, More Cuckoos in the Textual Nest . . ., JTS NS 24 (1973), 70–71.

II

Dans un certain nombre de cas, le doublet a une fonction différente selon les contextes. On peut distinguer à l'intérieur de ce groupe deux catégories: l'une où le destinataire reste le même, et l'autre où le destinataire change.

1) *Jer 16 14–15 et 23 7–8.* Au ch. 23, les v. 7–8 constituent la fin d'un oracle soigneusement structuré, comprenant deux parties. La première partie, qui prend la forme d'un chiasme, utilise essentiellement le langage métaphorique (v. 1–4): Yahweh condamne les bergers indignes, responsables de la dispersion du troupeau (v. 1–2) et annonce le rassemblement du troupeau et l'installation de nouveaux bergers (v. 3–4). La seconde partie explicite ces deux derniers points, selon l'ordre des thèmes aux v. 1–2, en deux morceaux introduits chacun par la formule »voici des jours viennent, oracle de Yahweh« (v. 5–6.7–8). Le v. 8 reprend le thème du v. 3, à savoir l'annonce du rassemblement des dispersés, rétablis dans leur pays. 8aβ correspond ainsi presque mot pour mot à 3aβ; de même, 8b correspond à 3bβ. Les v. 7–8 sont donc fort bien liés au contexte, autant du point de vue thématique que du point de vue structurel. Au ch. 16, ces mêmes versets font suite à un morceau d'une dureté étonnante, qui non seulement annonce la déportation, mais l'absence de toute possibilité de grâce. L'insertion de ce passage venu de 23 7–8 a eu pour objet d'infléchir le caractère radical de cet oracle par cette promesse de retour[13], qui seule est ici au centre de la préoccupation des rédacteurs. Il en est résulté une triple modification de l'archétype: le *yašăb* de 23 8b a été changé en un verbe *šûb*; le retour a été mis en relation explicite avec la promesse patriarcale; enfin et surtout, les rédacteurs ont nettement distingué entre la référence à une formule proverbiale (v. 14–15a) et une parole de Yahweh annonçant le retour (v. 15b), et ont modifié en conséquence la personne des verbes[14]. L'insertion de ce texte immédiatement après le v. 13, plutôt qu'après le v. 18, montre que l'objectif principal n'était pas tant l'annonce du retour, mais l'annulation du refus de la grâce divine. Les rédacteurs lui ont opposé cette autre parole de Yahweh, qui en prend le contre-pied.

Jer 32 43bα et 33 10aβ citent, dans le cadre d'un discours de Yahweh, une parole du peuple constatant la dévastation du pays. Les ch. 32 et 33 sont liés par une unité de lieu – la cour de la prison où Jérémie était

---

[13] Par ex. A. Weiser, Der Prophet Jeremia, ATD 20.21, 1960⁴, 140; J. Bright, Jeremiah, Anchor Bible 21, 1965, 113. *Ri'šônā*, en 16 18, pourrait provenir de la même main (J. Bright op. cit. 108).

[14] Les autres différences sont mineures et portent sur l'orthographe (*šam* en 23 8; *šammā* en 16 15; *ṣapônā* en 23 8, *ṣapôn* en 16 15) et la forme du verbe introduisant la citation (impf. qal, comme au v. 6, 3° pl. en 23 7; impf. ni., 3° sg. en 16 14). 23 8a est un peu plus long; l'expression *zæra' bêt* Israël/Jacob ne se retrouve qu'en Ez 20 5 et 44 22.

retenu —, et de thème — l'annonce du rétablissement —. Le ch. 33 se présente comme un second discours adressé par Yahweh au prophète (v. 1). 32 36–44 et 33 4–11 sont construits selon un schéma analogue: formule du messager (32 36 33 4), suivie d'une référence à la catastrophe imminente (32 36 33 4–5), annonce du rétablissement futur introduite par *hinᵉnî* + participe (32 37 33 6), nouvelle formule du messager (32 42 33 10) introduisant la citation et débouchant sur une description imagée de la situation future. La conclusion de ces deux morceaux est formulée de manière quasiment identique (32 44 33 11). Tout ceci corrobore l'impression que ces deux textes ont été rédigés de manière à se correspondre et ainsi à se compléter. Le texte même de la citation ne présente que peu de variantes. Au ch. 32, la citation fait référence à la situation de Juda en général[15], tandis qu'au ch. 33 elle se rapporte plus particulièrement à la situation de Jérusalem, ce qui a entraîné une modification du genre des pronoms personnels. 33 10 insiste sur l'absence de vie qui est résulté de cette dévastation, répétant le premier *meʾên* (repris encore trois fois dans la suite du verset), et soulignant de la sorte le caractère dramatique de la situation. Vues sur cet arrière-plan, les différences de contenu n'en sont que plus frappantes. 32 36–44 met l'accent sur l'alliance nouvelle (v. 37–41) et sur la reprise des activités commerciales (v. 43a.44), ceci en liaison étroite avec le geste symbolique des v. 6–15, dont le v. 43a reprend d'ailleurs la conclusion. 33 4–11, par contre, insiste sur l'aspect cultuel et présente le rétablissement en terme de guérison, purification et pardon (v. 6–8), la situation future étant décrite comme une reprise de la vie sociale et cultuelle (v. 11).

Il est peut-être possible ici de préciser le milieu qui est à l'origine de cette réinterprétation. Une indication nous est fournie par une autre variante dans le texte de la citation. Alors que 32 43 utilise l'adjectif *šᵉmamā*, courant chez Jérémie, pour décrire la dévastation du pays, 33 10 utilise l'adjectif *ḥareb*, qui n'y réapparaît qu'en 33 12. Or, cet adjectif, utilisé à propos d'un lieu, se retrouve deux fois en Ez 36 33–38 (v. 35.38)[16]. Jer 33 et Ez 36 33–38 sont également unis par une analogie thématique. Cette parenté est confirmée par la quadruple présence en Ez 36 du participe ni. de *šamăm* (v. 34.35.36) qui, en Jer, ne se trouve qu'en 33 10[17]. On peut donc légitimement en conclure que les auteurs de Jer 33 4–11 appartiennent au même milieu que ceux d'Ez 36 33–38, et qu'ils ont dû avoir connaissance de ce dernier texte.

---

[15] Au ch. 32 on a deux citations, la première référant à la situation de Jérusalem, livrée aux mains de l'ennemi (v. 36).

[16] Uniques autres attestations dans cet emploi: Agg. 1 4.9 Neh 2 3.17.

[17] Ailleurs uniquement en Am 9 14 Ez 29 12 30 7 32 15 Is 54 3 Ps 69 26. A noter également la mention des troupeaux en Ez 36 38 et Jer 33 12.

Cette intervention rédactionnelle, qui s'appuye sur la réutilisation d'une même citation, a eu pour objet de compléter une présentation trop unilatérale en mettant l'accent sur le côté cultuel. On trouve en 17 25a et 22 4b un autre exemple de ce type, la réinterprétation se faisant ici dans un sens rituel.

Jer 10 12–16 et 51 15–19 sont un hymne au Dieu créateur. Au ch. 10[18], cet hymne conclut un diptyque condamnant les idoles de fabrication humaine (v. 3–7.8–10), chaque élément de ce diptyque débouchant sur une doxologie (v. 6–7.10). Il souligne que ce créateur de l'univers, maître des éléments de la nature, alors que les idoles ne sont que néant, est aussi le Dieu d'Israël. En 51 15–19, cet hymne réapparaît dans le cadre de l'oracle contre Babylone. Le texte est quasiment le même, et les variantes sont purement orthographiques[19], à une exception près qui est l'absence de la mention d'Israël de 10 16a. Cette omission est d'autant plus étonnante que, pour le reste, la fidélité de la reproduction est assez remarquable. Certes, l'expression »Israël, tribu de son héritage« est rare et n'a de parallèle qu'en Ps. 74 2. Mais l'idée qu'Israël est l'héritage de Yahweh est fréquente. On comprendrait fort bien la suppression de *šebæṭ*, qui serait une harmonisation avec une formule courante. La disparition accidentelle »d'Israël« paraît, par contre, difficilement concevable. La solution de ce problème est liée à celui de la fonction de ce texte dans l'oracle contre Babylone. Il ne semble pas que le but des rédacteurs ait été la polémique contre les idoles, auquel cas ils auraient, selon toute vraisemblance, inséré ce texte à la suite de 51 44.47 ou 52, qui auraient constitué un excellent point de contact avec 10 15. Or, une des idées dominantes du contexte de 51 15–19 est l'idée que les nations sont l'instrument du châtiment entre les mains de Yahweh (v. 7.20–23 pour Babylone, v. 11 pour les Mèdes). Dans cet oracle, ce n'est qu'ici que ce thème est à ce point développé. On peut ainsi se demander si les rédacteurs n'ont pas voulu jouer sur le double sens de *šebæṭ*, tribu, mais aussi bâton, et donc instrument de châtiment. Le passage constituerait ainsi un commentaire théologique du v. 14. Yahweh est l'instrument de la vengeance d'Israël. Créateur et maître des éléments, il est aussi le maître de l'histoire. Les mouvements des nations, les bouleversements politiques qui agitent la région, se font à son initiative et trouvent leur explication dernière dans la relation privilégiée entre Israël et Yahweh, qui utilise les nations pour châtier aussi bien Israël que ses ennemis. Le mot même de *šebæṭ* devient le principe herméneutique de l'histoire de cette époque troublée.

---

[18] Sur 10 1–16, cf. P. R. Ackroyd, Jeremiah X.1–16, JTS NS 14 (1963), 385–390; T. W. Overholt, The Falsehood of Idolatry: an Interpretation of Jer X.1–16, JTS NS 16 (1965), 1–12; B. N. Wambacq, Jérémie, X.1–16, RB 81 (1974), 57–62.

[19] Outre les différences dans l'utilisation des matres lectionis, 51 16a a corrigé la forme rare *wăyyă‘ălē* (+ uniquement I Sam 7 9) en *wăyyă‘ăl*.

2) Dans tous les textes examinés jusque là, le destinataire était resté le même, à savoir Israël. Le but du doublet était essentiellement de préciser, de compléter ou d'interpréter. Dans d'autres cas, le destinataire change.

Jer 23 19–20 et 30 23–24. Au ch. 23, ce passage fait partie d'un oracle contre les prophètes qui disent leurs propres paroles et annoncent la paix (v. 16–22). Il est inséré entre v. 18 et v. 21–22, de contenu et de structure parallèles, qui soulignent l'autonomie de ces prophètes. N'ayant pas assisté au conseil divin, ils n'ont pu écouter les propos tenus par Yahweh qui, par ailleurs, ne les a chargé d'aucune mission. La parole qu'ils auraient pu entendre et qu'ils auraient dû transmettre est celle des v. 19–20[20], à savoir que la colère de Dieu va s'exercer contre les méchants, ceux-là mêmes auxquels les prophètes avaient promis la paix, en dépit de leurs mauvaises actions (v. 17. 22). Il s'agit donc ici d'un oracle de jugement contre Israël. Le ch. 30 annonce le retour et la restauration, opposant en deux tableaux l'angoisse et les malheurs du présent au bonheur à venir (v. 5–11.12–17), tandis que les nations qui avaient frappé Israël seront châtiées. Un tableau final souligne ce bonheur futur. Tout comme leur archétype, les v. 23–24 sont insérés entre deux morceaux semblables, qui en forment le cadre: Israël sera le peuple de Yahweh, Yahweh sera le Dieu d'Israël (30 22 31 1). A cette promesse correspond le châtiment des oppresseurs, qui sont ici les méchants contre lesquels s'exerce la colère divine (v. 11.16.20). Le retournement de cette parole primitivement adressée en oracle de jugement à Israël est tout à fait dans la ligne du reste du chapitre, où le futur est présenté comme une succession de retournements. Il en illustre ainsi parfaitement la thèse, même si, en en faisant le point culminant de ce morceau, il majore l'idée du châtiment des nations[21].

Jer 6 22aβ–24 et 50 41–43. Introduit au ch. 6 par la formule du messager, ce morceau constitue un oracle de jugement contre Israël. Il annonce la marche sur Jérusalem d'un peuple redoutable venu du Nord. Cet oracle fait suite à l'accusation de désobéissance (v. 16–17.19b) et développe la menace des v. 19a et 21. Au ch. 50, ce même passage apparaît dans le cadre de l'oracle contre Babylone. Inséré après l'annonce de la dévastation de Babylone, dont le sort est comparé à celui de Sodome et de Gomorrhe (v. 40), il précise quel est l'auteur de ces ravages. Il précède un autre morceau, également introduit par *hinnē* (v. 44–46), où le

---

[20] Ainsi J. Bright op. cit. 152.

[21] Le texte diffère de 23 19–20 sur les points suivants: absence de la coordination devant *śāʿăr.* et de *bînā* (fin 23 20); remplacement de la forme unique *ḥûl*, hitp. par *gûr*, hitp.; adjonction de *ḥᵃrôn* devant *ʾăp*. Il se pourrait que, pour ce dernier point, la modification ne soit pas simplement une adaptation à une formule courante. Cette expression se trouve en effet, à propos des nations en général, en 25 37.38 (cf. aussi 49 37 51 45), dans un contexte où apparaît aussi l'image de la tempête dévastatrice (25 32). Dans le même ordre d'idée, la lecture *gûr* serait-elle due à une confusion avec *ʿûr*, en 25 32 (faute d'audition)?

dévastateur est comparé à un lion. Cette analogie structurelle et thématique a incontestablement favorisé l'insertion de ce morceau à cet endroit. Le texte est pratiquement le même qu'en 6 22aβ–24, sauf pour les indispensables adaptations. Par ailleurs, c'est ici un ensemble de peuples qui monte contre Babylone (50 41b), et c'est l'attitude du roi de Babylone et non celle de son peuple qui est décrite au v. 43. Ces modifications sont autant d'adaptations au reste de l'oracle (cf. respectivement v. 9 et v. 17–18)[22].

Ce doublet est particulièrement intéressant en ce qu'il permet de déceler quels sont les mécanismes qui ont permis ce retournement. En effet, 6 22b–41b se retrouve, à propos des nations en général, en 25 32b, à ceci près que ce texte utilise la métaphore du vent pour désigner l'ennemi. Le ch. 25 fournit ainsi la clé de ce retournement par l'annonce que les nations expérimenteront le sort qu'Israël a subi en premier. Sur la base de cette prophétie, les rédacteurs ont appliqué à Babylone, l'adversaire par excellence, une menace qui, initialement, s'était réalisée à propos d'Israël. Comme Israël, Babylone va, à son tour, être frappé par un ennemi venu du Nord. Dans ce contexte, on peut aussi mentionner 9 10a et 51 37a, 9 15b et 49 37b, 15 2bβ et 43 11b[23].

III

Il nous faut examiner, enfin, deux textes dont chaque verset a son doublet et qui font ainsi l'effet d'une mosaïque.

Jer 7 30b–34a[24] se situe à la suite de deux sections qui développent les deux thèmes du discours du Temple (v. 3–15), en condamnant respectivement le culte aux autres dieux (v. 17–19), et le culte sacrificiel en général opposé aux voies de Dieu (v. 21–26). Notre passage se raccroche au constat que Yahweh a rejeté cette génération (v. 29b), une décision motivée de manière très générale par le fait que les fils de Juda ont fait le mal (v. 30a). La suite précisera ce en quoi consiste ce mal.

L'oracle peut se diviser en deux zones qui s'articulent autour d'un verset pivot (v. 32). La première zone est celle de l'accusation (v. 30b–31). Celle-ci porte sur les deux points suivants: la présence »d'abominations« dans le Temple (v. 30b), et la construction de *bamôt hăttopæt* dans la

---

[22] Les autres changements concernent l'usage des matres lectionis et des coordinations, et l'absence de 'æræṣ en 50 41a.

[23] Cf. aussi 21 14b et 50 32b. La menace est, certes, fréquente. Mais son usage, quasiment dans les mêmes termes, à propos de deux réalités différentes, crée un lien entre ces deux réalités. De même, il est certainement significatif que soit associée à Manassé (15 4a) une menace ailleurs proférée à l'encontre de Sédécias (24 9a 29 18bα 34 17bβ).

[24] Cf. notamment W. Thiel, Die deuteronomistische Redaktion von Jeremia 1–25, 1973, 128–132.

vallée de Ben-Hinnom, en vue de sacrifices humains (v. 31). Cette accusation s'intègre donc parfaitement à la thématique du ch. 7. Elle se retrouve sous cette double forme, et de manière quasiment identique, en 32 34—35a, à ceci près que les verbes qui, ici, sont au parfait (en accord avec 30a), y sont à l'imparfait (en accord avec 32 33). Par ailleurs, le doublet du ch. 32 met l'accent sur le caractère idolâtre de ces sacrifices humains: ils sont offerts à *Molèk* sur les hauts-lieux de *Baal*. La formulation de 32 35 semble influencée par II Rois 23 10, seul autre texte où le sacrifice à Molèk est mis en rapport avec le tophèt de la vallée de Ben-Hinnom[25], et par I Rois 11 7, où Molèk et »abomination« sont associés. La seconde partie de cette accusation de 7 30b—31 se retrouve aussi en 19 5[26]. Elle est ici tout particulièrement en situation, puisque la scène se déroule dans la vallée même où se pratique ce culte. Ce fait y a d'ailleurs rendu superflue la précision topographique de 7 31aα. Tout comme en 32 35, l'accent est mis sur le caractère idolâtre du culte, ici adressé, en toute logique, à Baal, en holocauste.

Le v. 32 fait passer de l'accusation à l'annonce du châtiment. Reprenant les deux indications de lieu de la seconde accusation, il annonce un changement symbolique de toponyme — la vallée s'appellera »vallée des tués« —, et de fonction — le tophèt deviendra un charnier. Absente du ch. 32 en raison de la fonction différente qu'y ont les v. 34—35 (rappel des transgressions d'Israël), cette prophétie se retrouve tout naturellement au ch. 19. Mais, en raison même de l'économie du texte, elle y est répartie sur les deux discours de Jérémie. 19 6 correspond à 7 32a, sauf que le changement de nom y est introduit par *qara'* ni. au lieu de *'amăr* ni. D'autre part, du fait même de son étroite association avec le lieu où se déroule cette scène, 19 6 a ajouté la précision »ce lieu« (cf. aussi v. 3.4.7). La seconde partie de la menace se retrouve en 19 11b[27], dans le second discours de Jérémie, en relation étroite avec le geste symbolique du v. 10, et se prolonge par une comparaison entre le sort du tophèt et celui de Jérusalem. Il convient de souligner le fait que ces menaces sont très étroitement liées à la seconde accusation, et d'ailleurs elles n'apparaissent que dans ce contexte. Ceci signifie aussi que l'association avec la présence

---

[25] A la différence de 7 31a, l'acte du sacrifice humain est exprimé en 32 35a, tout comme en II Rois 23 10, par *'abăr*, hi., une formulation qui ne se retrouve en relation avec Molèk qu'en Lev 18 21.

[26] 19 5 et 32 35 ont *'æt* après le verbe initial. 19 5a n'a pas la mention des filles comme victimes du sacrifice (cf. de même II Rois 17 31). La formulation de 7 31a ne se retrouve qu'en Deut. 12 31. 19 5b insère *lo' dibbărtî* entre les deux verbes de 7 31b. 32 35a accole au premier verbe un pronom suffixe.

[27] Les deux textes diffèrent toutefois dans l'ordre des mots — 19 11b mettant, ici encore, le lieu en relief — et le temps des verbes, pf. en 7 32, tout comme aux v. 30—31, impf. en 19 11b, en accord avec v. 11a.

»d'abominations« au Temple, aux ch. 7 et 32, ne va pas de soi. En fait, elle pourrait bien avoir été inspirée par Ez 20 30–31, lu à la lumière d'Ez 5 11, le seul autre texte où il est question d'une »abomination« dans le Temple de Jérusalem.

Dans la seconde zone de l'oracle, cette annonce de mort est prolongée, positivement par une parole sur le sort des cadavres livrés aux oiseaux et aux animaux (v. 33) et, négativement, par une parole sur l'absence de joie (v. 34a). Les deux menaces se retrouvent respectivement en 16 4b 19 7b 34 20b[28], et 16 9b 25 10a 33 11a[29]. Les rédacteurs de notre passage les ont sans doute empruntées à 16 1–9 où elles sont tout particulièrement en situation. Comme ici, la menace concernant les cadavres est étendue à tout le peuple, et non, comme dans les autres passages, aux seuls habitants de Jérusalem. Et dans les deux cas, le motif de l'absence de joie (étroitement en relation avec 16 2) est introduit par *šābat* hi. (au lieu de *'ābad* hi. en 25 10) et arrive en position finale.

L'authenticité de ce morceau est donc pour le moins suspecte, et il semble davantage être le produit d'un travail rédactionnel dont le but était de compléter de la sorte, à partir d'autres textes de Jérémie et d'Ezéchiel, le catalogue des péchés ayant conduit à la catastrophe. Pour ce faire, les rédacteurs ont gommé autant que possible les éléments spécifiques de Jer 19 5, en particulier la liaison étroite avec une situation historique précise et la mention de Baal, dont le culte avait d'ailleurs déjà été dénoncé au v. 9. Mais cette adjonction, qui associe aussi étroitement idolâtrie et formes aberrantes du culte avec le châtiment de mort, a aussi eu pour conséquence de déplacer le centre de gravité du ch. 7 et de nuancer, ou peut-être même de corriger, le caractère radical des affirmations de v. 21–22: ce que Yahweh a surtout interdit (v. 31b), c'est l'idolâtrie et le sacrifice humain. Ils sont les principales causes de la catastrophe. L'analogie entre 7 29a et le geste symbolique d'Ez 5 1–4 a pu servir de catalyseur

---

[28] Sur ce motif, cf. H. Weippert op. cit. 183–186. Pour l'A. il s'agirait d'une expression spécifique à Jérémie, sans influence deutéronomiste. En 19 7b la menace est introduite par *natăn* (cf. aussi Ps 79 2), avec Yahweh comme sujet, à cause du début du v. Pour le reste, la formulation est identique dans les différents passages, à ceci près que 7 33 explicite le pr. suff. ailleurs accolé à *nᵉbelā* (une précision que le contexte y rendait superflu). 33b ne se retrouve, dans ce contexte thématique, qu'en Deut 28 26b. En 34 20b, cette menace est, comme en Deut 28, liée à celle qui fait d'Israël un sujet d'effroi pour toutes les nations (34 17bβ Deut 28 25a), comme conséquence d'une rupture d'alliance.

[29] La formulation est identique dans les différents textes. Sous cette forme, cette série ne se trouve qu'en Jer. En 25 10 elle apparaît, amplifiée, dans le cadre d'un résumé de la prédication du prophète et est suivie, comme en 7 34b, de l'annonce de la dévastation du pays. En 19 8, l'annonce de l'abandon des cadavres est suivie de celle de la dévastation de Jérusalem, mais l'image utilisée est différente. 33 11 inverse la formule, qui devient ici promesse. A ces cris de joie que l'on entendra de nouveau s'ajoutent les cris de louange en provenance du Temple restauré.

à cette intervention rédactionnelle. Le résumé de Jer 32 26–35 connaît le ch. 7 dans sa forme actuelle et en reprend la séquence des accusations.

Jer 49 17b–22. La suspicion qui frappait la fin du ch. 7 atteint encore davantage la conclusion de l'oracle contre Edom, déjà suspect du fait que son début est lui-même en partie un doublet d'Abd 1–6. Cette conclusion peut se diviser en deux parties: une annonce du châtiment (v. 17–18) et une double comparaison de l'instrument de ce châtiment avec un lion (v. 19–21) et un aigle (v. 22).

a) Le v. 17a annonce la dévastation d'Edom, qui stupéfie et épouvante (*šamăm* et *šarăq*) tous ceux qui en voient les conséquences (v. 17b). Le v. 17b, qui décrit cette réaction, est un doublet exact de 19 8b, où l'image est employée à propos de Jérusalem, et de 50 13b, où elle est utilisée à propos de Babylone[30]. Dans ces trois textes, cette stupéfaction – verbe *šamăm* – vient du spectacle de la désolation – *šammā* – du lieu (19 8a 49 17a, *šᵉmamā* en 50 13a), un jeu de mot qu'on retrouve aussi en 18 16. L'emploi dans les mêmes termes à propos d'Edom et de Babylone d'un motif utilisé à propos de Jérusalem n'est peut-être pas fortuit. On retrouve, en effet, la même association *šammā* et *šᵉreqā* en 25 18[31], où la dévastation promise à Juda n'est que le début d'une longue série qui frappera l'ensemble des nations. Or, le rapprochement avec le ch. 25 est clairement établi par 49 12 (séparé du v. 17 par le doublet avec Abd 1–4), qui reprend à la fois la métaphore de la coupe (cf. 25 15.16 etc.), et la question rhétorique de 25 29, appliquant ainsi à Edom une argumentation qui, en 25 27–29, concernait toutes les nations.

Cette idée même de dévastation attire tout naturellement celle d'absence d'habitants, 49 18b = 49 33b = 50 40b. Le rapprochement est fréquent chez Jérémie (2 15 4 7 6 8 9 10 34 22 46 19 48 9 50 3.13 51 29.37.43.62) même si sous cette forme exacte le motif n'a pas de parallèle. 49 18a et 50 40a comparent cette dévastation à celle qui a frappé Sodome et Gomorrhe. Quoique leur formulation soit très proche, les deux textes présentent entre eux quelques variantes, légères mais significatives[32]. 49 18aα correspond, en effet, à Deut 29 22bα où, comme ici, c'est la vue des coups – *măkkôt* – infligés par Yahweh au pays qui amène la comparaison (49 17b, Deut 29 21b). 50 40aα, par contre, se retrouve mot pour mot en Am 4 11aα et, dans le cadre de l'oracle contre Babylone, en Is 13 19b. Aussi bien en 50 39 qu'en Is 13 18–22, l'accent est mis sur l'absence d'habitants. A la différence de

---

[30] En 50 13, l'objet de *'ăl* est explicité, une précision superflue dans les autres textes, du fait de la mention du lieu dans la première partie du v. On retrouve ce motif en Jer 18 16 I Rois 9 8 // II Chr 7 21 Lam 2 15.16 Soph 2 15, mais avec une formulation différente.
[31] Cf. aussi 18 16 19 8 25 9 51 37 Mi 6 16 II Chr 29 8.
[32] 50 40a précise le sujet de cette action, à savoir Elohim, et fait précéder les toponymes par *ӕt*. Au lieu de *'amăr* (Yahweh) (49 18), 50 40 a *nᵉ°um*. Cette même alternance apparaissait en 32 44//33 11, où la forme en *'amăr* était utilisée dans le texte secondaire.

Deut 29, c'est aussi sur ce point qu'insiste 49 18, en ajoutant, avec 50 40, à la série »Sodome et Gomorrhe« la précision »et ses habitants«. On a ainsi appliqué à Edom et Babylone une comparaison qui, en Deut 29 et Am 4, l'était à Israël.

b) L'oracle sur Edom se termine par deux morceaux, tous deux introduits par *hinnē*, et qui comparent le destructeur à un lion (v. 19–21) et à un aigle (v. 22).

La métaphore du lion pour désigner le destructeur est courante. Il convient toutefois de souligner que la série désolation — absence d'habitants — lion, se retrouve, dans un ordre différent, en 2 15 et 4 7 à propos d'Israël et, dans une séquence identique, à propos de Babylone, en 51 37–38 (cf. aussi, à propos des nations, 25 38). Les v. 19–21 sont un doublet de 50 44–46, où la séquence est interrompue par un morceau venu de 6 22aβ–24. Les deux textes sont quasiment identiques, sauf pour les nécessaires adaptations à leur destinataire respectif[33].

La métaphore de l'aigle est empruntée à l'oracle contre Moab (48 40aβb.41b). Elle se raccroche très bien au contexte, d'abord au v. 16 (parallèle à Abd 3–4), où apparaît également la métaphore de l'aigle, ensuite aux v. 19–21, par l'utilisation d'une autre métaphore empruntée au domaine zoologique. En ajoutant *yăʿălē* immédiatement après la mention de l'aigle — verbe qui n'apparaît pas en 48 40 — les rédacteurs ont eu le souci esthétique de souligner le parallèle avec le développement des v. 19–21, qui se voient ainsi introduits de la même manière[34]. Cette métaphore de l'aigle qui s'élance ne se retrouve qu'en Deut 28 49, à propos d'une nation venue contre Israël des extrémités de la terre en vue d'exercer le châtiment. Comme en 48 41b, cette image du destructeur est suivie d'une autre image qui décrit la victime (v. 22b). Elle s'intègre d'autant mieux que cette même dualité s'observe également pour les v. 19–21.

Nous nous trouvons ainsi en présence d'une section constituée à partir d'éléments venus de l'oracle contre Moab et surtout de celui contre Babylone. Tout comme au ch. 7, cette série de doublets se trouve à la fin

---

[33] Ainsi pour les toponymes en 49 20a//50 45a, et en 49 21//50 46. 50 46 a mis l'accent sur la prise de Babylone, et a utilisé de ce fait le vb. *tapăś* (au lieu de *napăl* en 49 21) qui, en Jer, n'est employé dans ce sens qu'en 50 24 et 51 41, toujours au ni. Les autres différences portent principalement sur des modifications de pr. suffixes, de la forme de *ra'ăś* (ni. en 50 46, unique dans l'AT), et l'orthographe de *zᵉʿaqā* (50 46, cf. aussi 51 54), écrit *ṣᵉʿaqā* en 49 21. Cette orthographe vient peut-être de 25 36, où se trouve d'ailleurs aussi l'association avec *qôl* (absente de 50 46). Cf. aussi l'analogie thématique.

[34] Outre les adaptations dues à la différence de destinataire, et notamment la suppression des précisions géographiques de 48 40b.41a, les autres différences concernent le temps du verbe *parăś* (ici à l'impf. en accord avec les deux vb. précédents) et l'emploi de *ʿăl*, au lieu de *ʾel* en 48 40. 48 41b et 49 22b sont identiques et sans parallèles sous cette forme. Par contre, la métaphore elle-même est fréquente. L'association guerrier — parturiente a sans doute conduit à l'insertion, en 49 26, d'une parole venue de 50 30.

de l'oracle. La liaison entre les différents éléments a été en partie imposée par l'existence de séquences fixes. Mais elle est aussi le résultat d'un effort de composition qui a eu pour effet de donner à cette section une structure originale. En empruntant la plupart de ces éléments à l'oracle contre Babylone, les rédacteurs ont voulu souligner une certaine solidarité dans le malheur entre ces deux nations. Toutefois, l'adjonction du v. 22, venu de l'oracle sur Moab, laisse entrevoir que tel n'était pas leur seul but. Ce qui frappe surtout, en effet, est l'accumulation d'éléments appliqués ailleurs à Israël et qui, ici, le sont à Edom, dont la singularité est encore soulignée par l'utilisation à son propos d'une parole qui, en 25 29, l'était à propos de toutes les nations. Edom, qui avait cru pouvoir échapper au sort commun, apparaît ainsi à la fois sur le même plan qu'Israël, subissant les mêmes épreuves que le peuple frère, et sur le même plan que Babylone, l'ennemi d'Israël par excellence, dont il partagera le sort. Cette conclusion de l'oracle fait ainsi l'effet d'un commentaire de la première partie. Son message se rapproche de celui du livre d'Abdias: solidaire de l'ennemi, au lieu de l'être avec Israël, Edom subira le sort des uns et des autres.

De cette rapide enquête on peut dégager les conclusions suivantes:
1) Les doublets ne sont pas répartis uniformément sur l'ensemble du livre de Jérémie[35]. Ils sont principalement concentrés sur les ch. 1–25, soit que les différentes attestations apparaissent dans cette même section, soit qu'on y trouve l'un des éléments d'un doublet dont l'homologue apparaît, à part à peu près égale, dans les sections 26–36 et 46–51. Les doublets à l'intérieur de ces deux dernières sections sont peu fréquents. Ceci pose à la fois le problème de la structure de 1–25 et celui de ses rapports avec le reste du livre.

2) L'insertion dans le contexte a été facilitée par la présence de mots clés, par une analogie thématique ou structurelle, par l'existence de séquences fixes, etc... Mais elle a été, dans la plupart des cas, le résultat d'un choix conscient, et s'est accompagnée d'un effort d'adaptation au contexte, autant sur le plan du contenu que sur celui de la forme. Le lieu même de cette insertion, tout comme d'ailleurs le choix des textes ainsi repris, est étroitement lié aux préoccupations des rédacteurs, et n'est pas le fait du hasard.

3) Les différentes interventions rédactionnelles traduisent un souci d'ordre pastoral. Les rédacteurs se sont adressés à une communauté à laquelle ils ont voulu donner les moyens d'assumer la catastrophe et de continuer à vivre. Ils ont dressé à son intention un catalogue des péchés ayant conduit à cette catastrophe, et en ont souligné certains, afin que, les mêmes causes produisant les mêmes effets, elle ne retombe pas dans des

---

[35] Pour une liste des doublets, cf. S. R. Driver, An Introduction to the Literature of the Old Testament, 1913⁹, 275–277.

errements qui se sont avérés fatals. Ils ont insisté sur l'élément rituel et surtout cultuel, indispensable à l'existence d'une communauté, et ont ainsi complété des textes trop unilatéralement centrés sur l'élément éthique individuel. Ils ont présenté Yahweh comme le maître de l'univers, qui utilise à son gré les nations, et l'ont ainsi désigné comme étant à l'oeuvre derrière l'apparent désordre des événements. Toutes ces interventions rédactionnelles procèdent, en dernier ressort, de la conception de Dieu des rédacteurs. D'une part, Yahweh est pour eux le Dieu d'Israël, qui a établi avec son peuple des relations privilégiées, en sorte que l'histoire universelle ne saurait être qu'israélo-centrique, et que la grâce ne saurait être que le dernier mot de Dieu pour Israël. D'autre part, ils sont convaincus de la continuité dans l'action de Dieu. Le doublet leur a permis d'illustrer cette continuité, et de montrer que le Dieu qui a châtié Israël est le même que celui qui châtie les nations et qui restaure Israël.

Dans ses différents emplois, le doublet nous apparaît ainsi, non comme un accident ou le signe d'une sclérose, mais comme un outil parfaitement adapté à son objet, utilisé pas des rédacteurs chez qui les préoccupations pastorales l'emportent sur le souci de la fidélité historique.

Syntax and style in the Book of Jonah: six simple approaches to their analysis

By Stanislav Segert

(Near Eastern Languages and Cultures, University of California, Los Angeles, California)

A contributor to a volume honoring Georg Fohrer has a wide choice of topics even if he limits himself to those areas of Old Testament studies in which Fohrer himself has been active. Methodology is represented among Fohrer's many publications by a book[1] of small size and great effectiveness, pluralistic in more than one respect: four former pupils joined their master to produce an introduction to the methodology of Old Testament exegesis. While the authors expressed their own views – the chapter on linguistic analysis was written by G. Wanke[2] – this team has succeeded in producing a tool for study, which is consistent and in its deep structure considerably unified. Even though the contributors have drawn from many and various sources, the result is not an eclectic mixture, but rather a pluralistic combination of approaches, some long proven, some waiting to be put into full use with the expectation of meaningful results.

The present contributor brings a few low-key approaches which may add to this pluralistic perspective. They were tested in a course[3] devoted to the Book of Jonah, a book which is admittedly the least typical of all the prophetic books. Its narrative has its closest counterpart in the Book of Ruth, while the Psalm of Jonah (2 3–10) consists of quotations from and imitations of older psalms. The juxtaposition of both narrative and poetic styles in the Book of Jonah offers an opportunity to analyze and characterize their contrasting features[4].

---

[1] G. Fohrer – H. W. Hoffmann – F. Huber – L. Markert – G. Wanke, Exegese des Alten Testaments. Einführung in die Methodik. First edition 1973, second revised edition 1976.
[2] 57–81.
[3] In a graduate course »Studies in Hebrew Biblical Literature« the active participation of students was enhanced by applying these simple new approaches. Mrs. Shoshana Berk and Mr. Stephen Reimer deserve to be mentioned for submitting papers in which they follow up some suggestions.
[4] In the following, the bibliographical references are limited to those indicating direct sources.

0. Preliminary remarks

Attempts to introduce new approaches seem to be characteristic of the present state of Old Testament studies. While at the beginning of the modern period biblical scholars were able to introduce methods then generally accepted, the ever-increasing specialization of linguistic and literary disciplines does not limit scholars working in individual literatures in their attempts to invent and develop new methods. More and more they have to rely on methods developed by researchers in other fields. This is not necessarily a disadvantage for students of the Bible; they become more open to approaches and trends in the study of other literatures, and thus better able to relate to other disciplines and cultures.

Some of the new methods offered for consideration in the study of biblical texts are presented as exclusive; their proponents claim that they will replace the imperfect and atomistic approaches of the past. It can perhaps be said that such claims to exclusiveness foretell a new method for failure. The usefulness of a new approach is greater the more it can be integrated with reliable and proven methods used hitherto.

Some of the new approaches are based on a sophisticated and complicated analytical apparatus. The demanding prerequisites for these approaches make their use difficult for students interested in their application to texts rather than in their theory.

There are many competing methods which demand attention from students of the Bible. Some are based exclusively on analysis of modern languages and literatures; as a whole they are not suitable for the study of a limited corpus of ancient texts, but many of their methodological devices can be used, some with adjustment, for biblical literature.

At present, methods using quantification are becoming increasingly refined, and their use requires increasingly technical skills[5]. On the other hand, in something of a reaction, whether intentional or unintentional, there are new approaches in which the personality of the researcher and his subjective views play a considerable role. Among these different approaches some methods are offered which lead to results not depending on subjective impressions, and, at the same time, their translation of the reality of the text would lead to exact but rather abstract formulas and schemes[6].

---

[5] Because of the small numbers appearing here, it seems that the application of statistical methods is not necessary.

[6] Even general linguists here and there feel the difficulties of too complicated methods, cf. R. P. Stockwell, Foundations of syntactic theory, 1977, xv–xvi.

1. Dependency syntax: Graphical presentation

The approach to a given ancient text is in principle cognitive. The generative method may be used only in reconstructing or emending a passage of text.

Dependency syntax has an advantage in its unequivocal determination of syntactic relations between the parts of a sentence. The mutual dependency between the constituents — subject and predicate —, the simple dependency of the components of these constituents or other components, and even double dependency of the complement, both to the verb and to the object or the subject, can be clearly indicated.

In modern syntactic literature the relations between parts of the sentence are frequently represented by the tree diagram[7]: the governing word is at the top, and the other parts are connected to it as branches. This method of presentation may be useful for isolated examples that serve to substantiate some theoretical points, but its use for syntactical analysis of connected texts would be cumbersome.

The presentation of each sentence on a separate line is more practical, but even this device does not show the relations between parts of the sentence clearly enough.

A very simple and effective graphical representation of dependency syntax is that introduced by Professor V. Šmilauer, which can be adapted to any language[8].

The individual words are written — preferably in transliteration — each on a separate line; prepositions, conjunctions and suffixed pronouns have to be indicated separately. The characteristics of the clause and its parts are presented in six columns. Those words which indicate the character of the clause, mostly conjunctions, are listed in the first column; the type of the clause may be indicated here too. In the second column the subject is characterized; in the third, the predicate. The fourth column is reserved for the direct object, while other adverbial components are indicated in the fifth column. In the sixth column can be listed all the adnominal components: apposition, adjectival and genitival attribute, and complement to the subject (predicative) or the object. Any necessary or useful morphological characteristics of a sentence part can be given: determination, number and gender for nouns, person, number, gender, mode and pattern for verbs.

---

[7] Cf. J. Lyons, Introduction to Theoretical Linguistics, 1969, 163. 167. 211. 219.

[8] This device is explained in the first edition of the book about the syntax of Modern Czech, Novočeská skladba, 1947. The second edition of 1966 does not contain this appendix. The author would like to thank Professor V. Šmilauer for his advice given in the early fifties.

This graphical representation gives at first glance a good picture of the word order and of certain repetitive features, such as those in the parallel cola in older Hebrew poetry. The delimitation of clauses and sentences follows their analysis. There is enough space to introduce other characteristics which may then be used for observation of other syntactic features and for stylistic analysis. The columnar arrangement provides a convenient basis for the quantitative analysis of syntactic phenomena.

Jon 1 4	Clause	Subject	Predicate	Object	Adverbials	Adnominals
wă	w-					
Yhwh		DN.				
hēṭîl	state-ment		perf. 3s.m. Hi.	N.		
rûăḥ				N(oun) f.		
gᵉdôlā						ATTRIBUTE Adj. f.
ʾæl					ʾl	
hăyyam					N det.	
Jon 2 8						
wăt-	w-					
tabôʾ			imperf. cons. 3s.f.			
ʾel-					ʾl	
-ékā					2s.m.	
tᵉpillat-		N-				
-î						ATTRIBUTE 1s.

2. Length of clauses

This very simple quantitative indicator can be used to single out clauses that are either too short or too long, and that therefore deserving special attention. The average length of clauses in a given section does not by itself give useful information, but when the average clause length in a certain section is compared with that in other sections, meaningful results can be obtained[9].

It would be possible to rectify the raw numbers by the exclusion of some elements, such as co-ordinating conjunctions, but the results would not be significantly affected.

In the narrative sections of ch. 1, 3 and 4 of the Book of Jonah the clause length varies between 2 and 11 words, in the direct speeches within

---

[9] V. Mathesius, Větné základy epického stylu v Zeyerově Kronice o sv. Brandanu, Slovo a slovesnost 8 (1942), 80—88.

these narratives between 1 and 15 words. No particular difference between these types of discourse can therefore be observed.

One particular clause in Jon 4 2, »you are the God ...«, consists of no less than 15 components. It can be characterized as a quotation of a previously fixed religious formula.

The numbers for the average length of a clause do not differ too much between narrrative sections and direct speech. No significant variance between ch. 1 and ch. 3 and 4 can be observed. The average length of clauses in ch. 1 and in ch. 3—4 is 6.2 and 4.6 words respectively, in the direct speeches 5.6 words and 5.0 words respectively.

For comparison another biblical book of similar length and similar literary character, the Book of Ruth, may be used[10]. The numbers indicating the length of narrative clauses in chapter 1 do not differ considerably. The clauses in direct speeches are only slightly shorter (4.7 words) than those in the narratives (5.45 words), while in the Book of Jonah the clauses in the direct speeches are, on the average, slightly longer.

This criterion of clause length may be applied to the poetic passages. Their prosodical patterns, however, have to be taken into consideration.

The Psalm of Jonah (2 3–10) follows an asymmetrical pattern ($q\hat{\imath}n\bar{a}$ verse). In this type of verse, the proportion of the first colon to the second may be expressed in terms of the accentuation prosody as 3:2, in terms of the alternation prosody as 4:3.

It could therefore be expected that a similar proportion would appear in the count of the words in clauses. This is true only in a limited number of verses (lines): 3b.4a(!).6a, cf. also 7c. In other verses the boundaries between clauses do not coincide with the caesurae between the two asymmetric cola: 3a.5a.7b. In several verses the boundaries of the clauses coincide with those of the verse; two subsequent cola together form one clause: 4b.5b.6b+7a(?).8a (with an infinitival construction). 8b.9.10a.

These various relations between the cola and the clauses may be counted and used for a quantitative specification of poetic techniques and styles. The number of words in clauses in Jon 2 3–10 varies between 2 and 7 in clauses coinciding with cola, and between 6 and 10 in clauses coinciding with verses (lines). The average length is 3.5 and 8.5 words respectively. The average for the entire poem is 5 words in a clause.

Considerably different results will appear in counting words in the clauses in Lamentations. The same $q\hat{\imath}n\bar{a}$ verse is used, but in the majority of the verses chapter 1 the clauses coincide with the verses (lines).

The asymmetric versification in the Psalm of Jonah may be compared to the poem which could be considered the most consistent representative of parallelistic poetry in the Hebrew Bible, Ps 29. With only three excep-

---

[10] Cf. F. I. Andersen – A. D. Forbes, A Linguistic Concordance of Ruth and Jonah: Hebrew Vocabulary and Idiom (The Computer Bible vol. IX), 1976.

tions its cola coincide with the clauses. The number of words in individual clauses varies within narrower limits, while the average length of a clause is also 5 words. In clauses coinciding with cola, the number of words varies between 3 and 7. There are 9 clauses with 4 words, and 6 clauses with 6 words.

3. Word categories

A tally of words according to their categories[11] can be made quite easily from the charts prepared for the syntactic analysis, as described above in section 1.

While there is no significant difference in the total numbers of words within clauses between narratives and direct speech in the Book of Jonah, the frequency of word categories differs considerably.

The relative number of nouns is about 25 percent in both ch. 1 and ch. 3 and 4. The same percentage appears in the passages in direct speech in ch. 3–4, while in direct speech of chapter 1 the nouns account for only 15 percent of the words. A significant difference may be seen in the frequency of pronouns: only 8 percent and 6 percent in the narratives; 30 percent and 18 percent in direct speech. Verbs are more frequent in the narrative sections: 24 percent throughout; less frequent in direct speech: 20 percent and 17 percent. The percentage of prepositions does not differ considerably: 18 percent throughout the narrative sections, 19 and 15 percent in direct speech. But the frequency of conjunctions is considerably higher in the narrative sections – 20 percent and 18 percent – than in the passages in direct speech – 10 percent and 12 percent, for ch. 1 and 3–4 respectively. Interjections occur only in direct speech.

More significant than the differences between narratives and passages in direct speech are those between prose and poetry, and even those between different types of poetry.

The proportion of nouns is higher in the Psalm of Jonah, about 30 percent, and it exceeds 50 percent in the parallelistic Ps 29. There are a few adjectives in the prose section of the Book of Jonah, none in the Psalm of Jonah, and only one in Ps 29. The percentage of pronouns – 22 percent – in the Psalm of Jonah is similar to that in the passages in direct speech in this book, but the frequency of pronouns in Ps 29 is much lower than in even the narratives passages of Jonah, only 3 percent. In indirect proportion to the nouns the verbs are less frequent in the poetry: only 20 percent in the Psalm of Jonah, and only 15 percent in Ps 29. There are few adverbs in the prose section of the Book of Jonah, mostly in direct speeches, but none in either of the poems. The frequency of prepositions

---

[11] Cf. n. 9.

appears more or less constant in all the different sorts of texts analyzed here: 19 percent in the Psalm of Jonah, 15 percent in Ps 29. But the frequency of conjunctions varies with the type of text: it is higher in narrative, lower in direct speech, and lowest in poetry — only 8 percent in both the poetic texts.

4. Semantic areas

A simple count can show how many words within a category or an area appear only once and how many are repeated. The proportion between the number of words in a given section and the number of different lexical items can give an idea of the variety or monotony of a given text.

In Ps 29 only 29 different lexical items are represented among the 63 nouns, while in the Psalm of Jonah there are no less than 32 different lexical items among 38 nouns. The poetry shows the greatest extremes here, while the prose passages of the Book of Jonah come in between. Only one adjective is used in all of the four occurrences of this category in Jonah 1: *rāb* »great«, which is also disproportionately frequent in the other prosaic sections. The variety of verbs is considerably higher. This kind of approach probably does not give significant results for prepositions and conjunctions. Quite obvious is the overwhelming frequency of the coordinating conjunction *w-* »and«.

More instructive is the proportion of words from different semantic areas[12]. The words for god and his names constitute about 8 percent of all words in Ps 29; they reach about 5 percent in the Psalm of Jonah and in the narrative in ch. 3 and 4. Different words for men attain about 7 percent in the narrative of ch. 1. There is no word of this area in the Psalm of Jonah, but of comparable function are the nouns indicating different parts of the human body — 8 percent of all words. Nouns that depict nature exceed 10 percent in both poems analyzed here, while the percentage of man-made objects is much higher in the prose of Jonah. Interestingly enough, the text with the highest percentage — about 16 percent — of abstract terms is Ps 29. It would be possible to make similar counts of different kinds of verbs, such as verbs of perception, sound, movement, feeling, etc.

The number and frequency for proper names in the Book of Jonah is significantly different from these parameters in the Book of Ruth. Only one person is given his proper name in the Book of Jonah, Jonah himself, 18 times, and once (1 1) the name of his father is mentioned. In the Book of Ruth, even if names in the genealogical appendix and those used for comparison are omitted, names of 8 persons appear together in 69 occur-

---

[12] The term »area« is used here for a broader complex than »semantic field«.

rences. The number and frequency of geographical names of places is relatively higher in the Book of Jonah: Joppa is mentioned once, Tarshish three times, and Nineveh nine times[13].

A difference between a fictitious narrative and a narrative based on historical tradition is reflected by these numbers.

5. Functional sentence perspective and related approaches

The basic idea of what is called in English functional sentence perspective was put forward by V. Mathesius[14] in 1939: It is possible to distinguish in a sentence what is previously known and what is new, or the point of departure and the kernel of the utterance. These parts, called theme and rheme, do not necessarily coincide with the formal division into subject and predicate[15].

The advantage of this approach can be seen if what precedes and what follows a sentence is taken into consideration[16]. Traditional syntactic analysis, limited to the sentence, is supplemented by the study of both the connections between sentences and the formation of longer units.

In difference to the previously mentioned approaches, no ready-to-use devices are available. In the following, the seminal ideas are indicated, and some attempts to apply them to the syntactic and stylistic analysis of Hebrew Biblical texts are reported.

In the narratives of the Book of Jonah, the clauses and sentences follow each other in straightforward manner. Nearly every clause brings a new information as the action proceeds. There is only one clause that interrupts this sequence which brings only a necessary description or explanation of the site of the city of Nineveh (Jon 3 6). Even the direct speeches serve the same purpose. It can be said that whithin the sentences of this straightforward narrative, the proportion of information previously known to the new information is very low.

Functional sentence perspective may bring more useful results in analysis of direct speeches by relating questions and answers.

---

[13] Cf. n. 10.
[14] V. Mathesius, O tak zvaném aktuálním členění věty, Slovo a slovesnost 5 (1939), 171–174.
[15] Cf. F. Daneš, A three-level approach to syntax, Travaux linguistiques de Prague 1 (1964) 225–240; J. Firbas, On defining the theme in functional sentence analysis, ib., 267–280; Z. Tyl, Materiály k bibliografii prací o aktuálním členění větném 1900–1970, 1970; F. Daneš, ed., Papers on functional sentence perspective, 1974.
[16] This aspect is developed in »text linguistics«; cf. W. Dressler, Einführung in die Textlingustik, 1972; B. G. Mortara, Aspetti e problemi della linguistica testuale, 1974.

Some ideas of the functional sentence perspective may be applied to poetry analysis. Here the proportion and relation between previously known and the new information appears significant in the analysis of the parallelistic features. In the most rigorous type of this poetry, the first colon in a complete clause gives some information — either new or known from the previous context — while the second colon repeats the information of the first, using the same syntactic construction and synonyms of the words. It is possible to count the occurences of such relations and to indicate their proportion to the entire length of a given poem. It is obvious that Ps 29 has a much higher proportion of this type of verses and sentences than the Psalm of Jonah.

In Ps 29 only v. 7 and 9a do not fit into parallelistic structure; this may be result of later interference. In the Psalm of Jonah only v. 3 can be considered as strictly parallelistic, while the parallelistic structure in v. 4 and 6–7a is looser. In v. 7bc and 9–10a a very loose parallelism may be seen. Vv. 5. 10b — and perhaps 8 — are not parallelistic.

The numbers would be 10:2 for Ps 29, indicating the proportion between parallelistic and non-parallelistic verses (lines). Comparable proportion for the Psalm of Jonah does not appear so clearly: 1 (+2 +2?): 2 (+1?). The difference between the two types of verses is obvious.

Another measurable concept may then be introduced, that the redundance. Those expressions which do not convey any new information, but only repeat the known in synonymous words, can be considered as redundant. In a strictly parallelistic poem the redundance, if we consider only the relations within verses or bicola, can reach 50 percent. Any lower number indicates a less rigorous parallelistic structure. An asymmetrical prosodic pattern will obviously lower the percentage of redundant expressions.

6. Narrative worlds

For a narrative like that in the Book of Jonah it is easy to apply some patterns known from the previous study of narratives. Especially the concept of equilibrium, its violation and its restitution, can be used.

The normal conditions are violated by the sinful behavior of the citizens of Nineveh. As a remedy, Jonah is sent there. As a remedy for his disobedience, the storm, the sailors and the big fish help to direct him to the right destination.

A useful approach may be that of different narrative worlds, as introduced by L. Doležel[17], on the basis of recent studies of modal logics[18].

---

[17] L. Doležel, Narrative Worlds, ed. L. Matejka, Sound, Sign and Meaning: Quinquagenary of the Prague Linguistic Circle, 1976, 542–552.
[18] L. Doležel refers to studies by G. H. von Wright and by J. Hintikka.

The concept of the alethic world is characterized by »classical« modality with categories of possibility, impossibility and necessity.

In the deontic world the categories are permission, prohibition, obligation, while those of the axiological world are goodness, badness, indifference. The fourth model, the epistemic world, deals with the categories of knowledge, ignorance, and belief.

For the narrative of the Book of Jonah the question of reality has been posed very often and very clearly. The human characters act within the limits of reality, while the big fish and the plant, usually characterized as a ricinus, act in terms not coincident with the everyday reality.

A strict application of the concept of possibility and impossibility apparently does not give a satisfactory solution, while the introduction of deontic and axiological models can lead to better understanding.

Jonah disobeyed God's command, and therefore a quite extraordinary vehicle was used to bring him closer to his destination. After Jonah misplaced his values, preferring his personal pride to the lives of thousands of innocent beings, his attitude was shown to be wrong by the rapidly growing plant which was destroyed by a worm. The following speeches by God himself only explained this.

It can be clearly seen that what appears as unreal serves the deontic and axiological purposes of the narrative.

It would be possible to adduce again the Book of Ruth, here for contrast: Everything in this book corresponds to reality as known and experienced in those times[19].

---

[19] For the improvements of English syntax and style the author is obliged to his daughter Eva and to his son Jan, both undergraduate students at U.C.L.A.

Hosea und die Außenpolitik Israels

Von J. A. Soggin

(Via Pietro Cossa 42, Roma)

1. *Die Nachwehen des syro-ephraimitischen Krieges, Hos 5 12–14 und 8 7–10.*

5 12 Aber ich werde* für Israel zum Wundbrand*,
    für das Haus Juda zum Knochenzerfall*!
13 Israel hat freilich seine Krankheit gespürt,
    und Juda sein Siechtum:
    So ist Israel nach Assur gezogen,
    Juda hat dem Großkönig* Boten gesandt.
    Doch dieser kann euch nicht pflegen,
    jener eure Wunden nicht heilen!
14 Ja, für Ephraim werde ich zum Löwen,
    für das Haus Juda werde ich zum Jungleu:
    Ich zerreiße und reiße aus,
    ich verschleppe, und niemand kann mich daran hindern!

8 7 Gewiß: Wer Wind sät, wird Sturm ernten.
    Getreidehalm, der nicht sproßt,
    der keine Frucht hervorbringt.
    Und wo er zufällig doch etwas hervorbrächte,
    werden Fremde den Ertrag aufessen.
8 Israel wird verschlungen,
    er steht jetzt unter den Völkern
    wie ein wertloser Topf!
9 . . . .
10 . . . .

V. 12: ʿāš I ist die »Motte«, ʿāš II die »Fäulnis«, u. a. als Folge einer eiternden Wunde, eines Wundbrandes, einer Infektion[1]. Die letzte scheint also die beste Übersetzung, wenn auch dagegen Th. H. Robinson, G.

---

[1] G. R. Driver, Difficult Words in the Hebrew Prophets, in: Studies in Old Testament Prophecy ... Th. H. Robinson, 1950, 52–72: 66f., angenommen von KB² und von manchen Kommentaren.

Rinaldi, E. Osty[2], G. von Rad, H. Donner und É. Jacob[3] ʿašī lesen möchten. *raqab* ist sowohl »Holzwurm« als auch »Karies«, »Krebs«. Diese zweite Bedeutung ist wohl die beste, besonders wenn wir im Vorherigen »Wundbrand« übersetzen, gegen die Anm. 2–3 genannten Autoren. Ich schreibe also »Knochenzerfall«. Es ist bekanntlich immer schwer, die Symptome der biblischen Krankheiten durch moderne medizinische Begriffe zu erklären; dies war wohl auch nicht die Absicht des alten Schriftstellers.

Im *v. 13* ist vielleicht, wie anderswo im Text, »das Haus Juda« zu lesen. Der Sinn des Textes wird dadurch nicht verändert. »Dem Großkönig«: wie 10 6, hebr. buchstäblich »dem König Jareb«, was allgemein, mit der Ausnahme von G. Rinaldi, als sinnlos empfunden wird. Die meisten nehmen die 1897 vorgeschlagene Korrektur in מלכי רב an, also mit einem jod compaginis[4], doch ist diese den konsonantischen Text respektierende Konjektur vielleicht gar nicht nötig: G. R. Driver seinerzeit, heute gefolgt von W. Rudolph[5], faßt *jareb* als Adjektiv aus der aramäischen Wurzel *jrb*, »groß sein« auf, was den gleichen Sinn bietet.

Die *v. 7–10* bilden eine schwierige, z. T. unverständliche Stelle; eine Rekonstruktion versucht zuletzt W. Rudolph. Der Sinn des v. 7 ist klar: es werden dort zwei Sprichwörter, das erste vollständig, das zweite unvollständig, zitiert und auf das Volk angewandt.

Einige Autoren[6] möchten die beiden Texte in der Zeit des von Menahem an Tiglat-Pileser III. gebrachten Tributs, also um 738, datieren, vgl. II Reg 15 19 und ANET[3] 283a, DOTT 54f., TGI[2] 55f. und VSBN 166, aber die beste Erklärung bleibt immer noch die von A. Alt, neuerdings gefolgt von L. Rost[7]: Israel und Juda stehen hier nicht mehr im Gegensatz zueinander, sondern sind nun Leidensgenossen; dies kann nicht vor dem Ende des syro-ephraimischen Krieges, sondern nur gegen dessen Ende oder kurz danach geschehen sein, als die beiden Staaten die Folgen einer verlorenen Krieges zu tragen hatten. »Juda« gehört also zum Text

---

[2] Th. H. Robinson – F. Horst, Die zwölf kleinen Propheten, HAT I, 14, 1954[2] (1964[3]); G. Rinaldi, I Profeti minori I, 1953, und É. Osty, Amos – Osée, BJ, 1960[2].

[3] G. von Rad, Theologie des Alten Testaments, II, 1965[2], 150; H. Donner, Israel unter den Völkern, 1964, 50f., und É. Jacob, Prophètes et politique, in: Parole et société 80 (1972), 3–19.

[4] R. Meyer § 45, 3. e.

[5] G. R Driver, Studies in the Vocabulary of the Old Testament. VIII, JThS 36 (1935), 293–301: 295f., und W. Rudolph, Hosea, KAT XIII,1, 1966, z. St.

[6] Th. H. Robinson, G. Rinaldi und E. Osty a. a. O. (Anm. 2).

[7] A. Alt, Hosea 5,8–6,6. Ein Krieg und seine Folgen in prophetischer Beleuchtung, 1919, in: Kl. Schr., II 1953, 163–181: 181ff.; H. Donner a. a. O. (Anm. 3) 51f. und L. Rost, Das Problem der Weltmacht in der alttestamentlichen Prophetie, TLZ 90 (1965), 241–250, Studien zum Alten Testament, 1974, 76–86; dagegen, m. E. nicht überzeugend, E. M. Good, Hosea 5 8–6 6: An Alternative to Alt, JBL 85 (1966), 273–286.

und ist kein späterer Einschub[8]. Auch Damaskus ist inzwischen gefallen, und von der anti-assyrischen Koalition bleibt nichts mehr übrig. Es ist ferner die Zeit, als Hosea, der Sohn des Ela, sich gegen Pekah, den »Sohn des Remaljahu« (Jes 7 4 8 6 usw.) verschwor, ihn tötete und die Macht an sich riß, worauf er sofort einen pro-assyrischen politischen Kurs einschlug, vgl. II Reg 15 30 und ANET^3 284a, DOTT 55, TGI^2 58f., VSBN 168f. Die assyrischen Annalen heben die Einsetzung Hoseas durch den Assyrerkönig hervor, wenn sie auch sonst die These vertreten, daß es »alle Einwohner ... des Hauses ʿOmrî« gewesen seien, weche Pekah »stürzten«[9].

Während also Juda im syro-ephraimitischen Krieg mehr oder weniger spontan, doch gewiß als souveräner Staat, entschieden hatte, sich der assyrischen Herrschaft zu unterwerfen, wenn auch gegen den Rat Jesajas, vgl. Jes 7 1ff.[10], mußte Israel, nach dem Fall von Damaskus und dem Auseinanderfallen der Koalition, sich nunmehr beeilen, dasselbe zu tun, wenn auch unter viel ungünstigeren Umständen, welche durch einen unmittelbaren Eingriff in seine Innenpolitik bedingt waren, also kaum noch als vollkommen souveräner Staat.

Gegen diese Unterwerfung richtet sich nun der Protest Hoseas, indem er dem Volk verkündet, sie sei ein ungenügendes Heilmittel gegen eine tödliche Krankheit. »Wundbrand« und »Knochenzerfall« sind, wie gesehen, in der biblischen Sprache Umschreibung tödlicher Krankheiten, bei denen keine Linderungsmittel helfen können: man mußte zuerst bis zu den Wurzeln des Übels vordringen, um es einmal genau zu diagnostizieren, um so mehr als sein Hauptgrund im strafenden Eingreifen Jhwhs lag. Doch gerade die Unterwerfung unter die Assyrer war so ein Linderungsmittel, das die Ursache im Dunkeln ließ!

Während bei Jesaja die Unterwerfung unter Assur als Abfall vom Glauben verurteilt wird[11], ja geradezu als negative Alternative zum Glauben erscheint, stellt Hosea die Lage anders dar: Es handelt sich um eine Fehldiagnose, auf die falsche Heilmittel folgen, die mit dem Ernst der Lage in keinem Zusammenhang stehen. Und während Jesaja eine theologische und politische Alternative vorschlägt: glauben, sich also nicht unterwerfen, beschränkt sich Hosea auf die Diagnose: Der Spielraum für politische Optionen war ja auch gering, wenn überhaupt vorhanden, angesichts des unmittelbaren Eingreifens Assurs in die inneren Angelegenheiten Israels.

---

[8] So richtig W. Rudolph.
[9] Vgl. E. Vogt, Die Texte Tiglat Pileser III. über die Eroberung Palästinas, Biblica 45 (1964), 348–354: 348f.
[10] Zu diesem Thema vgl. jüngstens die ausgezeichnete Studie von W. Dietrich, Jesaja und die Politik, 1976, 60–99 und passim im 3. Teil.
[11] W. Dietrich a.a.O.

Deswegen ist die von Gericht Jhwhs herbeigeführte Krankheit auch tödlich. Doch das Volk ist verantwortlich dafür, daß es soweit gekommen ist und daß man nicht einmal versucht, an die Wurzeln des Übels heranzugelangen!

2. Die letzten Jahre des Reiches Israel, 7 8–12, 11 5–6 und 12 2.

7 8   Ja, Ephraim hat sich unter die Völker gemischt*
      Israel wurde wie ein Fladen,
      den man im Ofen nicht umgekehrt hat.

9   Fremde haben seine Macht verzehrt,
    ohne daß er es wußte;
    grau wurde sein Haar,
    ohne daß er es merkte*!

10   Israels Herrlichkeit* wurde vor seinen Augen gedemütigt,
     doch zu Jhwh, seinem Gott, kehrte er nicht zurück,
     ungeachtet dessen hat er mich nicht gesucht.

11   Ephraim hat sich wie eine Taube benommen:
     leicht zu hintergehen, ohne Gedanken;
     er hat Ägypten angerufen,
     ist nach Assur gezogen
     . . . .(?).

11 5   Er wird* nach Ägypten zurückkehren müssen,
      Assur wird sein Herr sein,
      weil er sich weigerte, umzukehren.

6   Das Schwert wird seine Städte entleeren,
    seine Söhne ausrotten
    . . . .

12 2   Ephraim nährt sich von Luft,
      folgt dem Ostwind nach,
      hört nicht auf, Lügen und Gewalt zu mehren.
      Mit Assur schließt er ein Bündnis,
      nach Ägypten bringt er Öl.

Die v. 8–9 sind nicht leicht. *bll* heißt »den (Brot-)Teig mischen« bzw. »kneten«, kann aber im Akkadischen auch für die Völkermischung gebraucht werden, die aus den Deportationen hervorging[12], wenn auch dieser letzte Sinn nicht häufig ist. Es wäre in Betracht zu ziehen, daß Hosea diese Wurzel (anstatt der häufigeren, auch im Ugaritischen und im Akkadischen belegte Wurzel *lwš*) verwendet, indem er auf ihrem Doppel-

---
[12] W. von Soden, AHw I, 97f.

sinn ein Wortspiel aufbaut[13]. Der größte Teil des Reiches Israel ist ja schon besetzt und seine Bevölkerung z. T. deportiert, und dasselbe Los steht dem kleinen Überbleibsel bevor. Die Metapher des nicht umgekehrten Fladens ist von den Kommentaren verschieden gedeutet worden. S. M. Paul[14] denkt an die Unschlüssigkeit, in der sich die Führung des Landes befand. Mir scheint es aber besser, bei dem Bild des Fladens zu bleiben: auf der einen Seite verbrannt, auf der anderen ungebacken – ein gutes Bild für die prekäre Lage des Landes, zu deren Abhilfe angeblich immer zuviel oder zuwenig getan wurde. »Ohne daß er es merkte«: zrq_{II}, ein Hápax, darf auf Grund des Parallelismus so übersetzt werden.

Der *v. 10* dürfte ein homiletisch-katechetischer Zusatz sein, könnte aber auch vom Propheten selbst herrühren. Eine Diskussion des Problems bei H. Donner[15]. »Herrlichkeit«: nach S. M. Paul[16], nach welchem, ferner, am Ende des v. 11 eine Zeile ausgefallen ist.

Im *v. 5* wird das *loʾ* am Anfang meistens gestrichen: Der Text redet nämlich vom Exil und nicht davon, daß Israel nicht in das Exil gehen soll. LXX hat *lô* (αὐτῷ) gelesen, und zu v. 4 gerechnet; so neuerdings noch W. Rudolph und BHS. Die Möglichkeit, daß es sich um ein Lamed emphaticum handle, muß aber ernsthaft in Betracht gezogen werden[17]. Wir müßten dann übersetzen: »Gewiß, Ephraim wird . . .«.

V. 2: »Hört nicht auf . . .«: wohl wiederum ein homilitisch-kathechetischer Zusatz. Der Zusammenhang redet von internationalen Bündnissen, welche so helfen können wie die Luft zur Nahrung dient. ». . . Bringt es Öl«: Man liest meistens *jôbilû* (hif.) für *jûbal* (hof.), vgl. BHS und die Kommentare. »Öl bringen« steht im Alten Orient oft für das Schließen von Bündnissen[18]. Und dies versucht Israel sowohl mit Assur als auch mit Ägypten, in der Hoffnung, sich auf diese Art gegen beide, ohne daß sie das Doppelspiel bemerken, absichern zu können. Der Pro-

---

[13] Vgl. S. M. Paul, The Image of the Oven and the Cake in Hosea VII 4–10, VT 18 (1968), 114–120.
[14] A. a. O.
[15] H. Donner a. a. O. (Anm. 3) 78f.
[16] A. a. O.
[17] Vgl. meine kurze Wortstudie in BeO 9 (1967), 42f., jetzt englisch in: Old Testament and Oriental Studies, 1975, 223; siehe aber schon H.-W. Wolff, Dodekapropheton I, BK XIV, 1, 1962², z. St. (»beteuerndes לא«).
[18] Vgl. D. J. McCarthy, Hosea XII 2, Covenant by Oil, VT 14 (1964), 215–221, und neuerdings ders., Treaty and Covenant, 1978², 287, und K.-H. Deller, *Šmn bll* (Hosea 12,2), Biblica 46 (1965), 349–352; vgl. ferner L. Perlitt, Bundestheologie im Alten Testament, 1969, 140 und 143. Es ist für unseren Gegenstand unerheblich, ob wir traditionell mit »Bund« bzw. »Bündnis«, oder mit »Verpflichtung« und dergleichen übersetzen, vgl. E. Kutsch, Verheißung und Gesetz, 1973, 59 und passim. K.-H. Deller und D. J. McCarthy heben mit Recht, gegen W. Rudolph a. a. O. 266 Anm. 11, das außenpolitische Doppelspiel Israels hervor.

phet betrachtet eine solche Handlungsweise als ein noch schlimmeres Vergehen als ein Bündnis nur mit Assur, denn hier haben wir auch noch Doppelzüngigkeit und Betrug. Israel glaubt sich schlau, ist aber nur naiv wie eine Taube, 7 11; es reißt sich dadurch zugleich vom Jahwebund los: Anstatt unter dem Königtum Gottes, muß es nun unter demjenigen Assurs stehen, 7 11 und 12 2; es geht in der Verwirrung der Völker unter, ohne dabei etwas zu erreichen, 7 8.

Wie Jesaja sieht also Hosea die menschliche Initiative, hier konkret die Sicherstellung des Volkes durch internationale Verträge, als überfordert: Man verlangt von ihr, was sie nicht im Stande ist zu bieten: Sicherheit und Heil. Dies kann Israel nur von seinem Gott erhalten.

Die Texte lassen sich darum ohne Schwierigkeit in den letzten Jahren des Reiches Israel unterbringen, als seine Herrscher die äußersten, doch immer noch ungenügenden Mittel anwandten, um das Land vor seinem Untergang zu retten.

3. Schlußwort

Die Knappheit der Texte Hoseas, die von der Außenpolitik des Landes reden, und ihre prekäre textkritische Lage bilden die Schranke, die der Forscher nicht ungestraft überschreiten kann. Folgendes dürfen wir aber feststellen:

a) Hoseas Kritik an Israels Außenpolitik bietet, wie gesehen, weder eine theologische noch eine politische Alternative, wie dies z. B. bei Jesaja und Jeremia der Fall ist. Das könnte ein Zeichen dafür sein, daß der ganze Gedanke bei Hosea nicht genügend entwickelt ist. Doch, wie erwähnt, könnte es freilich auch zutreffen, daß der Prophet eine solche Alternative nicht sah, weil es sie tatsächlich nicht gab: Das würde übrigens gut zum Thema der *tödlichen* Krankheit passen. Andererseits scheint er doch an die Möglichkeit einer Heilung von dieser Krankheit geglaubt zu haben, wenn nicht durch menschliches Streben, dann durch Jhwhs Hilfe, vgl. 11 8–9 und 3 4–5.

b) Hosea verwirft die Bündnispolitik Israels und ist besonders scharf, wenn sie die unredlichen Züge eines Doppelspiels annimmt. Das Gottesvolk wird nicht durch menschliche Verträge und ähnliche Maßnahmen dem Gericht entgehen, denn das Gericht droht nicht von Menschen, sondern von Jhwh selber, wenn auch durch menschliche Täter. Linderungsmittel können hier also nicht helfen, und Bündnisse sind nicht viel mehr. Nur die Auseinandersetzung mit den Tatsachen und die darauffolgende Umkehr[19] bilden, vielleicht, eine letzte Möglichkeit für das Volk.

---

[19] H.-W. Wolff, Das Thema »Umkehr« in der alttestamentlichen Prophetie, ZThK 48 (1951), 129–148, in: Ges. Stud., 1973², 130–150: 141.142f., und der verehrte Jubilar, Umkehr und Erlösung beim Propheten Hosea, in: Studien zur alttestamentlichen Prophetie, 1967, 222–241.

Der Name des Propheten Amos und sein sprachlicher Hintergrund

Von Johann Jakob Stamm

(Neßlerenweg 16, Wabern bei Bern)

1

ʿamôs findet sich im Alten Testament nur als Name des Propheten (Am 1 1 7 8. 10–12 8 2)[1]. Es ist ein mit dem Verb ʿamǎs gebildeter Kurzname[2] nach dem Typus *qatul* (BL 466n^III). Weitere Kurznamen, die zugehören, sind *ᵃmaśá* und *ᵃmaśǎj*[3]. Der entsprechende Vollname ist *ᵃmǎsjā*. Wie ʿamôs ist auch dieser nur durch *einen* Träger im Alten Testament vertreten, einen Heerführer (*śǎr*) unter Josaphat (II Chr 17 16). Außerhalb des Alten Testaments hat *ᵃmǎsjā* sein Gegenstück in ʿmsʾl, einem Namen auf einem Siegel aus Ammān[4].

Einen mit der Wurzel ʿms gebildeten Satznamen kennt bereits das Amoritische mit *Ja-aḫ-mu-us-AN* = *Jaḫmus-Il/El* (Huffmon 198)[5]. Aus dem Ugaritischen ist der PN ʿms anzufügen, der in einer Liste von Leuten aus *Uškn* begegnet[6]. Diese sind alle als *bn* X, im vorliegenden Falle *bn* ʿms, aufgeführt. Wie A. Alt in dem Aufsatz »Menschen ohne Namen« wahrscheinlich gemacht hat[7], handelt es sich bei den auf solche Weise Bezeichneten um Dienstleute des Königs von Ugarit.

Eine beachtenswerte Rolle spielt das Verb ʿms in der phönikischen und vor allem in der punischen Namengebung. Neben dem Kurznamen ʿms (PNPhPI 172) finden wir die Vollnamen ʿmsmlk (a.a.O. 173), ʾšmnʿms (a.a.O. 72f.), bʿlʿms (a.a.O. 97) und mlqrtʿms (a.a.O. 141)[8].

---

[1] Abkürzungen nach L. Koehler–W. Baumgartner, Hebräisches und Aramäisches Lexikon zum Alten Testament, 2. Lieferung, 1974³ (= HAL).

[2] Vgl. dazu M. Noth, N. 38 und 178f.

[3] Der eigenartige PN *ᵃmǎssǎj* (Neh 11 13) ist nach M. Noth, N. 253b, eine Kombination der beiden orthographischen Varianten ʿmsj und ʿmśj, so auch W. Rudolph, EN 184. – Zu *ᵃmaśá* und *ᵃmaśǎj* vgl. Keilschr. *Amsi* (APN 22).

[4] Vgl. N. Avigad, Eretz–Israel 9 (1969), 8, F. Vattioni, Biblica 50 (1969) 380 nr. 204, und S. H. Horn, BASOR 205 (1972), 43–45.

[5] Vgl. dazu M. Noth, JSS 1 (1956), 325 = AbLAk, II, 1971, 237.

[6] Text UT 2021, 3 = KTU 4.335, 3.

[7] Kl. Schr., III, 1959, 198–213; zu den PN mit ʿms vgl. auch Gröndahl 109 und 377b.

[8] Vgl. auch PNPhPI 379f. und Z. S. Harris, Gr. 134.

2

a) Das Verb ʿāmăs heißt im Hebräischen im qal einerseits »aufladen«, nämlich eine Last auf ein Tier (Gen 44 13 Jes 46 1[9] Neh 13 15) — gelegentlich kann es auch von einem Stein, den man stemmt, gesagt werden (Sach 12 3) —, und andererseits bedeutet es »tragen«. Nach Neh 4 11 wären ʿomᵉsîm solche, die eine Last tragen, es wären dieselben, die unmittelbar vorher als hănnosᵉʾîm băssæbæl charakterisiert sind. Das Nebeneinander der gleichartigen Bezeichnungen ist aber unwahrscheinlich, und so empfiehlt es sich, für ʿomᵉsîm vielmehr nach G ḥᵃmusîm »gerüstet(e)«, »gewappnet(e)« zu lesen[10].

An den sonstigen Belegen (Jes 46 3 Ps 68 20) steht das Verb je in einem heilsgeschichtlichen Zusammenhang, indem es in bildlicher Redeweise das fürsorgliche Walten Gottes an seinem Volk beschreibt. Die beiden Stellen lauten:

»die ihr vom Mutterschoß von mir getragen (hăʿᵃmusîm)
und von Geburt an gehegt worden seid (hannᵉśuʾîm)«

(Jes 46 3b) und

»uns trägt (jăʿᵃmăs lanû) der Gott, der unsere Hilfe ist« (Ps 68 20b)[11].

Das Hi. kommt nur in der Wendung hæʿmîs ʿol ʿăl »jemandem ein drückendes Joch auferlegen« vor (I Reg 12 11 = II Chr 10 11).

b) Wir erwähnten schon, daß Sach 12 3 ʿāmăs vom Stemmen eines Steines gesagt wird. Der damit gemeinte Stein wird hier als ʾæbæn măʿᵃmāsā bezeichnet, d. h. als Stemmstein (für alle Völker). Bei Sirach (6 21) entspricht dem der Ausdruck ʾbn mśʾ. Sach 12 3 bietet den einzigen biblisch-hebräischen Beleg für ein vom Verb ʿāmăs abgeleitetes Substantiv, das von seinem Ursprung her soviel wie »Last« oder vielleicht noch eher »Gegenstand, den man trägt« bedeutet haben wird[12].

Im Mittelhebräischen kommt zum qal von ʿāmăs = »aufladen, belasten« das Part. pu. mᵉʿummas hinzu mit dem Sinn »belastet«[13]. — Für ein dem erwähnten măʿᵃmāsā entsprechendes Hauptwort bieten die Wörterbücher von G. Dalman und J. Levy keine Belege; dafür verzeich-

---

[9] Zum Text von Jes 46 1 vgl. C. Westermann, Das Buch Jesaja. Kap. 40—66 (ATD 19), 143 Anm. 1.
[10] So u. a. W. Rudolph, EN 126.
[11] Anders M. Dahood, Psalms, II, 1968, 143f. Er ändert die Verbalform in jᵉʾămmes (sog. pi. privativum, GK § 52h) und übersetzt: »Er entlastete uns«; ähnlch J. Gray, JSS 22 (1977), 24, der ʿummăs liest und übersetzt: »unsere Last ist von uns genommen«.
[12] Zu măʿᵃmāsā in seiner Verbindung mit ʾæbæn vgl. HAL 581a; anders G. R. Driver, ZAW 80 (1968), 180f.: ein großer Steinblock oder eine Masse schwerer Steine, die den Durchgang versperren.
[13] G. Dalman, Wb.³, 316a; hier auch das ja. Verb ʿᵃmăs »zusammendrücken«.

nen sie das Substantiv ʿômæs »Last«[14], eine Segolat-Bildung des *qutl*-Typus (BL 460h´´), die im älteren Hebräisch wohl nur zufällig nicht erhalten ist.

c) Im Ugaritischen ist über den PN ʿms hinaus das ihn bildende Verb in mythologischen und profanen Texten an den folgenden Stellen bezeugt:

1. ʿms mʿ lj ʾalʾijn bʿl (CTA 6 I 12 = KTU 1.6 I 12) (Anat zur Göttin Šapšu): »Lade mir doch Alijan Baal auf!«. Die Ausführung der Bitte hat den Wortlaut (a. a. O. Z. 14 f.) tšʾu ʾalʾijn bʿl lktp ʿnt »Sie lud den Alijan Baal auf die Schultern der Anat«. Das Verhältnis der Verben ʿms und nšʾa in Bitte und Ausführung entspricht ihrem Zusammengehen in Jes 46 1 und 3, eine Tatsache, auf die Y. Avishur, UF 7 (1975), 27, hingewiesen hat[15]. Der parallele Gebrauch wiederholt sich im Phönikischen, s. unten bei d.

2. bt ʾarzm jkllnh/ hm bt lbnt jʿmsnh (CTA 4 V 73 f. = KTU 1.4 V 10 f.) (Rede der Göttin *Aṭirat* an *Jammu*): »Ein Haus aus Zedern wird er vollenden, siehe, ein Haus aus Ziegeln wird er aufrichten«[16].

3. jʿmsn nn ṯkmn/ w šnm w ngšnn ḥbj (Ug. V 545 ff. = KTU 1.114, 18 f.) (über den vom Gelage zurückkehrenden El): »Es tragen ihn *Ṯkmn* und *Šnm*, und es nähert sich ihm *Ḥbj*«[17].

4. mʿmsh/ mʿmsk/ mʿmsj kšbʿ(t) jn (CTA 17 I 31 f., II 6.20 = KTU 1.17 I 30 f., II 6.20) (aus dem Katalog der Pflichten eines guten Sohnes): »der ihn/dich/mich trägt beim Voll-Sein von Wein«[18].

5. w ʾuḫj jʿmsn ṯmn (UT Text 2065, 19 f. = KTU 2.41, 20 f.) (aus einem Brief): »Und möge mein Bruder mir dort geben!«, wörtlich: »und möge mein Bruder mich dort beladen (mit dem, was ich wünsche)!«[19].

6. Ein von dem Verb ʿms abgeleitetes Substantiv ʿmsn[20] scheint vorzuliegen in dem Text UT 2067, 1 f. = KTU 4.370, 1 f.: spr bnš mlk dtʾaršn ʿmsn »Personnel of the king, who request a shipment«[21].

d) Im Phönikischen hat ʿms den Sinn von wegtragen. Bezogen auf das Wegtragen des Toten aus seiner Ruhestätte (*mškb*) wird es so dreimal im Ešmunazar-Sarkophag gebraucht[22]. Mit diesem Wegtragen ist das Hochheben bzw. das Entfernen des Sarges (*ḥlt mškbj*) verbunden, und dafür ist das Verb nšʾ verwendet (Z. 5, 7, 21). Wie J. C. Greenfield,

---

[14] G. Dalman, Wb.³, 308 a, und J. Levy, III, 663 b.
[15] Wegen der zu Neh 4 11 notwendigen Emendation kann diese Stelle nicht als weiterer Beleg für den Parallelismus der beiden Verben genannt werden.
[16] Übersetzung mit K. Aartun, Die Partikeln des Ugaritischen 1974, 70.
[17] Übersetzung mit M. Dietrich, O. Loretz und J. Sanmartín, UF 7 (1975), 110.
[18] Vgl. K. Koch, ZA 58 (1967), 216, und O. Eissfeldt, Kl. Schr., IV, 1968, 268.
[19] So mit K. Aartun a. a. O. (Anm. 16) 4 f.
[20] Zur Wortbildung mit der Endung n (ān) vgl. UT I § 8, 58.
[21] So mit UT III nr. 379.
[22] KAI Nr. 14 5–6·7·21.

Fschr. Albright, 1971, 260f., betont, ergibt das ein Nebeneinander der beiden Verben, wie es sich ähnlich Jes 46 1 und 3 findet, s. oben unter a.

e) Im Punischen ist ʿms zum Opferterminus geworden. Das Verb wird mit dem eine Opferart bezeichnenden Hauptwort ṣwʿt verbunden und meint »darbringen«[23]. Damit hat ʿms eine Sonderbedeutung gewonnen, indem der im Verb liegende allgemeine Sinn von »tragen« zu dem von »hintragen« spezialisiert wurde. Zum Vergleich ist an das griechische Verb προσφέρειν mit dem Substantiv προσφορά zu erinnern.

3

a) Zur Erklärung der mit ʿamăs gebildeten Namen zog M. Noth, N. 178f., vor allem die zwei folgenden Stellen heran[24]:

»Jahwe, dein Gott, trug dich ($n^e śa^{ʾa} ka$), wie ein Mann seinen Sohn trägt« (Dtn 1 31) und

»Denn seine Engel wird er für dich entbieten, dich zu behüten auf all deinen Wegen.

Sie werden dich auf Händen tragen ($jiśśaʾûnka$), daß dein Fuß nicht an einen Stein stoße« (Ps 91 11f.).

Inhaltlich stehen die Verben ʿamăs und naśaʾ einander so nahe, daß es sicher erlaubt ist, das eine durch das andere zu erklären, wie sie denn auch im Hebräischen, Ugaritischen und Phönikischen nebeneinander gebraucht sind[25]. Im Blick auf die beiden soeben zitierten Stellen wird man darum mit M. Noth, a.a.O., sagen dürfen: »tragen hat hier wohl den Sinn schützend auf seine Arme nehmen«. Das gilt sicher für die Satznamen ʿamăsjā und ʿmsʾl »Jahwe/El hat (schützend) getragen«. Entsprechend wird man auch den amoritischen PN Jaḫmus=AN(= Il/El) verstehen dürfen, und aus dem Phönikisch-Punischen die Vollnamen ʿmsmlk etc., s. oben 1.

Nicht ganz so eindeutig liegt es beim ugaritischen Kurznamen ʿms mit seinem phönikisch-punischen Gegenstück, s. wieder oben 1. Als perfektische Verbalform aufgefaßt, läßt sich das übersetzen durch: »Er hat getragen«; mit dem nicht genannten Subjekt kann nur eine Gottheit gemeint sein. Wagt man es, die Formen zu vokalisieren, so lauten sie für das Ugaritische ʿamasa und für das Phönikisch-Punische ʿamas bzw. ʿamōs[26]. Neben dieser Interpretation als finiten Verbalformen kommt

---

[23] Opfertarif aus Marseille (KAI Nr. 69, 13), aus Karthago (KAI Nr. 74, 8); zu ṣwʿt vgl. KAI II S. 85.
[24] Er weist dazu noch auf Ex 19 4 und Hos 11 3 hin.
[25] Vgl. dazu oben 2a, c und d.
[26] Vgl. Joh. Friedrich, Gr.², § 132.

wegen des hebräischen ʿamôs auch die als eines Verbaladjektivs in Frage. Auf den Sinn eines solchen werden wir sogleich (unter b) zurückkommen.

Zuvor sei für die Verbalsatznamen ʿᵃmăsjā, ʿmsʾl mit ihren Entsprechungen in den verwandten Sprachen die Frage berührt, auf wen sich das Tragen beziehe, auf das sie in ihrer Aussage dankend zurückblicken. Die Frage stellt sich, weil in den hebräischen PN, anders als in den akkadischen und ägyptischen, ein auf den Namensträger weisendes Suffix nicht üblich ist, es also nichts gibt, das einem akkadischen Irēmanni-ili »Mein Gott hat sich meiner erbarmt« ᵈSîn-irēmšu »Sin hat sich seiner erbarmt« und ᶠIrēmši-ᵈGula »Gula hat sich ihrer erbarmt« gleichkäme[27]. Bei einem hebräischen PN kann deshalb allein der Inhalt darüber entscheiden, ob in seiner Aussage das Empfinden der Eltern oder das des Kindes zum Ausdruck kommt. Dabei machen die Namendeutungen von Gen 29/30 es gewiß, daß in vielen Namen der Dank, den sie äußern, von den Eltern und nicht vom Kinde aus gesprochen ist. Ohne Zweifel ist das für PN anzunehmen, die mit den Verben šamăʿ, hæʾᵉzîn und zakăr gebildet sind. Bei anderen bleibt jedoch ungewiß, ob ihre Aussage sich mehr auf die Eltern oder mehr auf das Kind bezieht. Das mag für Namen mit ʿazār, milleṭ, pilleṭ und hôšîăʿ zutreffen.

Was nun das für uns wichtige ʿᵃmăsjā anlangt, so ist sicher das Kind Gegenstand des Dankes, der hier festgehalten ist, und das Gleiche darf für den inhaltlich nahestehenden PN sᵉmăkjahû angenommen werden. Der Dank für Heilung in rapaʾ und rᵉpaʾel ist am natürlichsten ebenfalls auf das schwache und am Anfang seines Lebens vom Tod bedrohte Kind zu beziehen[28]. Wie mir scheint, könnte es eine lohnende Aufgabe sein, die hebräischen Danknamen einmal daraufhin zu befragen, ob sie in ihrer Äußerung mehr an den Eltern oder mehr am Kind orientiert sind.

b) Nach den Belegen bei BL 466n''' hat der Typus qatul, mit dem ʿamôs gebildet ist, vorwiegend passivische Bedeutung. Danach hätte ʿamôs den Sinn: »Der (von Jahwe) Getragene«[29]. Als Bezeichnungsname würde es sich zum Satznamen ʿᵃmăsjā gleich verhalten wie der akkadische PN Šūzubu »Der Gerettete« zu ᵈNergal-ušēzib »Nergal hat gerettet«[30].

Unter den akkadischen Namen gibt es auch solche, die aus einem Part. act. des Grundstammes bestehen, wie z. B. Nāṣir(u) »Beschützer«, Mušēzib(u) und Ēṭir(u) »Retter«[31]. Sie haben Vollnamen neben sich wie ᵈMarduk-nāṣir »Marduk ist Beschützer« (ANG 115), Iṣṣur-ᵈSîn/ili »Sin/mein Gott hat (ihn) geschützt« (ANG 188), ᵈNabû/ᵈNergal-ušēzib »Nebo/Nergal hat (ihn) gerettet« (ANG 191), ᵈAdad/ᵈŠamaš-mušēzib »Adad/

---

[27] J. J. Stamm, Die Akkadische Namengebung, 1939, Neudruck 1968, 190 (= ANG).
[28] Anders M. Noth, N. 179.
[29] Vgl. dazu H. W. Wolff, Dodekapropheton 2. Joel und Amos (BK XIV/2), 1969, 153.
[30] ANG 112.
[31] ANG 115.

Šamaš ist Retter« (ANG 221) und *Ili-īṭiranni* »Mein Gott hat mich gerettet« (ANG 191).

Die zuerst erwähnten Partizipial-Namen werden am ehesten als Verkürzungen aus zugehörigen Satznamen zu verstehen sein. Aber daneben bietet sich noch eine zweite Möglichkeit an. Nach ihr läßt sich denken, »daß eine bewußte Doppeldeutigkeit beabsichtigt war: das beim Vollnamen von Gott ausgesagte Prädikat kann sich in der Verkürzung auch auf den Namensträger beziehen. »Retter« . . . und »Beschützer« heißt wohl ursprünglich der Gott, aber es läßt sich auch vom Kinde aussagen« (ANG 115).

Was bei diesen akkadischen Namen möglich scheint, ist vielleicht im Hebräischen für ʿamôs nicht ausgeschlossen. Die Form *qatul* wird zwar in der Regel, so sahen wir bereits, passivisch verwendet, aber die Adjektive ʾajom »furchterregend« und *jagôr* »fürchtend« lassen einen aktivischen Gebrauch als möglich erscheinen. Danach würde ʿamôs nicht allein »Der (von Jahwe) Getragene« bedeuten können, sondern auch »Der Träger«, d. h. derjenige, der (in der Zukunft) seinen Eltern oder später seiner eigenen Familie stützend zur Seite geht. Doch dürfte die erstere Auffassung die wahrscheinlichere sein, ohne daß dadurch die zweite ausgeschlossen würde. Zudem kann die Doppeldeutigkeit der akkadischen Namen vielleicht auch für ʿamôs in Anspruch genommen werden.

The authorship of the »prose sermons« of Jeremiah

By John V. M. Sturdy

(Gonville and Caius College, Cambridge)

One recent work on the so-called »prose sermons« of Jeremiah, Preaching to the Exiles, by E. W. Nicholson, has been widely recognised (perhaps especially in English-speaking countries) as a most important contribution to the study of Jeremiah (its more revealing subtitle is »A Study of the Prose Tradition in the Book of Jeremiah«), and his conclusions have been accepted by many scholars as a definitive statement of the right way to handle this material. The purpose of this article is to suggest a correction to Nicholson's views on just one point, which is nevertheless a significant one, requiring if accepted some modifications to his thesis, which in general the writer finds very convincing; and it is offered in the hope that it will at least be of interest to, even if it does not win the agreement of, Professor Fohrer, who has contributed so much of importance to the study of all the prophets, and among them of Jeremiah.

Nicholson argues that the prose sermons are the end product of a process of redaction, traditio-historical rather than purely literary in character, of material for the most part basically going back to Jeremiah, which the school of the Deuteronomists had worked over in the period of the exile in Babylon, consciously adapting it and reworking it to respond to the needs of their own time. In this view it is the insistence on a traditio-historical process of redaction that is distinctive. Earlier scholars[1] had attributed the language of the prose sermons to the Deuteronomistic school, and at this point Nicholson is reasserting an earlier view in rejecting the argument of J. Bright[2] that the sermons are the work of a circle of disciples of the prophet, sharing much of the language and thought of the Deuteronomists, but definitely separate from them. J. Bright built his case on a demonstration that of the 56 highly characteristic usages of the prose sermons which he isolated in his Appendix A (p. 30—35), 23 do not occur in the Deuteronomistic literature at all (including such distinctive expressions as »rising early and sending« (or, »speaking«, etc.); »amend your ways and your doings«; »sitting upon the throne of David«; »to present (my) supplication«; while of the 33 which do, 13 occur not more

---

[1] Such as B. Duhm, Das Buch Jeremia, 1901, X; S. Mowinckel, Zur Komposition des Buches Jeremia, 1914, 33 f.; G. Hölscher, Die Profeten, 1914, 382—384; and many others.
[2] The Date of the Prose Sermons of Jeremiah, JBL 70 (1951) 15—35.

than twice in it, and so »are hardly typical of it«, most of them occurring also in earlier literature; and very many of the stock phrases characteristic of the Deuteronomistic literature do not appear, or appear but rarely, in the Jeremianic prose sermons. J. Bright concluded that »the prose of Jeremiah is a style in its own right, akin to Dtr but by no means a slavish imitation of it«. This has the appearance of a well-made case.

Nicholson has nevertheless sought to overturn it, in an argument which looks conclusive. »It remains true«, he insists, »that there is an impressive array of parallels between the phraseology of these sermons in Jeremiah and that of the Deuteronomistic literature«. Some of the phrases, he allows, are part of a »common stock of well-worn clichés«. »There are, however«, he continues, »in addition to these a number of expressions of a strikingly individualistic nature which occur only once or twice and never more than three times in the whole of the Deuteronomistic corpus and elsewhere, with minor variations in some instances, only in the prose of Jeremiah«. The balance of probability lies, he concludes, with an involvement of the Deuteronomists themselves in the composition of these passages. He goes on to explain the presence of non-Deuteronomistic vocabulary and phraseology in the prose sermons as reflecting a substratum of the original language of the prophet Jeremiah[3].

It is this argument that I wish to scrutinize in more detail, and it will be necessary to quote first Nicholson's list of the decisive expressions. They are: »Their dead bodies will be food for the birds of the air and for the beasts of the earth (and none will frighten them away)«, in Jer 7 33 16 4 19 7, cf. 34 20, elsewhere only in Dtn 28 26; »and I will make them a horror to all the kingdoms of the earth« in Jer 15 4 24 9 29 18 34 17, elsewhere only in Dtn 28 25; »in the siege and in the distress with which their enemies shall afflict them« in Jer 19 9, elsewhere only in Dtn 28 53. 55. 57; »his ears will tingle« in Jer 19 3, elsewhere only in I Sam 3 11 II Kings 21 12; »from the iron furnace« in Jer 11 4, elsewhere only in Dtn 4 20 (cf. I Kings 8 51).

Although seen in print this is quite a substantial list, there are in fact only five separate items in it. I should wish first to urge that we should set aside the last two items. Neither of them is very long or strikingly distinctive, and while they can be allowed to be part of the terms common to the prose sermons and the Deuteronomistic literature, they are not enough to build a case for identity of authorship upon them. If then the remaining three items, upon which Nicholson's case now stands or falls, are examined, something very odd will be noticed about their distribution. While the instances in Jeremiah are from a variety of chapters (ch. 7. 15. 16. 19. 25. 29. 34) the parallels in the Deuteronomistic literature are all not just in one book of it, but in one chapter of one book, Dtn 28.

---

[3] Nicholson 29f.

It is hard to believe that this is not a fact of significance, and in need of explanation. If Nicholson's approach were correct, one would expect »expressions of a strikingly individualistic nature« occurring only rarely in the Deuteronomistic literature, and otherwise only in the prose sermons, to appear at a number of different places in the Deuteronomistic literature. There must be a more specific reason for the concentration of the longer parallels in just one chapter of Deuteronomy.

What are the possibilities? It is surely impossible to think of reasons why the prose sermons at different times should keep coming back to this one chapter of Deuteronomy as a source for lengthy citations. There could be two other possible explanations. The first is that the author of Deuteronomy ch. 28 in particular (who is then seen as different from and later than the authors of the Deuteronomistic literature as a whole) also wrote the prose sermons. This is not a likely view. While there are striking parallels at particular points between the two blocks of material, the language of Dtn 28 as a whole cannot be claimed to be the same as that of the prose sermons.

The second explanation is that Dtn 28 (or parts of it) is later than the prose sermons, and has drawn directly on their language. In favour of this solution there is supporting evidence to be adduced. For it is characteristic of Dtn 28 that it shares expressions with a number of other works, to a degree that is unusual among the books of the Old Testament. When I first scrutinized Nicholson's argument in detail I was reminded that B. Albrektson had already suggested contacts between Dtn 28 and some passages in the Book of Lamentations[4], which he argued were »too numerous and detailed to be dismissed as pure coincidence«. The passages he compared were Lam 1 3 with Dtn 28 65; Lam 1 5 with Deut 28 41. 44; Lam 1 9 with Dtn 28 43; Lam 2 20 4 1 with Dtn 28 53; Lam 3 45 3 14 with Dtn 28 37; and Lam 4 16 and 5 12 with Dtn 28 50. He thought it the most obvious view that Lamentations knew and was alluding to visitations already listed in Dtn 28 as the wages of sin. But if Dtn 28 has prima facie direct literary contacts with both the prose sermons of Jeremiah and the Book of Lamentations, there is clearly a case to be examined for suggesting it may itself be (either in whole or in part) a later composition, which has drawn consciously on already traditional material in Israel to build up its text.

If Dtn 28 is examined in more detail support will, I believe, be found for such an approach. This unusually lengthy chapter of blessings and curses has been widely thought to include later expansions, even if its core goes back to an Urdeuteronomium of whatever date this is given; and at least v. 25b–37 and 47–68 have been so regarded[5]. The latest commentary,

---

[4] Studies in the Text and Theology of the Book of Lamentations, 1963, 231–236.

[5] So G. von Rad, Das fünfte Buch Mose – Deuteronomium (ATD 8), 1964, 125 f., E.tr. Deuteronomy, 1966, 175.

by A. D. H. Mayes[6], traces a complicated development, with v. 3–6. 16–19 seen as the oldest surviving material in the chapter, material which unlike the rest lacks language typical of the other parts of Deuteronomy. V. 20–46 are the first expansion, on the basis of which v. 7–14 were added to the blessings. The next addition, v. 47–57, stands apart from the rest of the cursing material in containing unconditional curses. Their author also wrote v. 45–46 as a transition. Finally v. 58–68 are a last very late addition by yet another author. This is an attractive analysis, and would suggest that there may be different relations to earlier material in different parts of the chapter (A. D. H. Mayes recognizes v. 8b–14 as being strongly Deuteronomistic, and 47–57 as having »several contacts with Jeremiah«, though he does not seek an explanation for these); but in view of the variety of analyses that have been offered it is necessary to examine the whole chapter for close relations with other books, before concluding finally that one analysis rather than another is right.

It will be realized that there are many uncertainties in the attempt to establish whether or not a definite literary relationship of dependence can be established between two books. There are particular difficulties in examining the relation between the Deuteronomistic language of the chapter and that of the rest of the Deuteronomistic literature, and this material will be left aside here. But for the rest there may in fact be a direct relationship which is reflected only in general similarities of language and thought, none quite sufficient to establish for us such a relationship; and there may be phrases held in common which are in fact a literary or liturgical commonplace, and are not evidence for a relationship. We may miss this because we do not know the point of reference, and wrongly claim a relationship to be present. When however a pattern of relationship between two chapters begins to appear in more than one instance we may be increasingly confident that a relationship of dependence is present.

With these cautions, it is still clear that there is a definite relation to be found between Dtn 28 and the Jeremianic traditions, and particularly the prose sermons. Among the clear examples of this are

Dtn 28	Jeremiah
10	7 10. 11. 14. 30 and often
20	4 4 21 12 23 2. 22 25 5 26 3 44 22
25	15 4 24 9 29 18 34 17
26	7 33 16 4 19 7 34 20
48	28 14
49–51	5 15–19
52	5 17
53. 55. 57	19 9

[6] Deuteronomy (New Century Bible), 1979.

Of these perhaps not all would agree that v. 20 is a certain example, since the expression *roăʿ măʿălᵉlêhaem* is already found in Isa 1 16. But the distribution of the expression raises a serious question whether that passage may not be late itself. As further possibilities only may be added at least

Dtn 28	Jeremiah
36	16 13
63	32 41
64	9 15

The next most clear relationship is with Lev 26. There is a general similarity of subject matter between the two chapters, but no general closeness of language, and it has been argued that these are »two independent elaborations of the same theme«[7]. But there are some instances which suggest a definite verbal reminiscence of the one by the other. Of these Dtn 28 22 Lev 26 16, Dtn 28 23 Lev 26 19, and Dtn 28 65b Lev 26 16 seem firm instances, but the parallel of Dtn 28 53b is not as close with Lev 26 29 as it is with Jer 19 9. O. H. Steck, Israel und das gewaltsame Geschick der Propheten, 1967, 141 n. 4, would explain these instances as very late integration of Deuteronomic traditions into the priestly tradition. This is not impossible. Whether it seems likely if it can be established that there is a general movement of other traditions into Dtn 28 is the important question.

The connections with Lamentations pointed to by B. Albrektson are in fact not quite as strong as those with Lev 26. Most of his instances are of a similar pattern of thought rather than of similarity directly of language (as he recognises himself). But in the cases of Lam 1 3 with Dtn 28 65 and Lam 1 5 with Dtn 28 41 a verbal connexion can be recognised[8].

The strongest links with other works have been listed; but there is a surprisingly wide scatter of other apparently close similarities in language which can be listed as follows

---

[7] S. R. Driver, A Critical and Exegetical Commentary on Deuteronomy (ICC), 1902³, 304.

[8] B. Albrektson went on to point out that the verses showing parallels to Lamentations came from parts of Dtn 28 both that were held to be original and that were held to be secondary, and urged that this suggested a reconsideration of the integrity of Dtn 28; implying that the whole chapter might be part of Urdeuteronomium. But it may be the case that analyses he refers to are wrong, and that all the verses with parallels in Lamentations are secondary. »It would be absurd«, he goes on, »to regard Deut. 28 as an entirely later work, deliberately picking from Lamentations some of its expressions«. It is not clear to me that this is so absurd; whether it is the case depends on whether there is some core of Dtn 28, such as v. 3–6.16–19, which is early; that Dtn 28 deliberately picked from Lamentations some of its expressions is what I would argue has happened.

Dtn 28

8	Prov. 3 10 (the word $^{\,a}sam\ae ka$: not certain)
28	Zech 12 4
29	Job 5 14b
65	Gen 8 9
66	Job 24 22

Once again, one or two of these may be fortuitous, but it is not likely that all of them are.

Some scholars had already not only noted the links between Dtn 28 and Jeremiah but also explained them by a late dependence of Dtn 28 on Jeremiah[9]. In the light of the instances given it may be urged that there is a strong case for saying that the author of Dtn 28 drew expressions from a number of chapters of the books of the Old Testament (which were possibly already acquiring an authoritative character for him), and that Jeremiah (especially, but not exclusively, the prose sermons: cf. Dtn 28 52 with Jer 5 17, which is in verse), Lev 26 and Lamentations, works whose attractiveness to him and usefulness to him are obvious, were those most used. It will be seen that the verses in which such contacts have with reasonable certainty been found are 8. 10. 20. 22. 23. 25. 26. 28. 29. 41. 48. 49–51. 52. 53. 55. 57. 65 and 66. While it is possible that successive redactors of the chapter had similar working habits, it is more likely that recent redactional treatments of the chapter have become too complicated, and that through all these verses at least a single redactor is at work. That the whole chapter is late, and that we should be talking of a single author, seems to me, though less likely, not out of the question.

It is time to return to our starting point, the prose sermons of Jeremiah, and see what conclusions follow from this discussion. Our point of departure was that J. Bright had made a strong case for saying that though there are family likenesses between the language of the prose sermons and that of the Deuteronomists the divergences between the two are sufficiently extensive to make it impossible to equate these writers. We looked at Nicholson's persuasive attempt to overthrow this conclusion, and found that it failed to convince because all his parallels from the Deuteronomists of any length came from one chapter, and for this a different explanation seems much more likely. At this point it seems that J. Bright's case is stronger than Nicholson's[10].

---

[9] Notably H. W. Wolff, Das Kerygma des Deuteronomistischen Geschichtswerks, in: Gesammelte Studien zum Alten Testament, 1964, 318–321, who correctly sees the same relationship applying also to Dtn 30 1–10 and 4 29–31.

[10] Meanwhile further discussion of the problem has been going on in Germany. In two monographs published in the same year W. Thiel (Die deuteronomistische Redaktion

It might be argued that linguistic evidence is insufficient, and that there is such a close similarity in theological outlook between the two blocks of material that a case nonetheless holds. But in fact a disagreement between the two can be indicated on two very central matters which put in question an identification on theological grounds too. In relation to the monarchy the attitude both of Deuteronomy (cf. 17 14–20, and its silence otherwise) and of the Deuteronomists (cf. the negative evaluation of all but one or two of the kings of Judah) is decidedly cool, and it may be suspected that the Deuteronomists did not envisage a restoration of the monarchy after the exile. On the other hand it is precisely in prose material in Jeremiah (23 5–6 33 14–16) which in its present form bears the stamp of the prose sermon tradition (and which Nicholson does not believe goes back to an underlay in the teaching of Jeremiah himself[11]) that we find such a hope in Jeremiah. In relation to the centrality of the temple in Israelite worship, however, the characteristic position in Deuteronomy (12 5–7) and in the Deuteronomistic material (which displays a recurrent interest in the temple and its treasures) is firmly positive, and cannot easily be harmonized with the attitude found in Jeremiah 7 and 26, which in its present form clearly reflects the language of the prose sermon sections (though very probably this is underlain by material going back to Jeremiah himself), and displays a strong hostility to any trust in the temple and the Zion traditions.

If it can be established that the prose sermons display neither the precise language nor the theology of the Deuteronomistic school, the case for regarding them as later than Jeremiah himself, and the work of a school concerned to keep his message alive and to relate it to a living situation that Nicholson has made, still stands. We should then conclude that it is a continuing group of disciples of Jeremiah that is responsible for this tradition. And this is perhaps a more natural solution. Who would we expect to preserve the tradition of Jeremiah but his disciples?

---

von Jeremia 1–25, 1973) and H. Weippert (Die Prosareden des Jeremiabuches, 1973) took diametrically opposed positions, W. Thiel arguing for a more nuanced and complex picture of Deuteronomistic redaction, H. Weippert strongly denying the presence of Deuteronomistic elements, and arguing that more of the prose sermons may go back to Jeremiah himself than is usually allowed. Both books were published after Nicholson's, but largely written before its appearance, and although there is a reference to Nicholson in H. Weippert's book she does not cross swords with him directly. My concern in this article is with the correctness of Nicholson's argument, and I will not examine in detail the cases presented by these two authors; but basically I would share H. Weippert's rejection of the case for Deuteronomistic redaction, but not that for a return to Jeremianic authorship: we still have later and redacted material in the prose sermons, but there is no case for looking to the Deuteronomistic rather than to the disciples of Jeremiah as responsible for the redactional activity.

[11] Preaching to the Exiles 89–91.

If the Deuteronomistic school were responsible we should need to suppose that in some way they had incorporated in themselves the group of disciples of Jeremiah and taken over their traditions, or that in some other way unclear to us they had come to have control of these traditions. It is in fact the simpler hypothesis, as well as that which fits the evidence, that sees the disciples of Jeremiah themselves as directly responsible for the continuing development of this tradition.

If this is accepted, it is necessary too to disagree with Nicholson's argument for a setting in Babylonia for the redactional process. W. Thiel has already argued[12] from within the »Deuteronomistic« position that at this point Nicholson's arguments are not conclusive: the attack on remaining Judahites could well reflect not the hopes of the exiles, but the disappointment with their religious concern of Deuteronomistic authors in Palestine. If the authors are in fact a group of disciples of Jeremiah one would expect to find them in Palestine (or just possibly in Egypt) rather than in Babylonia; and nothing in the text is a real difficulty for this view.

It has been argued that at one rather central point Nicholson's thesis needs amendment, and this has consequences too for the location of the redactional process. But his broader thesis of a traditio-historical, rather than more narrowly literary, development of the Jeremiah tradition is not affected by this amendment: it would fit quite as well with an acceptance of disciples of Jeremiah as the group responsible, and it may still be accepted, as I would wish to do, as a valuable advance in the understanding of this important, but puzzling, part of the Jeremianic tradition.

---

[12] In his review of Nicholson, TLZ 97 (1972), 25–27.

Jeremias Besuch beim Töpfer

Eine motivkritische Untersuchung zu Jer 18

Von Gunther Wanke

(Am Röthelheim 58, Erlangen)

In der Auseinandersetzung um die vielschichtigen Probleme, die die Jeremiaüberlieferung der Forschung aufgibt, spielt Jer 18 1–12 eine nicht unerhebliche Rolle. Offenbar aufgrund seiner Gestalt und Struktur ist der Text zu einem der Schlüsseltexte des Jeremiabuches geworden, an dem sich die verschiedenen Erklärungsmodelle für die Entstehung des Prophetenbuches zu bewähren haben. Vor allem diejenigen Untersuchungen, welche der Frage nach dem Verhältnis des Jeremiabuches zur Deuteronomistik nachgingen[1], haben jeweils Jer 18 breitere Aufmerksamkeit geschenkt und in diesem Zusammenhang das Verständnis des Textes wesentlich gefördert. So darf es zum Beispiel gegenwärtig als anerkannt gelten, daß wenigstens Jer 18 1–6 zu der von G. Fohrer beschriebenen Gattung der Berichte über symbolische Handlungen der Propheten gehört[2].

Angesichts der intensiven Beschäftigung der Jeremiaforschung mit Jer 18 ist es besonders auffällig, daß der Kern des Textes – das Bild vom Umgang des Töpfers mit dem Ton – vergleichsweise geringe Beachtung gefunden hat. Seine Funktion und damit die Funktion wenigstens des ersten Teils des Textes Jer 18 1–6 werden meist nur auf dem Wege textimmanenter Interpretation bestimmt oder geraten überhaupt nicht in den Blick. Der folgende Beitrag möchte einige Beobachtungen zum Gebrauch des fraglichen Bildes vorlegen und auf mögliche Konsequenzen für die

---

[1] Es genügt in diesem Zusammenhang auf die Arbeiten von S. Herrmann, Die prophetischen Heilserwartungen im Alten Testament, 1965; W. Thiel, Die deuteronomistische Reaktion von Jeremia 1–25, 1973, und Helga Weippert, Die Prosareden des Jeremiabuchs, 1973, zu verweisen, zumal in ihnen ein ausreichender Überblick über die neuere Forschung geboten wird.

[2] Damit ist nicht mehr, aber auch nicht weniger gesagt, als daß Jer 18 1–6 die von G. Fohrer für die Gattung »Bericht über symbolische Handlungen der Propheten« erarbeiteten typischen Strukturmerkmale aufweist, s. G. Fohrer, Die Gattung der Berichte über symbolische Handlungen der Propheten, ZAW 64 (1952), 101–120, jetzt in: Studien zur alttestamentlichen Prophetie (1949–1965), 1967, 92–112. Die entsprechende Zuordnung des Textes hat G. Fohrer allerdings selbst nicht vorgenommen, sondern Jer 18 1–11 der Gattung Parabel zugewiesen (G. Fohrer, Einleitung in das Alte Testament, 1969[11], 343), eine Zuordnung, die bei H. Weippert a.a.O. (Anm. 1) 66 zumindest implizit wiederbegegnet.

Auslegung von Jer 18 hinweisen, ohne alle mit diesem Abschnitt des Jeremiabuches verbundenen Probleme zu behandeln. Gleichzeitig möchte der Aufsatz zeigen, welche zusätzlichen Aspekte für die Interpretation eines Textes gewonnen werden können, wenn der motivkritischen Fragestellung größere Aufmerksamkeit geschenkt wird.

I.

Wegen des begrenzten Untersuchungsziels und um den Aufsatz nicht mit zusätzlichen Problemen zu belasten, ist es einerseits nötig, den Umfang des zu analysierenden Textmaterials möglichst gering zu halten. Um jedoch andererseits eine Verzeichnung der Untersuchungsergebnisse tunlichst zu vermeiden, sollte zumindest von einer einfachen Einheit ausgegangen werden. Schon *literarkritische Erwägungen* legen es nahe, einen ersten Schnitt innerhalb von Jer 18 1–12 zwischen v. 6 und v. 7 anzunehmen. Denn abgesehen von der durch den Personenwechsel in v. 2 bedingten Spannung bieten die v. 1–6 einen in sich geschlossenen Gedankengang. Das durch v. 1 angekündigte Jahwewort folgt als Befehl und Ankündigung in v. 2. Die Ausführung des Befehls durch Jeremia und das damit verbundene Geschehen im Haus des Töpfers berichten die v. 3–4, die Verwirklichung der Ankündigung eines weiteren Jahwewortes die v. 5–6. Damit sind alle ab v. 1 geweckten Erwartungen erfüllt. Da außerdem in v. 5 f. keinerlei Vorweiser festzustellen sind, kann v. 6 als Textende angesehen werden. Mit Jer 18 1–6 läge also eine einfache Einheit vor. Allerdings nötigt der Wechsel von der 3. pers. v. 1 in die 1. pers. v. 2 zu der Annahme, daß diese Einheit bereits eine Überarbeitung erfahren hat, welche eine ursprünglich in der 1. pers. gehaltene Einleitung – etwa in der Gestalt von 13 1 oder 16 1 – durch eine andere ersetzt hat. V. 1 ist auch als eine für das Jeremiabuch typische redaktionelle Wendung erkannt (7 1 11 1 14 1 [?] 21 1a 30 1 u. ö.)³. Es müßte also streng genommen Jer 18 1–6 als ein erweitertes Fragment bezeichnet werden. Da jedoch die ursprüngliche Gestalt der Einheit mithilfe von 13 1 bzw. 16 1 als ein Selbstbericht rekonstruiert werden kann und da der fragmentarische Charakter der vorliegenden Einheit für die folgenden Überlegungen nicht von Belang ist, braucht dieser Tatbestand auch nicht weiter beachtet zu werden.

Der folgende Abschnitt 18 7–10 hebt sich durch seinen parallelen Aufbau, eigenständiges Vokabular, fehlenden Rückbezug auf die Töpfermetaphorik, von v. 6 abweichende Objekte des Handelns Jahwes (v. 6 Haus Israel; v. 7–10 Völker und Königreiche) und veränderten Redestil klar von v. 1–6 ab. Die einzige Verbindung zwischen beiden Texten ist syntaktischer Natur: V. 7–10 erscheinen als unmittelbare Fortsetzung der

---

³ Die Funktion dieses redaktionellen Eingriffs zu diskutieren, ist hier nicht der Ort.

durch v. 5 eingeleiteten Jahwerede. Ähnliche Spannungen bzw. Verknüpfungen sind für 18 11–12 zu beobachten[4], so daß beide Abschnitte als Erweiterungen von 18 1–6 bezeichnet werden können. Unabhängig davon, wie man — entstehungsgeschichtlich gesehen — nun im einzelnen den Zusammenhang von v. 1–6 und v. 7–12 auch beurteilen mag, kann aufgrund der literarkritischen Erwägungen Jer 18 1–6 als eine einfache Einheit behandelt werden, ohne daß der Ausleger Gefahr läuft, durch eine vorläufige Ausblendung der folgenden Erweiterungen wesentliche Aussageaspekte zu übersehen.

Diese Abgrenzung bestätigt sich auch nach der *formen- und gattungskritischen Analyse* des Textes. Eine solche Analyse, die im einzelnen hier nicht ausgebreitet werden kann, führt auf folgende Textstruktur:

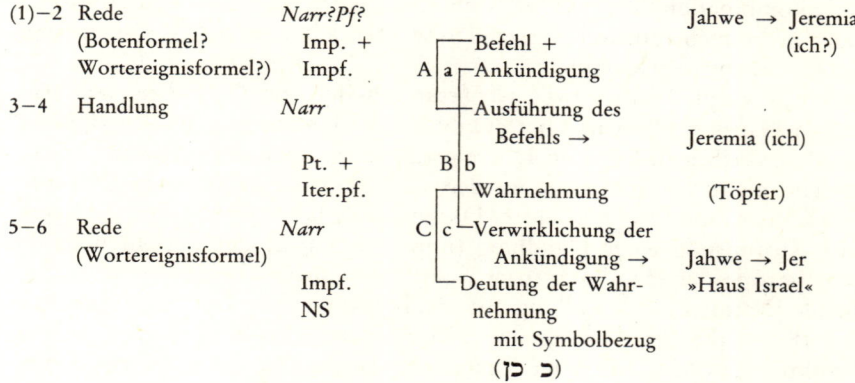

Die narrativischen Verbalsätze v. 1?. 3a. 5 bilden das knappe »Handlungsgerüst« des Textes, dessen dreiteilige Struktur klar erkennbar ist. Sie ist durch die Abfolge Rede–Handlung–Rede bestimmt. Die erste Rede stößt durch imperativische und futurische Ausrichtung das folgende Geschehen an. Dem knappen Handlungsteil v. 3a ist die Schilderung der Wahrnehmung v. 3b–4 untergeordnet, welcher Partizipien und iterative Perfekte beschreibenden Charakter verleihen. Erste Rede und Handlungsteil laufen auf die zweite Rede v. 5–6 zu, die somit den Höhepunkt des Textes bildet. Die Handlung hat allein dienende Funktion. Diesem recht einfachen und klaren Aufbau tritt eine kunstvolle Verschränkung der einzelnen Textelemente nach dem Schema A–B–a–C–b–c an die Seite

---

[4] Selbst wenn man mit H. Weippert a.a.O. (Anm. 1) 53ff. v. 7–12 eng mit v. 1–6 zusammensehen möchte, können die Erwähnung des Töpfers (*jôṣer*) in v. 4–6 und der Gebrauch des pt. *jôṣer* weder als Wortspiel analog Jer 1 11f. oder Am 8 2, noch als Wortspiel im Sinne ihrer eigenen Terminologie verstanden werden, nach welcher für ein Wortspiel Bedeutungsverschiebung bzw. -umkehrung — was immer das heißen mag — konstitutiv sind. Es liegt im besten Fall Stichwortanknüpfung vor.

(s. o.) Die handelnden Hauptpersonen sind Jahwe und Jeremia, wobei Jahwe immer als agierend, der Prophet immer als reagierend begegnen.

Auf die Frage nach der Funktion der Einheit, welche an ihrem Höhepunkt abzulesen ist, kann auf dieser Ebene der Untersuchung nur eine vorläufige Antwort gegeben werden. Die Verwendung der Frage (rhetorisch?) und die betonte zweimalige Endstellung von »Haus Israel« in v. 6 machen deutlich, daß der Text auf Reaktion aus ist. Welche Reaktion bei den Adressaten beabsichtigt ist — ob sie zur Anerkennung eines Sachverhalts bewogen werden sollen oder ob sie zur Änderung eines Verhaltens aufgefordert werden sollen — kann nicht eindeutig entschieden werden, da nicht alle Faktoren bekannt sind, die das vorauszusetzende Kommunikationsgeschehen bestimmen. Ebenso muß vorläufig offen bleiben, ob die Verbkombination 'ûkal la'ªśôt »ich kann euch tun« nur konjunktivisch oder nicht auch futurisch verstanden werden kann, so daß v. 6 auch einen Ankündigungsaspekt enthält.

Ein Vergleich dieser Textstruktur mit der von G. Fohrer beschriebenen Gattung »Bericht über symbolische Handlungen der Propheten«[5] zeigt an wichtigen Punkten Übereinstimmung, aber auch Abweichungen, welche nicht vernachlässigt werden dürfen. An gemeinsamen Strukturmerkmalen sind festzustellen: 1. Der meist als Jahwewort gestaltete Befehl zur Ausführung einer Handlung (imp., pf.cs.); 2. der Bericht über die Ausführung der Handlung (narr.) und 3. die meist als Jahwewort begegnende Deutung der Handlung mit Symbolbezug (k — kn). Somit liegen in Jer 18 1–6 alle für Berichte über symbolische Handlungen wesentlichen Strukturmerkmale vor. Der Text muß darum als durch diese Gattung geprägt angesehen werden[6]. Sitz im Leben dieser Gattung ist die prophetische Verkündigung in ihrer besonderen Ausprägung als symbolische Handlung. Da der durch die Gattung geprägte Einzeltext in der Regel den literarischen Niederschlag einer voraufgegangenen Verkündigungshandlung darstellt und damit die Handlungsaussage stabilisiert, darf die Funktion der Gattung von der Funktion der symbolischen Handlung abgeleitet werden: ». . . sie symbolisiert immer ein zukünftiges Geschehen«[7]. Die Funktion der Gattung kann also als symbolhafte Vorabbildung und damit Ankündigung künftigen Geschehens bestimmt werden.

Nun ist aber für Jer 18 1–6 schon mehrfach festgestellt worden, daß einerseits zwar die Strukturelemente der Gattung »Bericht über symbolische Handlungen« vorliegen, andererseits aber der Einzeltext nicht auf eine vorlaufende Symbolhandlung zurückgeführt werden kann, jedenfalls

---

[5] G. Fohrer a. a. O. (Anm. 2).
[6] Die Geschlossenheit der Textstruktur und das Vorliegen aller wesentlichen Strukturmerkmale der Gattung bestätigen das Ergebnis der literarkritischen Analyse und rechtfertigen die Begrenzung dieser Untersuchung auf Jer 18 1–6.
[7] G. Fohrer a. a. O. (Anm. 2) 112.

nicht auf eine Symbolhandlung, die der Prophet selbst zu vollziehen hat. In Jer 18 1–6 erscheint der Prophet vielmehr als passiver Beobachter eines Geschehens, an dem er selbst keinen Anteil hat. Die Handlung ist durch eine Wahrnehmnung ersetzt worden. Dies erklärt nun die Abweichungen, die zwischen der Textstruktur und dem Strukturmuster der Gattung festzustellen sind. Einmal tritt an die Stelle des durch narrativische Verbalsätze bestimmten Berichts über die Ausführung einer Handlung eine durch iteratives Perfekt und Nominalsätze bestimmte Schilderung eines vom Propheten wahrgenommenen (*hnh* + pt.) Geschehens. Daß es sich bei diesem Geschehen um ein den Symbolhandlungen vergleichbares qualifiziertes Geschehen handelt, wird innerhalb von Jer 18 1–6 durch die ausdrückliche Ankündigung eines Jahweworts, das im Zusammenhang mit ihm ergehen soll, herausgestellt. Diese Ankündigung bildet die zweite wesentliche Abweichung der Textstruktur von der Gattungsstruktur.

Die Verwendung der Gattung »Bericht über symbolische Handlungen der Propheten« und die in Jer 18 1–6 beobachteten Modifikationen erscheinen nur dann als sinnvoll, wenn angenommen wird, daß das vom Text vorausgesetzte Geschehen als ein den prophetischen Symbolhandlungen analoger Vorgang bestimmt werden soll, dessen eigentliche Funktion es ist, künftige Ereignisse anzukündigen. Damit wird die bereits ausgesprochene Vermutung gestützt, daß die Deutung nicht nur ein *mögliches*, sondern ein in der Zukunft auch *zu erwartendes* Handeln Jahwes im Blick hat.

II.

Wenn also Jer 18 1–6 ein bestimmtes Jahwehandeln ankündigt, dann darf erwartet werden, daß der Text auch etwas über die Qualität dieses Handelns zu erkennen gibt. Davon ist auch die Forschung — soweit ich sehe — unausgesprochen ausgegangen. Nur hat sie bislang recht unterschiedliche Interpretationen vorgelegt. Von der Annahme heilvollen Handelns Jahwes[8] bis hin zur Annahme unheilvollen Handelns Jahwes[9] sind alle möglichen Spielarten der Deutung schon vertreten worden, nicht zuletzt auch die Auffassung, daß der Text »als Gerichts- und/oder Heilswort«[10] verstanden werden kann. Und es ist der Text selbst, der solche unterschiedlichen Antworten auf die Frage nach der Qualität des Handelns Jahwes ermöglicht, denn er bleibt ohne Berücksichtigung des Kontextes

---

[8] Z. B. Sh. H. Blank, Jeremiah. Man and Prophet, 1961, 214ff.
[9] W. Thiel a. a. O. (Anm. 1) 213f. W. Thiel bietet auch einen knappen Überblick über die bislang vorgelegten Interpretationen, auf den hier der Einfachheit halber verwiesen werden darf.
[10] So z. B. H. Weippert a. a. O. (Anm. 1) 50.

bzw. ohne Erhellung des Situationshintergrundes mehrdeutig bzw. in seiner Aussage zu allgemein, wenn nicht gar banal.

Es braucht nicht betont zu werden, daß die Aussage des Textes der Wahrnehmung des Propheten, also dem, was er beim Töpfer zu sehen bekommt v. 3b–4, und der ihr durch klaren Symbolbezug zugeordneten Deutung v. 6 zu entnehmen ist. Dem alltäglichen Vorgang in einer Töpferwerkstatt wird Jahwes Handeln an Israel verglichen[11]. Jahwe kann mit Israel umgehen, wie der Töpfer mit dem Ton umgeht. Und dieser Umgang mit dem Ton ist ein souveräner Umgang: Der Töpfer verfährt mit dem Ton »wie es in den Augen des Töpfers recht war zu verfahren« v. 4bβ, also wie es ihm gefällt. Man sollte angesichts dieses Vergleichs »die sehr allgemeine Aussage der Souveränität Jahwes über die Geschicke seines Volkes« mit W. Thiel nicht zu rasch »als zu unbestimmt ausscheiden«[12], sondern daran festhalten, daß der Text, wie er vorliegt, nichts anderes als diese Souveränität Jahwes zum Ausdruck bringt. Allerdings – und hier hat W. Thiel etwas Richtiges gesehen – muß diese Aussage in den Augen des Israeliten als eine Selbstverständlichkeit erscheinen, und man wird fragen dürfen, ob es in der Tat das Ziel dieses Textes ist, mit nicht unbeträchtlichem Aufwand eine Banalität zu verkünden bzw. die Zustimmung der Israeliten zu einem allgemein anerkannten Glaubenssatz zu gewinnen (v. 6a [rhetorische] Frage!). Geht man einmal davon aus, daß dies nicht beabsichtigt war, will man also nicht annehmen, daß der Text nur von Banalitäten redet, sondern daß mit dem Hinweis auf das souveräne Handeln eine konkretere Absicht verbunden ist, dann muß dem Text eine zusätzliche Interpretation beigegeben werden, z. B. durch Erhellung von Kontext und Situationshintergrund.

Die bereits erwähnten unterschiedlichen Deutungen von Jer 18 1–6 sind dann auch das Ergebnis entsprechenden Vorgehens. So gewinnt Sh. H. Blank[13] seine heilvolle Deutung der »symbolischen Wahrnehmung« mit Hilfe der Datierung des Textes in die Zeit kurz nach der Eroberung Jerusalems 587, W. Thiel[14] dagegen seine Deutung als Gerichtswort über die Einordnung des Textes in die übrigen Symbolhandlungen Jeremias. H. Weippert[15] schließlich benötigt zur Auslegung von v. 6 den unmittelbaren Kontext Jer 18 7–12.

Ein solches Vorgehen ist ohne Zweifel methodisch zu rechtfertigen und für die Bestimmung des Aussagegehalts eines Textes notwendig. Doch sollten, ehe man sich der Kontextanalyse und der Rekonstruktion

---

[11] In der Beschreibung alltäglicher, selbstverständlicher Vorgänge zum Zwecke des Vergleichs ist Jer 18 4.6 den neutestamentlichen Gleichnissen verwandt.
[12] W. Thiel a. a. O. (Anm. 1) 214.
[13] S. Anm. 8.
[14] S. Anm. 9.
[15] S. Anm. 10.

des Situationshintergrundes zuwendet, alle Möglichkeiten ausgeschöpft werden, die der Text als sprachliches Gebilde anbietet. Und hier ist offenbar im Zusammenhang mit Jer 18 1–6 noch nicht alles getan, was getan werden kann. Denn im Blick auf das dem Text vorgegebene geprägte Gut sind zwar Formeln und typische Wendungen als geprägte Terminologie und die literarische Gattung als geprägte Struktur ausreichend untersucht und analysiert worden, geprägte Bedeutungssyndrome jedoch nicht erarbeitet[16]. Daß eine *motivkritische Untersuchung* von Jer 18 1–6 bislang noch nicht durchgeführt wurde, überrascht insofern etwas, als das für eine solche Untersuchung nötige Vergleichsmaterial durchaus bekannt ist[17]. Sie ist also dringend nachzuholen.

Wie wir gesehen haben, begegnet die zentrale Aussage des Textes in Gestalt eines Vergleichs: Jahwes Handeln an Israel wird im Bilde des Umgangs eines Töpfers mit seinem Ton veranschaulicht. Daß es sich bei diesem Bild (Umgang des Töpfers mit dem Ton — Bildthema: Souveränität von Jahwes Handeln an Israel) nicht um eine freie Schöpfung des Autors von Jer 18 1–6 handelt, sondern daß er sehr wahrscheinlich ein ihm vorgegebenes Bild aufgenommen, also ein geprägtes Bedeutungssyndrom verarbeitet hat, ergibt sich aus dessen Vorkommen auch an anderen Stellen des Alten Testaments.

a) *Jes 29 15–16*: Weh denen, die tief vor Jahwe
   ihren Plan verbergen,
so daß ihr Werk im Dunklen geschieht
   und sie sagen: »Wer sieht uns? Wer kennt uns?«
Oh, eure Verkehrtheit!
   Oder ist etwa der Töpfer dem Tone gleich zu achten,
daß das Werk zu dem, der's machte, sagte:
   »Er hat mich nicht gemacht!«
und das Gebilde spräche zu dem, der's bildete:
   »Er versteht nichts!«?[18]

Hier begegnet das Motiv innerhalb eines prophetischen Weherufs, in den Elemente des Scheltworts aufgenommen worden sind[19]. Der Text

---

[16] Zur Terminologie s. F. Huber, in: Exegese des Alten Testaments, 1976², § 8.

[17] Siehe hierzu die Verweise auf Jes 29 16 45 9 und 64 7 etwa bei B. Duhm, Das Buch Jeremia, 1901, 153; A. Weiser, Der Prophet Jeremia, ATD 20, 1966⁵, 159; W. Rudolph, Jeremia, HAT I/12, 1958³, 122.

[18] Die umstrittene Frage nach der Einheitlichkeit des Textes (vgl. z. B. O. Kaiser, Der Prophet Jesaja, Kapitel 13–39, ATD 18, 1973, 218f.; F. Huber, Jahwe, Juda und die anderen Völker beim Propheten Jesaja, 1976, 134f. Anm. 203) kann hier unbeantwortet bleiben, da v. 16 nur von v. 15 her interpretiert werden kann, unabhängig davon, ob er ursprünglich zu v. 15 hinzugehörte oder eine Erweiterung darstellt.

[19] S. hierzu L. Markert, Struktur und Bezeichnung des Scheltwortes, 1977, 268 (mit weiterer Literatur). Vgl. auch H.-J. Krause, *hôj* als profetische Leichenklage über das eigene Volk im 8. Jahrhundert, ZAW 85 (1973), 15–46 bes. 34f.

prangert Menschen bestimmten Verhaltens an und ruft über ihrem Tun das *hôj* der Leichenklage aus. Wer sein Handeln und Planen vor Jahwe zu verbergen trachtet und wer sein Werk im Dunkeln — wohl fern von Jahwe — vollbringt, ist dem Tode nahe. Mithilfe eines feststellenden Ausrufs wird die Verkehrtheit solchen Verhaltens herausgestellt und durch Anwendung des Bildes von Töpfer und Ton diese Verkehrung verdeutlicht und aufgedeckt. Daß das Bild auch hier wie in Jer 18 auf das Verhältnis Jahwe–Israel bzw. Judäer geht, ergibt sich unschwer aus dem Kontext, so daß auch das Bildthema das gleiche ist wie im Jeremiatext[20]. Bemerkenswert ist, daß das Bild im Rahmen einer direkten Anrede und als Frage stilisiert eingesetzt wird. Anrede und Frage verlangen nach Reaktion. Als solche kann Zustimmung zur Bildaussage — zur Souveränität des Töpfers über den Ton — erwartet werden. Mit der Zustimmung zur Bildaussage aber werden die Angeredeten genötigt, gleichzeitig die Verkehrtheit ihres eigenen Verhaltens zuzugestehen. Das Bild vom Verhältnis zwischen Töpfer und Ton wird also argumentativ zur Aufdeckung verkehrten Verhaltens verwendet; das ist seine Funktion in Jes 29 15–16. Das Bild ist außerdem integriert in einen prophetischen Wehe-Ruf, also in eine unheilkündende Gattung.

b) *Jes 45 9–10*: Weh dem, der mit seinem Bildner rechtet,
   eine Scherbe unter irdenen Scherben!
Oder sagt etwa der Ton zu seinem Töpfer: »Was machst du?«
   sein Werk: »Du hast keine Hände?«
Weh dem, der zum Vater sagt: »Was zeugst du?«
   und zur Frau: »Was kreißt du?«[21]

Auch in diesem bei Deuterojesaja überlieferten Spruch begegnet das Bild vom Töpfer innerhalb eines prophetischen Weherufs. Über das in

---

[20] Ob dieses geprägte Bild in der Schöpfungstradition seinen ursprünglichen Sitz hatte bzw. aus ihr direkt übernommen ist, wie das z. B. F. Huber a.a.O. (Anm. 18) explizit und H.-J. Krause a.a.O. (Anm. 19) implizit voraussetzen, kann hier offen bleiben. Nur soviel sei angemerkt: Notwendig ist eine solche Annahme nicht, auch wenn die Verwendung von Bildern aus dem Bereich des Töpferhandwerks im Rahmen von Schöpfungsaussagen geläufig ist bzw. eine starke Affinität zwischen Souveränitäts- oder Allmachtaussagen und Schöpfungsaussagen zugestanden werden muß. Das Bild ist auch ohne Assoziation von Schöpfungsvorstellungen voll verständlich. Und es erscheint mir wahrscheinlicher, daß umgekehrt die Schöpfungstheologie dieses Bild wegen seiner Verwendung angezogen hat.

[21] Der Text ist schlecht erhalten. Vor allem die letzte Halbzeile von v. 9 bereitet dem Verstehen Schwierigkeiten. Sie ist nach BHS rekonstruiert. Umstritten ist auch die Abgrenzung des Textes. Vgl. etwa G. Fohrer, Das Buch Jesaja, III 1964, 87, welcher den Spruch als selbständige Einheit betrachtet, mit J. Begrich, Studien zur Deuterojesaja (1938) 1963, 49ff., welcher den Text mit 45 11–13 zusammennimmt und in die Reihe der Disputationsworte stellt, allerdings nicht ohne gravierende Eingriffe in den Konsonantenbestand von 45 9f. vorzunehmen.

diesem unheilkündenden Spruch angeprangerte Verhalten kann man gerade noch so viel sagen, daß es sich um eine grundsätzliche Infragestellung Gottes durch Menschen handelt. Schon im einleitenden Satz wird das Bild vom Töpfer in die Aussage so integriert, daß sein Bezug auf das Verhältnis Schöpfer–Geschöpf und damit ja wohl auf das Verhältnis Jahwe–Israel deutlich genug zum Ausdruck kommt[22]. Wie in Jes 29 15–16 wird der Weheruf durch eine antwortheischende Frage fortgesetzt, welche unter anderem das Bild vom Töpfer und Ton einsetzt, um die Verkehrtheit des angeprangerten Verhaltens zu verdeutlichen. Das Bild wird also auch hier argumentativ verwendet, um die Zustimmung der Hörer zu gewinnen und sie zur Einsicht in die Todverfallenheit ihres Tuns zu führen.

c) *Jes 64* 7–8:   Aber jetzt, Jahwe:
          unser Vater bist du,
     wir sind der Ton
       und du unser Töpfer,
          ja, das Werk deiner Hände sind wir alle.
     Zürne nicht allzusehr, Jahwe,
         und gedenke unserer Schuld nicht für immer;
           ach, blicke doch her, dein Volk sind wir alle.

Diente in Jes 29 15f. und 45 9f. das Bild vom Töpfer als Argument zur Aufdeckung von Schuld, so begegnet es in Jes 63 15–64 11 im Rahmen eines Volksklageliedes[23] in engem Kontext von Sündenbekenntnis 64 4b–6 und Bitte um Beendung des Zürnens Jahwes und Vergebung von Schuld 64 8. Dabei bildet 64 7 eine Art überleitende Klammer zwischen Sündenbekenntnis und Bitte um Zuwendung, da der Text einerseits durch die Verwendung des Bildes vom Töpfer herausstellt, daß mit dem Sündenbekenntnis die Anerkenntnis Jahwes als des souverän Handelnden[24] verbunden ist und da der Text andererseits durch das Bekenntnis zu Jahwe als dem Vater, das auch schon am Beginn des Psalms ausgesprochen wurde 63 15f., andeutet, wo die Klagenden die Bedingung der Möglichkeit einer neuen Zuwendung Jahwes sehen. Die enge Verbindung des

---

[22] In Jes 45 9 ist der Zusammenhang des Motivs mit Schöpfungsaussagen nicht zu leugnen. Man hat den Eindruck, daß die Verwendung des Vergleichs 'Töpfer–Jahwe' innerhalb von Schöpfungsaussagen dazu führte, daß der Ausdruck 'Töpfer' zur Metapher für Jahwe werden konnte.

[23] S. C. Westermann, Das Buch Jesaja. Kapitel 40–66, ATD 19, 1966, 311ff.; G. Fohrer a.a.O. (Anm. 21) 246ff.

[24] Durch den Hinweis auf »das Werk deiner Hände« v. 7bβ wird auch hier das Bild in den Zusammenhang der Schöpfungsvorstellungen eingeordnet. Ob dieser Bezug ursprünglich ist (C. Westermann) oder sekundär (G. Fohrer) kann nicht mehr festgestellt werden. Jedenfalls ist auch dieser Text ein Beleg für die frühe Verknüpfung (exilisch?) des Bildes mit Schöpfungsaussagen.

Töpferbildes mit dem Sündenbekenntnis impliziert das Zugeständnis, daß früheres Verhalten der Klagenden als Infragestellung der Souveränität Jahwes zu verstehen ist. Damit ist auch in Jes 64 7 das Bild im Zusammenhang des Problemkreises Schuld—Verkehrtes Verhalten verwendet.

Fassen wir kurz zusammen: Die Rede vom Umgang des Töpfers mit dem Ton bzw. vom Verhältnis des Töpfers zum Ton kann als Motiv, und zwar als geprägtes Bild bezeichnet werden, da es an allen Stellen des Alten Testaments, wo es belegt ist, als Vergleich für die Souveränität Jahwes dient (= Bildthema). Seine Verwendung in unterschiedlichen Kontexten zeigt eine auffallende Affinität zu Fragen menschlichen Verhaltens angesichts der Souveränität Jahwes, vor allem menschlichen Fehlverhaltens und damit zu Schuld und Sünde. In Jes 29 15f. und 45 9f. wird das Motiv innerhalb einer Frage als Argument gebraucht, das zur Einsicht in verkehrtes Verhalten und damit in unheilvolles Geschick (prophetische Weherufe!) verhelfen soll, während es in Jes 64 7 die Anerkenntnis solchen verkehrten Verhaltens in der Vergangenheit und damit verbundenen Unheils (Jes 64 6!) zum Ausdruck bringt. In allen Texten ist deutlich, daß es nicht allein Funktion des geprägten Bildes ist, ein bestimmtes Bildthema zum Ausdruck zu bringen, sondern darüber hinaus und vor allem dieses Bildthema »Souveränität Jahwes« in seinen Konsequenzen für menschliches Verhalten herauszustellen. Es dient nicht einfach nur dazu, eine theologische Selbstverständlichkeit für Israel mit etwas anderen Worten auszusagen, sondern Israels Lebenspraxis auf dem Hintergrund dieser theologischen Einsicht zu beleuchten, eine Lebenspraxis, die dieser Einsicht nicht entspricht und darum Unheil zur Folge hat bzw. hatte.

III.

Wir kehren zu Jer 18 1—6 zurück, wo das Töpfermotiv in Gestalt einer prophetischen Wahrnehmung an die Stelle einer symbolischen Handlung getreten ist, als deren Funktion die Ankündigung künftiger Ereignisse angenommen wurde.

Von Jes 29 15f. 45 9f. und 64 7 herkommend, fällt zunächst auf, daß auch in Jer 18 das Motiv argumentativ eingesetzt ist. Die Deutung v. 6 ist in Frageform gehalten und fordert eine Antwort heraus, die nur in Zustimmung bestehen kann. Insofern steht Jer 18 den Weherufen Jes 29 15f. und 45 9f. besonders nahe. Während jedoch in den beiden Weherufen das Gewicht auf der Kritik menschlichen Handelns liegt und das daraus resultierende Geschick nur in dem einleitenden Wehe angedeutet wird, scheint in Jer 18 das künftige von Jahwe gewirkte Geschehen im Vordergrund zu stehen und die Aufdeckung von Schuld nur andeutungsweise zum Ausdruck zu kommen. In diesem Punkt steht Jer 18 wiederum Jes 64 7 nahe.

Daß in Jer 18 1—6 überhaupt menschliche Schuld im Blick ist bzw. Kritik an menschlichem Fehlverhalten anklingt, ist allerdings nur der

Verwendung des Töpfermotivs an den behandelten Stellen zu entnehmen. Eine Übertragung dieser Aspekte auf Jer 18 1–6 erscheint aber gerechtfertigt, wenn man davon ausgeht, daß der Vergleich Töpfer–Jahwe als geprägtes Bild aufgenommen wurde und seine Implikationen als bei den Adressaten bekannt vorausgesetzt werden durften. Nur von da aus, d. h. nur von der Voraussetzung einer bestimmten Kommunikationsituation her erklärt sich auch, warum der Bericht über Jeremias Besuch beim Töpfer nach seiner Verschriftung und damit losgelöst von seinem ursprünglichen Kommunikationskontext mehrdeutig werden mußte. Diese Mehrdeutigkeit – wenigstens mit einiger Wahrscheinlichkeit – auf Eindeutigkeit hin einzuengen, ist aber nur möglich, wenn es gelingt, Elemente und Bedingen des Kommunikationsprozesses aufzuspüren, dem der Text sein Entstehen verdankt. Ein solches Element ist offenbar, daß bei den Adressaten ein Vorwissen über die Verwendung des Töpfermotivs vorausgesetzt werden konnte.

Wenn diese Überlegungen auch nur einigermaßen zutreffen, dann kann auch mit aller Vorsicht eine Aussage über die Qualität des Jahwehandelns gewagt werden, das in der Deutung der symbolischen Handlung angesprochen ist und für welches der Text argumentierend Anerkennung fordert (v. 6 Frage!). Da in Jer 18 1–6 das Töpfermotiv wie in Jes 29 15f. und 45 9f. vom Propheten dazu verwendet wird, seinen Hörern zu einer bestimmten Einsicht zu verhelfen, und nicht wie in Jes 64 7 dazu dient, eine bereits gewonnene Einsicht bekenntnisartig zu formulieren, muß auch für die Beschreibung des Jahwehandelns in Jer 18 1–6 vom Gebrauch des Töpfermotivs in den Weherufen ausgegangen werden. Das heißt aber nun: Wenn die in den Weherufen explizit ausgesprochene Kritik an menschlichem Verhalten und seine Qualifizierung als Jahwes Souveränität infragestellendes Handeln in Jer 18 1–6 implizit zum Ausdruck gebracht ist, dann kann das ihm entsprechende Handeln Jahwes nur als Unheils- bzw. Gerichtshandeln verstanden werden.

Dieses Ergebnis der motivkritischen Untersuchung von Jer 18 1–6 ordnet sich gut in die oben angestellten sprachlichen und gattungskritischen Überlegungen ein. Die Verwendung der Gattung »Bericht über symbolische Handlungen der Propheten« erschien ja nur sinnvoll, wenn der Text die Ankündigung eines bestimmten Jahwehandelns zum Ziel hat. Darüber hinaus konnte eine Aussageabsicht rekonstruiert werden, ohne daß bereits durch die Einordnung des Textes in einen bestimmten historischen Kontext (Zeit- und Verfasserfrage) Vorentscheidungen für die Auslegung getroffen wurden; eine Aussageabsicht, welche es vielmehr umgekehrt erleichtert, den Situationshintergrund des Textes zu rekonstruieren. So legt es sich von der Verwendung der Gattung und vom Gebrauch des Motivs in diesem Rahmen her nahe, wenigstens den Selbstbericht 18 2–6 dem Jeremia zuzusprechen und ihn in die zweite Tätigkeitsperiode, die Regierungszeit Jojakims, zu datieren, zumal für die gleiche Periode Berichte über symbolische Handlungen als Selbstberichte unheilkündender Funktion vorliegen (Jer 13 1–11* 16 1–9* 19 1–2.10–11a*).

Daß dieses Ergebnis weiter Auswirkungen auf die Beurteilung der folgenden Verse 18 7–12 hat, ist selbstverständlich. Es sei hier nur angemerkt, daß ihre Einschätzung als Erweiterung nunmehr wahrscheinlicher erscheint als ihre ursprüngliche Zugehörigkeit zum Selbstbericht[25].

IV.

Gegen die vorgelegten Ergebnisse der motivkritischen Analyse könnte nun freilich eingewendet werden, daß sie ausschließlich aufgrund synchroner Betrachtung der Vergleichstexte gewonnen worden sind und eine diachrone Betrachtung unter Umständen zu einem völlig andern Resultat geführt hätte. Es kann ja in der Tat nicht ausgeschlossen werden, daß Jer 18 unter den behandelten Texten der älteste ist und damit prägend gewirkt hat[26]; also dürfe nicht von vornherein vorausgesetzt werden, daß in Jer 18 geprägtes Gut verarbeitet ist. Wenn nun aber unter einem Motiv »ein frei umlaufendes, d. h. nicht mit einem bestimmten Personenkreis verbundenes, geprägtes Bedeutungssyndrom verstanden« wird[27], dann kann ebensowenig selbstverständlich angenommen werden, daß ein bestimmtes Bedeutungssyndrom für denjenigen Text erst gebildet wurde, in welchem es seinen ältesten literarischen Niederschlag gefunden hat. Die Zufälligkeit des Gebrauchs von Motiven macht es wahrscheinlich, daß sie in den meisten Fällen auch in ihren ältesten literarischen Zeugnissen bereits als geprägt vorgegeben waren. Selbst für den Fall, daß man wirklich einmal an einen Text gerät, der ein Bedeutungssyndrom geprägt *hat*, ist synchrone Betrachtung für die Beschreibung des Motivs und seiner Verwendung methodisch gerechtfertigt, da für diesen Fall erst recht ein enger Zusammenhang zwischen Prägendem und Geprägtem vorausgesetzt werden darf.

---

[25] Gegen H. Weippert a. a. O. (Anm. 1) 66f.; G. Fohrer, Die Propheten des 7. Jahrhunderts, 1974, 98ff.; u. a.

[26] Vgl. etwa die Überlegungen von F. Huber a. a. O. (Anm. 18) 134f. zu Jes 29 15ff.. Zu beachten ist weiterhin, daß die andern beiden Texte, die das Motiv belegen, innerhalb von Deuterojesaja und Tritojesaja überliefert sind, also ebenfalls gut jüngeren Datums sein können als Jer 18.

[27] S. F. Huber a. a. O. (Anm. 16) 102.

Seid nicht wie eure Väter!
Bemerkungen zu Sacharja 1 5 und seinem Kontext

von A. S. van der Woude

(Domela Nieuwenhuislaan 57, Groningen)

Im Rahmen des als Fremdbericht gestalteten, zeitlich dicht hinter die von Haggai ausgesprochene Ermunterungsrede Hag 2 1ff. fallenden prophetischen Mahnwortes Sach 1 1–6 bereitet vor allem die Auslegung von v. 5 den Exegeten große Schwierigkeiten. Die Interpretation dieses Verses bestimmt auch die Erklärung des folgenden und dementsprechend die eines wichtigen Teiles des ganzen Abschnitts. Es dürfte sich daher lohnen, uns nochmals mit Sach 1 5 und seinem Kontext zu befassen, weil die bislang vorgetragenen Auslegungen des in Rede stehenden Verses sich bei näherem Zusehen als unbefriedigend erweisen. Mit diesem Beitrag möchte ich dem Jubilar meinen Gruß und meine herzlichen Wünsche sagen.

Das auf den achten Monat des zweiten Regierungsjahres des persischen Königs Darius I. datierte Mahnwort war wohl ursprünglich als Ich-Rede formuliert, in die ein späterer Redaktor durch die Änderung von einem »das Wort Jahwes erging an mich« in »das Wort Jahwes erging an den Propheten Sacharja, den Sohn Berechjas, des Sohnes Iddos« eingegriffen hat[1]. Andere Exegeten halten jedoch dafür, daß nicht nur dieser Vers, sondern auch 1 6b als historische Notizen insgesamt der Endredaktion zuzuschreiben sind[2], während W. A. M. Beuken[3] der Meinung ist, daß der ganze Abschnitt von ihr stammt. Die von 1 1 aufgegebenen überlieferungsgeschichtlichen Probleme können jedoch im Rahmen unserer Untersuchung unbesprochen bleiben, weil von ihrer Lösung die Auslegung des Mahnwortes als solches nicht betroffen ist. Auch die Fragen, ob v. 2 einen ursprünglichen Text ersetzt, in dem ein vor ואמרת (v. 3) zu erwartender Imperativ und eine Adresse gestanden hätten[4], oder ob hinter

---

[1] So auch H. G. Mitchell, Haggai and Zechariah (ICC), 1937², 107, und A. Petitjean, Les oracles du Proto-Zacharie, 1969, 6ff. Zur Frage der Authentizität von »Sohn Berechjas« und zur Datierung vgl. die Kommentare.
[2] Vgl. J. W. Rothstein, Die Genealogie des Königs Jojachin und seiner Nachkommen (I. Chron. 3 17–24) in geschichtlicher Beleuchtung, 1902, 46, und P. G. Rinaldi–F. Luciani, I profeti minori (La Sacra Bibbia AT), 1969, 160.
[3] W. A. M. Beuken, Haggai–Sacharja 1–8, 1967, 84ff.
[4] W. A. M. Beuken a.a.O. 85.

v. 1 eine Beauftragung Gottes an den Propheten ausgefallen ist[5], oder auch ob durch Umstellungen und Korrekturen in den überlieferten Text eingegriffen werden muß[6], können hier unerörtert bleiben, weil die Beantwortung dieser literarkritischen Probleme für die Erklärung der nachfolgenden Verse verhältnismäßig wenig einträgt. Dennoch dürften einige Bemerkungen zu v. 2 am Platze sein. Meiner Ansicht nach ist der Text von v. 2 und 3a völlig in Ordnung. Daß dem der eigentlichen Mahnung vorangeschickten Satz: »Jahwe ist sehr zornig gewesen auf eure Väter« ein Perf. consec. folgt, entspricht der syntaktischen Regel, daß ein Perf. consec., besonders wenn dieses einen Befehl oder einen Wunsch zum Ausdruck bringen soll, mit dem Vorangehenden öfters in losem Zusammenhang steht, vgl. Ges-K, Grammatik, § 112x, aa und I Reg 2 5–6 Dtn 10 15–16. Der literarische Aufbau von Sach 1 1–3 gleicht manchen Stellen im Buche Ezechiel, wo die Worte ואמרת bzw. אֱמֹר (mit hinzugefügtem כה אמר ויהי דבר יהוה אלי [אדני] יהוה) nicht unmittelbar der Einleitungsformel לאמר folgen, sondern davon durch einen oder mehrere Sätze geschieden sind. In diesem Zwischenstück finden sich Aussagen, die in einem mehr oder weniger direkten Zusammenhang mit dem eigentlichen Orakel stehen[7]. Das nun ist auch in unserem Text der Fall. Hier wird thesenartig die Erwähnung des bis vor kurzem das Los des Volkes beherrschenden Verhaltens Jahwes dem Folgenden vorangeschickt, weil auf jenem Hintergrund die eigentliche Mahnung ergeht. Daß also v. 2 nicht zum ursprünglichen Bestand der vorliegenden Prophetie gehören und Sacharja abgesprochen werden sollte, läßt sich weder aus syntaktischen noch aus überlieferungskritischen Gründen bestätigen und ist umso unwahrscheinlicher, wenn man beachtet, daß der Vers thematisch gerade einen charakteristischen Zug der Predigt des Propheten aufweist[8].

---

[5] So W. Rudolph, Haggai–Sacharja–Maleachi (KAT XIII/4), 1976, 66, und früher schon E. Sellin, Das Zwölfprophetenbuch, 1929/30[2.3], 479.

[6] K. Budde, ZAW 26 (1905), 4f., vesetzt v. 2 vor *šûbû* in v. 3 und fügt vor v. 3 ein »gehe« (bzw. »verkündige«) ein. W. Nowack folgt E. Sellin, indem er v. 2 als Glosse zu 7 12 betrachtet und 6 15b und 8 14–15 zwischen v. 6a und 6b einfügt (Göttinger Handkommentar zum AT III/4, 1922, 329). In der Gefolgschaft von F. Horst, Die zwölf kleinen Propheten, 1964[3], 216, versetzt Th. Chary, Aggée–Zacharie–Malachie (Sources Bibliques), 1969, 54, v. 2 hinter v. 6a, während er, wie E. Sellin, vor v. 3 ein: »Crie au reste de ce peuple«, einfügt. Nach K. Elliger, Das Buch der zwölf Kleinen Propheten (ATD 25), 1959[4], 102, ist die Einleitung v. 1–3 entweder durch Textbeschädigung oder durch ungeschickte Redaktion verstümmelt. H. G. Mitchell a.a.O. 110 betrachtet v. 2 als Interpolation und vermißt vor v. 3 einige Wörter.

[7] Vgl. dazu A. Petitjean a.a.O. 28.

[8] Vgl. Sach 1 15 7 12. »Zu ihnen« in v. 3 findet in »eure Väter« das notwendige Beziehungswort. Zum Suffix als Beziehungswort vgl. Ges-K, § 138f.

V. 3 bildet ohne Zweifel den Kern des Mahnwortes[9]. W. A. M. Beuken gesteht wenigstens theoretisch, daß der an die klassische Prophetie erinnernde und den Einfluß der deuteronomistischen Umkehrpredigt zeigende Spruch: »Kehrt um zu mir, so will Ich umkehren zu euch«, von Sacharja selbst stammen könnte. Diese Möglichkeit verringere sich seiner Meinung nach aber sehr, wenn man beachte, daß שוב als »Ausdruck der Bundestheologie«, außer in unserem Text, nirgendwo bei Sacharja vorkommt[10]. Dazu wäre zunächst zu sagen, daß man einem Propheten eine bestimmte Aussage nicht deswegen absprechen sollte, weil in ihr eine Verwendung einer Vokabel begegnet, die sonst bei ihm nicht belegt werden kann. Auf unseren Fall bezogen müßte man dann auch Mal 3 7 als sekundär betrachten, weil שוב in der dort vorkommenden Bedeutung anderswo bei Maleachi nicht gefunden wird. W. A. M. Beuken meint tatsächlich, daß wir diesen Text als spätere »Erweiterung« zu betrachten haben, was mir allerdings zweifelhaft erscheint, weil so die eigentümliche Struktur der Diskussionsrede des Propheten erheblich beeinträchtigt wäre[11]. Daß gerade Maleachi und auch der Chronist (II Chr 30 6) die Worte: »Kehrt euch zu mir, so kehre Ich mich zu euch« aufgegriffen haben, könnte darauf hinweisen, daß dieser Spruch als Bestandteil der deuteronomistischen Predigt in nachexilischer Zeit geläufig war. Auch wäre nicht von vornherein auszuschließen, daß Sacharja mit den Worten: »Kehrt euch zu mir« die Forderung der klassischen Propheten übernommen und um die Worte: »So kehre Ich mich zu euch« erweitert hat[12]. Hinzu kommt, daß es m. E. keinen ausreichenden Grund gibt, Sacharja eine völlig andersartige Verwendung von שוב in 1 3 auf der einen Seite und in 1 16 8 3 auf der anderen Seite zu unterstellen. Was »umkehren« in 1 3 bedeutet, läßt sich zwar nicht mit aller gewünschten Eindeutigkeit bestimmen, aber einiges ist dazu doch wohl mit ziemlicher Sicherheit zu sagen. Aus dem folgenden v. 4 dürfen wir wenigstens den Schluß ziehen, daß die geforderte Umkehr der Gemeinde sich auf gehorsamen Handel und Wandel gemäß den Worten und Anordnungen Jahwes bezieht. Diese Interpretation wird durch Sach 7 8 f. und 8 16 f. 19 bestätigt. Eine solche sittliche Umkehr ist Voraussetzung einer neuen Heilszeit bzw. dafür, daß Jahwe sich zu seinem Volk kehrt und nicht wieder zürnt (v. 2)[13]. Voraussetzung der neuen Heilszeit ist für Sacharja, wie für Haggai, aber auch der Bau des Tempels. Mit »Umkehr zu Jahwe« ist somit nicht bloß sittlicher, sondern auch kultischer Gehorsam gemeint, Aspekte des Gehorsams, die ohnehin im alten Israel kaum

---

[9] A. van Hoonacker, Les douze petits prophètes, 1908, 588, betrachtet dagegen v. 3 als beiläufige Mahnung einer Prophetie, die das Los der Väter ins Gedächtnis rufen wollte.
[10] A. a. O. 92 f.
[11] Vgl. zur Struktur der erwähnten Stelle Mal 1 6 f.
[12] Vgl. etwa Jer 18 11 f. 25 5 f.
[13] Dieses Moment wird besonders von W. Rudolph a. a. O. 68 betont.

voneinander zu trennen waren. Konkret mußte also der Ruf zur Umkehr in jenen Tagen *auch* bedeuten, sich am Bau des Tempels zu beteiligen[14]. Es ist auffallend, daß die Worte: »Kehrt euch zu mir, so kehre Ich mich zu euch« bei Maleachi und beim Chronisten in einem kultischen Kontext begegnen[15]. Ein Entweder-Oder im Sinne einer sittlichen Umkehr oder einer kultischen Beteiligung am Tempelbau sollte man aus den Worten: »Kehrt euch zu mir« also nicht herauslesen, um in dem einen Fall Sacharja als Kritiker der Predigt Haggais auszumalen, in dem anderen ihn dasselbe wie sein prophetischer Kollege sagen zu lassen. Dementsprechend wird auch die »Umkehr« Jahwes zu seiner Gemeinde nicht nur im Sinne einer künftigen Spendung des Segens, sondern auch als Rückkehr zu seinem Tempel und Jerusalem zu verstehen sein[16]. So interpretiert, unterscheidet sich die Bedeutung von שוב in 1 3 nicht erheblich von der in 1 16 8 3. Die öfters beklagte Tatsache, daß die Tragweite von שוב in 1 3 weder im Fall der Umkehr des Volkes noch in dem der Umkehr Gottes klar umrissen ist, könnte Absicht des Propheten sein: die Umkehr des Volkes soll umfassend sein, weil auch die neue Hinwendung Jahwes zu seinem Volk allumfassend sein wird.

»Es ist schon längst aufgefallen, daß der nur vier Wörter umfassende Bußruf durch die dreimalige Versicherung, daß es sich um *Jahwes* Wort handelt, um mehr als das Doppelte anschwillt« (W. Rudolph)[17]. Diese Tatsache berechtige nach Ansicht von W. Rudolph zu der Annahme, daß die Worte Sacharjas eine Spitze gegen die Ankündigung Haggias enthalten, der wenige Wochen zuvor »mit derselben Plerophorie« den Anbruch der Heilszeit wegen des in Angriff genommenen Tempelbaus verkündet hatte (Hag 2 4–9). Sacharja habe die Predigt seines Kollegen dahingehend kritisiert, daß die Bereitwilligkeit zum Tempelbau zur Umkehr nicht genüge: letztere müsse tiefer gehen und sich stärker auswirken[18]. Ob man aus der Betonung, mit der Sacharja den Ruf zur Umkehr als Wort *Jahwes* vorbringt, so weitgehende Schlüsse ziehen darf, scheint mir zweifelhaft. Es dürfte besser sein und der Tendenz des ganzen Abschnitts entsprechen, die Akzentuierung als Wort Jahwes von den folgenden Versen her zu deuten: dieses neue Gotteswort soll nicht in den Wind geschlagen werden, denn das Wort Gottes erweist sich als wirkungsmächtig.

Die in v. 4 formulierte Warnung davor, dem schlechten Beispiel der Väter, die die Predigt der früheren Propheten in den Wind geschlagen hatten, zu folgen, ist sprachlich zum allergrößten Teil in jeremianisch-

---

[14] Dieses Moment wird besonders von A. Petitjean a.a.O. 36, H. Junker, Die zwölf Kleinen Propheten (Die Heilige Schrift des AT, VIII/3/II), 1938, 118, W. Nowack a.a.O. 329 und G. Fohrer, Die Propheten des Alten Testaments, V, 1976, betont.

[15] Vgl. A. Petitjean a.a.O. 36.

[16] So auch H. G. Mitchell a.a.O. 111 und K. Elliger a.a.O. 101.

[17] A.a.O. 68.

[18] A.a.O. 68.

deuteronomistischer Tradition verwurzelt[19]. Demgemäß sollte man den Begriff »eure Väter« hier nicht zu eng fassen und nicht von vornherein auf die Generation der nach Babel verschleppten Exulanten beschränken[20]. Dem entspricht, daß die *früheren Propheten*, eine für Sacharja eigentümliche Wendung[21], grundsätzlich alle vorexilischen Künder des Gotteswortes umspannen.

Wie in v. 2 hebt sich auch in v. 5 das Vokabular deutlich von deuteronomistischer Tradition ab. Nach dem Rückblick auf die Zeit des Ungehorsams der Väter erwartet man in diesem Vers einen Hinweis auf das Strafgericht, das sie getroffen hatte. Dieser Erwartung kommt v. 5a tatsächlich entgegen, indem der Prophet seine Zuhörer in rhetorischer Art und Weise fragt: אבותיכם איה־הם, »eure Väter – wo sind sie?« Diese Worte werden oft so erklärt, daß die Väter im Exil geblieben und auf fremder Erde gestorben sind[22]. W. A. M. Beuken[23] hat aber gezeigt, daß der Sinn und die Bedeutung der Frage mit dieser Interpretation nicht genügend erfaßt werden. Obgleich auch er meint, daß das zweite Glied von v. 5 (von ihm mit: »Und leben die Propheten ewig?« übersetzt) die vorangehenden Worte der Bedeutung nach so zuspitzen, daß vom Verschwinden der Väter vom Schauplatz der Geschichte die Rede sei, hat er doch mit Recht betont, daß die dem Streitgespräch entnommene Frage: »Wo ist/sind nun ...« gestellt wird, »wenn jemand auf etwas seine Hoffnung setzte und sich getäuscht sieht, oder wo feindliche Mächte wegfallen«. So wird den von Feinden verfolgten Gerechten vom Gegner spöttisch gefragt: »Wo ist nun dein Gott?«[24], und wird dem abtrünnigen Israel die Frage gestellt: »Wo sind nun eure Götter?«[25] So fragt auch Jeremia den sich an ihn klammernden König Zedekia: »Wo sind nun eure Propheten, die euch weissagten: ›Der König von Babel wird nicht über euch und über dieses Land kommen?‹«[26], ohne daß er damit behaupten wollte, daß die falschen Propheten schon alle gestorben seien, vgl. auch Nah 2 12 3 18 Jer 13 20 Ez 13 12. Die Spottfrage: »Wo sind sie?« will also nicht zuallererst oder gar ausschließlich den *Tod* der Väter hervorheben, sondern das schmähliche Los, das ihnen infolge ihres Ungehorsams widerfuhr. Nicht der Tod der Väter steht im Mittelpunkt des Interesses, geschweige denn der Tod im fernen Land des Exils, sondern das, was aus den Vätern geworden ist: die

---

[19] Zu den Einzelheiten vgl. A. Petitjean a.a.O. 39 und W. A. M. Beuken a.a.O. 95ff.
[20] In der jeremianisch-deuteronomistischen Literatur bezieht sich die Wendung auf viele vorangehende Generationen bis zur frühesten Zeit Israels.
[21] Vgl. Sach 7 7.12.
[22] Vgl. W. Rudolph a.a.O. 69 und E. Sellin a.a.O. 479; F. Horst a.a.O. 217; H. G. Mitchell a.a.O. 112; W. Nowack a.a.O. 330; A. Petitjean a.a.O. 42.
[23] A.a.O. 99.
[24] II Reg 18 34 Jer 17 15 Ps 42 4.11 79 10 usw.
[25] Dtn 32 37.
[26] Jer 37 19.

ganze Geschichte der Enttäuschung, der Schmach und des Elends, die sie über sich gebracht haben.

Mit dieser wohl kaum zu beanstandenden Bedeutung der Frage: »Eure Väter, – wo sind sie?«, verträgt sich nun aber die folgende, offenbar im parallelismus membrorum angeschlossene weitere Frage: »Und die Propheten, leben sie ewig?« besonders schlecht. Wenn diese Übersetzung von v. 5b dem Urtext entspräche, hätten wir hier tatsächlich einen Hinweis auf das befristete Leben bzw. den Tod der Propheten vor uns. Der Gedanke eines Strafgerichts läßt sich mit dieser Aussage nicht vereinbaren. Aber auch in ganz anderer Hinsicht hat der Text von v. 5b den Erklärern seit langem große Schwierigkeiten bereitet. Welche Propheten sind hier gemeint, die klassischen Schriftpropheten oder die falschen Propheten? K. Elliger, A. Petitjean u. a. haben vorgeschlagen »die Propheten« mit den in v. 4 erwähnten früheren Propheten, die in v. 6 von Jahwe als »meine Knechte, die Propheten« bezeichnet werden, zu identifizieren. Aus den Worten von v. 5 gehe hervor, daß sich der Kanon des Alten Testaments ankündige: »Mögen die Väter, das Objekt der Verkündigung, und die Propheten, das Subjekt der Verkündigung, nicht mehr vorhanden sein, so ist doch der Inhalt ihrer Verkündigung noch da[27].« Noch ganz abgesehen davon, ob in v. 5 zuallererst vom Verschwinden der Väter die Rede ist und ob Sacharja (gemäß der Verwendung des Ausdrucks »die früheren Propheten«) sich selbst nicht als Prophet verstand, hat W. A. M. Beuken gegen obige Erklärung mit Recht eingewendet, daß sie nicht nur die Bedeutung von השיגו in v. 6, das stets »als Glück oder Unglück treffen« und niemals ein neutrales »erreichen« bedeutet, verkenne, sondern auch den offensichtlichen parallelismus membrorum von v. 5 mißachte: »Der ungünstige Ton, der aus dem »Wo sind nun eure Väter?« zu hören ist, überträgt sich durch den Parallelismus auch auf: »Und leben die Propheten ewig?« Daher müsse, wie schon Hieronymus vorgeschlagen hatte, in unserem Vers von den falschen Propheten die Rede sein[28]. Gegen diese Interpretation hat W. Rudolph[29] neulich wieder einmal betont, daß 14.6a und 77.12 die Deutung von »die Propheten« im Sinne von Pseudopropheten nicht erlauben und daß die Hinzufügung von »meine Knechte« in v. 6a nicht einen Gegensatz zu v. 5b zum Ausdruck bringt. Man müsse deswegen der schon im Targum geäußerten[30] und von A. van Hoonacker[31]

---

[27] K. Elliger a. a. O. 101; vgl. auch K. Marti, Das Dodekapropheton (KHzAT XIII), 1904, 400; H. Junker a. a. O. 119; G. Fohrer a. a. O. und R. Mason, The Books of Haggai, Zechariah and Malachi (The Cambridge Bible Commentary), 1977, 33.

[28] W. A. M. Beuken a. a. O. 100.

[29] A. a. O. 69.

[30] »Eure Väter wo sind sie? und wenn ihr sagt: Leben denn die Propheten ewig? – nein, die Propheten leben nicht ewig.«

[31] A. a. O. 589.

befürworteten Erklärung folgen, daß in v. 5b eine aggressive Entgegnung der Zuhörer des Propheten vorliege. Nach W. Rudolph hätten die Gegner Sacharjas ihm entgegengehalten: »Die Propheten, diese Gottesmänner, sind doch auch nicht am Leben geblieben, wie kannst du dann mit solcher Sicherheit behaupten, daß der Tod der Väter als Strafe anzusehen ist?«[32] Hätte aber, wenn hier tatsächlich ein Einwand der Zuhörer vorläge, das nicht deutlicher gesagt werden müssen? Hätte man, wenn die Zuhörer Sacharjas das Exil nicht als Strafe Jahwes betrachten wollten, ihren Einwand gegen die Umkehrpredigt des Propheten nicht vielmehr nach v. 2–3 erwarten müssen, etwa im Sinne der Entgegnung der Zuhörer Maleachis? Ist wirklich anzunehmen, daß die eben aus dem Exil zurückgekehrte Gemeinde oder auch die im Lande zurückgebliebene Bevölkerung die Verwüstung Jerusalems und die Verbannung nicht als Strafe Jahwes erfahren hätten? Für die gegenteilige Auffassung fehlt, wenn ich recht sehe, in der uns überlieferten Geschichte, Prophetie und Poesie jener Zeit jede triftige Begründung. Ist schließlich zu erwarten, daß v. 5, der offenbar poetisch gestaltet ist, auf zwei Sprecher aufgeteilt werden muß?

Weil die genannten Erklärungen von v. 5 einen nicht befriedigen können, muß gefragt werden, ob das Übel nicht im überlieferten Text steckt. Das dürfte tatsächlich der Fall sein, obgleich Worte wie העולם und יחיו zunächst nicht den Schein erwecken, verschrieben zu sein. Unter Beibehaltung des Konsonantenbestandes (die Änderung von *yod* in *waw* ausgenommen) läßt sich der Text von v. 5b bei einer anderen Trennung der Buchstaben folgendermaßen lesen: וְהַנְּבִאִים הַלָעוּ לָמוֹ, »und (wo sind) die Propheten, die unsinnig zu ihnen redeten«. Dabei setzt sich die Form הַלָעוּ aus einem sog. *hă*-relativum und der 3. Pers. Plur. perf. qal von לעע, »irre, unsinnig, unbedacht reden« (vgl. arab. *lagā*), zusammen, während למו das Äquivalent von להם bildet. Die restlichen Buchstaben (חיו) sind zu v. 6 zu ziehen, s. unten. Nicht nur ist das *hă*-relativum in der nachexilischen Zeit gut belegt[33], sondern auch למו kann wegen der poetischen Gestaltung von v. 5 nicht als unmöglich bezeichnet werden, vor allen Dingen deswegen nicht, weil es eben im kontemporären Schrifttum öfters begegnet[34].

Bei der vorgeschlagenen Lesung von v. 5b verschwinden auf einmal alle Schwierigkeiten, die wir vorhin erwähnt haben und die einem befriedigenden Verstehen im Wege standen. Wie schon von Hieronymus vermutet und von neueren Auslegern bestätigt, handelt es sich bei den hier genannten Propheten tatsächlich um die vorexilischen Pseudopropheten.

---

[32] A.a.O. 69f., vgl. auch C. F. Keil, Biblischer Commentar über die zwölf Kleinen Propheten, 1888³, 536.
[33] Vgl. Ges-K, § 138i.
[34] Von den insgesamt 55 Belegen entfallen 4 auf Dtn 32–33, 5 auf Deutero- und Trito-Jes, 4 auf Thr, 10 auf Hi und 22 auf Ps (mehrere aus nachexilischer Zeit).

Der erschlossene Relativsatz weist sie ja als solche aus. Schon Zephanja hatte sie als Großsprecher und Männer des Betrugs angeprangert (Zeph 3 4, vgl. Ez 22 28), und Jeremia hatte sie der Lüge und des Schwindels bezichtigt (Jer 23 32). Unsere Erklärung gibt also nicht nur eine geläufige Bezeichnung der falschen Propheten her, sondern hat auch den Vorteil, daß sie den erwarteten parallelismus membrorum berücksichtigt und den schon im ersten Glied des Verses anklingenden ungünstigen Ton wahrt. Sacharja fragt also seine Hörer, was nun aus den ungehorsamen Vätern und den Propheten, denen sie gefolgt, geworden ist. Die Antwort auf diese Frage braucht er nicht eigens zu formulieren: Jeder weiß Bescheid! Diesem schlechten Beispiel des Nichthörens auf die Worte Jahwes sollte keiner in Zukunft folgen!

Nachdem der Prophet in v. 4–5 anhand der Geschichte der Väter seinen eindringlichen Ruf zur Umkehr erläutert hat, indem er auf die folgenschwere Enttäuschung hinweist, welche die Väter infolge ihres Nichthörens auf Gottes Wort und ihrer Hinwendung zu den falschen Propheten erlitten haben, wendet er sich in v. 6 abermals dem Thema Wort Gottes zu, jetzt aber von einem anderen Blickpunkt aus. In diesem Vers wird die Wirkungsmächtigkeit der Worte und Anordnungen Jahwes betont, die die Väter bejahen mußten. Obgleich nicht zu leugnen ist, daß v. 6 Beziehungen zu v. 4–5 aufweist, da ähnliche Begriffe und Wendungen aufgegriffen werden und auch hier die vergangene Geschichte paränetisch ausgewertet wird, ja sogar v. 6 in einem gewissen Gegensatz zu v. 5 steht, sollte doch mehr als üblicherweise geschieht, die relative Eigenständigkeit der Thematik von v. 6 ins Auge gefaßt werden.

Die letzten drei Buchstaben von v. 5 sind zu v. 6 zu ziehen und als חָיוּ, »sie sind lebend« (3. Pers. Plur. perf. qal von חיה), zu deuten. Ähnlich wie in Gen 7 23 (»Noach *jedoch* blieb übrig«) betont das vor dem Subjekt (»meine Worte und Anordnungen«) stehende אך, daß, während die Väter und die falschen Propheten sich nicht behaupten konnten, die Worte und Anordnungen, welche Jahwe seinen Knechten, den Propheten, anvertraut hatte, *jedoch* wirksam und lebenskräftig waren und sind (zu dieser Bedeutung des perf. vgl. Ges-K, § 106 g–l). Das Qal von חיה hat hier wohl die Bedeutung »wirksam existent sein«, entsprechend der Verwendung des Piʻels in Hab 3 2, wo »sich wirksam realisieren« gemeint ist. Betont ist also nicht in erster Linie, daß Gottes Wort für immer besteht, während die Väter und die Propheten gestorben und also nicht mehr da sind, sondern daß es sich wirkungsmächtig gestaltet und nicht ein leeres Wort ist (Dtn 32 47). Daß dem so ist, belegt Sacharja seinen Zuhörern dadurch, daß er sie auf die Tatsache hinweist, daß Jahwes Worte und Anordnungen, als wären sie Personen, die Väter nicht entkommen ließen: die in den mit den Bundesbestimmungen verknüpften Sanktionen stipulierte Strafe traf sie, vgl. Dtn 28 15.45. Sie mußten zum Schluß bekennen, daß tatsächlich das geschehen war, was ihnen vorausgesagt wurde.

Ganz abgesehen davon, daß die Worte הלוא השיגו אבתיכם, die nach unserer Analyse von v. 5–6 als Anfang eines *neuen* Satzes (und nicht als Fortsetzung eines als eine Art von casus pendens konstruierten v. 6a) zu betrachten sind, kaum den Abschluß der Mahnrede bilden können, gibt es auch weiter keinen ausreichenden Grund, v. 6b statt als direkte Fortsetzung des Vorangehenden als historische Schlußnotiz des Endredaktors zu interpretieren, so daß das Subjekt der Verbalformen וישובו und ויאמרו die Zuhörerschaft Sacharjas wäre[35]. Ganz im Gegenteil! Weil nach »eure Väter« in v. 6 kein neues Subjekt eingeführt wird, spricht der Kontext dafür, sie als Subjekt der Verbalformen zu betrachten[36]. Durch die Verwendung von דרכים und מעללים greift der Prophet sprachlich auf v. 4 zurück, wo von den Wegen und Werken der *Väter* die Rede ist. Die als Gerichtsdoxologie[37] stilisierten Worte von v. 6b sind als Schuldbekenntnis kaum im Munde der Zuhörer Sacharjas zu erwarten, weil im Vorangehenden von *ihrem* Ungehorsam nicht gesprochen wird und Texte wie I Reg 8 46 ff. Dtn 4 29–30 30 1 ff. entschieden dafür sprechen, daß die wegen ihrer eigenen Sünden Gestraften ihre Missetaten bekennen. Alle uns zur Verfügung stehenden Daten weisen also darauf hin, daß das in v. 6b erwähnte Schuldbekenntnis *von den Vätern* gesprochen wurde. Daraus hat J. Wellhausen[38] den Schluß gezogen: »In der Folge der Warnung bekehrten sie sich nicht, wohl aber, als es zu spät war, infolge der Strafe.«

Diese Interpretation stellt uns nach W. A. M. Beuken[39] vor große Schwierigkeiten. Sie untergrabe die eigene Darlegung Sacharjas in v. 4, wo der Prophet ausdrücklich dazu aufruft, dem schlechten Beispiel der Väter nicht zu folgen. Die Bekehrung der Väter wäre doch nicht als schlechtes Beispiel zu bezeichnen! Es habe weiter in der Linie der Predigt auch keinen Sinn, nach v. 5 noch einmal zu erwähnen, daß die Väter »infolge der Strafe« zur Bußfertigkeit kamen, denn »mit v. 5 ist die Erwähnung der Väter zu Ende«. Man müsse also nach Beuken v. 6b für eine historische Schlußnotiz über das Verhalten der Zuhörer des Propheten halten. Dazu wäre zunächst zu bemerken, daß auch in v. 6a ausdrücklich von »eure Väter« die Rede ist, denn es wird gesagt, daß die Worte Jahwes sie »als tödliche Geschosse« (G. Fohrer)[40] getroffen hatten. Was W. A. M. Beuken aber offenbar meint, formuliert er an anderer Stelle weniger mißverständlich: Nachdem er die Bedeutung von השיגו im Sinne eines neutralen Erreichens als falsch abgewiesen hat, schreibt er: »Es hätte keinen Sinn, im

---

[35] So W. Nowack a.a.O. 400; W. A. M. Beuken a.a.O. 86ff. und R. Mason a.a.O. 33.
[36] Eine Änderung von »eure Väter« in »euch« (so E. Sellin, K. Elliger usw.) ist ebensowenig erforderlich als die von »sie bekehrten sich« in »sie wurden zuschanden« (F. Horst, G. Fohrer).
[37] Dazu vgl. W. A. M. Beuken a.a.O. 103ff.
[38] J. Wellhausen, Die Kleinen Propheten, 1963⁴, 177.
[39] A.a.O. 87.
[40] A.a.O.

Verlauf dieser Predigt zu bemerken, daß die Väter das Wort Gottes doch hörten, wohl aber daß Gottes Wort, die Bundesbestimmungen und die damit verknüpften Sanktionen, die Väter einholte, m. a. W., daß sie dem, was Gottes Wort bewirkt, wenn es nicht angenommen wird, nicht entkommen konnten[41].« Es ist zuzugeben, daß die von W. A. M. Beuken signalisierte Diskrepanz sich nur mit Mühe durch die oben zitierte Schlußfolgerung J. Wellhausens beheben läßt. Daß es aber »in der Linie der Predigt« keinen Sinn habe von der Bußfertigkeit der Väter zu reden, hängt völlig davon ab, wie man die Linie der Predigt einschätzt. Meiner Ansicht nach zergliedert sich die historisch-paränetische Begründung des Aufrufs zur Bekehrung in zwei Teile (v. 4–5.6), wenn diese auch nicht ganz unverbunden nebeneinander stehen. Im ersten Teil handelt es sich um das Nichthören auf Gottes Wort und um die Enttäuschung, die die Väter infolgedessen erlitten (vgl. unsere Erklärung von v. 5). Im zweiten Teil handelt es sich um die Wirkungsmächtigkeit des göttlichen Wortes, der auch die Väter nicht entgehen konnten und die sie schließlich anerkennen mußten. Beide Sachen werden erwähnt, um die Zuhörer vor Mißachtung des eigenen, von Sacharja im Namen Jahwes gesprochenen Mahnwortes zur Umkehr zu warnen. Dem entspricht die von W. A. M. Beuken signalisierte Diskrepanz, die aber nur dann besteht, wenn man die – wenn auch relative – Zäsur zwischen v. 5 und v. 6 nicht beachtet. Die Erwähnung der Väter ist in v. 5 insofern zu Ende, als dem in v. 4–5 Gesagten nichts mehr hinzugefügt zu werden braucht. Die Väter erscheinen aber wieder in einem neuen Zusammenhang in v. 6. Es ist sogar fraglich, ob beide Male mit »eure Väter« genau dasselbe gemeint ist. Wir haben gesehen, daß die Verwurzelung von v. 4 in der jeremianisch-deuteronomistischen Tradition dafür spricht, in den Vätern und den früheren Propheten grundsätzlich zahlreiche vorexilische Generationen zu sehen. In v. 6 handelt es sich aber wohl zuallererst um die Väter, die die Verschleppung nach Babel erlebten bzw. um diejenigen, die in miserablem Zustand im Lande zurückblieben, vgl. Thr 2 17. Die doppelte Ausrichtung der der vergangenen Geschichte entnommenen Paränese kann gewisse Unterschiede zwischen v. 4–5 und v. 6 verständlich machen. Dementsprechend mußte, ähnlich wie in v. 5, in v. 6 gesagt werden, wie es den Vätern erging bzw. wie sich Gottes Wort bei ihnen auswirkte. Daß die Bekehrung der Väter zur Bußfertigkeit, wie W. A. M. Beuken ausführt[42], kein topos der nachexilischen Überlieferung sei, läßt sich bezweifeln. Eine derartige Bekehrung ist gerade in der deuteronomistischen Literatur vorgesehen, vgl. I Reg 8 46ff. Dtn 4 29–30 30 1ff. Daß in v. 6b die *Zuhörer* des Propheten in historischer Solidarität mit den Vätern die Sünde des Abfalls

---

[41] A. a. O. 101.
[42] A. a. O. 87.

und des Ungehorsams bekennen, läßt sich deswegen auch nicht motivgeschichtlich bestätigen[43].

Daß man, wie W. Rudolph sagt[44], in v. 6b »die notwendige Anwendung auf die Hörer« erwarten müsse und daher statt der erzählenden Tempora die Imperative ושובו ואמרו brauche, kann nicht überzeugen. Unbeschadet der Tatsache, daß eine solche Änderung des überlieferten Textes jede Stütze in den Versionen vermissen läßt, ist nicht klar, weshalb gerade an dieser Stelle eine Anwendung auf die Hörer stehen müsse, so daß diese zu einer Umkehr und zu einem Schuldbekenntnis aufgefordert seien. Denn von *ihrer* Schuld ist im ganzen Abschnitt Sach 1 1-6 niemals die Rede, und der Aufruf zur Umkehr war schon in v. 3 an sie ergangen. Dieser brauchte nach der folgenden Prämisse nicht wiederholt zu werden.

Unsere Untersuchung des in mancher Hinsicht umstrittenen Mahnwortes Sach 1 1-6 hat zu zeigen versucht, daß man in diesen Abschnitt weder textlich noch literarkritisch tief eingreifen sollte. Nur könnten die von uns vorgeschlagene Abtrennung der Buchstaben in v. 5b und der sich daraus ergebende Satz vielleicht zum besseren Verständnis des aus der vergangenen Geschichte begründeten Rufes zur Umkehr beitragen. Die öfters zwischen v. 4 und v. 6b signalisierte Spannung, die darin bestehe, daß sich die Aufforderung, dem schlechten Beispiel der Väter nicht zu folgen, nicht vertrage mit der Bußfertigkeit der Väter, läßt sich beheben, wenn man die doppelte Begründung des Rufes zur Umkehr (v. 3) in v. 4-5 und v. 6 beachtet: Nichthören auf Jahwes Wort führt zu Enttäuschung und Schande; Jahwes Wort ist wirkungsmächtig und führt zur Anerkennung der eigenen Schuld. Beides läßt sich aus der Geschichte der Väter beispielhaft belegen.

Den Abschnitt Sacharja abzusprechen, liegt kein ausreichender Grund vor. Zwar findet sich weder in unserem Mahnwort noch in Sach 7 4-14 vieles für den Propheten Eigentümliches, obgleich charakteristische Züge dann und wann deutlich erkennbar sind. Die Tatsache, daß diese Züge zum größten Teil von der deuteronomistischen Tradition überlagert sind, ist bei der Gestaltung des Mahnwortes als Homilie nicht befremdend.

---

[43] Vgl. auch Thr 2 17 Ps 79 9.
[44] A. a. O. 70f.

Das Phänomen der »Fortschreibung« im Buche Ezechiel

Von Walther Zimmerli

(Herzberger Landstraße 26, Göttingen)

I

Propheten sind Gestalten, die in konkrete Geschichte hinein aufgeboten sind und in sie hinein den Gottesbescheid sagen. Geschichte aber ist kein ruhendes Phänomen, sondern ein Prozeß, der, wie es das Wort »Geschichte« sagt, »geschehend« sich bewegt. Die Forschung an den Prophetenbüchern weiß sehr wohl um diesen Prozeß und die besonderen Probleme, die er gerade ihrem Verständnis stellt.

Die Bewegung der Geschichte kann schon für die Zeitspanne zwischen dem mündlich gesprochenen und dem schriftlich aufgezeichneten Wort bedeutsam werden, ist dort allerdings angesichts der Ungreifbarkeit des mündlichen Zeugnisses besonders schwer zu fassen. Aber wenn sich etwa beim Verständnis von Jes 6, wo doch wohl der Bericht des Propheten über seine Berufungsstunde zu lesen ist[1], die Frage stellt, wie weit sich in der Formulierung dieses Berichtes nicht schon spätere Erfahrungen des Propheten, etwa aus der Zeit des sog. syrisch-ephraimitischen Krieges niedergeschlagen haben, dann könnte auch hier später Erfahrenes die Schilderung des früheren Erlebnisses mitgestaltet haben.

Deutlicher faßbar ist demgegenüber die literarische »Nachgeschichte«[2] der schon schriftlich aufgezeichneten Texte, in der diese, oft sehr deutlich erkennbar, Umgestaltungen und Ergänzungen aus einer neuen Zeitsituation heraus erfahren haben, wobei dann auch u. U. das ursprüngliche Bild der prophetischen Rede stark verwischt werden konnte.

G. Fohrer, dem die folgenden Erwägungen in Dankbarkeit für seine umfangreiche Arbeit am Alten Testament und die länderweite Vermittlung der Forschung am Alten Testament in der ZAW und ihren Beiheften gewidmet sind, hat in der Vorarbeit zu seiner Kommentierung des Ezechielbuches auch dieser Nacharbeit seine Aufmerksamkeit geschenkt und die nachträglichen Erweiterungselemente in feste Kategorien der

---

[1] Anders O. H. Steck, Bemerkungen zu Jesaja 6, BZ NF 16 (1972), 188–206.
[2] Zu diesem Terminus vgl. H. W. Hertzberg, Die Nachgeschichte alttestamentlicher Texte innerhalb des Alten Testaments, BZAW 66, 1936, 110–121.

»Glossierung« eingeordnet³. So unterscheidet er die folgenden Kategorien der Erweiterung des vom Propheten selber stammenden Textes: 1. wiederholende, 2. erklärende, 3. ergänzende, 4. ändernde, 5. redaktionelle und 6. unverständliche Glossen, wobei im einzelnen die Absicht der jeweiligen Glosse noch weiter differenzierend charakterisiert werden kann.

Andere haben dann in stärker geschichtlicher Fragestellung nach bestimmten durchgehenden Schichten der Nachbearbeitung des Prophetenwortes und seiner redaktionellen Zusammenfügung zur Gestalt des vorliegenden Prophetenbuches gefragt und sind dabei z. T. zu radikalen, keineswegs immer überzeugenden Thesen für die Vorgeschichte des Ezechielbuches gelangt[4]:

Wenn hier nun unter dem Stichwort »Fortschreibung« ein Teilgebiet erweiternder Zusätze zum ursprünglichen Ezechieltexte aufgegriffen wird, so geht es um eine engere Fragestellung. Es soll nicht das Buchganze des Ezechielbuches betrachtet werden, wo wir wohl von einer schlüssigen Gesamtsicht noch weit entfernt sind. Vielmehr möchte die Frage gestellt werden, wieweit sich an einzelnen Stellen einigermaßen kontrollierbar erkennen läßt, daß eine zunächst in sich geschlossene Texteinheit unter einem neuen Aspekt nochmals aufgenommen und weitergeführt wird. Vor allem möchte darauf geachtet werden, wie neue geschichtliche Erfahrungen Anlaß zur Fortschreibung schon geformter Worteinheiten werden können[5]. Die Frage, wieweit solche Fortschreibung, hinter der sich der Fortgang der Geschichte abzeichnet, u. U. noch vom Propheten selber stammen könnte, darf dabei nicht unterdrückt werden, so schwer hier natürlich an manchen Stellen ein sicheres Urteil möglich ist. Dem Axiom allerdings, daß neue geschichtliche Situationen nicht zu neuartigen Formulierungen und evtl. sogar zum Griff nach neuen Formen führen können, glaube ich nicht huldigen zu können[6]. Angesichts des Umbruchs der geschichtlichen Lage zur Zeit Ezechiels wird man sich für die Möglichkeit solcher »Fortschreibung« der Verkündigung durch den Propheten selber ungleich stärker offenhalten müssen und diese nicht a limine als unmöglich erklären dürfen.

---

[3] G. Fohrer, Die Glossen im Buche Ezechiel, ZAW 63 (1951), 33–53 (=BZAW 99, 1967, 204–221), danach Ezechiel, HAT I 13, 1955.

[4] Vgl. dazu jetzt mein Vorwort zur 2. Auflage des Kommentars zu Ezechiel, BK XIII/1, 1979, IX–XVII.

[5] Die Wahl des Stichwortes möchte vor allem dieses geschichtliche Fortschreiten zum Ausdruck bringen.

[6] Wenn etwa H. Schulz, Das Todesrecht im Alten Testament, 1969, 166, deklariert: »Mit verschiedenen Schaffensperioden Ezechiels zu rechnen, heißt die Literarkritik durch ein vorgefaßtes Prophetenverständnis unmöglich machen«, so dürfte in solcher Formulierung eben gerade das »vorgefaßte Prophetenverständnis« vorliegen, das Möglichkeiten nicht in Erwägung zieht, die sich vom literarischen Dokument des Textes selber her anbieten könnten.

II

An den Anfang sei ein Beispiel gestellt, das zeigt, wie ein abgeschlossen vorliegendes Element prophetischer Rede durch Heraushebung eines weiteren Aspektes eine Fortschreibung in neuer Richtung erfährt, ohne daß sich dahinter schon eindeutig eine geschichtliche Weiterentwicklung erkennen ließe.

Ez 16 1–43 enthalten in ihrer Grundlage, die in einer gehobenen Erzählsprache in knappen, parataktisch gereihten Kurzsätzen redet[7], die in sich gerundete Geschichte Jerusalems im Bilde von Aufstieg, Fall und göttlicher Bestrafung eines von Jahwe am Leben erhaltenen und später zur Ehe genommenen Findelkindes. Diese erreicht in der Schilderung des Vollzugs des Gerichtes durch die Rechtsgemeinde der Liebhaber der Frau ihren klaren Abschluß. Das Ziel der Erzählung ist erreicht[8]. Die Erzählung kündet in ihrer Zielaussage dem treulosen Jerusalem das Gericht an. Es wird an den Mächten, denen es sich zum Liebesdienst preisgegeben hat, zu Fall kommen. Die ganze Erzählung hat in der auf die zwei Israelreiche bezogenen Geschichte von den zwei von Ägypten her hurerisch veranlagten Frauen von 23 1–27 ihre ganz ebenso geschlossene Parallele. Beide Erzählungen sind als Gerichtsankündigungen des Propheten vor der endgültigen Katastrophe von 587 zu verstehen.

In 16 44ff. nun ist eine Erweiterung angeschlossen, welche auf ein Element zurückgreift, das in der Erzählung von 16 1ff. deutlich angelegt ist. Wenn dort von der Herkunft des Kindes festgestellt wird: »Dein Vater war ein Amoriter, deine Mutter eine Hetiterin«, und darin auf die kanaanäische Vorgeschichte Jerusalems angespielt ist, so trifft die im knappen Sprichwort gehaltene Einleitung der Weiterführung: »Wie die Mutter, so die Tochter« (44), sachlich ohne Zweifel das schon in 1–43 Beabsichtigte. Die fragwürdige Herkunft ließ bei dem Mädchen nichts Besseres erwarten. Der Gedanke wird aber über das in v. 3 Gesagte hinaus ausgeweitet, indem auch die beiden Schwestern Samaria und Sodom herangezogen werden und Jerusalem zugleich als die Schwester ihrer Schwestern gekennzeichnet wird. Dazu tritt noch das in Ez 23 vorliegende Motiv der Steigerung hinzu. Jerusalem treibt es übler als seine Schwestern und schafft dadurch jenen eine eigentümliche »Rechtfertigung«[9]. Diese

---

[7] Der Grundtext 16 1–43 ist heute durch starke Wucherungen, z. T. in Kontamination mit dem verwandten Kap. 23, erweitert. Zu den Einzelheiten der Textgestaltung sei auch für alles Folgende auf die Analysen im BK XIII verwiesen.

[8] Das entspricht den Kriterien, die vor allem von W. Richter, Exegese als Literaturwissenschaft, 1971, zur Abgrenzung der »Kleinen Einheit« postuliert hat. Dazu ist zu fügen, was F. Hossfeld, Untersuchungen zu Komposition und Theologie des Ezechielbuches, 1977, 20ff., in seinen methodischen Vorerwägungen zum Spezifischen der prophetischen Literatur zu erwägen gibt.

[9] Vgl. die Verwendung der Verben ṣdq und pll in v. 51f.

Erweiterung scheint schon das über Jerusalem vollzogene Gericht vorauszusetzen, hebt dieses aber nicht besonders heraus, so daß man die hier vorliegende »Fortschreibung« von v. 1–43 in v. 44 ff. eigentlich nur als eine zweite Ausführung der schon dort verwendeten Elemente in neuer Richtung bezeichnen kann.

III

An anderer Stelle tritt demgegenüber die weiterlaufende Geschichte als inhaltliche Triebkraft zur weiteren Ausgestaltung deutlicher heraus. Man kann dabei formal zwei verschiedene Typen der Weiterführung unterscheiden. Es kann sich auf der einen Seite um eine tief in den zunächst vorliegenden Text eingreifende, diesen umgestaltende Form der Fortschreibung handeln, die der Rekonstruktion der Erstfassung desselben Schwierigkeiten bereitet. Daneben ist aber auch die andere Form einfacher Erweiterung zu finden, in der die Erweiterung in der Art, wie es schon in Ez 16 zu sehen war, das Vorgefundene einfach durch einen weiterführenden Zusatz ergänzt und den Grundtext unberührt läßt.

Die erstgenannte Form ist besonders deutlich in der Einheit 12 1–16 zu erkennen. Hier liegt der Bericht über eine Zeichenhandlung des Propheten vor, die sachlich eng zusammengehört mit der ursprünglichen Komposition von 3 Zeichenhandlungen in Ez 4 f., die schon G. Hölscher[10] klar herausgearbeitet hat. Geht es dort um Beginn, Höhe und Ende der Belagerung Jerusalems, so in der Zeichenhandlung «Exilsgepäck» von 12 1–16 um die zeichenhafte Darstellung der Wegführung der zur Exilierung bestimmten Bevölkerung Jerusalems, welche Belagerung, Hungersnot und Fall der Stadt lebend überstanden hat. In dem Zusammenbinden des Bündels an Habe, das die Deportierten auch nach Ausweis der bildlichen Darstellungen der Zeit, über den Rücken geschultert, mit auf den Weg nahmen, bringt der Prophet seiner Umgebung, die diesen Vorgang aus dem eigenen Erleben des Jahres 597 in persönlicher Erfahrung kennt, das bevorstehende Geschehen in Jerusalem zu Gesicht.

In die Darstellung dieser in sich geschlossenen Handlung ist im heutigen Text die Darstellung des besonderen Geschickes des letzten Jerusalemer Königs Zedekia eingearbeitet, wie es uns aus II Reg 25 4–7 (Jer 52 7–10) bekannt ist. Dort ist erzählt, wie Zedekia, als schon Bresche in die Stadtmauer gelegt war und die Babylonier in die Stadt einzudringen begonnen hatten, zur Nachtzeit mit seiner Truppe an anderer Stelle »durch das Tor zwischen den beiden Mauern, welches beim Königsgarten liegt«, zu entkommen sucht, dabei bis in die Jordansenke bei Jericho gelangt, dort aber von den verfolgenden Babyloniern eingeholt wird.

---

[10] G. Hölscher, Hesekiel. Der Dichter und das Buch, 1924, 62.

Gefangen wird er zu Nebukadnezar, der sein Hauptquartier in Ribla in Syrien aufgeschlagen hat, geführt und von Nebukadnezar gerichtet: Seine beiden Söhne werden vor seinen Augen niedergemacht, der König selber geblendet in Ketten nach Babylonien geführt.

Der Hinweis auf dieses Geschehen ist nachträglich in den Bericht über die Zeichenhandlung »Exilsgepäck« eingearbeitet worden, wobei das Geschick Zedekias zeitlich ganz in die Deportationserfahrung der Jerusalemer eingewoben wird. II Reg 25 8ff. führen darauf, daß zwischen dem Fall der Stadt und dem Eintreffen der im Hauptquartier Nebukadnezars eingeholten Weisungen vier volle Wochen verstrichen sind. Nach dem Eintreffen der königlichen Weisung werden Stadt und Tempel eingeäschert. Jetzt erst wird die Deportation der überlebenden Bevölkerung vorgenommen worden sein. Jer 40 1 legt die Annahme nahe, daß die Bevölkerung zuerst nach Rama evakuiert und dort der Transport nach Babylonien zusammengestellt wurde. Zedekia und sein Gefolge dürfte unmittelbar nach seiner Gefangennahme mit den Boten, die nach Ribla abgingen, dorthin gebracht, dort bestraft und von dort nach Babylonien deportiert worden sein.

Diese zeitliche Differenzierung der Behandlung von König und Volk entfällt im vorliegenden Text, der die Zeichenhandlung Ezechiels schildert. Bei der Einwebung von Zedekias Geschick in dasjenige der übrigen Deportierten ist die Verschiebung des Skopos der ganzen Zeichenhandlung durch den überschriftartig zugesetzten v. 10b: »Auf den Fürsten geht dieser Spruch – in Jerusalem, und das ganze Haus Israel, das in seiner Mitte ist« ausdrücklich markiert worden[11]. Die Absicht des Nachtrags, die Deportierten des »Hauses Israel« mit dem König, auf den die »Fortschreibung« nun vor allem bezogen ist, zu verbinden, ist in der ungelenken Konstruktion des vorliegenden Verses noch deutlich zu erkennen. Die beiden letzten Zielrichtungen – diejenige der Grundlage, die von der Deportation des »Hauses Israel«, und diejenige der Erweiterung, die von der Deportation des Fürsten redet – sind im heutigen Text von v. 10b nebeneinander genannt. Schwieriger ist die Herauslösung der »Fortschreibung« in den diesen Deutungsvers umgebenden Nachbarversen. Bis hin zu v. 4 scheint die ursprüngliche Zeichenhandlung noch rein vorzuliegen: Am Morgen soll der Prophet sein Bündel packen und sich für den Abend zum Weggang bereithalten. Man wird den Marsch nicht in der Mittagshitze angetreten haben, sondern erst gegen Abend, wenn es kühler zu

---

[11] B. Lang, Kein Aufstand in Jerusalem. Die Politik des Propheten Ezechiel, 1978, 19, urteilt über v. 10: »Ein Redaktor hat den Satz aus zwei Marginalnotizen zusammengebastelt, die er nicht richtig beziehen konnte.« Er glaubt hier wie dann auch in seiner Behandlung von Ez 17 und 19 das Phänomen der »Fortschreibung« (von ihm S. 126f. ungenau als »Weiterschreibung« zitiert), das schon in BK XIII registriert worden ist, ablehnen zu müssen und mit einer einfachen Glossierungstheorie durchzukommen.

werden begann. Aber wenn dann v. 5 sagt, daß der Prophet sich ein Loch
in die Wand graben[12] und das Gepäck durch dieses Loch hindurch-
befördern soll — wenn in v. 6aα gesagt wird, er soll das Gepäck »in der
Dunkelheit« herausbringen, nachdem v. 5b zuvor schon gesagt hatte, er soll
sich sein Gepäckbündel »vor ihren Augen« aufladen[13], wenn zu dem Ver-
hüllen des Angesichtes, was die Trauer der Deportierten zum Ausdruck
bringt, in v. 6aγ noch der Satz gefügt wird, daß »er das Land nicht sehen
soll«, was nach dem Wortlaut auf den auf den Fürsten zu beziehenden
Finalsatz v. 12bβ vorausweist, wonach dieser als ein an den Augen Geblen-
deter das Land nicht mehr mit Augen sehen kann — dann scheint darin
schon ein Stück Vorwegnahme der auf den Fürsten umgedeuteten Zeichenhandlung vorzuliegen. Die gleichen Fragen stellen sich bei v. 7, der den
Vollzug des von Jahwe Befohlenen berichtet, und in dem sich die gleichen
Erweiterungen finden wie in v. 5f. Ist in der Erwähnung des Fürsten in
v. 10 die Erweiterung deutlich zu erkennen, so scheint v. 11 wieder weitgehend dem Grundtext zuzugehören, während dann die Weiterführung in
v. 13f. als ganze zur nachträglichen Erweiterung auf den Fürsten hin gehört. Dafür spricht auch die enge Berührung mit den Aussagen von
17 20f. in der Auslegung der Parabel, die den Treubruch Zedekias gegenüber Nebukadnezar zum Gegenstand hat.

Das Phänomen der »Fortschreibung« liegt hier in klarer Weise vor.
Hatte der Prophet selber in seiner Zeichenhandlung ganz auf der Linie des
Grundtextes der Dreizeichenkomposition von Ez 4f. die bevorstehende
Deportation der Jerusalemer Bevölkerung angesagt, so schreibt die Erweiterung diesen Text im Lichte des dann im besonderen mit König Zedekia
Geschehenen fort. Man wird diese Fortschreibung, die den Text der ursprünglichen Zeichenhandlung eigenartig unklar macht, schwerlich noch
dem Propheten selber zuschreiben können. Andererseits wird man sie
aber auch nicht zu weit von dem ganzen Geschehen abrücken wollen, da
das Schicksal Zedekias sichtlich noch als etwas besonders Erschreckendes
nachhallt. Keinesfalls empfiehlt es sich, darin erst eine späte literarische
Zufügung aufgrund des dtr. Berichtes von II Reg 25 zu sehen, da hier
über jene Angaben hinaus vom Tode Zedekias in Babylon geredet ist. Terminus ante quem non dürfte also der Zeitpunkt des Todes Zedekias sein,
über den wir nicht informiert sind. Es bleibt reine Vermutung, wenn wir
annehmen, daß er an den Folgen der Mißhandlung in Ribla dann wohl
bald danach gestorben sein wird. Da da letzte Wort Ezechiels (29 17) ins

---

[12] B. Lang a. a. O. 23 findet, daß diese Übersetzung des hebr. ḥtr den Text »durch tenden-
ziöse Übersetzung ... vereindeutigt«, da in seinem doppelgipfligen Verständnis der ursprünglichen Texteinheit auch das Hinausgehen des Volkes durch die Breschen der
Mauer Raum bekommen muß. Das Verb ist aber hier wie in 8 8 nicht wohl anders zu
verstehen.
[13] Diese unklare Verdoppelung wird von B. Lang a. a. O. übersehen.

27. Jahr Jojachins, d.h. 571 datiert ist, würde es sich zeitlich nicht verbieten, noch im Propheten selber den Ergänzer zu sehen. Was dagegen spricht, liegt auf der Ebene der literarischen Zerstörung des in sich zunächst klaren Grundtextes[14].

IV

Mit allen Vorbehalten mag in diesem Zusammenhang auch auf das nicht spannungslose Nebeneinander der Gerichtsaussage in der Grundlage von Ez 10 neben derjenigen von Ez 9 gewiesen werden. Auch hier hat man den Eindruck, daß der von Ez 8 zu Ez 9 hin angelegte Spannungsbogen eigentlich mit Ez 9 10 sein Ende erreicht. Nachdem der Prophet in seiner Entrückungserfahrung nach Ez 8 die vier Greuel im Jerusalemer Tempel geschaut hat, sieht er nach Ez 9 sieben Gestalten in den Tempel eintreten, von denen sechs Vernichtungswerkzeuge (wohl Waffen) in den Händen tragen, die siebte, priesterlich gekleidete das Schreibzeug eines Schreibers. So wird diese zunächst ausgesandt, in der Stadt alle die Menschen an der Stirne zu zeichnen, die »seufzen und stöhnen ob all der Greuel, die in ihrer Mitte begangen werden« (9 4). Im Anschluß daran werden die 6 Bewaffneten mit dem Auftrag ausgesandt, in der Stadt ohne Ansehen des Alters alle zu erschlagen, die nicht das schützende Zeichen an der Stirn tragen.

Wieder gewinnt man den Eindruck, daß damit eigentlich das Ziel der Handlung erreicht ist. Auf die Begründung (Ez 8) folgt der Gerichtsvollzug, der nur einen Rest verschont. Die Aufgabenverteilung der sieben Gestalten ist dabei eindeutig und klar: die priesterliche Gestalt übt das Amt der Bereitung zur Verschonung, die sechs bewehrten Gestalten üben das eigentliche Amt der Vernichtung. Der Rückblick auf das Geschehen beim Auszug aus Ägypten, wo zwar nicht die Menschen, wohl aber die Häuser der Israeliten das Zeichen der Verschonung empfangen, der »Verderber« aber durch alle nicht gezeichneten ägyptischen Häuser geht und dort die Erstgeborenen tötet, legt sich dabei nahe. Ausdrücklich ist in Ez 9 festgehalten, daß das Gericht beim Hause Jahwes, dem Tempel, anhebt. Es ist vom Vollzug des Gerichtes, das bei den in 8 16ff. zuletzt genannten Männern vor dem Tempelhaus beginnt und sich dann in die Stadt hinaus ausweitet, berichtet. Und über dem ganzen Geschehen ertönt der Schrei des Propheten, der Jahwe fragt, ob er wirklich den Rest Israels in seinem Gericht verderben wolle (9 8). Der Schrei kehrt in einer auffallenden Wiederholung im Abschluß des nachträglichen Erweiterungs-

---

[14] Auf das Element des bewahrten »Restes« innerhalb der wohl noch jüngeren Erweiterung durch v. 15f. wird in späterem Zusammenhang zurückzukommen sein.

stückes 11 1–13 wieder und markiert dort deutlich das Ende der Teileinheit.

Es wird nun überraschen, daß daraufhin in 9 11 ausdrücklich die Rückkehr der linnengekleideten priesterlichen Gestalt berichtet wird, die den Vollzug des ihr Aufgetragenen meldet. Dieser Vers soll unverkennbar die Weiterführung in Ez 10 vorbereiten, in welcher der Linnengekleidete in einer anderen, inhaltlich sehr veränderten Funktion auftritt. Daß Ez 10 zunächst in ganz anderer Hinsicht Probleme bietet und daß in seiner erneuten Theophanieschilderung eine Schicht der Nacharbeit abzuheben ist, hat man schon seit längerer Zeit gesehen. Nach Ablösung dieser Bearbeitungsschicht[15], welche die Erscheinung der Jahweherrlichkeit mit leicht veränderter Wiederaufnahme des Vorstellungsgutes von Ez 1 schildert, bleibt ein knapper Grundbestand übrig, der davon berichtet, daß der Linnengekleidete den Auftrag bekommt, heiliges Feuer aus dem *galgäl*[16] unter dem Keruben in die Hände zu nehmen und über die Stadt zu werfen. Auch hier wird in 10 7b der Vollzugsbericht: »Er nahm es (das vom Keruben dargereichte Feuer) und ging hinaus (in die Stadt)" ausdrücklich hinzugefügt.

Der nach dem Gerichtsbericht von Ez 9 überraschende Neueinsatz mit einer zweiten Gerichtsschilderung, und die ebenso überraschende neue Funktion des Linnengekleideten, der anders als in Ez 9 selber zum Gerichtsvollzieher wird, legen die Frage nahe, ob in alledem nicht eine nachträgliche Fortschreibung des ursprünglich nur 8 1–9 10 umfassenden Berichtes vom Gericht über Jerusalem zu finden ist. Nach Ez 9 kommt die ganze Bevölkerung Jerusalems mit Ausnahme der vom Linnengekleideten Gezeichneten um. Von einem Rest an noch zu Richtenden in Jerusalem ist dabei nicht mehr die Rede. Demgegenüber redet die Weiterführung in Ez 10 lediglich mehr vom Brande der Stadt. Die Frage kann aufgeworfen werden, ob darin nicht die ausdrücklich von Nebukadnezar angeordnete, einen runden Monat nach dem Fall der Stadt vollzogene Verbrennung derselben in der Gestalt einer Fortschreibung des Textes unter dem Eindruck des tatsächlich Geschehenen erweiternd nachgetragen ist.

Offen bleibt in alledem die Frage, wie der weitere Bericht vom Wegzug der Jahweherrlichkeit aus dem Tempel zuzuordnen ist. Hat dieser Bericht zunächst direkt an das Geschehen von Ez 9 1–10 angeschlossen? Oder gehört er mit der ersten Fortschreibung zusammen? Man möchte dann allerdings erwarten, daß Jahwes Auszug aus dem Tempel vor der

---

15 Zur Analyse vgl. BK XIII. Zu den einzelnen Anschauungselementen vgl. jetzt O. Keel, Jahwe-Visionen und Siegelkunst. Eine neue Deutung der Majestätsschilderungen in Jes 6, Ez 1 und 10 und Sach 4, 1977.
16 Nach O. Keel a. a. O. 161 »ist an das Geschiebe, an das Geröll, an den sich daherwälzenden Haufen von Wolkendunkel, von glühenden Kohlen und Blitzen zu denken, der die Erscheinung Jahwes begleitet«.

Verbrennung der Stadt (und dann wohl auch des Tempels) berichtet worden wäre. So ist die Wahrscheinlichkeit größer, daß der Bericht über den Weggang der Jahweherrlichkeit aus dem durch die Greuel verunreinigten Tempel schon mit dem Grundtext 8 1–9 10 verbunden war.

Im Blick auf die Fortschreibung von Ez 8f. durch die Grundlage von 10 1–7 braucht nicht bezweifelt zu werden, daß diese Erweiterung sehr wohl noch von der Hand des Propheten selber stammen könnte[17]. Die literarische Zerstörung und Verundeutlichung des Textes geschieht dann erst durch die Übermalung mit einer erneuten Schilderung der Thronherrlichkeit Jahwes in Ez 10. Diese wird aus den gleichen Erwägungen, die zu 12 1–16 anzustellen waren, nicht der eigenen Hand des Propheten zu verdanken sein.

V

Ein schönes Beispiel für die Art, wie ein Text durch eine leicht ablösbare Zufügung unter dem Eindruck neuen geschichtlichen Geschehens fortgeschrieben werden kann, bietet die dritte Zeichenhandlung der ursprünglichen Dreizeichenkomposition von Ez 4f. Diese dritte, in 5 1f. angeordnete Zeichenhandlung kündet den Fall der Stadt an. Ein Drittel der Bevölkerung soll durch Feuer, ein Drittel durchs Schwert umkommen und ein letztes Drittel in alle Winde versprengt werden. Das in 5 1f. angesagte Geschehen ist in sich gerundet. Auch die ursprüngliche Anlage der drei Zeichenhandlungen, welche Beginn (4 1f.), Höhe (4 9–11)[18] und Ende (5 1f.) der Belagerung der Stadt ansagen, läßt keine Weiterführung erwarten.

Da muß es überraschen, daß in 5 3–4a der Aufforderung an den Propheten, sich die Haare abzuhauen, diese zu dritteln und an jedem Drittel eine Vernichtungshandlung bildlich zu vollziehen, noch eine Weiterführung angefügt ist. »Und du sollst einige wenige an Zahl nehmen und sie in deinen Gewandzipfel einbinden. Und von ihnen sollst du nochmals einige nehmen und sie mitten ins Feuer werfen und sie mit Feuer verbrennen«. In dieser Hinzufügung ist ein Doppeltes ausgesagt. Es ist zunächst davon die Rede, daß nicht alle von der Katastrophe Jerusalems Erfaßten ums Leben kommen, sondern daß Jahwe einen Rest behütet. Das könnte an die vom Linnengekleideten nach 9 4 Gezeichneten erinnern, die in Jerusalem dem Gericht entgehen. Sachlich könnte man dabei an eine Möglich-

---

[17] Man wird dann hier nicht einfach mit einem Marginalzusatz rechnen dürfen, sondern, da es sich um eine Einfügung in einen zuvor geschlossenen Kontext handelt, an eine Zweitschrift durch den Propheten selber.

[18] Zur Ausscheidung der Zusätze, die den Text heute mit den eingeschobenen Stücken, welche die Exilsymbolik enthalten, verklammern vgl. BK XIII.

keit denken, wie sie Jer 40 1 für Jeremia berichtet, der aus der Schar der zur Deportation Bestimmten herausgenommen und im Lande belassen wird. Die lose Anknüpfung von v. 3 an das Vorhergehende durch *miššam* läßt aber doch eher an eine Weiterführung der an dritter Stelle genannten Strafform der »Zerstreuung« (unter die Völker), d.h. an ein Geschehen unter den von Jerusalem Fernen denken, bei denen dann im weiteren für Ezechiel auch allein die Hoffnung einer neuen Zukunft Israels liegt[19]. Auffallend bleibt aber auf jeden Fall das eigentümliche Nachklappen dieser lose angeknüpften Bewahrungsaussage hinter der vollen Schilderung der drei Formen des Gerichtes. Die Aussage wirkt deutlich als Nachtrag.

Aber nun ist die Bewahrungsaussage ihrerseits nur Überleitung zu der in v. 4a ausgesagten weiteren Gerichtsaussage. Diese weitere Gerichtskatastrophe betrifft die dem Gericht über Jerusalem lebendig Entkommenen. Einige von ihnen sollen in der Bildhandlung des Propheten mit Feuer verbrannt werden. Man wird hier die bestimmte Vermutung wagen dürfen, daß darin das Geschehen bis zu einem Ereignis »fortgeschrieben« wird, das sich unter den Deportierten ereignet hat. Es sind einige von ihnen »mit Feuer verbrannt worden«. Ein solches Geschehen ist in Jer 29 22 (allerdings noch für die Zeit vor 587) angedeutet. Jeremia bedroht hier Heilspropheten unter den Verbannten. Zwei Propheten Ahab und Zedekia nennt er ausdrücklich mit Namen und sagt ihnen einen schrecklichen Tod an, so daß man mit ihrem Namen in Zukunft einen Fluch formulieren wird: »Jahwe mache dich wie Zedekia und Ahab, die der König von Babel mit Feuer verbrannt hat.« Man wird dabei die geschichtliche Frage aufwerfen, ob solches im Zeitpunkt des Jeremiabriefes, d.h. vor dem Fall Jerusalems schon geschehen ist. Dann würde es sich zeitlich nicht mit dem in Ez 5 3f. Erkennbaren decken. Ebensogut aber besteht die Möglichkeit, daß es sich beim Jeremiawort um eine vorwegnehmende Androhung handelt, die immerhin davon weiß, daß bei den Babyloniern Aufrührer verbrannt werden konnten. Vgl. dazu auch Dan 3. Daran, daß in der auffallenden Erweiterung 5 3f. eine Fortschreibung des Geschehens auf ein unter den Exulanten geschehenes Ereignis nachhallt, ist nicht zu bezweifeln. Man wird diese Fortschreibung zeitlich nicht zu stark vom Jahre 587 abrücken und dann auch eine mögliche Ergänzung durch den Propheten selber, der ja in ganz anderer Weise »schreibender Prophet« ist als die Propheten des 8. Jahrhunderts, nicht unbedingt ausschließen dürfen[20].

---

[19] Entsprechend 11 15ff. 33 24ff. auch Jer 24.
[20] Auf der gleichen Linie könnte die Erweiterung der ersten Zeichenhandlung 4 1f. durch 4 3 liegen. Der Neuansatz mit: »Du aber nimm dir . . .« macht es wahrscheinlich, daß hier mit einer etwas späteren Erweiterung zu rechnen ist. Das Motiv derselben liegt dann wohl in der Absicht, die Schilderung der Belagerungshärte (eiserne Backplatte) weiter zu steigern.

An anderer Stelle ist die Fortschreibung über das einschneidende Ereignis von 587 hinweg, die schon in 5 3f. erkennbar wurde, noch viel deutlicher zu greifen. So bieten 19 1–9 ein Klagelied über die beiden aus Jerusalem deportierten Könige Joahas, der nach Ägypten verschleppt wurde (II Reg 23 34), und Jojachin, zu dessen Deportationsgruppe Ezechiel selber gehört. In solcher klagenden Äußerung über den deportierten Jojachin liegt eine Parallele zu dem nach seinem Stil (Tripelfrage) unverkennbar jeremianischen Wort Jer 22 10 über Joahas vor. Ez 19 1–9 nun faßt die Klage über die beiden deportierten Könige in eine einzige Redeeinheit zusammen, wobei die Klage über Jojachin das Schwergewicht enthält. Diese Deutung ist innerhalb von 19 1–9 ganz klar.

Nun ist aber in 19 10–14 noch ein wesentlich anders gestaltetes, auch anderes Bildmaterial verwendendes Wort angefügt, in dem man den Rückblick auf das einst unmittelbar mit Ez 19 verbundene Kapitel Ez 17 nur schwer übersehen kann[21]. Das Phänomen der »Fortschreibung« ist auch hier wieder mit Händen zu greifen. Die Liste der deportierten Könige ist nach dem Fall Jerusalems um eine ziemlich anders gestaltete Strophe, die sich mit Zedekia befaßt, erweitert worden. Und dieses ist zu einem Zeitpunkt geschehen, in dem Ez 19 noch direkt an Ez 17 angeschlossen war. Darf man auch hier den (hinterher dann noch durch wuchernde Zusätze entstellten) Grundtext von 19 10–14 noch vom Propheten selber herleiten, was darauf führen würde, daß er selber noch die Kombination von Ez 17 und 19 vollzogen hätte? Man wird es nicht zwingend ausschließen können.

VI

Auf eine auffallend transformierende Form der Fortbildung der prophetischen Aussagen stoßen wir bei den Aussagen über den aus dem Gericht geretteten Rest[22]. Nach Ez 9 ging die linnengekleidete priesterliche Gestalt vor dem Einbruch der Katastrophe in die Stadt hinaus und zeichnete alle »die seufzen und stöhnen ob all der Greuel, die in ihrer Mitte begangen werden«, mit einem Schutzzeichen. Dann erst hielten die sechs Gerichtshelfer mit ihren Vernichtungswerkzeugen ihr schonungsloses

---

[21] Daß Ez 18 erst in einer späteren Redaktionsphase dazwischengeschoben worden ist, wird durch die fehlende Wortereignisformel zu Beginn von Ez 19 nahegelegt, vgl. BK XIII 420. 429. Es ist daher durchaus sinnvoll, daß J. Garscha, Studien zum Ezechielbuch. Eine redaktionsgeschichtliche Untersuchung von Ez 1–39, 1974, gerade beim Zusammenhang Ez 17/19 einsetzt.

[22] Es handelt sich dabei um eine inhaltlich-sachliche »Fortschreibung« der prophetischen Botschaft. Diese stellt einen anderen Typ dar als die einfache Forterzählung unter dem Eindruck inzwischen geschehener Geschichte oder die einfache Entfaltung eines Themas, wie sie in den zuvor aufgeführten Beispielen zu erkennen war.

Gericht. Die Schau läßt erwarten, daß aus der großen Vernichtung Jerusalems einige wenige als »Rest« gerettet werden. In der Folge aber fällt in der Verkündigung des Propheten auf, daß von einem geretteten »Rest« in Jerusalem nirgends mehr die Rede ist. Vielmehr erfolgt in Ez 33 23–29, wo der Prophet auf »die Bewohner der Trümmerstätten im Lande Israels« zu sprechen kommt, d. h. doch wohl die Menschen, welche die Vernichtung Jerusalems im Lande überlebt haben, ein denkbar scharfer Angriff und eine erneute Gerichtsankündigung. Diese Menschen trösten sich zwar in scheinbar frommer Zuflucht zur alten Väterverheißung mit den Worten: »Ein einzelner war Abraham und er bekam das Land zu eigen. Wir aber sind viele. Uns ist das Land zum Besitz gegeben«. Aber sie tun weiter Unrecht: »Mitsamt dem Blut eßt ihr (Opferfleisch), und solltet das Land zum Besitz bekommen?« Sie werden erleben, wie das Land »zur entsetzlichen Öde wird«.

Dafür taucht die Gestalt der dem Gericht lebend Entkommenen überraschend in ganz anderem Zusammenhange auf. In 33 21 f. ist es zunächst ein einzelner, der »Pleite« Entkommener[23], der dem Propheten Kunde vom Ende Jerusalems überbringt. Im weiteren aber wird sehr bewußt über die Funktion der so »Entkommenen« nachgedacht. In 14 12–23 ist eine ganze Redeeinheit auf die Frage abgezielt, was denn nun die der Katastrophe Jerusalems lebend Entkommenen von Jahwe her für einen Auftrag haben. Nachdem zunächst v. 12–20 in ganz stereotyp wiederholter Durchführung von 4 großen Gerichtsplagen, die Jahwe wider ein sündiges Land sendet, geredet und festgestellt hatten, daß selbst die drei großen Frommen der Vorzeit, Noah, Daniel und Hiob in solcher Situation nur ihr eigenes Leben retten könnten, kommen v. 21–23 auf das unmittelbar Erlebte zu sprechen. Da sind nun doch Menschen dieser Totalität des Gerichtes über Jerusalem entkommen und lebend zu den Exulanten gelangt. »Die werden zu euch herauskommen, und ihr seht ihren Wandel ... und ihr werdet erkennen, daß ich all das, was ich an ihm (d. h. Jerusalem) getan habe, nicht grundlos getan habe«. Ich sehe keinen wirklich zwingenden Grund dafür, diese Einheit Ezechiel abzusprechen. Auch die Zerreißung in eine ältere lehrhafte Ausführung v. 12–20, die dann (durch Fortschreibung) um v. 21–23 erweitert worden wäre[24], erscheint nicht zwingend erforderlich. Vielmehr dürfte das Wort von vornherein

---

[23] Das *palîṭ* wird man hier nicht mit »Flüchtling« übersetzen dürfen. Ein »Flüchtling« pflegt wohl kaum je gerade in die Mitte des Bereichs der Macht zu entfliehen, vor der er flüchtet. Vielmehr handelt es sich um einen lebend aus der Katastrophe Jerusalems Entkommen (dazu die »Fortschreibung« 5 3, s. o.), der in der Schar der Deportierten nun als Augenzeuge des Falls der Stadt nach Babylonien gekommen ist. So ganz deutlich dann in 14 21 f. Daß hier das kollektive *peleṭā* »Entkommenenschar« gebraucht wird, kann gerade zu der Frage rufen, ob das sing. *palîṭ* von 33 21 f. nicht auch schon in kollektivem Sinne zu verstehen ist.
[24] So manche Kommentatoren.

auf die Spitzenaussagen v. 21–23 hin gebildet sein, die den »Rest«-Gedanken aus der konkreten Erfahrung nach dem Eintreffen »Entkommener« ($p^eleṭā$), die »Söhne und Töchter herausgebracht haben«, neu wenden. Der Gedanke ist auch in der Erweiterung von 12 1ff. in v. 16 in wörtlicher Anlehnung aufgenommen worden: »Und ich werde einige wenige von ihnen übriglassen vom Schwert, dem Hunger und der Pest, damit sie unter den Völkern, zu denen sie kommen[25], all ihre Greueltaten erzählen, damit sie erkennen, daß ich Jahwe bin«.

In diesen Zusammenhang muß auch Ez 6 8–10 eingereiht werden, eine in das Gerichtswort gegen Berge und Hügel Israels eingefügte »Fortschreibung«. »Wenn von Euch dem Schwert Entronnene unter den Völkern sind, wenn ihr in die Länder zerstreut werdet, so werden eure Entronnenen unter den Völkern, dahin sie weggeführt sind, an mich denken ... Und sie werden sich in ihr Angesicht hinein ekeln ... wegen all ihrer Greuel und werden erkennen, daß ich, Jahwe, ... geredet habe[26].

Die Aussage über den um seiner Frömmigkeit willen mit dem Leben davongekommenen Rest ist an allen diesen Stellen (unter dem Eindruck der tatsächlichen Begegnung mit der $p^eleṭā$ von 587?) transformiert, in neuer Gestalt »fortgeschrieben«. Die Entkommenen erfüllen nun eine Funktion im Zusammenhang der radikalen Anklage Jahwes gegen sein Volk, die auch sonst die Verkündigung Ezechiels kennzeichnet. Anders als bei anderen Propheten ist sie nicht zur Vorstellung vom »heiligen Rest« weitergebildet, wie man es eigentlich von 9 4 her erwarten müßte. Diese überraschend eigenwillige Weiterbildung des Verständnisses der Funktion derer, die dem Gericht über Jerusalem entkommen sind, hängt sichtlich zusammen mit dem Gesamtverständnis des Propheten vom Ort, von dem Jahwes Heil nach der Gerichtszeit seinen Ausgang nimmt. Anders als bei Jesaja wird nicht auf das von Jahwe auf den Zion gelegte Heil geschaut. Der Neuansatz des Lebens über das Gericht hinaus wird im Bereich der Exulanten gesehen[27].

VII

Das Jahr 587 hat für Ezechiels Verkündigung eine einschneidende Wende gebracht. Zwar ist aus undurchsichtigen Gründen die bestimmt zu

---

[25] Über 33 21 f. und 14 12ff. hinaus ist nun ausweitend von Entkommenen »zu den Völkern« geredet. So dann auch 6 8–10. Unter diesen »Entkommenen« können nun auch »Flüchtlinge« (vgl. etwa die nach Jer 42 nach Ägypten »Fliehenden«) sein.

[26] Vgl. auch Anm. 25. Zur Textanalyse BK XIII.

[27] Daß die Errettung dann auch wieder zum Zion zurückführt, wird das gleich zu behandelnde Kap. 20 in seiner »Fortschreibung« zeigen. Der Name »Zion« ist aber bei Ezechiel anders als bei dem die Verkündigung des »neuen Exodus« aktualisierenden Deuterojesaja nie gebraucht. Ezechiel ist kein »Zionstheologe«. Die Rede vom »hohen Berg Israels« (17 23 20 40 ist von einer anders formulierenden »Theologie« her gebildet.

vermutende einleitende Datumsangabe der Vision von der Wiederbelebung der Totengebeine in Ez 37 1–14 getilgt worden. Daß diese Vision, die den Propheten der Neubelebung des Toten, d. h. ohne Bildrede der Rückführung der Verbannten in das »Land Israels« gewiß macht, in die Zeit nach 587 gehört, daran kann kein Zweifel bestehen.

Nun fehlt es nicht an Belegen im Ezechielbuch, welche die Fortschreibung früher formulierten Wortes auch über diese andersartige Schwelle hinweg erkennen lassen — eine Fortschreibung älterer Verkündigung, die nach der vollendeten Katastrophe mit dem verheißenen Neuanfang zu rechnen wagt. Besonders eindrücklich ist in diesem Zusammenhang Ez 20. Dieses Kapitel enthält in seiner ersten Hälfte (v. 1–31), auf die sich die einleitende Datierung in die Zeit vor 587 (20 1) beziehen dürfte, die ganz bildlos gehaltene Sündengeschichte des Volkes. Diese beginnt in Ägypten, setzt sich bei der ersten Wüstengeneration fort und löst bei der zweiten Wüstengeneration bei Jahwe den Entschluß aus, dieses Volk einst unter die Völker zu zerstreuen, ja, ihm böse, ins Verderben führende Gebote zu geben. V. 32 setzt dann deutlich nach der geschehenen Katastrophe neu ein mit dem Zitat von Worten des in der Tiefe der Verlorenheit sitzenden Volkes, das sich nihilistisch fallen lassen und seiner Umwelt assimilieren will. Da aber greift Jahwe mit leidenschaftlichem Schwurwort ein, indem er einen neuen, zweiten Exodus aus den Völkern in die »Wüste der Völker« hinaus ankündigt, der über ein Scheidungsgericht in der Wüste hin zum neuen Einzug ins Land führt. In der »Fortschreibung« ist hier die anfängliche Rede vom Exodus neu aufgenommen und darin auch das Stichwort für die etwas spätere volle Verkündigung Deuterojesajas vom neuen Exodus gegeben[28]. Die Fortschreibung geschieht hier anders als in den zuletzt erwähnten Beispielen nicht im Blick auf schon geschehene geschichtliche Wende, sondern im Hören auf die von Jahwe verheißend zugesagte kommende Wende. Im Hören auf diese Zusage ist schon in der Tiefe politischer Verlorenheit eine neue Situation gegeben, in die hinein der Prophet ältere Verkündigung in neuer Gestalt aufnehmen, und, das Gerichtswort in neuer Weise fortschreibend, die Exodusaussage in neuer Form der alten Erzählung anfügen kann.

In analoger Weise zeigt auch Ez 17 die Fortschreibung einer anfänglichen Unheilsaussage aus der Zeit vor 587 zur Heilsverkündigung. In der allegorischen Bildrede von der Zeder, dem Weinstock und den zwei Adlern war das Schicksal Jojachins und das treulose Verhalten Zedekias gegenüber seinem Oberherrn geschildert, das in die Katastrophe ausmünden sollte. Die Fortschreibung von v. 22–24 schildert unter Aufnahme des Bildes vom Wipfel der Zeder die kommende neue Geschichte der

---

[28] Ob die ganze weitere Ausführung bis hin zu v. 44 einen von Anfang an geschlossenen Zusammenhang darstellt oder ihrerseits weiter angereichert worden ist, braucht hier nicht erörtert zu werden.

Wiederherstellung des Gerichteten. Ob in dieser Fortschreibung in Form einer Verheißung noch des Propheten eigene Hand am Werke gesehen werden darf, ist strittig[29].

VIII

In diesen Zusammenhang muß aber noch eine weitere Erscheinung im Buche Ezechiel eingefügt werden. Es fällt hier auf, daß dem großen Berufungsbericht in Ez 1 1–3 15, der in 3 15 seinen deutlichen Abschluß erreicht, in 3 16–21, heute auf ein Datum »nach 7 Tagen« fixiert, eine Art zweiter Berufungsgeschichte, nach welcher der Prophet zum Späher und Warner seines Volkes berufen ist, folgt. Schärfere Analyse zeigt, daß 3 16–21[30] die Ausführungen sowohl von 33 1–9, wo das Späherbild voller ausgeführt ist, wie auch von Ez 18 voraussetzen, Einheiten, die aus des Propheten eigener Hand hergeleitet werden können. Das Stück 3 16b–21 stellt sich dagegen als das Werk eines Redaktors dar, der hier eine »Fortschreibung« der Berufungsgeschichte geglaubt hat direkt an den ursprünglichen Berufungsbericht anfügen zu müssen. Die innere Ratio dieser Fortschreibung ist unschwer zu erkennen, wenn man die Bedeutung der Einheiten Ez 18 und 33 1–9 erwägt[31].

Das einleitende Zitat von Worten des Hauses Israel in 18 2 führt in die Zeit der tiefen Resignation des Volkes nach der großen Katastrophe von 587 hinein. Es spiegelt die zynische »Bewältigung« dieser Katastrophe, die Jahwe den Fehdehandschuh hinwirft und alle wirkliche göttliche Gerechtigkeit in Frage stellt: »Die Väter essen Herlinge und den Söhnen werden die Zähne stumpf«. Wer das Zitat 33 10 danebenhält, auf welches die Erwägungen von Ez 18 in einer Art Kurzraffung folgen, findet dort die gleiche Verzweiflung im Gewande frommer Resignation zum Ausdruck gebracht: »Unsere Vergehen und unsere Sünden liegen auf uns und in ihnen siechen wir dahin; wie könnten wir da leben?« In die zynische Resignation hinein verkündet das Prophetenwort von Ez 18 3–20 zunächst die strenge göttliche Regel der Behaftung jeder einzelnen Generation für ihre eigene Schuld. Daran schließt in v. 21–34 die stärkere Engführung,

---

[29] Strittig ist auch die Frage, ob die Stelle königsmessianisch oder auf das Volk bezogen zu verstehen ist.

[30] Die Datumsangabe 3 16a gehörte ursprünglich zu 3 20ff.

[31] H. Schulz a. a. O. 163–187 findet in diesem ganzen Textbereich einen zeitlich weit abzurückenden »Deutero-Ezechiel« am Werk, was (modifiziert) von J. Garscha a. a. O. u. a. aufgenommen wird. Vgl. dazu meine Ausführungen in »Deutero-Ezechiel?«, ZAW 84 (1972), 501–516. Die innere Nähe der ersten und zweiten »Berufung« verrät sich auch etwa in der klaren Reflexion über die (begrenzte) Verantwortung des prophetischen Auftrags im Blick auf seinen Erfolg. Vgl. 2 5.7 3 11 mit 3 19.21 (33 8f.).

die nun auch im Ablauf des Einzellebens noch das Heute als das von Gott zur Rechenschaft Gezogene unterstreicht: Der Mensch kann so wenig von seiner Gerechtigkeit von gestern zehren, wie er umgekehrt verzweifelt sein Heute vom Gestern her als endgültig gescheitert beklagen muß. Die eigentliche Spitze der Ausführungen von Ez 18 ist im Blick auf Gott in der Aussage erreicht, daß Gott zum Leben hin parteilich ist, indem er das Leben und nicht den Tod des Sünders will. Im Blick auf den Menschen führt das auf den entschlossenen Umkehrruf. In des Menschen Umkehr liegt für jeden die Möglichkeit des Lebens[32].

Diese Verkündigung führt eindeutig in die Situation nach 587, wo das Volk, wie es auch das einleitende Zitat der Fortschreibung 20 32ff. verriet, in der Gefahr der Selbstaufgabe steht – sei diese dann zynisch oder in frommer Resignation formuliert. In dieser Situation ist nun aber auch 33 1–9 beheimatet. Infolgedessen ändert sich des Propheten Amt in der Situation nach 587. Er hat nicht mehr apodiktisch das kommende Unheil anzukündigen. Israel steht ja nun mitten im Unheil drin. Sein Tun erschöpft sich aber auch nicht nur im Hinweis auf eine gottverheißene Zukunft, wie sie in 37 1–14 am gewaltigsten zum Ausdruck kommt. Er hat in des Volkes Heute hinein zu sprechen, wenn dieses fragt, was es denn nun im Heute angesichts der bestehenden Möglichkeit von Zukunft zu tun hat. In dieses Heute hinein verkündigt er die Gebote. Umkehr zu Jahwe heißt im Heute nichts anderes als treues Hören auf den Ruf Jahwes in seinem Gebot. In der Funktion des Erinnerers an die Gebote aber wird der Prophet in einer ganz neuen Weise zum Späher und Warner. Was in Ez 33 1–20 (mit der volleren Ausführung von v. 11–20 in Ez 18) mit Recht in die Verkündigung der Zeit nach 587 hineingenommen ist, hat der Redaktor in seiner Ergänzung von 3 17–21 unmittelbar hinter dem ersten Berufungsbericht im Sinne einer »Fortschreibung« der prophetischen Berufung auch schon gleich an den Anfang gerückt. Die neue Zeitphase gibt dem Amt des Propheten ein neues Gesicht. Zum Ankündigen kommenden Gerichtes (Ez 2 8–3 3) tritt das warnende Mahnen und die Bereitung der Gemeinde für die Möglichkeit von »Leben« durch seine warnende Mahnung[33].

IX

Geht es in den letzterwähnten Beispielen nicht mehr eigentlich um ein Fortschreiben usprünglicher Aussagen im Lichte der fortschreitenden

---

[32] Die Zerreißung von Ez 18 in die getrennten Einheiten 1–20 und 21–32 »enthauptet« die Ausführungen von 1–20 und macht sie zur Entfaltung einer zeitlos allgemeinen »Lehre von der gerechten Vergeltung«. Ähnliches gilt von der Zerreißung von 14 12–20 und 21–23.

[33] W. Zimmerli, »Leben« und »Tod« im Buche des Propheten Ezechiel, ThZ 13 (1957), 494–508 (= Gottes Offenbarung. Gesammelte Aufsätze zum Alten Testament, 1963, 178–191).

Geschichte, sondern um einen neuen Zukunftsraum der Erwartung, der sich in des Propheten Verkündigung hinein abzeichnet, so soll ein Beispiel aus dem Bereich der Fremdvölkerworte schließlich wieder zurück in die Völkergeschichte führen. In Ez 26—28 finden sich Worte gegen Tyrus und seinen König, die in verschiedener Weise, in eigentlicher und in Bildrede vom Untergang des Angeredeten reden. Die Sammlung der Tyrusworte wird durch das an ihrem Kopf stehende Datum Ez 26 1 ins 11. Jahr datiert. Daneben soll das späteste, ins 27. Jahr datierte Wort des Prophetenbuches 29 17—20, das in die Sammlung der Ägyptenworte einbezogen ist, gestellt werden.

Dieses Wort ist darum in den Zusammenhang der Erwägungen über das Phänomen der Fortschreibung im Ezechielbuche einzureihen, weil es nun deutlich in den späteren Zusammenhang der Geschichte von Tyrus führt. Dieses ist für Nebukadnezar und die babylonischen Truppen nicht so zur reichen Beute geworden, wie es die früheren Tyrusworte angekündigt hatten. Auf dieses so anders erfolgte Geschehen mit Tyrus, wie immer dieses sich vollzogen haben mag, erhält der Prophet den Auftrag, im Namen Jahwes zu verkündigen, daß die Nebukadnezar und seinen Kriegern entgangene Löhnung ihnen in Ägypten zuteil werden solle. Ägypten soll zur Beute Nebukadnezars werden.

In einer ganz eigenartigen und in dieser Art einmaligen »Fortschreibung« des Tyrus-Nebukadnezarwortes unter veränderten geschichtlichen Verhältnissen zu einem Ägypten-Nebukadnezarwort geschieht hier ein prophetisches Folgen hinter geschehener Geschichte her in eine neue Situation hinein. Das anfängliche Gotteswort erfährt in dieser zu einer eigenen literarischen Worteinheit verselbständigten Aussage eine ausdrückliche Umpolung auf eine andere politische Größe hin. Die strenge Bezogenheit prophetischen Wortes auf konkrete Geschichte und das Nachgehen hinter der Geschichte her wird hier in ungewöhnlicher Deutlichkeit klar.

X

In allen vorgeführten Beispielen sind sehr verschiedenartige Phänomene von »Fortschreibung« erkennbar geworden. Neben die in literarischer Analyse abhebbaren Elemente heute zusammenhängender Textkomplexe, die einen jüngeren zeitlichen Standort verraten, treten ganz selbständige Einheiten, die strukturell in der gleichen Art zu beurteilen sind.

Man müßte nun natürlich von hier aus den Blick auf andere Prophetenbücher richten und fragen, ob dort nicht auch solche Phänomene der Weiterführung älteren Prophetenwortes aus der Geschichtssituation späterer Zeit heraus erkennbar sind.

In diesen weiteren Zusammenhang gehörte auch das von W. Thiel herausgestellte Phänomen im Jeremiabuch[34], daß zunächst apodiktisch formulierte Gerichtsansagen des Propheten in dtr. Bearbeitung in die Form der sog. Alternativpredigt, welche die apodiktische Gerichtsansage zur konditionalen Aussage macht, umgesetzt worden sind. Auch hinter diesem Phänomen steckt im Grunde eine Weise der Fortschreibung. So ist etwa die in Jeremias Tempelrede zunächst apodiktisch angesagte Zerstörung des Tempels in der Zeit des Deuteronomisten schon Wirklichkeit geworden. Auf die Frage, ob damit die prophetische Ankündigung überholt und vergangene Geschichte geworden sei, antwortet der dtr. Bearbeiter in einer Zeit, die zu hoffen wagt, daß Gottes Geschichte mit seinem Volke noch Zukunft habe, durch seine Umsetzung der die apodiktische Unheilsansage begründenden Gebote in ein das Volk im neuen Heute zum Gehorsam rufendes konditionales Wort. Die Lebensmöglichkeit wird auf jeden Fall verbunden sein mit dem Halten der Gebote. Der Überschritt, der im Ezechielbuche von der apodiktischen Gerichtsansage zu Ez 18 oder 33 1–20 hin vollzogen ist, vollzieht sich ganz so in der »Fortschreibung« der Tempelrede in eine neue Zeitphase hinein[35].

Aber es ist hier nicht der Ort, diesen Vorgang über das Ezechielbuch hinaus zu verfolgen. Die Fragestellung die sich auch anderswo stellt und hinter der sich letztlich die Frage nach der Lebendigkeit Gottes für jedes Heute verbirgt, dürfte von den Aussagen des Ezechielbuches her deutlich geworden sein.

---

[34] W. Thiel, Die deuteronomistische Redaktion von Jeremia 1–25, 1973. Dazu jetzt auch meine Ausführungen: Vom Prophetenwort zum Prophetenbuch, ThLZ 104, 1970, 481–496.

[35] In diesen Zusammenhang gehört auch, was G. von Rad, Theologie des Alten Testaments, II 1960⁴, 54–57, an Beispielen aus dem Jesajabuch (besonders eindrücklich am Sebnawort Jes 22 15–25) unter dem Stichwort »Produktiver Traditionsprozeß« ausführt.

List of Professor Georg Fohrer's Publications

I. Bücher

1. Der heilige Weg. Eine religionswissenschaftliche Untersuchung. Phil. Diss. Bonn. Düsseldorf 1939.
2. Die symbolischen Handlungen der alttestamentlichen Propheten. Theol. Diss. Marburg/Lahn 1944 (Maschinenschrift).
3. Das Buch Hiob. Übertragen und herausgegeben. Krefeld 1948.
4. Glaube und Welt im Alten Testament. Das Alte Testament und Gegenwartsfragen. Frankfurt a. M. 1948.
5. Die Hauptprobleme des Buches Ezechiel. BZAW 72. Berlin 1952.
6. Die symbolischen Handlungen der Propheten. Abhandlungen zur Theologie des Alten und Neuen Testaments 25. Zürich 1953. 2. überarb. und erw. Aufl. 1968 (Nr. 54).
7. Ezechiel. Mit einem Beitrag von Kurt Galling. Handbuch zum Alten Testament, I 13. Tübingen 1955.
8. Elia. Abhandlungen zur Theologie des Alten und Neuen Testaments 31. Zürich 1957. 2. überarb. und erw. Aufl. 1968 (Nr. 53).
9. Messiasfrage und Bibelverständnis. Sammlung gemeinverständlicher Vorträge und Schriften aus dem Gebiet der Theologie und Religionsgeschichte 213/214. Tübingen 1957.
10. Das Buch Jesaja. Zürcher Bibelkommentare.
    1. Band Kapitel 1–23. Zürich/Stuttgart 1960. 2. erw. und verb. Aufl. 1966.
    2. Band Kapitel 24–39. Zürich/Stuttgart 1962. 2. erw. und verb. Aufl. 1967.
    3. Band Kapitel 40–66. Zürich/Stuttgart 1964.
11. Studien zum Buche Hiob. Gütersloh 1963.
12. Das Buch Hiob. Kommentar zum Alten Testament, XVI. Gütersloh 1963.
12a. Das Buch Hiob. Kommentar zum Alten Testament. Berlin 1967.
13. Überlieferung und Geschichte des Exodus. BZAW 91. Berlin 1964.
14. Einleitung in das Alte Testament (= Sellin-Fohrer, 10. Aufl.). Heidelberg 1965.
    2. (11.) durchges. und erw. Auflage 1969.
    3. (12.) überarb. und erw. Auflage 1979.
15. Studien zur alttestamentlichen Prophetie (1949–1965). BZAW 99. Berlin 1967.
16. Geschichte der israelitischen Religion. Berlin 1969.
17. Das Alte Testament. Erster Teil. Gütersloh 1969. 2. überarb. Aufl. 1977.
17a. Das Alte Testament. Erster Teil. Berlin 1971.
18. Studien zur alttestamentlichen Theologie und Geschichte (1949–1966). BZAW 115. Berlin 1969.
19. Das Alte Testament. Zweiter und dritter Teil. Gütersloh 1970. 2. überarb. Aufl. 1977.
19a. Das Alte Testament. Zweiter und dritter Teil. Berlin 1972.
20. Theologische Grundstrukturen des Alten Testaments. Berlin 1972.
21. Die Propheten des Alten Testaments. Band 1: Die Propheten des 8. Jahrhunderts. Gütersloh 1974.

22. Die Propheten des Alten Testaments. Band 2: Die Propheten des 7. Jahrhunderts. Gütersloh 1974.
23. Die Propheten des Alten Testaments. Band 3: Die Propheten des frühen 6. Jahrhunderts. Gütersloh 1975.
24. Die Propheten des Alten Testaments. Band 4: Die Propheten um die Mitte des 6. Jahrhunderts. Gütersloh 1975.
25. Die Propheten des Alten Testaments. Band 5: Die Propheten des ausgehenden 6. und des 5. Jahrhunderts. Gütersloh 1976.
26. Die Propheten des Alten Testaments. Band 6: Die Propheten seit dem 4. Jahrhundert. Gütersloh 1976.
27. Die Propheten des Alten Testaments. Band 7: Prophetenerzählungen. Gütersloh 1977.
28. Geschichte Israels. Von den Anfängen bis zur Gegenwart. Heidelberg 1977. 2. durchges. und erw. Auflage 1979.
29. Glaube und Leben im Judentum. Heidelberg 1979.

Ia. Bücher gemeinsam mit anderen Verfassern

1. Hebräisches und aramäisches Wörterbuch zum Alten Testament. In Gemeinschaft mit H. W. Hoffmann, F. Huber, J. Vollmer, G. Wanke. Berlin 1971.
1a. Hebrew and Aramaic Dictionary of the Old Testament. London 1973.
1b. Hebrew and Aramaic Dictionary of the Old Testament. New York 1973.
2. Exegese des Alten Testaments. Von G. Fohrer, H. W. Hoffmann, F. Huber, L.Markert, G. Wanke. Heidelberg 1973.
   2.durchges. und überarb. Aufl. 1976.
   3. Aufl. 1979.
3. Salut. Par W. Foerster et G. Fohrer = IVa.

Ib. Übersetzungen

1a. Introduction to the Old Testament. Nashville/New York 1968.
1b. Introduction to the Old Testament. London 1970.
2a. History of Israelite Religion. Nashville/New York 1972.
2b. History of Israelite Religion. London 1973.
3a. Hebrew and Aramaic Dictionary of the Old Testament. London 1973.
3b. Hebrew and Aramaic Dictionary of the Old Testament. New York 1973.
4. Introdução Antigo Testamento, Vol. 1. São Paulo 1978. Vol. 2. São Paulo 1978.

II. Aufsätze zum Alten Testament

1. Schuld im Alten Testament. Frankfurter Hefte 1 (1946), S. 56—66.
2. Das Leid im Alten Testament. Frankfurter Hefte 2 (1947), S. 170—180.
3. Jeremias Tempelwort 7,1—15. ThZ 5 (1949), S. 401—417.
4. Die zeitliche und überzeitliche Bedeutung des Alten Testaments. EvTh 9 (1949/50), S. 447—460.
5. Die Judenfrage und der Zionismus. Judaica 7 (1951), S. 45—64.

6. Die Glossen im Buche Ezechiel. ZAW 63 (1951), S. 33—53.
7. Psalm 30, Psalm 126. Lyrik des Ostens, hrsg. von W. Gundert, A. Schimmel und W. Schubring, München 1952, S. 21—23.
8. Die Gattung der Berichte über symbolische Handlungen der Propheten. ZAW 64 (1952), S. 101—120.
9. Die wiederentdeckte kanaanäische Religion. ThLZ 78 (1953), Sp. 193—200.
10. Über den Kurzvers. ZAW 66 (1954), S. 199—236.
11. Vom Israel des Alten Testaments zum Judentum. Das Banner 28 (1955), Folge 3, März 1955, S. 5, 10.
12. Die Propheten des Alten Testaments im Blickfeld neuer Forschung. Das Wort im evangelischen Religionsunterricht, Schuljahr 1954/1955, Nr. 6 (Mai—Juni), S. 15—24.
13. Umkehr und Erlösung beim Propheten Hosea. ThZ 11 (1955), S. 161—185.
14. Zum Text von Jes. xli 8—13. VT 5 (1955), S. 239—249.
15. Ich bin der Herr, dein Gott. Vocati sumus ad militiam Dei vivi, Rundbrief der Evangelischen Studentengemeinde in Österreich, Folge 20 (November 1955), S. 3—10.
16. Die Frage der Kriegsdienstverweigerung im Lichte der Bibel. Der Mann vor Christus, Rundbrief für die Seelsorge am evangelischen Mann, 1955—56, Nr. 2, S. 16—23.
17. Der Arme im Alten Testament. Innere Mission, April 1956 Folge 4, S. 26—28.
18. Der Mensch vor Gott und in der Welt. Vocati sumus ad militiam Dei vivi, Rundbrief der Evangelischen Studentengemeinde in Österreich, Folge 22 (Juli 1956), S. 3—8.
19. Zur Vorgeschichte und Komposition des Buches Hiob. VT 6 (1956), S. 249—267.
20. Vorgeschichte und Komposition des Buches Hiob. ThLZ 81 (1956), Sp. 333—336.
21. Zu Jes 7,14 im Zusammenhang von Jes 7,10—22. ZAW 68 (1956), S. 54—56.
22. ». . . und sündige hinfort nicht mehr!« (Joh. 8,11). Der Mann vor Christus, Rundbrief für die Seelsorge am evangelischen Mann, 1956—57, Nr. 1, S. 25—28.
23. Israels Staatsordnung im Rahmen des Alten Orients. Zu Eric Voegelin, Israel and Revelation. Österr. Zeitschrift für Öffentliches Recht 8 (1957), S. 129—148.
24. Messiasfrage und Bibelverständnis. Das Wort im evangelischen Religionsunterricht, Schuljahr 1957/58, Nr. 1 (Sept.—Okt.), S. 9—19; Nr. 2 (Nov.—Dez.), S. 9—19.
25. Das Symptomatische der Ezechielforschung. ThLZ 83 (1958), Sp. 241—250.
26. Nun aber hat mein Auge dich geschaut. Der innere Aufbau des Buches Hiob. ThZ 15 (1959), S. 1—21.
27. Form und Funktion in der Hiobdichtung. ZDMG 109 (1959), S. 31—49.
28. Überlieferung und Wandlung der Hioblegende. Festschrift Friedrich Baumgärtel, Erlanger Forschungen, Reihe A Band 10. Erlangen 1959, S. 41—62.
29. Der Vertrag zwischen König und Volk in Israel. ZAW 71 (1959), S. 1—22.
30. Theologische Züge des Menschenbildes im Alten Testament. Das Wort im evangelischen Religionsunterricht, Schuljahr 1959/60, Nr. 1 (Sept.—Okt.), S. 9—21.
31. Die Struktur der alttestamentlichen Eschatologie. ThLZ 85 (1960), Sp. 401—420.
32. Die Weisheit des Elihu (Hi 32—37). AfO 19 (1959/60), S. 83—94.
33. Das Gottesbild des Alten Testaments. Das Wort im evangelischen Religionsunterricht, Schuljahr 1960/61, Nr. 1 (Sept.—Okt.), S. 8—16.
34. Tradition und Interpretation im Alten Testament. ZAW 73 (1961), S. 1—30.
35. Eisenzeitliche Anlagen im Raume südlich von nāʿūr und die Südwestgrenze von Ammon. ZDPV 77 (1961), S. 56—71.
36. Remarks on Modern Interpretation of the Prophets. JBL 80 (1961), S. 309—319.
37. Forscher mit Bus und Fernglas. Deutsche Professoren suchen eine alte Grenze. Evangelischer Pressedienst B Nr. 2 vom 11. 1. 1962, S. 10—12.

38. Gottes Antwort aus dem Sturmwind, Hi. 38—41. ThZ 18 (1962), S. 1—24.
39. Erwägungen über das Leid im Buche Hiob. Das Wort im evangelischen Religionsunterricht, Schuljahr 1962/63, Nr. 1 (Sept.—Okt.), S. 9—20.
40. Jesaja 1 als Zusammenfassung der Verkündigung Jesajas. ZAW 74 (1962), S. 251—268.
41. Der Aufbau der Apokalypse des Jesajabuches (Is 24—27). Catholic Biblical Quarterly 25 (1963), S. 34—45.
42. 4Q Or Nab, 11Q tg Job und die Hioblegende. ZAW 75 (1963), S. 93—97.
43. The Origin, Composition and Tradition of Isaiah I—XXXIX. The Annual of Leeds University Oriental Society 3 (1961/2), S. 3—38.
44. »Priesterliches Königtum«, Ex. 19,6. ThZ 19 (1963), S. 359—362.
45. Das Hiobproblem und seine Lösung. Wissenschaftliche Zeitschrift der Martin-Luther-Universität Halle-Wittenberg, Gesellschafts- und sprachwissenschaftliche Reihe, 12 (1963), S. 249—258.
46. Prophetie und Geschichte. ThLZ 89 (1964), Sp. 481—500.
47. Das sogenannte apodiktisch formulierte Recht und der Dekalog. Kerygma und Dogma 11 (1965), S. 49—74.
48. Die Sage in der Bibel. Sagen und ihre Deutung, Göttingen 1965, S. 59—80.
49. Universal Ideas in the Ancient Canaanite and Biblical-Israelite Religions. Parliament of Religions, Calcutta 1965, S. 59—67.
50. Prophetie und Magie. ZAW 78 (1966), S. 25—47.
51. The Centre of a Theology of the Old Testament. Ned. Geref. Teologiese Tydskrif 7 (1966), S. 198—206.
52. Die Vorgeschichte Israels im Lichte neuer Quellen. Das Wort im evangelischen Religionsunterricht, Schuljahr 1965/66, Nr. 2, S. 2—10.
53. Altes Testament — »Amphiktyonie« und »Bund«? ThLZ 91 (1966), Sp. 801—816, 893—904.
54. Die Sprüche Obadjas. Studia Biblica et Semitica, Theodoro Christiano Vriezen dedicata, Wageningen 1966, S. 81—93.
55. The Personal Structure of Biblical Faith. Fourth World Congress of Jewish Studies, Papers, Vol. I, Jerusalem 1967, S. 161—166 (neuhebr. Zusammenfassung S. 218).
56. Wandlungen Jesajas. Festschrift für Wilhelm Eilers, Wiesbaden 1967, S. 58—71.
57. Micha 1. Das ferne und nahe Wort, Festschrift Leonhard Rost, Berlin 1967, S. 65—80.
58. Action of God and Decision of Man in the Old Testament. Biblical Essays 1966, 1967, S. 31—39.
59. Israels Haltung gegenüber den Kanaanäern und anderen Völkern. Journal of Semitic Studies 13 (1968), S. 64—75.
60. Der Mittelpunkt einer Theologie des Alten Testaments. ThZ 24 (1968), S. 161—172.
61. Twofold Aspects of Hebrew Words. Words and Meanings, Cambridge 1968, S. 95—103.
62. Das Geschick des Menschen nach dem Tode im Alten Testament. Kerygma und Dogma 14 (1968), S. 249—262.
63. Die israelitischen Propheten in der samaritanischen Chronik II. In Memoriam Paul Kahle, Berlin 1968, 129—137.
64. Stellvertretung und Schuldopfer in Jesaja 52,13—53,12 vor dem Hintergrund des Alten Testaments und des Alten Orients. Das Kreuz Jesu, Göttingen 1969, S. 7—31.
65. Kritik an Tempel, Kultus und Kultusausübung in nachexilischer Zeit. Archäologie und Altes Testament, Festschrift für Kurt Galling, Tübingen 1970, S. 101—116.
66. Glaube und Hoffnung. Weltbewältigung und Weltgestaltung in altestamentlicher Sicht. ThZ 26 (1970), S. 1—21.

67. Das Alte Testament und das Thema »Christologie«. EvTh 30 (1970), S. 281—298.
68. Offenbarung und Altes Testament. Grundlagen des Glaubens, Tutzinger Texte Nr. 8, München 1970, S. 31—51.
69. Priester und Prophet — Amt und Charisma? Kerygma und Dogma 17 (1971), S. 15—27.
70. Zur Einwirkung der gesellschaftlichen Struktur Israels auf seine Religion. Near Eastern Studies in Honor of William Foxwell Albright, Baltimore 1971, S. 169—185.
71. Die alttestamentliche Ladeerzählung. Journal of Northwest Semitic Languages 1,1 (1971), S. 23—31.
72. Vollmacht über Völker und Königreiche. Beobachtungen zu den prophetischen Fremdvölkersprüchen anhand von Jer 46—51. Wort, Lied und Gottesspruch, Festschrift für Joseph Ziegler, Würzburg 1972, Band II, S. 145—153.
73. The Righteous Man in Job 31. Essays in Old Testament Ethics (J. Philip Hyatt In Memoriam). New York 1974, S. 1—22.
74. »Gesetz« und »Gerechtigkeit« oder Tora und Rechtverhalten nach dem Alten Testament. Das neue Erlangen Heft 45 (März 1978), S. 3300—3307.

IIa. Aufsätze in Übersetzung

1. Altes Testament »Amphiktyonie« und »Bund«?, I.—II., in: מוסד »האמפיקטוניה« בישראל העתיקה, 1976, 7—24.

IIb. Aufsätze in Nachdrucken

1. Die Struktur der alttestamentlichen Eschatologie, in: H. D. Preuß (hrsg.), Eschatologie im Alten Testament, Darmstadt 1978, 147—180.
2. Bemerkungen zum neueren Verständnis der Propheten, in: P. H. A. Neumann (hrsg.), Das Prophetenverständnis in der deutschsprachigen Forschung seit Heinrich Ewald, Darmstadt 1979, 475—492.

III. Andere Aufsätze

1. Deutscher Theologentag in Marburg/Lahn. ThZ 6 (1950), S. 151—155.
2. Zulassung von Frauen zum Pfarramt. Amt und Gemeinde 6 (1955), Nr. 4, S. 13—14. (Auszugsweise in: Evangelische Welt, Informationsblatt für die Evangelische Kirche in Deutschland 9 (1955), Nr. 19, S. 586f.)
3. Das Problem von Lehrfreiheit und dogmatischer Bindung in der evangelischen Theologie und Kirche. ThZ 13 (1957), S. 260—284.
4. Über Freiheit und Bindung. Amt und Gemeinde 9 (1958), Nr. 4, S. 26—27.
5. Geleitwort. ZAW 75 (1963), S. 1—2.
6. Für oder wider eine Münchner evangelisch-theologische Fakultät? Nachrichten der Evangelisch-Lutherischen Kirche in Bayern 19 (1964), Nr. 17, S. 268—271.
7. Der XXVII. Internationale Orientalisten-Kongreß und die Folgerungen. ZAW 79 (1967), S. 367f.

IV. Artikel in Lexika

1. Evangelisches Kirchenlexikon:
    1. Joel. Band II, Sp. 354f.
    2. Jona. Band II, Sp. 375.
    3. Micha. Band II, Sp. 1327f.
    4. Nahum. Band II, Sp. 1498f.
    5. Obadja. Band II, Sp. 1643f.
2. Die Religion in Geschichte und Gegenwart, 3. Auflage:
    1. Elia. Band II, Sp. 424—427.
    2. Elisa. Band II, Sp. 429—431.
    3. Fabel II. Im AT und NT. Band II, Sp. 853—854.
    4. Gleichnis und Parabel II. In der Bibel. 1. Im AT. Band II, Sp. 1615f.
    5. Korach. Band IV, Sp. 15.
    6. Levi und Leviten. Band IV, Sp. 336f.
    7. Leviticus. Band IV, Sp. 339f.
    8. Mahlzeiten, kultische II. Im AT und NT. Band IV, Sp. 607f.
    9. Noah. Band IV, Sp. 1501f.
    10. Numeri. Band IV, Sp. 1542f.
    11. Priesterschrift. Band V, Sp. 568f.
    12. Sittlichkeit III. Im AT, Band VI, Sp. 66—69.
3. Calwer Bibellexikon, 5. Bearbeitung:
    1. Alphabetische Lieder. Sp. 43.
    2. Amos, Amosbuch. Sp. 52—54.
    3. Baruch. Sp. 127f.
    4. Buchrolle. Sp. 173.
    5. Cantica. Sp. 181.
    6. Daniel. Sp. 193—195.
    7. Danklied. Sp. 196.
    8. Debora, Deboralied. Sp. 202f.
    9. Elihu. Sp. 254.
    10. Ethan. Sp. 294f.
    11. Festrollen. Sp. 315.
    12. Fremdvölkersprüche. Sp. 333f.
    13. Gottesknecht. Sp. 441f.
    14. Habakuk. Sp. 451f.
    15. Haggai. Sp. 455.
    16. Hallel. Sp. 456f.
    17. Halleluja. Sp. 457.
    18. Heman. Sp. 491.
    19. Hesekiel. Sp. 513—515.
    20. Hiob. Sp. 523—527.
    21. Hoheslied. Sp. 542f.
    22. Hosea. Sp. 545—547.
    23. Hosianna. Sp. 547.
    24. Immanuel. Sp. 555.
    25. Jael. Sp. 576.
    26. Jeduthun. Sp. 590.

27. Jeremia. Sp. 592—595.
28. Jesaja. Sp. 613—619.
29. Kijjun. Sp. 714.
30. Kleine Propheten. Sp. 724.
31. Klugheit. Sp. 725.
32. Kosmologie. Sp. 747f.
33. Lehre, lehren. Sp. 789f.
34. Lehrer. Sp. 790.
35. Lehrerin. Sp. 790f.
36. Lehrgedicht. Sp. 791.
37. Lernen. Sp. 795f.
38. Magnifikat. Sp. 831.
39. Maleachi. Sp. 838f.
40. Mene, Mene, Tekel, U-pharsin. Sp. 867f.
41. Mesach. Sp. 875.
42. Ohola und Oholiba. Sp. 963.
43. Propheten. Sp. 1052—1060.
44. Raubebald, Eilebeute. Sp. 1085.
45. Rest Israels. Sp. 1101f.
46. Sacharja. Sp. 1128—1130.
47. Schear-jaschub. Sp. 1165.
48. Sprichwort, Spruch. Sp. 1248.
49. Sprüche, Buch der. Sp. 1248—1250.
50. Sulamith. Sp. 1273.
51. Symbolische Handlungen. Sp. 1276f.
52. Symbolische Namen. Sp. 1277.
53. Tag des Herrn. Sp. 1283—1285.
54. Theophanie. Sp. 1310—1313.
55. Tobias, Tobiasbuch. Sp. 1322.
56. Tor, töricht, Torheit. Sp. 1326f.
57. Uz. Sp. 1354.
58. Weisheit, Buch der. Sp. 1392f.
59. Weisheitsdichtung. Sp. 1393f.
60. Weissagung. Sp. 1394.
61. Wortspiele. Sp. 1409f.
62. Zephanja. Sp. 1429f.
63. Zitate. Sp. 1436f.
64. Zusätze, spätere. Sp. 1441.

4. Theologisches Wörterbuch zum Neuen Testament:
    1. Zion-Jerusalem im Alten Testament. Band VII, S. 291—318.
    2. σοφία, σοφός, σοφίζω: B. Altes Testament. Band VII, S. 476—496.
    3. σῴζω und σωτηρία im Alten Testament. σωτήρ im Alten Testament. σωτήριος. Band VII, S. 970—981, 1013, 1022—1023.
    4. υἱός, υἱοθεσία: B. Altes Testament; C. Judentum I. 1a. Band VIII, S. 340—355.

5. Biblisch-Historisches Handwörterbuch:
    1. Aberglaube. Band I, Sp. 9—11.
    2. Abwehrmittel. Band I, Sp. 19.
    3. Amme. Band I, Sp. 81f.

4. Amulett. Band I, Sp. 90f.
5. Arm. Band I, Sp. 129.
6. Astarte. Band I, Sp. 142f.
7. Backe. Band I, Sp. 189.
8. Barfuß. Band I, Sp. 198.
9. Bart. Band I, Sp. 200f.
10. Begräbnis. Band I, Sp. 211f.
11. Berggötter. Band I, Sp. 220.
12. Beschwörung. Band I, Sp. 225f.
13. Bett. Band I, Sp. 235f.
14. Beutel. Band I, Sp. 236f.
15. Binde. Band I, Sp. 253.
16. Blick, böser. Band I, Sp. 257.
17. Bogen. Band I, Sp. 264, 267.
18. Braten. Band I, Sp. 270.
19. Brauchtum. Band I, Sp. 270f.
20. Brust. Band I, Sp. 276.
21. Butter. Band I, Sp. 293.
22. Dämonen. Band I, Sp. 315f.
23. Daumen. Band I, Sp. 324.
24. Dirne. Band I, Sp. 346.
25. Ehernes Meer. Band I, Sp. 372.
26. Eimer. Band I, Sp. 378.
27. Eingeweide. Band I, Sp. 379.
28. Entwöhnung. Band I, Sp. 415.
29. Essig. Band I, Sp. 444.
30. Fackel. Band I, Sp. 462f.
31. Falle. Band I, Sp. 463.
32. Fett. Band I, Sp. 479.
33. Finger. Band I, Sp. 481f.
34. Geburt. Band I, Sp. 528.
35. Gewürz. Band I, Sp. 566.
36. Gießerei. Band I, Sp. 570f.
37. Glas. Band I, Sp. 573–575.
38. Gottesberg. Band I, Sp. 594.
39. Gottessöhne. Band I, Sp. 598.
40. Götzendienst. Band I, Sp. 602–604.
41. Grundbesitz. Band I, Sp. 612f.
42. Hand. Band II, Sp. 631f.
43. Hebamme. Band II, Sp. 664.
44. Heer. Band II, Sp. 670–673.
45. Hefe. Band II, Sp. 674.
46. Hiram. Band II, Sp. 727.
47. Kahlköpfigkeit. Band II, Sp. 918.
48. Kalmus. Band II, Sp. 922.
49. Kelter. Band II, Sp. 939.
50. Kesselwagen. Band II, Sp. 944.
51. Keule. Band II, Sp. 946.

52. Klageweib. Band II, Sp. 961.
53. Kleidung. Band II, Sp. 962—965.
54. Knie. Band II, Sp. 973.
55. Koch. Band II, Sp. 974.
56. Kopfbedeckung. Band II, Sp. 985f.
57. Kopfbund. Band II, Sp. 986.
58. Körper. Band II, Sp. 995.
59. Krongut. Band II, Sp. 1015.
60. Kultgeräte. Band II, Sp. 1018—1020.
61. Lauge. Band II, Sp. 1054.
62. Leinwand. Band II, Sp. 1072.
63. Lende. Band II, Sp. 1074.
64. Lichtschneuze. Band II, Sp. 1083.
65. Lilith. Band II, Sp. 1093.
66. Lippe. Band II, Sp. 1095.
67. Messer. Band II, Sp. 1197.
68. Metrik. Band II, Sp. 1208f.
69. Moreseth-Gath. Band II, Sp. 1238.
70. Mörser. Band II, Sp. 1239.
71. Most. Band II, Sp. 1245.
72. Mund. Band II, Sp. 1249.
73. Nase. Band II, Sp. 1288.
74. Nieren. Band II, Sp. 1311.
75. Ofen. Band II, Sp. 1329.
76. Ohr. Band II, Sp. 1336.
77. Onan. Band II, Sp. 1343.
78. Parallelismus. Band III, Sp. 1388—1389.
79. Pech. Band III, Sp. 1409.
80. Prosa. Band III, Sp. 1514—1515.
81. Qinavers. Band III, Sp. 1533—1535.
82. Rauschtrank. Band III, Sp. 1557.
83. Ring. Band III, Sp. 1603—1604.
84. Rosinenkuchen. Band III, Sp. 1622.
85. Rötel. Band III, Sp. 1622.
86. Ruß. Band III, Sp. 1625.
87. Rüstung. Band III, Sp. 1626—1628.
88. Sack. Band III, Sp. 1638.
89. Sarg. Band III, Sp. 1671—1672.
90. Scham. Band III, Sp. 1684—1685.
91. Scheren. Band III, Sp. 1690—1691.
92. Schild. Band III, Sp. 1698.
93. Schlauch. Band III, Sp. 1701.
94. Schleier. Band III, Sp. 1702.
95. Schminke. Band III, Sp. 1706.
96. Schmuck. Band III, Sp. 1706—1708.
97. Schönheitspflege. Band III, Sp. 1710.
98. Schuhwerk. Band III, Sp. 1738.
99. Schuppenpanzer. Band III, Sp. 1744.

100. Schwert. Band III, Sp. 1750—1751.
101. Selbstmord. Band III, Sp. 1763.
102. Sichelschwert. Band III, Sp. 1781.
103. Sonnenuhr. Band III, Sp. 1822—1823.
104. Spiegel. Band III, Sp. 1831—1832.
105. Stab. Band III, Sp. 1845.
106. Tempeldirne. Band III, Sp. 1948—1949.
107. Tempelquelle. Band III, Sp. 1949.
108. Teraphim. Band III, Sp. 1952.
109. Text. Band III, Sp. 1957—1960.
110. Tiegel. Band III, Sp. 1984.
111. Totengeist. Band III, Sp. 2014.
112. Unzucht. Band III, Sp. 2059—2060.
113. Waffen. Band III, Sp. 2124—2127.
114. Wein. Band III, Sp. 2149—2150.
115. Weinberg. Band III, Sp. 2150—2151.
116. Windel. Band III, Sp. 2175.
117. Zauberei. Band III, Sp. 2204—2205.
118. Zeichendeuter. Band III, Sp. 2209—2210.
119. Zottenrock. Band III, Sp. 2248.
6. Theologische Realenzyklopädie
    1. Ahab. Band II, S. 123—125.
    2. Ahas. Band II, S. 125—127.
    3. Ahia von Silo. Band II, S. 127—128.

Va. Forschungs- und Literaturberichte

1. Neuere Literatur zur alttestamentlichen Prophetie. 1. Teil: Literatur von 1932—1939. ThR NF 19 (1951), S. 277—346.
2. Neuere Literatur zur alttestamentlichen Prophetie. 2. Teil: Literatur von 1940—1950. ThR NF 20 (1952), S. 192—271, 295—361.
3. Orientalistik. Der Hellenismus in der deutschen Forschung 1938—1948, hrsg. von E. Kiessling, Wiesbaden 1956, S. 31—50.
4. Zehn Jahre Literatur zur alttestamentlichen Prophetie (1951—1960). ThR NF 28 (1962), S. 1—75, 235—297, 301—374.
5. Hin zu den Quellen. ZAW 78 (1966), S. 225—229.
6. Neue Literatur zur alttestamentlichen Prophetie (1961—1970).
    ThR NF 40 (1975), S. 193—209, 337—377;
    ThR NF 41 (1976), S. 1—12, 337—377.

Vb. Rezensionen und Buchanzeigen

Von 1950—1979: 2765 Rezensionen und kürzere Buchanzeigen, vornehmlich in der »Bücherschau« der ZAW.

Vc. Kurzberichte

Von 1956–1979: Kurzberichte über erschienene Aufsätze in der »Zeitschriftenschau« der ZAW.
Kurzberichte über eigene Aufsätze in: Internationale Zeitschriftenschau für Bibelwissenschaft und Grenzgebiete, von Bd. 4 (1955/56) an.

VI. Herausgebertätigkeit

a) 1. Emil Balla, Die Botschaft der Propheten. Tübingen 1958.
   2. Curt Kuhl, Die Entstehung des Alten Testaments. Zweite, überarbeitete Auflage. Bern/München 1960.
   3. In Memoriam Paul Kahle. (Mit Matthew Black.) Berlin 1968.
b) Zeitschrift für die alttestamentliche Wissenschaft: von Jahrgang 72 (1960) an.
c) Beihefte zur Zeitschrift für die alttestamentliche Wissenschaft: von Beiheft 79 an.
d) Zürcher Bibelkommentare (gemeinsam mit H. H. Schmid und S. Schulz).
e) Theologische Realenzyklopädie: 1. Hauptherausgeber,
                                    2. Herausgeber Altes Testament.
   Zu 1.: Februar 1971–April 1974,
   Zu 2.: April 1968–April 1974.

VIIa. Biographisches I

1. o. Prof. Dr. Fritz Wilke †. Österreichische Hochschulzeitung 10 (1958), Nr. 1, 1. Jänner 1958, S. 2.
2. Fritz Wilke. Archiv für Orientforschung 18 II (1958), S. 489–490.
3. Fritz Wilke †. Jahrbuch der Gesellschaft für die Geschichte des Protestantismus in Österreich 75 (1959), S. 139–148.
4. Johannes Hempel †. ZAW 77 (1965), S. I–III.
5. Professor D. Martin Noth †. ZAW 80 (1968), S. 288.
6. Otto Eißfeldt. 1. 9. 1887–23. 4. 1973. ZAW 85, Heft 2 (1973).

VIIb. Biographisches II

1. Ein Uerdinger ordentlicher Professor in Wien. Uerdinger Rundschau 4 (1954), Nr. 21/22, November 1954, S. 21.
2. Georg Fohrer, Wien. Österreichische Hochschulzeitung 7 (1955), Nr. 5, 1. März 1955, S. 3.
3. Theologische Literaturzeitung 89 (1964), Sp. 150f.
4. E. Feinendegen, Männer der evangelischen Kirche aus Uerdingen. Uerdinger Rundschau 15 (1965), Nr. 3, S. 9–14 (12).
5. J. Gray, Georg Fohrer, D theol, Professor of Old Testament Studies, University of Erlangen. Aberdeen University Review 43,2, No. 142 (1969), S. 194f.

Hebräisches und aramäisches Wörterbuch zum Alten Testament

Herausgegeben von Georg Fohrer in Gemeinschaft mit Hans Werner Hoffmann, Friedrich Huber, Jochen Vollmer und Gunther Wanke

Oktav. X, 331 Seiten. 1971. Ganzleinen DM 28,–
ISBN 3 11 001804 7

Hebrew and Aramaic Dictionary of the Old Testament

Edited by Georg Fohrer in cooperation with Hans Werner Hoffmann, Friedrich Huber, Jochen Vollmer, and Gunther Wanke

Octavo. XVI, 332 pages. 1973. Cloth DM 28,–
ISBN 3 11 004572 9

Georg Fohrer

Geschichte der israelitischen Religion

Oktav. XVI, 435 Seiten. 1969. Gebunden DM 38,–
ISBN 3 11 002652 X   de Gruyter Lehrbuch

Georg Fohrer

Studien zur alttestamentlichen Theologie und Geschichte (1949–1966)

Groß-Oktav. X, 372 Seiten. 1969. Ganzleinen DM 74,–
ISBN 3 11 002580 9
(Beiheft zur Zeitschrift für die alttestamentliche Wissenschaft, Band 115)

Preisänderungen vorbehalten

Walter de Gruyter      Berlin · New York

Georg Fohrer
Theologische Grundstrukturen des Alten Testaments
Oktav. X, 276 Seiten. 1972. Kartoniert DM 38,−
ISBN 3 11 003874 9
(Theologische Bibliothek Töpelmann, Band 24)

Georg Fohrer
Studien zur alttestamentlichen Prophetie (1949−1965)
Groß-Oktav. XII, 303 Seiten. 1967. Ganzleinen DM 60,−
ISBN 3 11 005582 1
(Beiheft zur Zeitschrift für die alttestamentliche Wissenschaft, Band 99)

Gerald T. Sheppard
Wisdom as a Hermeneutical Construct
A Study in the Sapientializing of the Old Testament

Large-octavo. XII, 178 pages. 1980. Cloth DM 78,−
ISBN 3 11 007504 0
(Beiheft zur Zeitschrift für die alttestamentliche Wissenschaft, Band 151)

J. A. Loader
Polar Structures in the Book of Qohelet
Large-octavo. XII, 138 pages. 1979. Cloth DM 62,−
ISBN 3 11 007636 5
(Beiheft zur Zeitschrift für die alttestamentliche Wissenschaft, Band 152)

Preisänderungen vorbehalten

Walter de Gruyter  Berlin · New York

DATE DUE	
OCT 24 1995	
MAY 10 1996	
MAY 24 1996	
JAN 20 1998	
NOV 18 1997	
FEB 16 2000	
NOV 29 1999	
GAYLORD	PRINTED IN U.S.A.